Snapshots of Bloomsbury

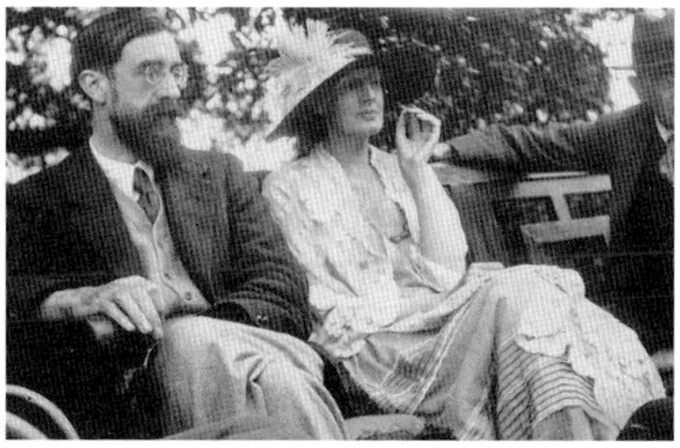

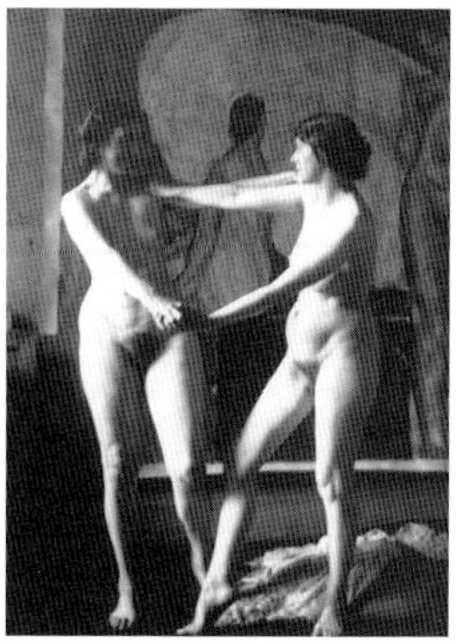

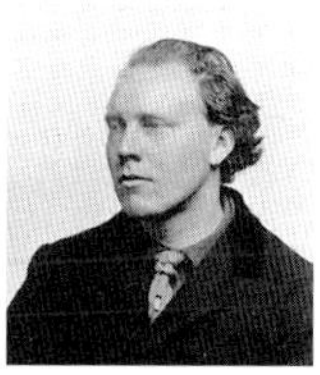

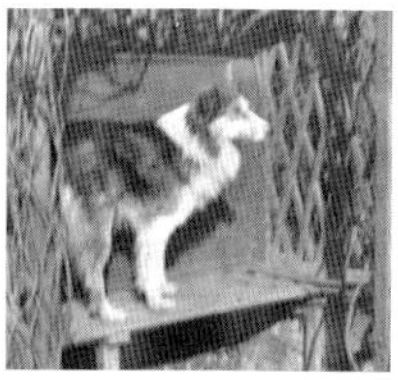

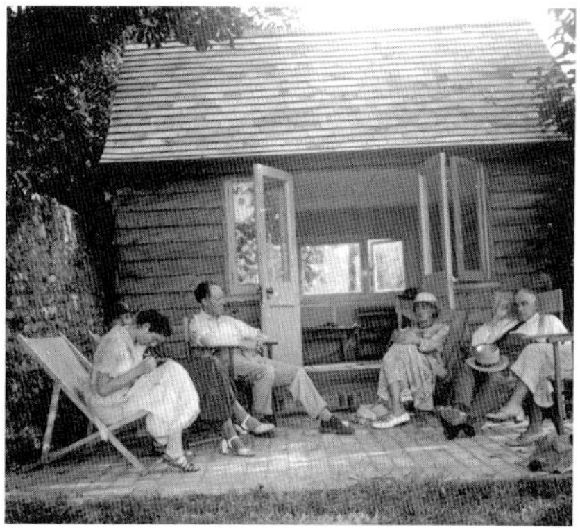

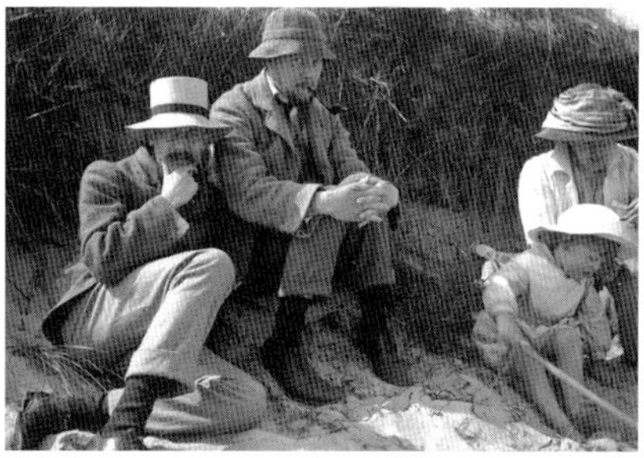

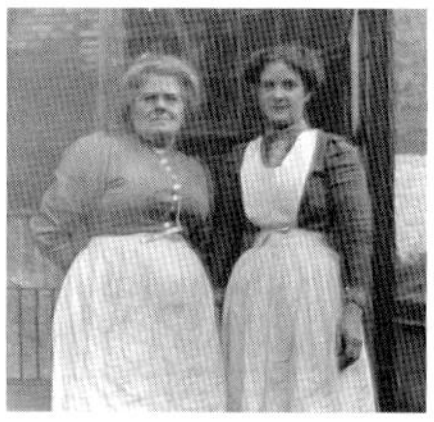

SNAPSHOTS *of* BLOOMSBURY

The Private Lives of Virginia Woolf and Vanessa Bell

MAGGIE HUMM

RUTGERS UNIVERSITY PRESS
NEW BRUNSWICK, NEW JERSEY

LIBRARY OF CONGRESS CATALOGING-IN-PUBLICATION DATA

Humm, Maggie.
Snapshots of Bloomsbury : the private lives of
Virginia Woolf and Vanessa Bell / Maggie Humm.
p. cm.
Includes bibliographical references (p.) and index.
ISBN 978-0-8135-3706-1 (cloth : alk. paper)
1. Woolf, Virginia, 1882-1941—Portraits. 2. Novelists, English—20th century—
Portraits. 3. Bell, Vanessa, 1879-1961—Portraits. 4. Painters—Great Britain—Portraits.
5. Sisters—Great Britain—Portraits. 6. Bloomsbury group—Pictorial works. I. Title.
PR6045.O72Z7255 2005
823'.91209—dc22 2005009513

A British Cataloging-in-Publication record for this book is available from
the British Library

Illustrations on page ii by permission of the Harvard Theatre Collection,
the Houghton Library, and the Tate, London, © 2004

Manufactured in Canada

Contents

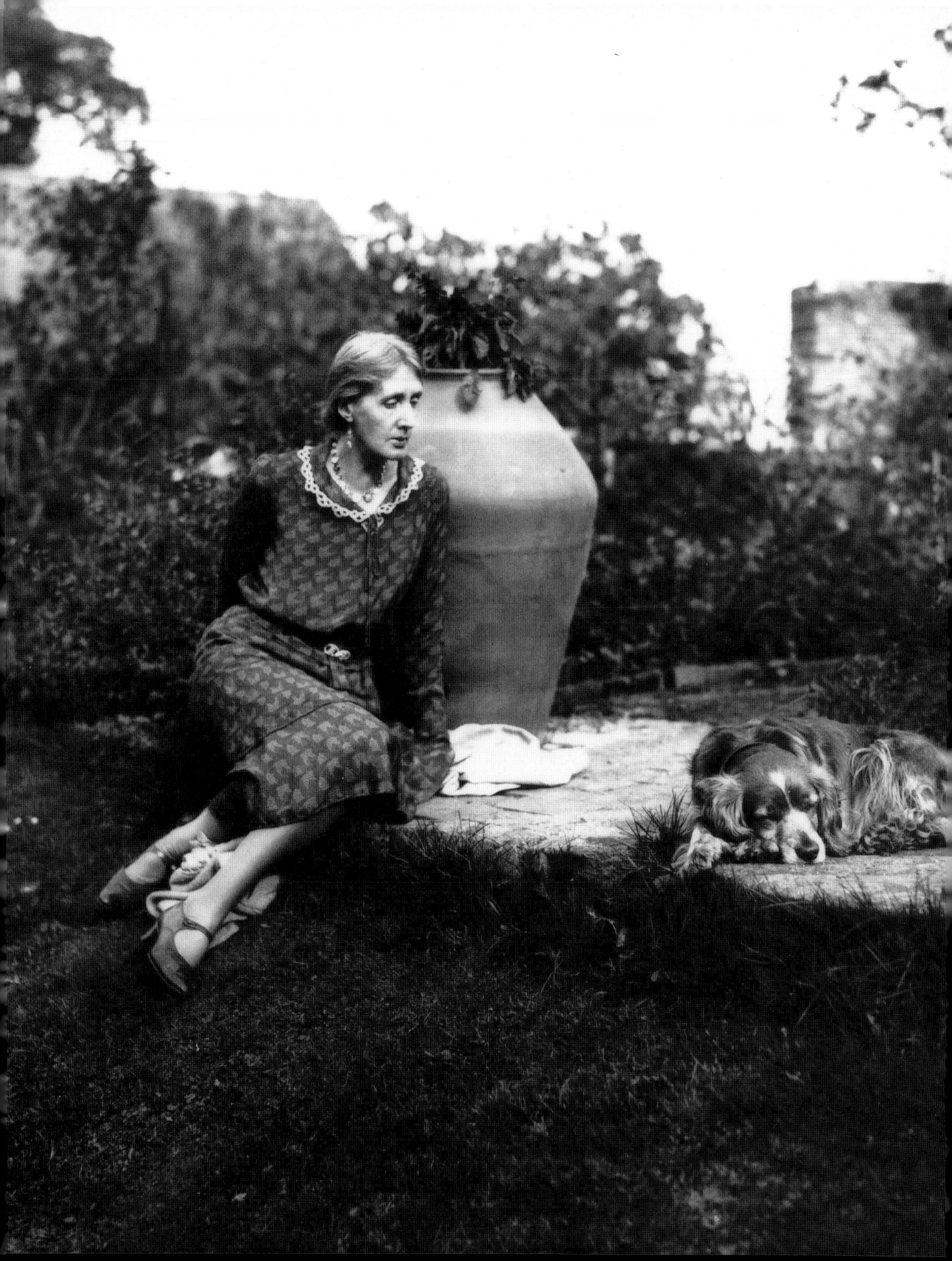

Preface and Acknowledgments

"Isnt it odd how much more one sees in a photograph than in real life?"

— VIRGINIA WOOLF

FIGURE 133 *Virginia Woolf, Monk's House, August 1931. Reprinted by permission of the Harvard Theatre Collection, the Houghton Library.*

PHOTOGRAPHS OF VIRGINIA WOOLF, from youth and beauty as one of the famous Stephen sisters to maturity, are inseparable from her status as a writer and her public image. She was photographed by Man Ray, Lenare and Gisèle Freund, as well as by her sister, family, and circle of Bloomsbury friends and artists. Indeed, one of the National Portrait Gallery's most popular postcards is of her. Images of Woolf are everywhere and familiar to those who have never read her writing. But even in her own day, Woolf was not aloof from popular culture. She might have understood, as critics of modernism now do, this crossover from high to public art. It is my intention here, as well, to locate Virginia Woolf and Vanessa Bell in that wider world outside of Bloomsbury's gallery.

The current state of domestic black-and-white and color photography is not an auspicious one, however. Even Kodak (the maker of some of the cameras that Woolf and Bell themselves used) has closed its film laboratories and processing plants on both sides of the Atlantic, having moved on to new technologies. Yet photographs in photo albums are often crucial to our sense of identity because they expose issues of memory and representation, and aesthetic frameworks of identity. Although it is again fashionable to read an artist's aesthetics through the small lens of subjective experience, and everyday experiences were very important to Bell and the Woolfs, reading an artist's photo albums is not easy. Generally speaking albums and photobooks are the work of auteurs collaging images within a personal framework. But photobooks are events often organized around a particular theme.

Albums have their own syntax, their own codes and indices and are hybrid entities. Albums are not only objects of perceptions; they also structure perceptions. In addition the meaning of albums, draws on biographic and cultural moments and traditions. To date there is no "theory" of amateur photography. Although John Szarkowski established a snapshot aesthetic at the Museum of Modern Art as long ago as 1966, with the exhibition Toward a Social Landscape, amateur photographers are thought to lack picture awareness. Szarkowski's aim was to appropriate and formalize a snapshot photographic vocabulary *detached* from its vernacular tradition, and this aim carries through into more recent exhibitions such as Cruel and Tender at the Tate Modern in 2003.

Histories of photography frequently endorse this formalism by creating a canon of "great" photographers of the everyday (for example, Paul Strand, Garry Winogrand, Martin Parr). Even cultural studies of vernacular photography allow the snapshot only a limited number of features such as "legibility" and "social function" (Shinkle, 173). Although the social and political uses of photography have received more attention, as, for example, in John Tagg's analysis of nineteenth-century criminal photographs, Tagg ignores the range of amateur photography's contingent meanings. Sociological analyses of camera clubs and ethnographic accounts of colonial photography see photography in terms of class/occupational groups or in terms of constructions of race and the gaze (Bourdieu; Clifford). Recent innovative work in narrative studies has developed critical methodologies for examining "everyday" photography, but necessarily within a sociological frame (Harrison). Family and memory studies of amateur photography go much further in decoding possible psychic and familial pressures shaping forms of composition (Hirsch; Spence and Holland). Notions of loss, photographic mnemonics and gender constructions are crucial themes that impact on amateur selections and on the Bloomsbury snapshots. But family studies are sometimes content driven at the expense of technical and economic variables.

Feminist artists and critics have examined the relationship between women's lack of economic and social status and depictions of femininities and masculinities in the family album—most famously in Jo Spence's 1979 exhibition at the Hayward Gallery, Beyond the Family Album. But Spence and others often aim to "fix" family photographs in a new feminist framework by means of detailed textual captions. Trauma studies are devoted to amateur photography but necessarily serve as a recovering of a historical project. Susan Sontag and John Berger are postmodern, even Situationist, photographic theorists in their shared attack on the manipulation of photographs as spectacle. Certainly the constructed nature of representations and the culturally mediated nature of visual experience are key issues. But Sontag, although an inspirational critic, writes largely about professional photography and in *Regarding the Pain of Others* she uncritically conflates narrator with author in her critique of Woolf's *Three Guineas*, and Berger works collaboratively with a professional photographer.

My own approach to these photographs is necessarily hybrid—drawing on cultural history, discourse analysis, Bloomsbury biographies and criticism, and photographic and psychoanalytic studies. Woolf herself, as Brenda Silver argues, frequently transgresses the margin between popular and intellectual cultures. In any case domestic photographs themselves always negotiate private and public domains because they are taken by one person, with or without the consent of the subject and usually share a private vision among many.

Snapshots of Bloomsbury is a companion volume to *Modernist Women and Visual Cultures*. That book discussed a wider range of the visual cultures of modernism, including avant-garde cinema and cinema journalism alongside domestic photographs. *Snapshots of Bloomsbury* now focuses on the photographs, providing a catalogue of images as well as a survey of Bloomsbury cultures. I draw on the many Bloomsbury diaries, letters, and autobiographies to identify people, places, and dates, and in the captions I hope to evoke both the moment of the snapshot as well as an emotional response in the viewer. In addition, there are close parallels between details in the photographs and descriptive details in Woolf's autobiographies. Often in these works Woolf seems to be describing not an *actual* memory but as if describing a photograph in front of her in the albums. For example, Woolf's descriptions in "Reminiscences" of Vanessa match photographs (fig. 19), and the famous opening of "A Sketch of the Past" matches plate 36f in Leslie Stephen's photo album.

While indexing the photographs for *Modernist Women*, I realized that descriptions of many of the sisters' photographs were omitted from Elizabeth Richardson's otherwise summative *A Bloomsbury Iconography*, as well as from lists of Woolf archives (See "Guide to Library Special Collections"). My catalogue raisonné of the Monk's House Albums and photographs, the first catalogue of the Woolfs' domestic photographs, was needed. Together with the captions and photographs, this information is intended as a reference for researchers from different disciplines: art historians interested in Bell's and Grant's paintings, some of which are visible in a few photographs; social historians interested in class and economic indices of dress and objects; cultural and photographic historians interested in technologies (for example camera models are deducible from my measurements of the prints); as well as Woolf scholars and the general public.

I have included previously published photographs where these are considered important images of Bell and the Woolfs so that *Snapshots* can be a more complete record. In discussion with Woolf experts, it became clear that many early photographs would be welcome even if they were of poor technical quality. However, in these photographs (figs. 31–33, 35–40) taken just after the deaths of her mother, Julia Stephen, and half-sister Stella Duckworth, Virgnia's deep melancholy is palpable. I have included as many photographs of Virginia Woolf as possible because of the high interest in her images. A few photographs appear twice (albeit with different formats) because they appear in both Bell's and the Woolfs' albums, indicating how important such images were and how much photographic memories were shared.

I have arranged the photographs in approximate chronology, using the same loose time periods as the introductory overview. In each section, photographs from the Woolfs' Monk's House Albums come first, followed by ones from Bell's albums. Although my use of chronology may seem to go against the grain of Woolf's approach in her albums and writings, it should allow readers to look historically and to place the photographs in conversation. Bell's and the Woolfs' photographs can look at each other again, and the suspended daily conversations or letters between Virginia and Vanessa are re-activated. The Woolfs' and Bell's black-and-white photographs and favored midbody shots are formats that sweep viewers into the frame. There is an exchange of emotion between the photographs and, hopefully, between photographs and contemporary viewers who can share that conversation in contemplative collaboration.

Snapshots of Bloomsbury owes much to academics around the world who invited me to give papers at conferences and universities. I am grateful to Karen Kukil for her invitation to Woolf in the Real World: the Thirteenth Annual Conference on Virginia Woolf, at Smith College in 2003, and for her generous gifts of Woolf photographs; to JoAnne Neff van Aertselaer for inviting me to give a keynote address at VII Jornadas de Estudios de la Mujer, at Madrid Complutense University in 2003; to Susan Shifrin for inviting me to give a plenary at the Picturing Women Symposium, at Bryn Mawr College in 2004; to Gina Vitello and Lisa Shahriari for inviting me to give a plenary at Back to Bloomsbury: the Fourteenth Annual Conference on Virginia Woolf, at the University of London in 2004; to Sas May for inviting me to speak at the Photography and Literature Colloquium, at the University of Westminster in 2004; to Gabriele Griffin for inviting me to give a commemorative address at the University of Hull in 2004; to Adalgisa Giorgio for inviting me to give a keynote at Contemporary European Women Writers: Gender and Generation, at the University of Bath in 2005; to Ana Gabriela Macedo for inviting me to give a plenary at Intertextual Dialogues, at the Universidado do Minho, Portugal, in 2005; and to Andrea Noble and the vice chancellor of Durham University for his invitation to the annual research dinner and to give a paper at the inauguration of Durham's Centre for Advanced Photography Studies in 2005.

I am especially grateful for British Academy Small and Overseas Conference grants and for an Arts and Humanities Research Council Research Leave Award (no. 111689).

I am indebted to the curators and librarians who allowed me to explore their collections and for permissions to reprint. In particular I thank Kathleen Coleman, formerly of the Harvard Theatre Collection, for her heroic work of arranging for reproduction and permission; and Fredric Woodbridge Wilson, the curator of the collection, for his expert support; Laura Whitton and Dominic Persad of Tate Enterprises and the Tate Picture Library; Elizabeth Inglis, formerly of Sussex University Library, for sharing her knowledge of the albums; Jeremy Crowe and Lisa Dowdeswell, Society of Authors on behalf of the Virginia Woolf Estate; and librarians at King's College Cambridge, the National Portrait Gallery, and the Berg Collection of the New York Public Library.

Every effort has been made to contact copyright holders for their permission to reprint material. The publishers would be grateful to hear from any copyright holder who is not here acknowledged, and of any citation and sourcing errors, an inevitable possibility in a text of this detail, and will undertake to rectify any errors or omissions in future editions of this book.

My special thanks to members of the Executives of the British and American Woolf Societies, especially Stephen Barkway and Stuart Clarke, and former members, particularly Vanessa Curtis for her expert knowledge of early Stephen photographs, and to Colin Ford for sharing his Cameron expertise.

For this publication I have been particularly fortunate to benefit from the support and Bloomsbury expertise of Leslie Mitchner, associate director and editor in chief at Rutgers University Press; and Jackie Jones, deputy managing director of Edinburgh University Press, for introducing me to Leslie, and for her continuing support.

Finally my thanks go to colleagues and students at the University of East London for their vibrant discussions, especially Karen Cross for her always reflective and informed comments; special thanks to Becky Beasley, Anna Snaith, and Tory Young for inviting me to co-organize the British Modernism Research Seminar, University of London, and for sharing their stimulating ideas; to Helen Taylor, Julia Watson, and Gabriele Griffin, without whose support this book would not have emerged; to Dan and Male for their love and moral support and for inviting me to Alejandro's wonderful birth, and to Rodger most of all, for his visual expertise and continuing encouragement in everything.

PART ONE

Bloomsbury Histories and Photography

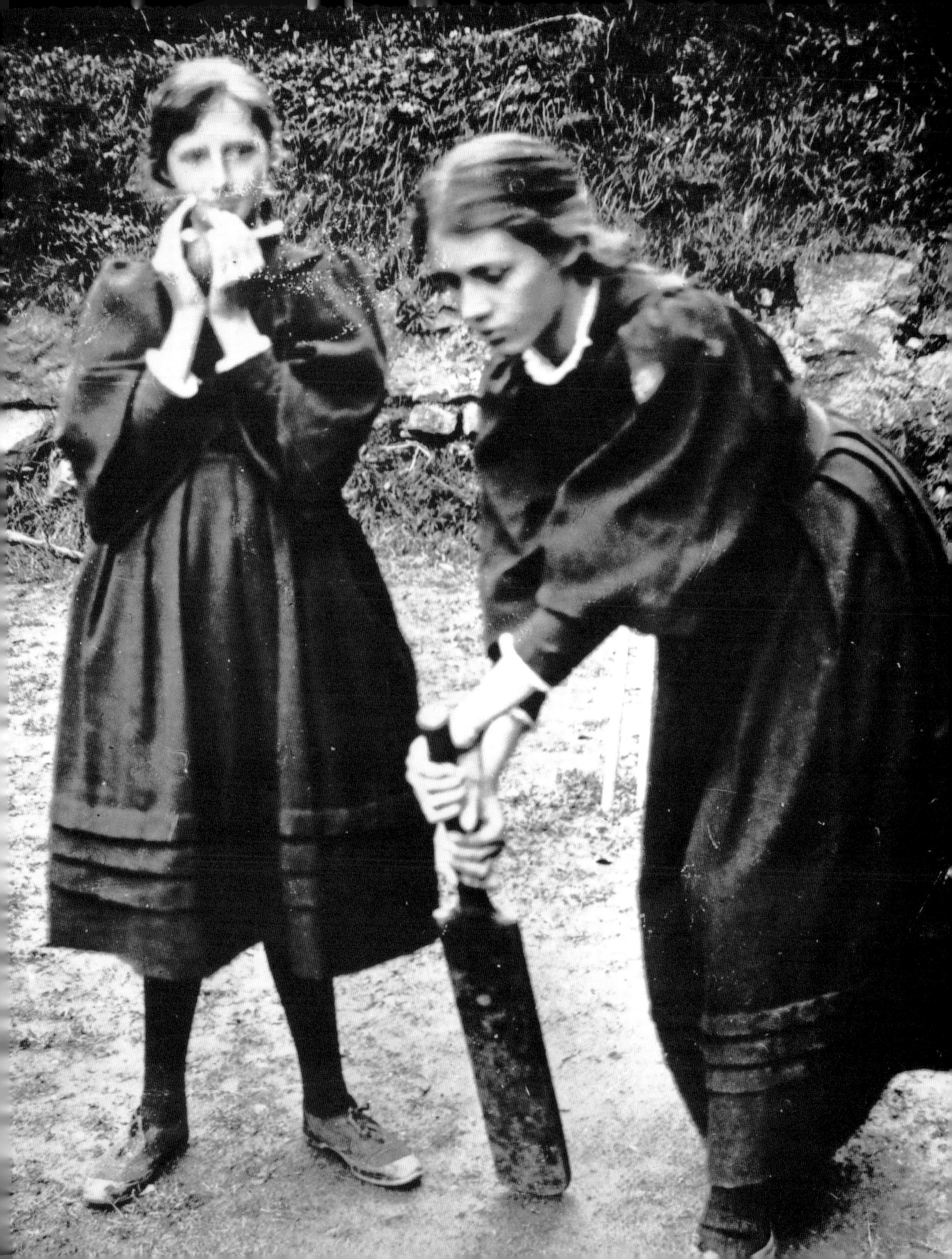

The Early Years

FIGURE 19 *Virginia and Vanessa Stephen, St. Ives, ca 1893–1894. Reprinted by permission of the Harvard Theatre Collection, the Houghton Library.*

VIRGINIA WOOLF the writer and her sister Vanessa Bell the artist created self-portraits, portraits of their friends and family, and also studies of the places where they lived. Both were autobiographical artists whose portraits draw on visual memories that shaped fictional identities and painted figures. Any artistic expression of identity draws on such repositories of memory. As autobiographical artists, Woolf and Bell provided insights into their work and lives through their domestic photographs. In envisioning the ways that identity is shaped by imagery and memory, the sisters were able to see themselves "as other" by means of photography. For most of Woolf's and Bell's lives, photography was, if not an obsession, then a continual ritual, one shared by family and friends including Lady Ottoline Morrell and Lytton Strachey, at a time when photography was permeating popular culture. Photography was also a constituent component of their visual inheritance from Julia Margaret Cameron, the famous Victorian photographer and their great-aunt, and from the photo albums of their father, Leslie Stephen, and their half sister Stella Duckworth.

Constructions of visual identity always involve questions of memory and speculation about how to record the thickness and malleability of personal lives. In what would now be termed a form of "life caching" or "memory prosthesis," Woolf and Bell used photo albums extensively as autobiographical narratives. Domestic photographs mounted in albums also invite viewer participation in constructing pictorial narratives from these domestic aide-mémoire. Scholarly and artistic accounts of amateur photography have become part of critical discussion since John Szarkowski's promulgation of a "snapshot aesthetic" in postwar exhibitions at New York's Museum of Modern

sisters regularly took and developed photographs, sometimes at the family home Hyde Park Gate but more often, like other amateurs, at holiday locales: St. Ives, Warboys, and Fritham. There are more than twenty references to photography in the initial year (1897) of entries to Woolf's first published journal. Woolf reveals how the sisters shared a wide range of visual experiences—seeing demonstrations of Roentgen rays (X-rays), frequently visiting the National Gallery, and acquiring and producing photographs. A favorite card game was played with family photographs in which "the ugliest took the trick" (Spater and Parsons, 3).

Woolf's diary entries provide irrefutable evidence of the significance of photography to the Stephen sisters. In March 1897, "Marny [Vaughan] came to tea with us, and asked about Stella's wedding present—to be a photograph or a picture" (*EJ*, 60). Photography's role as memorial of major events such as weddings extended into more diurnal moments. On holiday at the Old Vicarage, Painswick, in August 1897, "Marney & Emma arrived to pay us a visit. We photographed them. We developed after they were gone. Some rather good ones" (*EJ*, 121). The sisters shared a growing exploration of photography. Virginia and Vanessa almost always photographed when together, sharing one camera. At Bognor in February 1897, "the Frend [*sic*] arrived from Becks, in a new box, all rubbed up and beautiful, smelling strongly of Jargonel. We tried shutting Nessa up in the cupboard to put in the films, but there were too many chinks. Then she suggested being covered by her quilt, and everything else that I could lay hands on—She was accordingly, buried in dresses and dressing gowns, till no light could penetrate. Soon she emerged almost stifled having forgotten how to put the film in" (*EJ*, 34).

Adrian possessed his own camera, and all the children prioritized the financing of photographs even before birthday presents. "We shall have to be very economical. What with photographs, birthdays etc" (*EJ*, 12). Similarly, on holiday with "Georgie" Duckworth in 1896, Vanessa believed that mentioning photography first would be of more interest than describing a potentially erotic play. "We took a lot of photographs, but we haven't had time to develop any yet . . . on Saturday we went to a very improper French play" (VB/L, 6). Woolf is always very precise about her photographic technical needs. Writing to Thoby in January 1897, she states, "the size of the film is 3½ × 2⅝" (*L*, 1:3). The sisters took on differing but complementary technical skills, just as they pursued different artistic careers. "We found that the Frend [*sic*] would not work . . . when Nessa wound the shutter and mended it. . . . I have toned all the other photographs" (*EJ*, 38). The Frena employed a complicated notched film and eccentric handle, and by 1899 the style was modified (Lothrop, 122). Just as the observation of persons is a crucial feature of Woolf's narration and the outline of figures is crucial in Bell's paintings, so too were the sisters' careful documentation of their friends and animals in photographs essential sources for their memory and reflection.

It is, however, at their favorite home, Talland House, St. Ives, where the sisters, with their family, photographed continuously, documenting everyone who visited (figs. 13 and 16). Leslie Stephen had discovered Talland House on a walking expedition taken just before Virginia's birth, when the children were ages 13 (George), 12 (Stella), 11 (Gerald and Laura), 2 (Vanessa), and 1 (Thoby). Until 1894 the children, together with the later-born Virginia and Adrian, shared the activities of butterfly chasing, cricket playing, and rock climbing as well as photography and exploring the gardens of Talland House, in "intense domestic happiness" (L. Stephen, 63).

In the summer of 1892, Woolf, aged ten, wrote a novel titled *A Cockney's Farming Experiences* and a sequel, *The Experiences of a Pater-familias*, for the family newspaper, the *Hyde Park Gate News* at Talland House (DeSalvo,

134). Although Louise DeSalvo suggests that some of Woolf's later accounts of 1892 Cornwall, as revealed in letters, indicate Woolf's unhappiness during that year, certainly Cornwall represented to Woolf "cream, solitude, sublimity" (L, 2:464). Crucially for Woolf's subsequent photography, in 1892 Vanessa took a key photograph of Woolf, together with their mother Julia and father, sitting in the library at Talland House (fig. 10). All three sisters' albums—those of Virginia, Vanessa, and Stella—contain this 1892 photo in which Virginia gazes at Vanessa as camera operator as if sharing a "primal scene." Woolf's father also memorializes the image in his *Mausoleum Book,* written about the dead Julia, and includes it in his album (although dating it 1893). "When I look at certain little photographs—at one in which I am reading by her side at St. Ives with Virginia . . . I see as with my bodily eyes the love, the holy and tender love" (L. Stephen, 58–59). Woolf uses the photograph as a major frontispiece in Monk's House Album 3. Frances Spalding suggests that Vanessa's visual consciousness (just as Virginia's) grew out of "a need to repair a sense of loss, to reconstruct that sense of oneness with the world experienced by infants at the breast," after the death of Julia when Virginia was thirteen and Vanessa fifteen (Spalding, *Bell,* 19).

The need to recreate details from this childhood photograph appear again and again in the Woolfs' album sequences. As I argued in *Modernist Women and Visual Cultures,* childhood bereavement often finds artistic expression in visual memories and visual creations. Woolf's and Bell's photographs are layered images of familial presences and absences. The early photographs also have an ontological function, providing documentary evidence of the figures who were key players in the sisters' childhood and adolescence. Woolf's attachment to mother surrogates, for example, Stella, Vanessa, and Violet Dickinson, re-created for Woolf this pre-Oedipal attachment to the mother. Dickinson (fig. 43) cared for Woolf during Virginia's second breakdown, after her father's death in 1904. Violet was Virginia's "woman," and after their initial meeting in 1902 she was addressed by Woolf with playful erotic intimacy as "kangaroo" (Lee, 168). Dickinson's undated smaller photo album (4¾ × 7½ inches) does not contain the 1892 photograph but does have photographs of Woolf on both the frontispiece and cover; it contains as well Woolf's erotic euphemisms—"I hope to see you, Sparroy is firmly planted in that cabbage patch you call your heart." In Dickinson's separate autograph book, Virginia, Vanessa, Thoby, Adrian, George, and Gerald Duckworth have all signed autographs for the year 1904.

Before her death, Stella Duckworth was a major mother surrogate for Woolf, who accompanied Stella and Stella's fiancé, Jack Hills, to Bognor (the holiday during which "Nessa" was covered with her quilt). Stella Duckworth's album in the Berg Collection contains fifty-five photographs, mostly 4 × 3 inches, which repeat many of those in the Woolf and Bell albums (fig. 11), although Stella's contains additional pictures of their mother Julia. One of these, together with the 1892 photo, is mounted on a heavy protective card, as Woolf does with her photo of Julia in the later Monk's House Album 3, as if their mother's photographs are significant icons.

Other photographs taken during the sisters' adolescence are also palpably resonant. As Hermione Lee suggests, in photos of George Duckworth with his sisters "he is always standing too close to them" (fig. 22). When Julia Stephen died, George was twenty-seven, and from then, and increasingly after Leslie Stephen's death, he became the sisters' "unofficial guardian and their passport to the outside world" (Lee, 151). Louise DeSalvo has detailed the possible incestuous relationship between the older brothers and their half sisters at this time and earlier.

Other portraits taken during the sisters' childhood are less traumatic in resonance. George was secretary to Charles Booth, the social reformer and author of *Life and Labour of the People in London,* and Booth visited St. Ives together with J. A. Symonds, the painter and critic who taught Roger Fry (fig. 13). A more cosmopolitan friend was the Florentine Rezia Rasponi, who married a Corsini prince and brought her husband (fig. 41) to meet the Stephens at Fritham House one summer. Vanessa later painted an incomplete, and now missing, portrait of Rezia in Florence in 1909. Photographs, like portraits, are also selective records and fictions. But photographs were important mementos for Virginia and Vanessa. In 1898, writing to Thoby, Woolf thought that a photo of "Nessa by Cousin Henry" (Henry Herschel Cameron, the son of their great-aunt Julia Margaret Cameron) would be "the best present I can think of" (L, 1:18). Woolf was more self-conscious about her own photographic representations, which were often "like an ancient beast of my acquaintance" (L, 1:29).

THE WOOLFS' ALBUMS

The Woolfs' seven photo albums, called the Monk's House Albums, together with four boxes containing over two hundred additional loose photographs, are housed in the Frederick Koch Collection of the Harvard Theatre Library and are uncatalogued. There are many signs of disturbance in the albums, with blank areas and excised or lost photographs, presumably due to the removing of photographs by Leonard Woolf and by George Spater and Ian Parsons for their books published after Virginia's death. Woolf states in her letters that "I keep a family album," in the singular, and the majority of the album captions are in her hand (L, 6:169). But many are in Leonard's shaky script, and the albums seem to be dialogic. Leonard and Virginia often take turns photographing each other sitting in the same chair or position. Yet Leonard's obsessional numeration of life events in chronological order in his diaries and ephemera, for example, the precise dates of cacti flowering and of central heating use, is very unlike the albums' associative meanderings and suggests that Virginia may have had more responsibility for the albums' compilation. And there are few entries after her death.

Two of the albums are somewhat less significant small albums, one consisting primarily of cartes-de-visite and cabinet photographs of well-known public figures from the 1860s, and the other almost empty except for three photographs, dated "Sweden July 28th 1911," of Elia and Gertrude between Lysekil and Fishbrackil. But the remaining five much larger albums are a major record of the Woolfs' lives and friendships. The albums are fully notated in the "Catalogue of the Monk's House Albums and Photographs," in this volume, but there are typological characteristics I wish to highlight here to illustrate the nature of the Woolfs' visual storytelling.

One feature of the albums is the large number of Victorian photographs that predate the Woolfs' lives and are carefully captioned (fig. 2). This panorama suggests, perhaps, a longing for a confirmed familial world. Duncan Grant remembered that "she was fascinated by the old familiar figures of her childhood, the friends and relatives of her father . . . some shrivelled by time, some still brightly vigorous, some horribly decaying" (Grant, "V. Stephen," 157). Family photographs directly shade the Woolfs' and Bell's personal landscapes. For example, in Monk's House Album 1, a studio portrait of Stella Duckworth is succeeded by further photos of the Stephen family, including one of Virginia's half sister Laura as a baby, held by her father Leslie Stephen, and Bell's Album 1 has photos of her mother Julia holding the infant Gerald Duckworth (figs. 17, 4, 26). As Nigel Nicolson recalled, on Virginia's first visit to Vita Sackville-West, "she liked the feeling of this vast continuity of portraits hanging on the walls, forming a sort of second set of occupants of the house watching their descendants" (Nicolson, 74).

A second feature is the contingency of the photographs, the Woolfs' refusal of conventional chronology. Album 1 jumps from Victorian cartes-de-visite, to Leonard's Ceylon photographs ca. 1907 (pp. 27–42), and returns to Victorian family photographs (p. 51). The albums lack of chronological logic matches Woolf's refusal of narrative realism in her fiction and illustrates the intertextuality of past and present. In Album 3 the past vividly "narrates" the present. The framing frontispiece is a large 6 × 7½ photograph of Julia Stephen (fig. 3; see the Catalogue for attribution), immediately followed by the 1892 St. Ives photograph of Julia, Leslie, and Virginia Stephen, yet page 3 is marked "August 1931."

The chronology of Monk's House Album 4, like its predecessors, is very eclectic. The album is dated 1939, but the first photographs are of Roger Fry taken by Lenare and a *News Chronicle* clipping dated 1938, followed by photographs taken at Ottoline Morrell's in 1923 (fig. 61) and Carrington, Ralph Partridge, and Lytton Strachey at Ham Spray in the 1920s (fig. 57). Monk's House Album 5 too is shaped by Virginia's childhood memories. Pages 1–14 contain photographs of Virginia's favorite childhood home—Talland House, St. Ives—together with studio portraits of Leslie Stephen. There is no closed, hierarchical system; for example, photographs of servants (fig. 14) are not separated from family photographs, and past photographs impact on contemporary scenes. The Woolfs' love of repetitive sequencing is impregnated by Gerald Duckworth's much more rigorous, "anthropological" sequential photographs of servants at Talland House in 1892 (fig. 15).

A third feature is the repetition of monumental portraits. The camera is inscriptive, not transcriptive, in its visibility—for example, the portraits of Ethel Smyth and the Keyneses in the 1930s (figs. 134 and 140). The psychological consistency of composition in these photographs suggests a subtle relationship between photographers and subjects through the sitters' strong self-presentations. In many ways, all these features suggest a foregrounding and subversion of the conventional nature of albums and the Woolfs' refusal of artificial family histories.

VANESSA BELL'S ALBUMS

Vanessa Bell's ten family albums are in the Hyman Kreitman Research Centre Archive and Special Collections, at the Tate in London. These comprise a unique documentary record of her family and friends, as well as of her aesthetic interests and enthusiasms. The first album (1A) opens with photographs dated 1896 (Bell was born in 1879), and album 9 ends with photographs of Fitzroy Square, dated 1939 (Bell died in 1961). Bell carefully paginates her albums and groups photographs by dates of composition as well as place and personae. The layout is clear and quasi-chronological, although the albums are not in proper sequence. Album 1 figures family scenes at St. Ives and elsewhere, dated 1890, which precedes the 1896 date of Album 1A. Bell's albums expansively capture her community and family in a progressive narrative. As Naomi Rosenblum points out, in the 1910s and 1920s, women photographers found "genre themes particularly appealing," particularly narrative genres (Rosenblum, 100).

Bell's mode of collection and organization mimics her familial and domestic roles. For example, Bell welcomes into her collection many photographs taken by others just as Bell warmly welcomed visitors to stay in Charleston and Cassis. Bell includes in her albums family photographs taken before her birth (fig. 25), and photographs taken by Virginia and Leonard as well as photographs of Angelica "taken by Mrs. Curtis" (Album 7, pp. 14 and 15); of Julian Bell by Lettice Ramsey, a professional photographer and one of Julian's girlfriends (fig. 183) (Album 7, pp. 22 and 23); a Charleston interior taken by Barbara Bagenal in 1936 (Album 8, p. 20); Janie Bussy's family photographs; and Angelica "taken by Mrs. Gladwyn Jebb" in 1935 (Album 8, pp. 3 and 4). There are many additional photographs in the Bell archive that Bell chose not to mount in her albums. For obvious reasons, the several photographs (some reproduced here) of herself, Molly MacCarthy (fig. 102), Duncan Grant (fig. 99), and other models posing naked are not mounted in albums.

Although the detailed captions as well as the many family portraits in Bell's albums might seem to match those of the Woolfs' albums and Leslie Stephen's photo album, Bell does not contextualize the present in a family past in the way the Woolfs do by their use of Julia Stephen's photograph as a significant frontispiece that dominates their album construction. Vanessa Bell's photographs vary enormously in size, genre, and quality. The most imposing are monumental portraits of family and friends, such as those of Duncan Grant and Roger Fry (figs. 89 and 83), that are corporeally expressive. Others, some of family events at Charleston, are small snapshots no larger than 2½ × 3¼ inches, and some photographs are even of photo booth, or passport photograph, scale (1 × 1½ inch). Bell seems less concerned with a progressive development of her photographic techniques than with making full and detailed firsthand studies of her world. For example, images are repeated with regularity in differing scales, particularly photographs of Bell's children. Repetition is not a simple act but indicates how loath Bell was to discard images; it also is important as a doubled act of remembrance. As Martha Langford argues, "the condition of memory, or something that reminds us of memory, is figured and absorbed through repetition" (Langford, 141).

The domestic arena, whether at Charleston or the London studios, is a paradigmatic space. Bell shared this attachment with her great-aunt. In *Annals of My Glass House*, Cameron's autobiography, she describes how her "habit of running into the dining room with my wet pictures has stained such an immense quantity of table linen with nitrate of silver." As it would be later for Bell, the domestic arena provided not only the site of Cameron's photographs but also their representational coordinates. Looking at the prizewinning photograph in the first exhibition to which she submitted, Cameron noted "that detail of table-cover, chair and crinoline skirt were essential to the judges of the art" (Cameron, 13).

The performativity of Cameron's photographs is reflected both in Bell's *Orlando* photographs of Angelica (figs. 125 and 126) and in Woolf's love of mock biographies supported by photographs, for example, *Flush*. As Anny Thackeray Ritchie, Leslie Stephen's sister-in-law suggests, "People like clear hard outlines, and have a fancy to see themselves and their friends as if through opera-glasses, all complete, with the buttons, &c. nicely defined. These things Mrs. Cameron's public may not always find, but in their stead are very wonderful and charming sights and suggestions" (Ford, 57).

A similar tension between documentation and "sights and suggestions" informs the Woolfs' and Bell's photo albums. Bell's albums follow a rough diachronic chronology of production, whereas the photographs in the Woolfs' albums are grouped more by subject matter. But the question of the relationship between kinds of depiction and biographical referents is basic to the medium of photography itself as well as to photo albums. Often photographs contain details that may have escaped the photographer's perception, and photographic decoding is a complex activity in which microscopic analysis can be enormously productive for artistic and cultural understandings.

READING ALBUMS

Domestic photographs can be read symptomatically through the observation of detail as well as through choices of framing. Snapshots are apparently informal depictions of everyday experience, but the Woolfs' and Bell's portraits are frequently contemplative, composed images, and family albums, as the U.S. photographer of family life Garry Winogrand suggests, are the "most carefully made photographs that ever happened" (Campany, 35). In any case, Bloomsbury members as a group consistently used the term *amateur* in a positive sense to articulate a detachment from *professional*, that is, associated with trade and artistic consumerism. And photography, as Susan Sontag suggests, is the only major art in which amateurs can excel.

The Woolfs' and Bell's family albums involve a careful choreography of professional and private lives. The Woolfs' albums become a history of the literary and artistic figures they knew and the wider cultural relationships such friendships inspired. Bell's photographs often act as artistic prequels for her later art (figs. 199 and 200). In addition, Bell's fabric of family life is a self-conscious narrative. While family photographs may be fragile moments of personal perceptions often hermetic and opaque to the general reader, they are also "technologies of memory." In *Tangled Memories* Marita Sturken argues that photographs are technologies of memory because they are transactions between "personal memory, cultural memory and history" (Sturken, 178). For example, for the Woolfs and Bell, photographs were important talismans in a personal sense (Virginia in particular used photographs as talismans against her fear of death), but the Bloomsbury photographs also become technologies in our contemporary present through which we can construct and situate a Bloomsbury past. From this perspective, the Woolfs' and Bell's photographs need not be sentimentally revered as romantic auteur objects but read culturally. Rather than crudely romanticizing each image, we can read the photographs as material practices and technologies of memory as well as, of course, biographically. In an obvious way, any album's aggregate of photographs is an index of private imaginaries because people only photograph what interests them.

For Virginia, in particular, photography was an elegiac art. Photography's role as a memorial agent is now a commonplace of critical discussion following Roland Barthes's seminal *Camera Lucida*. "Ever since cameras were invented in 1839, photography has kept company with death" (Sontag, *Pain*, 21). Certainly in the early history of photography, many people were actually photographed for the first and last time in their coffins. But the Woolfs' attention to memorial photography supplements these critical and historical themes. Woolf was an elegiac modernist writer, for example, subtitling *To the Lighthouse* "an elegy" for her brother Thoby Stephen, and photographs of friends were important memento mori in her personal life. In March 1925 Woolf pleaded with Gwen Raverat, after the death of Jacques Raverat, the French painter, for "a snapshot or any photograph of him? I go on making things up to tell him" (fig. 64), an affiliative urge Woolf had felt from childhood in all her friendships (*L*, 3:172–173). As many critics of modernism have noted, the creation of a usable past is also crucial to modernism's confrontation with the perceived fragmentation and transitory quality of modernity.

By the time the sisters entered womanhood following the move to Bloomsbury in 1904, photography was a constant presence in their lives and a constant reflection of their evolving visual consciousness. And it was photography, particularly the mass circulation of Kodaks, that made, arguably, the greatest contribution to the changing visual consciousness of modernity as a whole. The widespread dissemination of photographs, together with the general public's increasing knowledge of photographic processes, marked a change in modern perceptions and was symbolized domestically by the Stephen sisters' happy relocation to the white, light interiors of Bloomsbury albeit hung with their Cameron photographs, away from the dark interiors of Hyde Park Gate. As Ann

Ardis argues, many cultural experiences that we imagine as "distinctively modern"—she cites as examples shopping and cinema but we could add photography—"are closely tied up with the experience of women in the modern world" (Ardis, 292).

Similarly, neat boundaries cannot be drawn between the realms of Woolf's and Bell's more avant-garde work and their delight in the popular culture of amateur photography in their daily lives. The conceptual polarities of aesthetic and popular culture are inappropriate for Bloomsbury since the aesthetic meant a significant way of looking. A major consequence of abandoning this classic binary is that the distinction between affect and knowledge dissolves. The affect of photographs becomes a form of cognition, particularly when the display of albums is a narrative performance. So-called banal snapshots might be a vernacular process, but inevitably they contributed to the Stephen sisters' visual experience and knowledge. In *Bloomsbury Rooms* Christopher Reed convincingly argues that Bloomsbury's domestic aesthetic is a significant contribution to modernism. In Woolf's writings the domestic space is a creative space: for example, Clarissa Dalloway's parties and Rezia's and Clarissa's domestic sewing in *Mrs. Dalloway.* Similarly Bell's *Nursery Tea* displays maternal intimacy as well as the class differences of modernity. Although women's use of domestic space can be marked as stereotypically "feminine," for many complex socioeconomic and historical reasons women do have a different relationship to space than men do. Looking at visual modernities from the perspective of the gendered domestic space and the everyday, while simultaneously refusing to read everyday memories as simply "real" life, is a tricky balance but matches new modernism's focus on visual technologies in both domestic and public spaces.

"The Light and the Air": 1904 to 1929

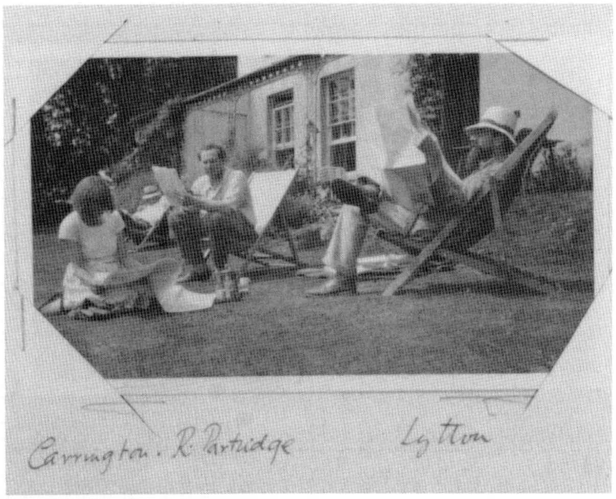

FIGURE 70 (DETAIL) *Dora Carrington, Ralph Partridge, and Lytton Strachey, Ham Spray dated 1930. Reprinted by permission of the Harvard Theatre Collection, the Houghton Library.*

DAME JANET Vaughan remembered that when "asked about my memories of Bloomsbury I got out my mother's tattered old scrapbook. I found faded photographs of Leslie Stephen and Julia standing out in the snow at Davos. . . . there were photographs also of Leslie Stephen seated in his armchair in the Hyde Park study and a very lovely one of Julia looking out of the same window as she pulled aside the curtain to let the light fall full on her face" (Vaughan, 9).

The multiple domestic photographs and albums produced by the Stephen family preserve not only memories but also different visual stories of each family member's sense of its generational place. There are seven photographs, taken in Switzerland by Gabriel Loppé, in Leslie Stephen's album (series VII, 1889, leaf 39), possibly because the Stephens' Swiss photographs crystallized for Sir Leslie an imaginary of his marriage with his performance of alpine masculinity. So that Virginia and Vanessa's move to Bloomsbury, after Stephen's death in 1904, was not just a geographical move but a move to a new and freer psychocultural space, a public world of culture and politics away from their enclosed Victorian home. In "Old Bloomsbury" Woolf describes how Gordon Square became "the headquarters of Bloomsbury" (OB, 173).

Both sisters experienced this new domestic space visually. "In October 1904 it was the most beautiful, the most exciting, the most romantic place in the world . . . the light and the air after the rich red gloom of Hyde Park Gate were a revelation" (OB, 162). In the light painted rooms of 46 Gordon Square, reached through a hallway of Julia Margaret Cameron photographs, including photographs of Julia Duckworth, the sisters joined Thoby and his Cambridge friends on Thursday evenings in animated conversations. "There was now nothing that one could not say, nothing that one could not do, at 46 Gordon Square. It was, I think, a great advance in civilisation" (OB, 174). The Stephen sisters enjoyed the free space of cultural debate, albeit a space entered through a maternal photographic iconography. Not surprisingly, the post-1904 photographs, taken at a range of places, including Brandon Camp, Charleston, Asheham House, Firle Park, and Monk's House, display a life growing far beyond the confines of the Stephens' Victorian family.

As the geo-social boundaries of Bell's and the Woolfs' world became more cosmopolitan and fluid in the 1920s, with many new friendships, their marriages, and frequent changes of houses, studios, and landscapes, photography could map familial onto cultural networks. The photographs in this period are self-confident portraits of their many friends and family, including Margaret Llewelyn Davies (fig. 55), Vanessa's children (fig. 113), and artists and writers including T. S. Eliot (fig. 56), Walter Sickert with Roger Fry (fig. 86), and E. M. Forster (fig. 59). The portraits are set into the reflective space of multiple albums that the sisters had began compiling during their childhood, before their father's death and their marriages. By 1904 Virginia had completed one album and Vanessa was halfway through a second album.

As a genre, photo albums are conventionally read as documents of "real" family life. Indeed snapshot photography is frequently assessed by its ability to document indices of the real. And "Kodaking" is often seen as a mundane cultural practice. But it would be wrong to believe that photo albums by their very "reality" somehow escape modernist ambivalences just because they are sources of family and historical evidence. Equally, to divide domestic practices from public cultures is to be caught up in a reactionary and now outmoded critical stance. Although the scenes and people recorded by the Woolfs and Bell are snapshots of everyday Bloomsbury, the camera viewpoints and framing look attentively beyond the snapshot moment into the sisters' past and outward into moments of modernity. The seemingly trivial detail and events in the photographs, such as household objects and pursuits, are elements of the everyday but can be cognitively viewed from different angles.

A further problematic, following the issue of evaluating marginalia, is how to know, except by indexical, cultural, and biographical analysis, the photographs' likely "readership" and Bell's and the Woolfs' reasons for shooting and selection, since this is not always evident in the many diaries or letters. To purloin Alex Zwerdling's very pertinent questions about Woolf's autobiographical memoirs: For whom are the photo albums constructed—"for the nuclear family, for an inner circle," or the anticipation of a wider circle? "And for what purpose: to honor the dead? . . . To make the past cohere? to produce the official record? to amuse and entertain? To illustrate a representative way of life? to confess? to understand oneself?" Zwerdling concludes, in relation to writing, that the "multigenerational Stephen internal tradition of memoir writing illustrated all these options" (Zwerdling, 168–169). The Bloomsbury photo albums equally illustrate all these options. Most Stephen family members (Leslie, Stella, Vanessa, Virginia, Julian) and friends kept photo albums and kept albums in constant circulation. For example, while visiting her friend Violet Dickinson in June 1904, February 1907, and December 1910, Virginia contributed whimsical greetings to Dickinson's album: "I besieged your very heart in Manchester Square" (Dickinson, 6).

How then to read this marginal minutiae of modernism? It is both tautological because self-evident and yet not enough to argue that the portraits represent the sisters' intense desire for a supportive social/cultural group of like-minded friends and family. There are questions of appropriate femininities and masculinities that remain unspoken as well as questions of class and generational rebellions and visual inheritances. In many ways photo albums resemble what Edward Soja, in the context of urban geographies, calls a "third space," which combines the real and the imagined, as well as Foucault's concept of heterotopology. Foucault coined this term to define marginal sites of modernity, such as Parisian arcades, whose role was to create a kind of virtual reality. Foucault's idea has greatly influenced contemporary architectural studies, as, for example, in Charles Jencks's application of the term *heteropolis* to Los Angeles' combination of modernism with sites of difference.

By applying Foucault's concept to photo albums, I do not intend to imply that photography is purely spatial or only a collection of measurable representations. This illusion of clarity would oversubstantiate the snapshot world. But focusing on spatial arrangements in album photographs is potentially fruitful not least because it allays a common belief that all amateur photographers are unable to aesthetically manage spatial dimensions. Space is socially produced and actively shapes our subjectivity, whether in visual sites such as photographs or in urban geographies. Where everyday representations are often below the threshold of art history, heterotopology, on the contrary, illuminates the psychodynamics of snapshots. Spaces of representation in snapshots embody complex emotions, the multiple perceived and unconscious spaces of the camera operator, and the photographed figures and viewers. These complex symbolisms are sometimes coded, for example, by learned artistic conventions, and sometimes not. In third space, or heterotopology, physical measurable space is interdependent with symbolic and imaginative spaces. For example, in the iconography of nineteenth-century cartes-de-visite, the 1892 photograph of Woolf's parents reading at St. Ives suggests simply an intimate family space. But heterotopologically, Virginia's look to Vanessa behind the camera suggests an explicit sorority projected in the sisters' symbolic space of the primal scene (fig. 10).

One good example of a heterotopological "method" is Bell's and the Woolfs' use of photo album captions. Their frequent use of nomenclature, with Virginia captioning her own images "VW" and giving full names to friends—for example, "Roger Fry"—and Vanessa using initials for each individual (including her children), is unusual. The sisters clearly did not need to remind themselves of Fry's identity and certainly not of their own. At first glance, Bell and the Woolfs' "objectivity" might seem the antithesis of heterotopology because the function of titles is didactic, even mechanistic. Recording titles is a way of collating information, like a catalogue or dictionary does, into predetermined spaces. John Tagg has read the history of photography in this way as documentary evidence of institutions of social control. Walter Benjamin agrees that captioning photographs "literarises the relationships of life" (Benjamin, "Photography," 25). What both ignore is gender and how even documentary records can have multiple meanings.

The role of photo albums in their lives more resembles Foucault's account of the role of a mirror in heterotopology, which "enables me to see myself there where I am absent" (Foucault, 24). A more pertinent question to ask is: *Why* should Bell and the Woolfs wish to constantly name themselves and their friends in albums? What does this action reveal about their imaginary configuration of friends and family? The album captions suggest an implied viewer and also suggest that Bell and the Woolfs were motivated by several of the possibilities that Zwerdling outlines: to honor the dead, to make the past coherent, to understand themselves. The album captions suggest the sisters deep desire for a visual remembrance of life and friendships, reinforcing close-up portraits with verbal stress, and matching Bell's domestic aesthetic and the Woolfs' daily diaries and letter writing. The albums become memento mori in the very act of construction. They are slices of time, precarious spaces both temporary and permanent. The albums picture present moments shaped by a past that is never permanently past. Objects and places in Bell's and the Woolfs' snapshot photographs stand in for the irretrievably lost childhood home at St. Ives, just as the past sometimes informs Virginia Woolf's stance in her more formal studio portraits.

For example, while as Brenda Silver rightly points out, the *Vogue* photographs taken of Woolf reflect the "growing visibility of her public persona," the place of Woolf's studio portrait for *Vogue* on April 27, 1925 (fig. 66), taken by Maurice Beck and his partner Helen Macgregor, was Marylebone Mews, a house in which Thomas Woolner the sculptor had proposed a sitting and marriage to Woolf's mother Julia (who refused both) (Silver, 132). Woolf's decision to wear gloves for this photograph, together with her composed, demure decorum, recalls that earlier time, which Woolf refers to in her diary. "I have been sitting to Vogue, the Becks that is, in their mews, which Mr Woolner built as his studio, & perhaps it was there he thought of my mother, whom he wished to marry" (*D*, 3:12). And for the first *Vogue* photograph, taken in 1924 (fig. 65), Woolf chose to wear her mother's dress. It is Woolf's inability to exclude memory referents from all her photographs, including those she saved that were taken by others, which makes Woolf's albums so pregnant with meaning. In addition, as Silver acutely notes, there are few professional photographs that capture Virginia's direct gaze (169). The domestic photographs, in which Woolf repeatedly interacts with the viewer, become even more significant with their projective point of view.

The photo albums of the Woolfs and Bell can be read as performing a virtual space, in interlocking circles of friendship and family and Bloomsbury culture. The Woolfs' and Bell's photographs document real events and people, but the portraits are also transformational spaces, containing multiple stories of the way in which the sisters wished to textualize their worlds. The panoramic picture of domestic Bloomsbury is sometimes idealized but necessarily is also part of the new panorama of avant-garde and consumerist cultures of pre- and postwar Britain. There was the Dreadnought Hoax in February 1910, involving Virginia and Adrian, which took on the British naval establishment and drew on Adrian's earlier Cambridge Zanzibar Hoax (fig. 45), and the Post-Impressionist Ball, when the sisters dressed as "South Sea savages" to match Roger Fry's inclusion of African art in his 1910 exhibition (*L*, 1:455).

The years 1910 to 1930 were a period in which Vanessa Bell, Duncan Grant, and Roger Fry became key cultural figures, following the two Post-Impressionist exhibitions in London of 1910 and 1912, which influenced museum and private collections. The Woolfs too shaped cultural opinion through their books, journalism, and political activism. The founding of the Omega Workshop and the Hogarth Press, and Leonard's editorship of key journals, including the *International Review* and the *Nation*, were the compass points of a cultural configuration that included Bell and Grant's influential visits abroad to the Paris studios of Matisse and Picasso, anticonscription work, and the international modernity of the Woolfs' political and friendship networks.

It was a time when London modernity became qualitatively international in new, exciting, but often confused ways. Patterns of consumption were changing with the arrival of American department stores such as Selfridges in 1909, and the rise in postwar wages reduced class differences in patterns of leisure and consumption. London doubled its size between 1917 and 1939, with the London County Council's "greatest amount of rebuilding . . . since the Great

Fire of London" (Ross, 116). Gramophones, wirelesses, and cinema followed the growth of other technological modernities such as photography. It was estimated by the *Daily Mail* in August 1905 that there was, roughly speaking, "one camera user in every ten of the population" (Gernsheim, 425). Public and private modernities are always in tension. Vanessa Bell's constant photography of her young children matched a growing interest in child care in this period, with the 1906 Education Act providing food for schoolchildren, the 1908 Children's Act preventing parental neglect, and the 1910 Midwives Act requiring midwife certification. H. A. L. Fisher, the sisters' cousin, designed the 1918 Education Act, which raised the age at which a child could leave school to fourteen. The postwar improvement in British education matches Virginia's interest in common readers and marginalized figures. Leonard optimistically records in *Sowing*, one of his autobiographies, that "We were not part of a negative movement of destruction against the past. We were out to construct something new; we were in the van of the builders of a new society which should be free, rational, civilized, pursuing truth and beauty. It was all tremendously exhilarating" (*S*,138).

The version of modernity that emerges from Leonard's liberal account is of a pre- and postwar grand progress sweeping over the less equitable irregularities of gender disparities, and the defeat of the General Strike. Virginia, more "gloomy," knew immediately that "Labour, it seems clear, will be effectively diddled again," and indeed trade union membership fell by 1930 to less than half its former number (*D*, 3:85). These differing meanings of the 1910s and 1920s impact unevenly on the Woolfs' and Bell's domestic photography in terms of particular choices of photographic events, such as parties, and in less conscious choices of image. Virginia wrote to Vanessa on November 13, 1918, more negatively than to Leonard about the immediate aftermath of World War I: "The clocks strike incessantly, in a very disordered way . . . there's practically no one in London now whom I can talk to either about my own writing or Shakespeares. I'm beginning to think that I'd better stop writing novels" (*L*, 2:293).

This conjunction of public and private change that the Woolfs and Bell tried to ameliorate with photography, and in turn with their photographs, just as much as with their art and writing, was inevitably caught up in a re-imagined urbanity. Lady Ottoline Morrell's photographs of Woolf taken at Garsington (fig. 60) and those of the naked Vanessa (fig. 102), George Mallory the Everest climber (fig. 94), and a cross-dressing Duncan Grant "pleat" with more formal modernist low-angle photographs of Roger Fry (fig. 109) and Duncan (Serrès). The formation of new gender identities marked this period of transition, which started with the 1910 anti-corset campaign onward. It is a commonly remarked-on feature of the 1920s that it was a decade in which the popular press, fiction, and science gave great attention to re-visioning femininity, female portraits featured in modernist photography, including nude portraits by Edward Weston and Man Ray, and the 1920s cinema created "auto-erotic images of sexuality" (Maltby, 23). This focus on women's images responded to women's newly commodified sexuality as well as to women's very real new economic and political enfranchisement. Sexuality became a more public issue with the prosecution of Radclyffe Hall's *The Well of Loneliness*, for which Woolf was to appear as a witness for the defense, and with Woolf's own play with gender roles in *Orlando*, a best seller for the Hogarth Press—or indeed when the Prince of Wales posed in drag for the camera.

The frequent cross-dressing at Bloomsbury parties was always more than simply snapshots of fancy dress; indeed, it often seemed to indicate its participants' antipathy to modernist machismo, as Woolf struggled to define in her diary. "My present reflection is that people have any number of states of consciousness: & I should like to investigate the party consciousness, the frock consciousness &c. . . . These states are very difficult (obviously I grope for words) . . . it is something real. You must keep it up; conspire together" (*D*, 3:12–13). Woolf suggests that costume parties, which Bell carefully documented in photography, somehow expressed a diversity of consciousness, a diversity of sexualities perhaps akin to Woolf's multiple fictional modernist subjectivities.

Bloomsbury's "party consciousness" was mirrored publicly. Clive Bell pinpointed this moment of modernity by citing the visits to London of Diaghilev's ballet in 1911 and 1919, when "suddenly the arts became the preoccupation of Society (with the capital S) which twelve months earlier had been preoccupied with military and political intrigue. Abruptly, and unexpectedly the wheels of civilisation began to turn" (Bell, as quoted in Ross, 54). The influence of the Russian ballet on Bloomsbury design was profound, bringing a new fluidity to figures in Duncan Grant's *The Queen of Sheba* (1912) and his window panels at 38 Brunswick Square, and later affecting the posing of Angelica in Russian clothing in Bell's photographs for *Orlando* (figs. 125 and 126).

Domestic and public visual worlds always reflect. For example, Nijinsky's choreography for the 1913 ballet *Jeux*, created for Diaghilev's company, drew on Nijinsky's delighted observation of a Bloomsbury tennis party at Lady Ottoline Morrell's house in Bedford Square, although Grant had already constructed a tennis player mural in 1912–1913 for the first-floor sitting room at Brunswick Square (Shone, *Portraits*, 96; Reed, 97). By 1925, personal and public worlds became more intimate with John Maynard Keynes's marriage to Lydia Lopokova, the famous Russian ballet dancer, who "emoted as powerfully as any silent film star" (Ross, 53). Other hostesses, Lady Sibyl Colefax and Christabel McLaren, joined Ottoline Morrell in combining domestic and cultural concerns with support for Bloomsbury. McLaren and Colefax coordinated the MacCarthy fund with Woolf's assistance to cover Desmond MacCarthy's debts and to finance a holiday for him and his wife. In six months £730 (£30,000 at today's prices) was collected, with E. M. Forster's very generous starting contribution of £125 (£5,000 today), a marked difference from the earlier T. S. Eliot fund, which had only managed £77 (Barkway).

This "pleating" of friendship networks into fancy dress parties, exhibitions, and theater was matched in the sisters' art, writing, and photography. Bell's photograph of Sophie Farrell and Maud (fig. 108), taken at the rear of Brunswick Square, both marks the servants' significant social role in 38 Brunswick Square's new domestic freedoms, with its mixed ménage of Grant, Keynes, Adrian, and Virginia and Leonard Woolf dependant on supportive domestics, as well as Duncan's exhibition art. Grant's studio was located on the rear ground floor, and the window in the photograph's background displays Grant's sure knowledge of modernist art with its reworking of Matisse's figures, the centerpiece of the 1912 Post-Impressionist exhibition.

The public spaces of Bloomsbury leisure during the 1910s and 1920s weave in and out of imaginary spaces. Brandon Camp near Thetford, in August 1913, was a masquerade of an organic community, with key Bloomsbury figures: the Olivier sisters, Ka Cox, Rupert Brooke, the Raverats, Molly MacCarthy, and Roger Fry came together with Clive, Vanessa (fig. 96), Duncan bringing a bottle of champagne, and Adrian. Although Vanessa slept in nearby accommodations, wishing "we were all healthy, young women like the O[livier]s," she delighted in the rural escapade part of a general Edwardian fascination with pastoralism (VB/L, 140). "Today luckily has been lovely again, warm and sunny . . . Roger of course has been painting hard . . . and I am sitting over the fire keeping watch on a wonderful stew R has made"

(VB/L, 140). The camp's "primitive" life inspired Bell to innovative abstractions: *Summer Camp* (1913), her boldly schematic Omega designs *Painted Omega Screen Tents and Figures* (1913) and *Design for Omega Rug* (1914), and photography. The activity resembles what Lisa Tickner has called, in reference to Augustus John's similar caravanning, "a dream of the restored plenitude of the maternal body" (*Modern Life*, 77).

More private, psychobiographic spaces emerge in other ways, however. Both Bell and Woolf try to incorporate the maternal into their modernism, albeit with different understandings of the mother figure. Woolf's writings are flooded by the melancholy memory of her mother, and Bell paints strong representations of motherhood in her use of children's toys and women's figures. These cultural-psychic maternal presences are as residually present in Bell's and Woolf's photography as they are in the sisters' better-known art and writing, and they shape the sisters' techniques in both art and photography. Pamela Caughie argues that in *Jacob's Room*, with its strong maternal figure, written during this period, Woolf uses the camera devices of close-up and scoping, although "it is more a matter of modernist techniques and new technologies mutually shaping one another than of direct influence" (Caughie, xxv–xxvi). Often the very structure of Woolf's sentences, for example, Woolf's frequent use of ellipses, creates an implied reader, much like the repetition of objects in the Woolfs' photography needs an active spectator. The Woolfs' constant photography practice and Virginia's early knowledge of photographic techniques, including framing, space, and distance, would unconsciously shape her fictional use of frames.

Certainly Vanessa Bell and the Woolfs took photography very seriously. Leonard's diaries record a regular expenditure showing their addiction to photography, and the amounts are as revealing about British class divisions as about technologies. In April 1922 Leonard spent ten shillings on photography but paid their servant Lottie only two shillings (LW/D). In 1923 the Woolfs spent one pound, two shillings (or twenty-two shillings), on photography, and a year later, on May 30, 1924, one pound and one shilling, but gave Nellie only five shillings. Some idea of the scale of photographic expenditure can be had when we see that the Woolfs paid exactly the same amount, one pound, one shilling, for a refrigerator in May 1925. Domestic refrigeration did not become commonly available in Britain because of its expense until the late 1950s.The income from Virginia's capital "had shrunk to less than half its original sum by 1918–19" and was even lower in the 1920s, at a time when their joint earnings were often in deficit (Spater and Parsons, 90), yet the Woolfs' photographic costs remained fairly constant, with spending in August 1929 at one pound, ten shillings (LW/D).

Similarly Bell's frequent use of enlargements and her love of repetitive photographs, especially of her children Julian, Quentin, and Angelica, are a material celebration of the domestic. Bell enlarged her familial worlds into epic "spaces" with a sure sense of scale and frame. Photographs taken by Bell in 1912 illustrate this issue of framing and relationships. The portrait of Duncan Grant and John Maynard Keynes taken at Asheham (fig. 88), measuring 8 × 6 inches, is striking. Both figures are in profile in a carefully structured design. The camera is in marked close-up to each figure. Although it is useful to note, as Mary Ann Doane argues, that the close-up in "other national cultures" does not necessarily connote "proximity, intimacy, knowledge of interiority," Bell's close-ups do suggest identifications and intimacy ("Close-up," 107). The framing and enlargement of figures might reflect Vanessa's nascent regard for Duncan in 1912, when she shared Christmas Day "reading passages aloud from her father's *Mausoleum Book*" and painting alongside Duncan at Asheham (Spalding, *Bell*, 119). Keynes's relaxed pose also hints at a residue of his former sexual relationship with Duncan.

An equally interesting use of framing marks Bell's photograph of Walter Sickert and Roger Fry in 1912 at Newington House (fig. 86), the home of the American painters Ethel Sands and Nan Hudson. The en plein air yet formal, photograph might be Vanessa's antidote to the "refined" Ethel and Nan. As Vanessa explained in a letter to Fry, "I was a little alarmed at their excessive elegance and 18th century stamp. It isn't what we want even for our minor arts, is it? . . . I must say that seeing them in their own chosen surroundings did give me rather the creeps" (VB/L, 121).

In her "minor art" of photography, Bell makes the frame as significant as the relationship between the two men by placing each figure at opposite sides of the photograph and in relation to two pillars. In some ways this device betrays Bell's seasoned modernist eye yet also the presence of a certain autobiographical intensity. Fry, through his gaze, coyly interacts with Vanessa, while Sickert is aloof in shadow under his wide-brimmed hat. In 1912 Vanessa and Roger began to share ideas, love, and their lives, while Walter Sickert by 1912 was less enamored with Fry. Although both artists had been youthful friends and Fry admired Sickert's painting, Sickert became suspicious of Fry's championing of Post-Impressionism, and his face remains, photographically speaking, in distant shadow. And Sickert, with a misogynistic streak, excluded Nan Hudson and Ethel Sands from membership in his masculine Camden Town Group (Reed). Bell's photographs, like those of the Woolfs', are hybrid entities, with multiple connotations, heteropologies of past and present.

As Richard Shone argues, Bell's subject matter in her paintings "was resolutely domestic—her family and friends, her immediate surroundings or places on whose familiarity she could count." And that subject matter is charged with a matrilineal photographic inheritance. In *The Garden Room,* Bell "views the women of her family with both warmth and detachment in a manner reminiscent of the photographic tableaux of her great-aunt Julia Margaret Cameron" (Shone, *Art of Bloomsbury,* 18). Lisa Tickner points out that Bell's portrait *The Red Dress* (1929) re-creates a Julia Margaret Cameron photograph of Julia Jackson ca. 1866 ("Mediating Generation," 24–25). Woolf too was creating "stills" of her mother in *To the Lighthouse,* while editing and writing the introduction to a collection of Cameron photographs and being photographed for *Vogue.* During times of personal and historical changes, the sisters' photography creates a sense of stability by means of re-visioning matrilineal figures as well as a domestic spatial "belonging."

Asheham House was the setting for a number of the Woolfs' and Bell's photos earlier in this period (fig. 90). Leonard Woolf describes finding Asheham in 1912: "We came upon an extraordinarily romantic looking house . . . from its windows and, terrace in front of the house you looked across the great field and the Ouse Valley." In February there was a Bloomsbury house-warming party with "Virginia, Vanessa, Clive, Adrian, Roger Fry, Duncan Grant and myself. . . . I have never known a house which had such a strong character, personality of its own—romantic, gentle, melancholy, lovely" (*BA,* 56, 57). Virginia makes use of Asheham's domestic beauty in her short story "A Haunted House," in which the ghosts' memories of domestic comfort provide the pulse of the story, and in photographs of Vanessa with Duncan. Bell used the trope of the terrace and space at Asheham both in photography and painting.

There were further dislocations and instabilities facing Bell. As a conscientious objector, Duncan Grant had to undertake rural work, and in 1916 Vanessa became involved in locating work for Duncan and his lover David Garnett and relocating herself, Grant, and the children to Charleston. Bell lived at the three-storey farmhouse for the rest of her life. "It's most lovely," Bell wrote to Roger Fry in October 1916, "inside the house the rooms are very large . . . one I shall make into a studio. It is very light and large, with an east window" (VB/L, 201). Over the years, Duncan and Vanessa, with other Bloomsbury artists, decorated Charleston's walls, furniture, and doors, creating textiles, ceramics, and a flourishing garden. Charleston is the dominant subject of many of Bell's paintings and is named as such in *The Pond Charleston* (1916) and *The Dining Room Window, Charleston* (1940). Similarly, the domestic security that Charleston offered is the frequent subject of Bell's photographs as much as in her paintings. Bell's need for a stable matrilineal psychic space carries into all the photographs she took of her children at Asheham and Charleston, yet the tension between that psychic desire and visual traditions of objectification is an interesting issue in relation to Bell's photographs of her naked children.

Vanessa Bell's albums contain over fifty photographs of her children naked and approximately ten photographs in which the naked children appear with fully clothed adults. David Garnett remembered how "Julian and Quentin often went naked . . . Vanessa sometimes followed them about stealthily, a Kodak in her hand" (Garnett, 177). As I have detailed elsewhere, the photographs taken at Asheham in 1913 frame Julian (fig. 97) stretching across Asheham's French windows. To examine Bell's practice further here touches on the issue of album categorization and whether domestic depictions are unmediated. It could be argued that many of the photographs of Bell's children are strongly erotic in the sense that Bell makes use of strong bright sunlight to capture the topography of their bodies in close-up (figs. 106 and 107). But Bell seems to unfix the category of the erotic by revealing the domestic innocence of childhood as well as its sensuality. There is reciprocity between photographer and "models." The children are not often passive but collude with Bell as camera operator. For example, the children look intimately and directly to the camera (fig. 88). There is an implied exchange of looks, suggesting a reciprocity of pleasure. Bell collects photographic memorable moments in a syncretic rather than objective manner.

By placing many different shots of her naked children, taken at different moments, into her albums, Bell is documenting a long period of matrilineal attachment through to adulthood. In addition there is often an off-frame effect in the photographs. As Bell suggested in a letter to Virginia, "they're really very independent and have lots of games of their own" (VB/L, 224). The album photographs need to be seen as inseparable from Vanessa's interest in childhood, progressive education, and the psychic traces of her mother, and importantly, in relation to Bell's continual artistic practice. As Christopher Reed notes, Bell used her own photograph of her son Quentin naked in the garden for a figure of Bacchus in the room that Bell and Grant decorated for the poet Dorothy Wellesley in 1929. There is a tension too between Bell's depictions and her own matrilineal inheritance; for example, Julia Margaret Cameron's *Devotion* (1865) adopts a similar convention of the naked infant. And, as I have argued, Cameron, like Bell, used the domestic arena as the space of her photographs, photographing her children and close relatives to engage with allegorical meanings of gender and art. A Cameron photograph appears in Bell's later painting *Flowers in a Jug* (1948–1950), on a table and supporting the jug as if acting as the foundation of Bell's art (Reed). In a similar gesture Woolf ends her play *Freshwater*, about Cameron's life, by citing Cameron's maternal photographic legacy: "take my lens. I bequeath it to my descendents. See that it is always out of focus" (F, 83).

Bell's and the Woolfs' photo albums are the "mirrors," or heterotopologies, of their domestic, family, and cultural worlds. Although the albums encompass a surprisingly wide range of technical formats, including expressionist low-angle shots, the portrait is the most consistent genre. A good number of contemporary women photographers create portrait performances. Cindy Sherman's reconstruction of sexual and cultural stereotypes of femininity is the most obvious example of a play with identity and otherness. The Woolfs' and Bell's portraits are not performances in this contemporary sense, just as Virginia's writing is more suggestive of images rather than re-creating an image-repertoire, and Bell's painted portraits are often lyrical.

In addition, while Bell's and the Woolfs' multiple portraits in this period are documents of friends and family visits and events, they also contain the opposing register of the psychic in vivid personal presences. The earlier portrait of Leonard and Virginia taken by George Duckworth during their visit to Dalingridge Place in 1912 (figs. 50 and 85) is a good example of the pressure of the psychic. The photograph's low angle (which might derive from Duckworth's use of a Frena rather than a more up-to-date Kodak) renders the couple with great presence. In July 1912 the Woolfs were engaged, and yet the pose is one of two separate "unengaged" people. Virginia, unconventionally, wore the same clothes here and again on her wedding day. It would be anachronistic to read the photograph through a contemporary lens by expecting the couple to fondly touch or look to the camera with smiles or mutual gazes. Studio portraits of couples in this period usually depict separate figures with sitting males and standing females or vice versa. But physical contact is often centered in these studio photographs with one figure's right hand resting lovingly on the other's left shoulder. The scene of the Woolfs' engagement is mournful, as taut as Leonard's buttoned-up jacket and Virginia's glove clutching. Both gaze into a distant future rather than at each other or toward the camera.

As Virginia had written very honestly to Leonard the month before, "I don't know what the future will bring. I'm half afraid of myself. . . . I go from being half in love with you . . . to the extreme of wildness and aloofness. . . . As I told you brutally the other day, I feel no physical attraction in you" (*L*, 1:496). And, knowing that "Leonard and I shall be alone" over Bank Holiday, Virginia wrote pleadingly to Ka Cox, "will you come to Asheham this week, Saturday, and spend Bank Holiday" (*L*, 1:506). The photograph carries Virginia's corporeal resistance in its intense haptic quality. Engagements are public events often involving a whirl of social engagements, a social technology of public relationships. The photograph, with its poses, incorporates into that sociality Woolf's more private fears. Perhaps Woolf's photographic refusal of affiliative looking at the body of Leonard might parallel her attention to the limits of the body in her fiction writing at this time, for example, in *The Voyage Out*, before her more explicit turn to the interiority of modernist fiction in the succeeding decade.

On the one hand, portrait photography gave both the Woolfs and Bell the possibility of affiliative stasis in family tableaux, but that authoritative figuration is often undercut by enigmatic interiorities. It is interesting to note that Bell chose to take many close-up photographs during a period when her painted portraits had absent faces. In her paintings Bell delights in a Post-Impressionist radical simplification. There is little chiaroscuro in her modernist paintings and no faces. With blank faces Bell's figures cannot see or gaze at the painter/viewer. The absent gaze suggests a hidden inner self through body physiognomy. The gap of the face represents the unwritten life and opens up the formation of identity to past and present, enhancing portrait spectatorship. In contrast, Bell's and the Woolfs' photographic *plan rapproché*, or head-and-torso shot, is a method of overcoming distance between sitter/viewer, a kind of portraiture revealing a desire "to overcome the separation of absence and death" (Woodall, 8).

A good example is Bell's 1913 portrait of Lytton Strachey (fig. 104). The photograph is minimalist, with full lighting highlighting in silhouette Strachey's remarkable features. Strachey is stabilized and immobilized in enlargement. The photograph complements Bell's color figurations in her painted portrait of Lytton, also in 1913, with its simplified forms and minimalist physiognomy. Woolf later wrote to Vanessa of her "contented state of mind. I heard from Lytton who feels the same, and says he would like to live with you for ever" (*L*, 2:108). Lytton's death in 1932 made Vanessa realize "I have loved him ever since the time when Thoby died and he came and was such an inexpressible help and made one think of all the things most worth thinking of" (Spalding, *Bell*, 257).

As the period progressed, the Woolfs began to allow their cameras more direct access to the private spaces hidden in their engagement photograph. The Woolfs preference for paired self-portraits of themselves and their friends makes the issue of identity part of the portrait and constitutes a veritable repetitive visual autobiography. The Woolfs assent to each other's camera gaze. Each is a very central presence in the frame, as if each is making a lengthy visual analysis of the other's distinctive image. Such close-up figuration creates embodiment, disrupting the normal separation of camera and subject. These repetitive paired sequences go beyond the conventions of candid or instant photography. In their use of repetition, the photographs are dialogic, encouraging dialogue between the sitters and between husband and wife as camera operators. Similarly, Virginia's use of a dialogic form in her essays "constitutes Woolf's greatest separation" from conventional academia in the 1920s (Cuddy-Keane, 79).

The constant pairing of husband and wife and of friends over decades (fig. 135) is a dialogic practice in which relationships are staged in the photographic encounter. The portraits are not static but use space as an "other space," Foucault's synonym for heterotopologies. "The space in which we live, which draws us out of ourselves, in which the erosion of our lives, our time and our history occurs, the space that claws and gnaws at us, is also, in itself a heterogeneous space" (Foucault, 23). Taken as a whole the Woolfs' and Bell's albums are transactional, containing performances of intimate exchange within the genre of formal portraiture, going beyond what we normally find in family albums but synchronizing with a period that witnessed a renaissance of the literature of personality. Bell and the Woolfs confidently express their individuality to each other through their bodies, just as Virginia in fiction frequently creates meaning through character physiognomy and gesture.

Frances Spalding has noted how Bell's paintings of this period also delineate strong powerful figures, particularly *Studland Beach*. But Bell's photographs are familial and autobiographically revealing as a visual aggregate. Traces of sorority in them can be usefully compared to her more resolved distillation of the maternal in painting. Bell's Album 1 contains photographs of Clive Bell together with Virginia taken at Studland Beach in 1910. Clive and Virginia are cooperative models, but their gazes are not fully direct. In both photographs there is deliberate repetition. The two figures are in complimentary positions with arms and legs in synchronic patterns (figs. 75 and 76). The visual ordering and spacing of their relationship are compounded by the inclusion of paired shoes and beach huts within the frame. In one photograph the raised seams of Virginia's gloves parallel the swollen veins of Clive's downward pointing hands. The persistence of any photographic motif, for example, a pattern of pictorial relations, confirms its importance and accrues excess through repetition. Any choice, whether conscious or unconscious, of organizational pattern necessarily involves a latent language. It is as if the echoing patterns of Clive's and Virginia's positions are a corporeal allusion to other correspondences in their lives.

After the birth of Vanessa's first child, Julian, in February 1908, Clive and Vanessa interrupted their sex life, and Clive began to flirt with Virginia. Hermione Lee suggests that "from this time—May of 1908—they began to play a game of intimacy and intrigue which lasted for perhaps two years," that is, until the Studland photographs of 1910 (Lee, 249). The Studland photographs carry this hidden hint of sororial absorption in the repetitions and patterning of each image. In contrast, in Bell's painting *Studland Beach* (1911–1912) the figures, with their backs to the viewer, have no gazes. The painting's subjects are all women and children, and are presented in clear, spatially distinct forms. Lisa Tickner rightly suggests that *Studland Beach* may have evoked, for Bell, memories of St. Ives and her mother Julia (*Modern Life*, 138). Bell's sororial photographic tensions are resolved in her painting's maternal phantasmagoric space. The artist is in full control, using confident abstractions and a careful color palette. *Studland Beach* consciously distills experience, while the photographs reproduce unconscious experience.

Other portraits carry more transparent referents. The photographs of the naked Vanessa and Molly MacCarthy (fig. 102), taken in 1913 in Bell's studio at 46 Gordon Square, mirror Bell's and Grant's paintings. The painting by Bell in the rear of the photograph is *Design for Overmantel* (1913), "Bell's massive nudes, indebted to Matisse, their schematic form related to her own paintings such as *Street Corner Conversation* (1913)" (Shone, *Art of Bloomsbury*, 147). But Vanessa and Molly also adopt poses frequently favored by Duncan in paintings, for example, in *Dancers* (1912) and in the mural that Duncan completed for John Maynard Keynes's rooms in King's College, Cambridge (1910–1911). Similarly the photographs of Duncan naked at Asheham (figs. 99–101), one assumes taken by Vanessa for her own pleasure and Duncan's pleasure and use, because the male nude is not a feature of Bell's work, could have been used by Grant as photographic prequels for his several versions of *The Bathers*. Grant used photographs of himself naked, taken by J. M. Keynes during their travels in Greece and Tunis, for *Queen of Sheba* (1912). It is possible, though *highly* unlikely, that Keynes may have taken the Asheham photographs, but certainly Vanessa treasured these photographs until her death. And as Douglas Turnbaugh suggests, Duncan's "fascination with the male body never ceased" (*Erotic Art of Grant*, 8).

The photographs of George Mallory (figs. 94 and 95) are sourced to Grant by the Tate, although Spalding suggests that "Duncan did not take photographs. When asked to take a photograph, Duncan was baffled by the camera, despite being instructed which hole to look through, and which trigger to press" (Spalding, *Grant*, 488). However, Duncan did take photographs of later models, including Toni Asserati, and commissioned a professional "physique" photographer to take pictures of a later lover, Paul Roche, in 1946, although Roche too spoke of Duncan's technical ineptitude. Certainly Mallory and Grant were lovers, and Mallory posed for Duncan at 38 Brunswick Square and colludes with Duncan as camera viewer by adopting these complicated poses. The painted portrait *George Mallory* (1912) is an oil on panel in the National Gallery. At Charleston, Virginia noted Bell's frequent informality and nakedness. "Nessa seems to have slipped civilisation off her back, and splashes about entirely nude, without shame, and enormous spirit" (L, 2:147).

The photograph of Bell's family at Charleston looking for "newts" in a tub (fig. 90) also reflects a painting, Bell's *The Tub*, in a shared use of tilted planes, more perhaps than Bell's possible knowledge of Degas's *Le Tub* (1886), or as Reed argues, the painting's "abstract harmonies of Post-Impressionism" (Reed, 194). But these apparently transparent references are always in tension with familial dynamics. And here I depart from Diane

Filby Gillespie's otherwise very learned analysis in *The Sisters' Arts*, where Gillespie suggests that "the sisters never fully developed their potentials for dual creativity" (7). Bell and Woolf's most dualistic creations are their photographs. Many photographs are duplicated in both sets of albums, for example, the photograph of Vanessa with Quentin and Angelica (fig. 166) in Italy in 1935 (Bell Album 8, p. 4; and Monk's House Album 3, p. 60). In addition, the sisters share a love of personalized objects and mimic each other in spatial particularities in depth of field. For example, the trace of Bell and Woolf's favorite photograph of their father and mother in the library at Talland House (favorite because the photograph is given a significant place in both sisters' albums) recurs both in Woolf's use of punctum from that photograph and in Bell's recurrent motif of the chair in her paintings. Richard Shone argues that the chair in Bell's paintings embodies "a sense of personal loss" (*Art of Bloomsbury*, 218). As the contemporary photographer Wright Morris pinpointed in his equivalent use of a chair motif, they are "saturated with the quality of life that I find both poignant and inexhaustible. I don't want to sit on them; I want to look at them" (Dow Adams, 201). Bell's and the Woolfs' photographic use of objects such as chairs should be read much more in terms of Adorno's idea that the enigmatic quality of art objects is linked to suffering, rather than Benjamin's view of objects and the bourgeoisie in which "a dwelling place becomes a kind of casing," enabling the bourgeoisie to "remove objects from the profane eyes of non-owners" (Benjamin, *Baudelaire*, 46–47).

Bell and the Woolfs share the same traces in their photography, but the photographs are also varied reconstructions of their worlds, replete with complex psychic layers. The photographs voice the unsaid, like quasi subjects. Studying these domestic photographs in terms of affect might help with the troubling issue of quality. How do we read domestic photographs that acknowledge their often profoundly complex traces without categorizing the photographs as technically banal? In a fresh rethinking of the high/low binary in modernism, Andreas Huyssen suggests welcoming "the issue of medium (oral/aural, written, visual) in all its historical, technical and theoretical complexity rather than continue to rely on the traditional binary notion of media culture as low and its high literary other in traditional modernist fashion" (Huyssen, 370–371).

Domestic photography is a medium that is best read, following Huyssen, for its complex interweaving of technical with historical and personal issues. In addition, photographs in photo albums, for all their superficial fixity, are constantly exchanging meanings with each other and with different viewers. Speaking of the Woolfs' and Bell's moment of modernity and the end of the 1920s, Dora Russell, in her autobiography *The Tamarisk Tree*, says of the 1929 stock market crash, "there are periods in human history, when, without apparent reason, at first imperceptibly, the movement in one direction goes into reverse, the change occurs not only in the economics and politics of the time, but even in the motivation of human lives" (Russell, 216).

In 1929 both Virginia and Vanessa were entering new aesthetic fields. Bell, as Lisa Tickner argues, had moved far from the direction of Watts and the Royal Academy, not "imperceptibly" but dramatically, following Clive Bell's purchase in 1911 of Picasso's *Pots et citron* (1907), the first Picasso in a British private collection. In 1928 Woolf published *Orlando*, *To the Lighthouse*, and "The Cinema," Britain's first essay on avant-garde cinema. But, as Russell suggests in *The Tamarisk Tree*, a complete rupture with the past is never possible. Woolf and Bell entered the 1930s, just as they had entered the twentieth century, by laminating together past familial echoes with present moments of friendship.

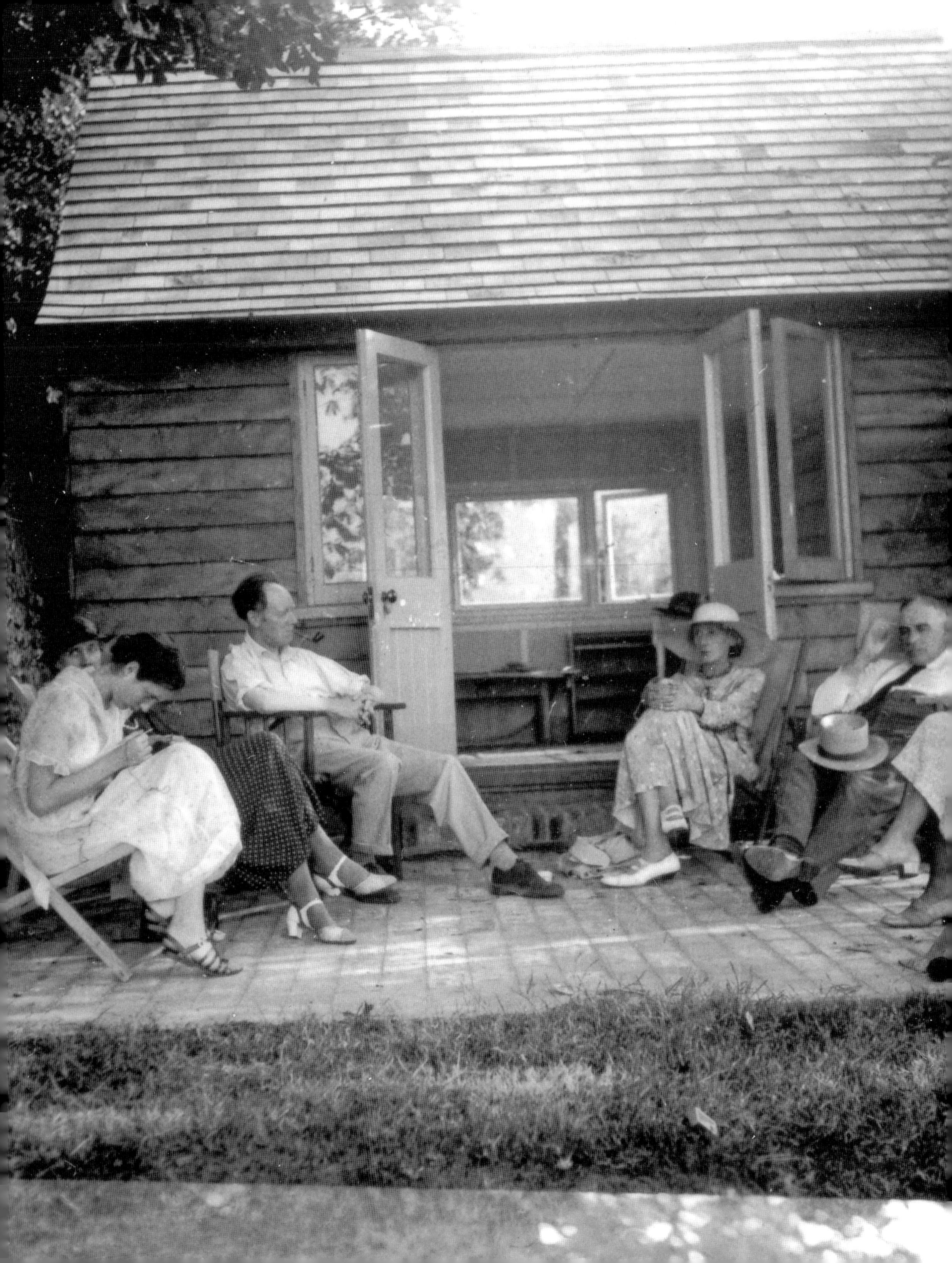

The 1930s

FIGURE 168 Angelica and Clive Bell, Virginia Woolf, and Maynard Keynes, Monk's House, August 6, 1935. Reprinted by permission of the Harvard Theatre Collection, the Houghton Library.

THE PHOTOGRAPHS taken by the Woolfs and Vanessa Bell in the 1930s are important examples of portraiture and represent an extensive narrative of themselves and their friends. Photographic portraits as a genre are very composed, constructed forms that suggest the photographer's identification with the subject. By incorporating traces of their makers' histories as well as the everyday moment, the photographs by the Woolfs and Bell continue to mediate between past and present. Monk's House Album 3 contains photographs taken between 1931 and 1934 of many of the Woolfs' friends: Roger Fry, Lydia and Maynard Keynes, John Lehmann, Alice Ritchie, Charles Siepmann, Angus Davidson, Molly and Desmond MacCarthy, Tom and Vivienne Eliot, Stella Benson, Wogan and Rosamond Phillips, Peter and Prudence Lucas, and Vita Sackville-West, as well as relatives: Ann and Judith Stephen, Vanessa Bell, Clive Bell, Duncan Grant, and Vanessa's children. The disparate locales in the photographs include Greece, Italy, and Ireland, but Monk's House, where Leonard and Virginia developed their photographs, is the preferred setting.

In the albums, sitters are photographed with distinct presences, and deeper meanings are suggested through the accumulation and sequencing of photographic motifs. The large number of repeated portraits reveals the Woolfs' need for a constant visual discourse of friendship during the 1930s. Vanessa Bell's photographs of the 1930s share this concern. Bell captures the thickness of friendship in a large number of portraits, including those of Roger Fry, Frederick Ashton, Aldous Huxley, and family members: Duncan, the children, and the Woolfs. Bell's photographs of fancy dress parties and Charleston entertainments during the 1930s are like photo-stories, cohesive sequences of familial relationships. Her focus on group compositions shows how significant personal relationships were to Bell at a time of further public changes. The fancy dress party at 8 Fitzroy Street in January 1930 (fig. 181), to celebrate Angelica's twelfth birthday, was "a most hectic affair" involving "any stray members of Bloomsbury" (VB/L, 357–358). Later in the 1930s Bell thought that she had "never seen anything quite so indecent" as Duncan's Spanish Dancer created for a Charleston entertainment (fig. 192), and Bell wanted to "try and get photos of all of them" to post to her son Julian, then in China (VB/L, 419). Portraying the density of friendship by means of repetition clearly expressed the Woolfs' and Bell's desire for a collective "history" at a time of great social and cultural change.

This period of photography is concurrent with a time, in Virginia's diaries and letters, of almost constant descriptions of the contemporary deaths of many of her friends as well as her reminiscences of earlier family deaths, particularly those of her brother Thoby and father Leslie Stephen, which the contemporary reflections evoked. Vanessa mourned the deaths of Lytton Strachey and Dora Carrington and, in this decade, suffered the two most catastrophic deaths in her life: her son Julian, killed in the Spanish Civil War, and the sudden death of her former lover Roger Fry. And Bell began to feel that "there's something of death in all partings" (VB/L, 402).

Leonard and Virginia were involved in many social and political developments in the 1930s, and Vanessa's children Julian and Quentin were active Labour supporters, "driving canvassers to meetings" (Spalding, *Bell*, 255). The worldwide Depression following the General Strike and U.S. stock market crash was met in Britain by the downfall of Ramsay MacDonald's Labour government and his formation of a national government on August 24, 1931. For those like Vanessa with properties in France, the national government's withdrawal from the gold standard in September 1931 precipitated a rapid decline in the value of the English pound in relation to the French franc, with the pound dropping in 1934 to 62 percent of its 1929 value in relation to the franc (Stephenson, 41). As Hermione Lee argues, Leonard, as the co-editor of the *Political Quarterly* founded in that year, "was caught up, from now on, in what he called 'the intelligent man's way to prevent war'" (Lee, 617).

The year 1931 was one of unprecedented and brutal developments both at home and abroad. Japan's invasion of Manchuria in September 1931 weakened Leonard's faith in the League of Nations. Public demands for women's emancipation diminished during the 1930s, with feminist efforts subdued by the realities of economic recession and the rise of Fascism. The 1931 Anomalies Act, although introduced by a woman minister, Margaret Bondfield, made it difficult for unemployed married women to qualify for benefits, disqualified 80,000 married women, and was attacked by Woolf's friends, including Selina Cooper, at Central Hall in 1933 (Rowbotham, *Century of Women*, 174). The year before the act was passed, in 1930, Virginia wrote the introduction to the collected letters of the Women's Co-operative Guild as an autobiographical heuristic understanding of working-class women's social and political injustices.

The response of the Woolfs' Hogarth Press to these developments took the form of a generational divide. The press published pamphlets about the League of Nations and other political institutions, and Virginia's "Letter to a Young Poet" in 1932. As Harold Nicolson argued, the pamphlets were "epistles in which the generation of 1910 confronts the generation of 1932" (Lee, 618). The publications represent not so much an estrangement from present change as a mediation of that change through a discursive past.

The Woolfs and Bell, however, contributed to modernity as a social formation. The Woolfs lived in the modern world, broadcasting on the BBC (Leonard's "The Modern State"—a series of six talks he delivered in October and November 1931), going to movies, enjoying constant photography as well as visits to the 1931 Olympia Motor Exhibition, and approving a car, "The Star, which indeed we could buy if we wished," probably the Little Comet Fourteen costing £345 (D, 4:50). The Woolfs' income rose dramatically in the 1930s. *Flush* (1932) sold 50,000 copies, and by 1937 *The Years* was a best seller in the United States, second only to *Gone with the Wind*, and Man Ray's photograph of Virginia appeared on the cover of *Time* (Silver, 79). Vanessa was less materialistic but equally conscious of the satisfactions of domestic technology, wanting to give Roger Fry's partner, Helen Anrep, a reconditioned Frigidaire after Roger's death (VB/L, 426). Taxation began to favor the middle classes more in the 1930s than it had in the 1920s and contributed to the expansion of consumer industries. Amateur photography flourished. By 1937 there were over three hundred photography clubs and societies. The editor of *Amateur Photographer* and the *Photograms of the Year*, Frances J. Mortimer, attributed "the greater and continued enthusiasm" to the "miniature camera . . . these little instruments are to be seen on all sides on every occasion and in most unexpected places," and in 1936 he presented a series of BBC radio programs on the topic of amateur photography (Mortimer, 3–4).

This more complex experience of modernity/modernism, as a disparate formation interweaving past and present, high and popular cultures, and Virginia's defense of the amateur "common reader," is at odds with many of modernism's contemporary critics. For example, the architect Reginald Blomfield, hostile to Roger Fry's ideas, claimed that "since the war, Modernism, or *Modernismus*, as it should be called on the German precedent, has invaded this country like an epidemic . . . its attack is insidious. . . . whether it is communism or not, 'Modernismus' is a vicious movement which threatens that literature and art which is our last refuge from a world that is becoming more and more mechanized everyday" (Blomfield, 52–53). *The Studio* art journal editorial in 1932 agreed: "Britain is looking for British pictures of British people, of British landscapes" (*The Studio*, 64).

This common fear of modernism as foreign is far removed from Bloomsbury's association with international modernism, for example, Vanessa Bell's and Duncan Grant's attention to the work of Matisse and the French avant-garde. In Britain, Vanessa and Duncan worked with cutting-edge modern industrial techniques, joining forces with Allan Walton, one of the most forward-looking textile producers of the 1930s, who transferred more than fifteen of Bell's and Grant's painterly designs onto a gleaming rayon-faced cloth that intensified and reflected light (Mendes). The fabrics sold at Fortnum and Mason's and major London outlets.

The Woolfs too link modernism and modernity. One result of that attention to a more mass-mediated imaginary are their photographs, but also Virginia's writings about painting, for example, *Walter Sickert: A Conversation*. Sickert had asked Woolf to write about a retrospective exhibition of his paintings, in November 1933 at Agnew and Son, because he felt that Woolf would best represent the literary qualities of the work. But Woolf, more interestingly, begins her essay with one of her favorite dinner party scenes in which guests discuss whether driving in London is helped or hindered by the "new system of coloured lights," a discussion Woolf transmogrifies into an extended analysis of color and spectatorship (*WS*, 5).

The introduction in Britain of three-color traffic lights in 1928 and 1929 was followed by the Road Traffic Act of 1934, which introduced a 30 mph speed limit in urban areas, driving tests, fines for jaywalking, and "sanctuary lanes" (pedestrian crossings). Just as modernism was considered to be too risky and Continental by many critics in Britain, so too were traffic lights, although they had been adopted in the

United States by 1918 and in France by 1922. By 1931 in Britain there were over a million private cars. Vanessa, like the Woolfs, loved driving but was conscious of traffic dangers. Duncan Grant hit a Humber car, whose owners tried "to get £3 or so out of me. . . . Roger writes that he has again (most curiously) knocked down a cyclist who ran, but not deliberately this time, into him" (VB/L, 373). And the Woolfs give a whole album page to a photograph of their new Lanchester car (fig. 152).

Virginia was equally attentive to other new technologies, happy that Leonard bought, on July 23, 1931, "a superb Zeiss camera" (probably the Lloyd or Nixe rather than the more expensive model Cocarette of 1929) and pleased that "my Kodak can be made perfect for 5/- [five shillings]" (L, 4:361). In 1931 a Kodak 120 film of eight exposures cost one shilling (the same price as one packet of twenty cigarettes or two packets of Pears soap). Equally Vanessa was delighted that she could send superior photographs to Julian in China, taken by Barbara Bagenal, of "the interiors of this house [Charleston], with some wonderful German camera" (VB/L, 422). Sickert himself was very aware of photographic techniques and, during the 1930s, transfigured newspaper photographs into formal paintings. Sickert's *Edward VIII* (1936) endows a popular media image of the king with advanced modernist painterly handling. The king, when Prince of Wales, was archetypally modern. He persuaded the Post Office to use up-to-date phones, loved fast cars, and supported the Royal Academy's first modernist exhibition, British Art in Industry, by affirming that "simplicity in line form and decoration is, I think, what modern taste demands" (Hogben, 68).

Beginning in 1931, Woolf collected photographs and newspaper cuttings (fig. 170) in her effort to document the differing social, economic, and cultural positions of men and women. The photographs and cuttings, together with quotations and letters, Woolf mounted into three scrapbooks whose pages, which included extensive information about education, sexuality, politics, and social values, were sources for *Three Guineas*. Woolf's prescient "montage" of text, published photographs, and "narrated" photographs of the Spanish Civil War, which were not published in *Three Guineas*, produced a complex multigeneric work of feminist visual modernism (Humm). Woolf's use of photography is in advance of the typical newspaper photographic reproductions of the 1930s in which photographs are subordinate to stories, until the arrival of *Picture Post* in 1938. And neither newspapers nor magazines created compelling testimonials about gendered photographic affect in juxtaposition with published photographs, as Woolf does in *Three Guineas*. In some ways, Woolf's technique resembles the modernist photographer August Sander's universal language of photography with which "we can communicate our thoughts, conceptions, and realities" (North, 109).

The 1930s for Woolf were also a period of self-reflection, particularly about her past and about death. Woolf's diaries and letters for 1931–1934 contain detailed thoughts about the contemporary deaths of fourteen people, all of whom, apart from the king of Belgium, were personally known to Woolf, including her intimate friends Lytton Strachey, Dora Carrington, and Roger Fry, her half brother George Duckworth, and Leonard's sister Clara. Woolf's "witnessing" of multiple contemporary deaths during the 1930s and her memories of family deaths emerge in her writing: "the end of The Waves. I wrote the words O Death fifteen minutes ago," and shape the Woolfs' repetitious photographs (*D*, 4:10).

There is one surprisingly tangential account, written in the 1930s, in which the writer's frame of reference and technology of memory are very close to Woolf's. Freud too at this time was creating an explanatory narrative of memories of his dead father in the context of social change and threats of war. Both Virginia Woolf and Sigmund Freud decided to revisit the Acropolis in the 1930s, Woolf in person and Freud in his memories and in writing. Woolf's first visit to Athens, with Vanessa, Thoby, and Adrian, was in 1906 at the age of twenty-four, whereas Freud was forty-eight when he first visited in 1904.

In 1936 Freud decided to celebrate the birthday of his admired friend the writer, musicologist, and Nobel Prize winner Romain Rolland by writing an account for Rolland of Freud's 1904 Acropolis visit, together with an explanation for why the visit "kept on recurring in my mind" and frequently troubled Freud during the intervening years (Freud, 239). Freud's eightieth birthday was also celebrated by an address signed by nearly two hundred writers, including Rolland and Virginia Woolf. In May 1932 Woolf traveled to Greece, together with Leonard, and Roger and Margery Fry. Perhaps not surprisingly, at the Acropolis Woolf thought that "my own ghost met me" and had recurring memories of the death of her brother Thoby, who had died of typhoid after the 1906 visit, and of her father Leslie Stephen (*D*, 4:90).

Freud's love of Hellenic culture is evident early in his life in his desire to name his brother Alexander the Great. In *Freud and the Non-European*, Edward Said describes Freud's knowledge of the Greco-Roman world that Freud drew on repeatedly for "psychoanalytic images and concepts" (Said, 15). Said's main focus is on Freud's representation of Moses as a non-European and how this destabilizing history of Jewish identity is a model for identity in the modern world. But Said notes that for Freud, Athens was a "city of the mind," representing "Freud's lifelong dedication to intellectual achievement" (38).

Freud shared Woolf's faith that narrative could free a selective blockage of memory. He articulates the case study as a linear narrative of self-analysis, but as in all his writings the self-analysis is impregnated with similes and literary figures, and Freud himself is the central character in his story of "a phenomenon . . . which I myself had experienced a generation ago, in 1904, and which I had never understood, has kept on recurring in my mind. I did not at first see why; but at last I determined to analyse the incident" (Freud, 239). In 1904 Freud and his brother decided to travel to Corfu by way of Trieste, but while visiting a business acquaintance of Freud's brother in Trieste, they were persuaded instead to visit Athens. Waiting for the boat office to open, Freud and his brother wandered "about the town in a discontented and irresolute frame of mind" (240). Finally arriving at the Acropolis, Freud changed into his best shirt for the occasion.

Only now, many years later, does Freud come to understand that what motivated his earlier behavior is a sense of guilt or inferiority, but why, Freud asks, does the guilt arise in "such a distorted and distorting disguise." It "is known as a feeling of derealization [Entfremdungsgefuhl]," a similar phenomenon as depersonalization or double consciousness. All these behavioral phenomena, Freud argues, "serve the purpose of defence; they aim at keeping something away from the ego" (Freud, 243–245).

What Freud realizes he was keeping away from his ego in Trieste and at the Acropolis is his sense of guilt at having surpassed his father. The "limitation and poverty of our conditions of life in my youth" meant that the joy of seeing the Acropolis was "beyond the realms of possibility" for Freud's father. Freud and his brother experience extreme guilt in going "further than one's father, and as though to excel one's father was still something forbidden" (Freud, 246–247). Freud's "guilt" is still very much present in the 1930s, as is evident in his defensive switch to the impersonal pronoun *one*. The episode is replete with generational tensions and struggles with the technologies of memory, as well as with Freud's conceptualizations of psychic structures in relation to memory—all tensions and struggles shared by Woolf.

Woolf's actual meeting with Freud later in January 1939 was not auspicious. "Dr Freud gave me a narcissus . . . A screwed up shrunk very old man . . . Difficult talk." (*D*, 5:202). But after Freud's death, in September of that year, Woolf was "gulping up Freud" and applying Freud's concept of "ambivalence" to her mixed feelings about shopping (249). And Freud's exploration of memories of his father in his Acropolis letter and other case studies very much resembles Woolf's incorporation of memory fragments into her writings and photographs in the 1930s. Both resurrect memories by means of unreliable narrators who are relentlessly self-reflexive. Both adopt framing devices of discreditation. For example, Freud suggests that his Acropolis letter "is the gift of an impoverished creature" who has "seen better days" (Freud, 239). Woolf, with less justification, felt that she too was ageing: "I'm getting old myself—I shall be fifty next year" (*L*, 4:397).

In 1932 Woolf, like Freud, engaged with the fear of, or guilt at, surpassing the father. On February 28 Woolf was invited to deliver the Clark Lectures. "This, I suppose, is the first time a woman has been asked; & so it is a great honour—think of me, the uneducated child reading books in my room at 22 H. P. G.—now advanced to this glory" (*D*, 4:79). Woolf's father Sir Leslie Stephen gave the first Cambridge Clark Lectures (founded in honor of William Clark, vice-master of Trinity) in 1893, taking eighteenth-century literature as his subject. Although Woolf wanted to believe that her "father would have blushed with pleasure" that his daughter "was to be asked to succeed him," she immediately rejected the invitation, although three days later she could "think of nothing else; my mind is swarming with ideas for lectures" (*D*, 4:79–80). Woolf's declared reasons for rejecting appear to be practical. Writing to Clive Bell, Woolf claimed that the "honour is not overwhelming," and in her diary records the writer's usual panic at sudden writing requests: "how could I write 6 lectures, to be delivered in full term, without giving up a year to criticism" (*L*, 5:27; *D*, 4:79).

Two days later "the devil" is whispering that Woolf had already "six lectures written in Phases of Fiction; & could furbish them up & deliver the Clark lectures, & win the esteem of my sex" (*D*, 4:79). Woolf's "devil" or mental "disturbance" resembles Freud's understanding that "the essence of success was to have got further than one's father . . . and as though to excel one's father was still something forbidden" (Freud, 247). Precisely because giving the lectures would be an antipatriarchal project "winning the esteem of my sex," Woolf cannot envisage accepting. Woolf's fear of surpassing the father is clear. Undertaking the lectures would, Woolf claims, make her "2 or 3 years distant from The Waves" (*D*, 4:80). The excess in Woolf's reaction betrays a defense mechanism.

By 1940, when Woolf was reading Freud and writing "A Sketch of the Past," she understood her relationship with her father in Freudian terms, now using Freud's term ambivalence to describe her feelings about her father, but in 1932, the year of Woolf's visit to the Acropolis (fig. 145), Woolf famously claimed unfamiliarity with the works of Freud. Just before visiting Greece, writing to an American undergraduate, Woolf stated, "I have not studied Dr Freud or any psychoanalyst—indeed I think I have never read any of their books; my knowledge is merely from superficial talk" (*L*, 5:36). Returning from Greece, Woolf repeated her disclaimers in a further letter to the American: "I may say that I have never read Bergson and have only a very amateurish knowledge of Freud and the psychoanalysts; I have made no study of them" (91). But one of the three books published about Woolf in that year was *Le roman psychologique de Virginia Woolf* by Floris Delattre, and members of Woolf's family circle had great expertise in Freud's works and a lively awareness of the impact of psychoanalysis on popular culture—as had Woolf.

James Strachey and Adrian Stephen studied with Freud professionally in the 1920s, and Lytton

Strachey's biography *Elizabeth and Essex* in 1928 was informed by interpretative psychology. The Stracheys went on to translate Freud's works for the Hogarth Press. Leonard, as early as 1914, had reviewed *The Psychopathology of Everyday Life* for the *New Weekly* and read *The Interpretation of Dreams* (Kurzweil and Phillips, 248). Virginia makes a direct reference to Freudianism in her 1920s book review of J. D. Beresford's novel *An Imperfect Mother* (now published as an essay in *Contemporary Writers*), and in *A Room of One's Own* she creates an imaginary "psychopathology of everyday life" in her portrait of Professor von X. Inevitably, by April 1932 when Virginia and Leonard, together with the Frys, left for Greece, Virginia would perceive her memories of the past, which the Acropolis triggered, in a more complicated way than simply as nostalgia. Roger Fry himself was fascinated, as early as 1919, by the relationship between collecting objects and Freud's idea of anal complexes, and Fry's discussions with Woolf influenced Woolf's short story "Solid Objects" (Harvey).

In Woolf's letters from Greece, and in the accompanying diaries, there are close parallels between her memories of 1906 and the present of 1932. Although in a two-line letter to Ottoline Morrell Woolf facetiously says of Athens, "this is where we are, not much like Gower Street," her more autobiographical descriptions reveal complex mediations in which the past is not unproblematically screened off by direct transference to present images but acts as an informing level of reality (*L*, 5:60). For example, Woolf largely repeats in her diary an entry she made in August 1906 describing the mind's ability to create spontaneous visual images. Woolf reverts to displacement in a classic Freudian sense by screening her own responses onto those of Roger and Margery Fry (fig. 146). "Roger is a fair shower bath of erudition—Not a flower escapes him. And if it did, Margery would catch it" (*L*, 5:54). It is Fry who notices Woolf's ability to disassociate. "Margery caught me smiling the other day at my own thoughts and said no Fry had ever done that. 'No' said Roger, 'we have no power of disassociation'" (*L*, 5:56).

What Woolf experiences is precisely what Freud, in his Acropolis letter, defines as "derealization," a defense mechanism that, for Freud, was a defense against the guilt of surpassing his father (Freud, 244). Woolf frequently recalls the past in other forms of displacement. Returning to Athens from Corinth, "I thought of the lights of the herring fleet at sea; everyone holding a yellow taper along the street and all the lights coming out in the windows" (*L*, 5:59).Woolf's structure of feeling here is her childhood memories of St. Ives, which Woolf reincarnated in *To the Lighthouse*. "The lights were rippling and running as if they were drops of silver water held firm in a wind . . . the lights of the town and of the harbour and of the boats" (*Lighthouse*, 79).

Woolf's Greek descriptions are antipatriarchal. Greece offered Woolf an alternative to her father, to linear masculine history: "This is England in the time of Chaucer" (*D*, 4:92). Woolf loves Greece's "uncivilised, hot new season to be brought into our lives . . . sloughing the respectable skin" (97). Woolf knew that Vanessa would share this feeling and enjoys recounting sexual memories in a letter to her sister: "if ever I had a turn towards Sapphism it would be revived by the carts of young peasant women in lemon red and blue handkerchiefs" (*L*, 5:57). Woolf realizes that Greece has become as significant to her as the St. Ives childhood. "And I could love Greece, as an old woman, so I think, as I once loved Cornwall, as a child" (*D*, 4:97). The impact of Greece on Woolf was immense. "Since we came back, I'm screwed up into a ball; cant get into step; cant make things dance; feel awefully detached; see youth; feel old; no, thats not quite it; wonder how a year or 20 perhaps is to be endured . . . the inane pointlessness of all this existence" (102). Woolf's mind "will present me, unasked, with visions, as I walk, of Aegina, of Athens—the Acropolis with the incandescent pillars . . . not yet complete enough for me to have detached pictures," which the Woolfs would capture in photographs (100).

The period is one in which the Woolfs and Bell were overwhelmed by unchained *dispotifs* of death; it was as well the time of their most active album construction. Photographic frames offer self-contained spaces, refuges from the affective contemporary deaths they were witnessing. In March Arnold Bennett died, making Woolf "sadder than I should have supposed . . . an element in life—even in mine that was so remote—taken away. This is what one minds" (*D*, 4:15–16). In April Woolf praises Beatrice Webb's "justification of suicide. Having made the attempt myself [in 1913], from the best of motives as I thought" (*L*, 4:305). Returning to Tavistock Square and her diaries, Woolf decides that "Percy [Woolf's gardener at Rodmell] could burn the lot in one bonfire. He could burn them at the edge of the field where, so we think, we shall lie buried" (*D*, 4:24).

When Woolf's headaches returned in May, Woolf realizes that "if it were not for the divine goodness of L. how many times I should be thinking of death," and memories of death inevitably recall Woolf's father (*D*, 4:27). On September 3 each year, Woolf writes the same words in her diary: "the battle of Dunbar: the battle of Worcester . . . ," because she remembers "father saying that at St Ives on this day" (43). In the same month Woolf changes the location of her burial in a letter to John Lehmann (fig. 138): "in 50 years I shall be under the pond, with the gold fish swimming over me" (*L*, 4:381). Delighted by Vanessa's reaction to *The Waves*—that the book was "a lullaby capable of singing him [Thoby] to rest"—Woolf replied that she had Thoby (fig. 46) "so much in my mind,—I have a dumb rage still at his not being with us always" (390–391).

Lytton Strachey's fatal illness in December depressed Woolf still further. "Talk to L. last night about death: its stupidity; what he would feel if I died" (*D*, 4:55). And "L. & I sobbed on Christmas Eve" (56). Dining at the Keyneses' on Christmas Day, the couples talked about death and immortality. "L. said death was stupid like a motor accident," but Maynard Keynes wished that "there should be death arranged for couples simultaneously, like himself & Lydia, me & Leonard. But he always supposed he would die before Lydia, & I, I said, before Leonard. Then Lydia & Leonard will marry. They will combine all these dogs" (56).

It was photography that the Woolfs turned to in the last days of the year. Photography offered the Woolfs a form of oppositional memorializing. When the Keyneses came the next day to Monk's House for Boxing Day tea, the Woolfs took photographs that embed the Christmas Day discussion about couples and immortality (fig. 140). The presence of death is an informing referent in the sequencing of the photographs. Reinforcing the solidity of their friends by means of photographic repetitions is a form of visual narrative acting against the instabilities of death. By photographing the Keyneses as quasi-formal images, partially replicating sitting positions with clear lighting and two frontal gazes, the Woolfs give the Keyneses a very strong presence and exaggerated significance. The photographs are like studio photographs in which the Keyneses are performing themselves. The portrait presences are full and unmistakably self-confident, preserved by the Woolfs from oblivion. The photographs are agents of memory framing, linking the Keyneses and exaggerating the quality of coupledom. John Maynard Keynes and Virginia Woolf did die earlier than their respective partners (Keynes in 1946 and Woolf in 1941), but of course Lydia and Leonard did not marry.

Similarly, Vanessa Bell's paintings in the 1930s became more circumstantial in that she included figures that were no longer anonymous. As Frances Spalding argues, these domestic scenes may have celebrated motherhood but were "also poignantly about loss" (*Bell*, 251). Bell countered the impact of the deaths of Dora Carrington and Roger Fry, and her geographical distance from Julian, by compiling photographs. In Bell's letters to Julian, photographs become a memory technology offering her some comfort. "I'll send 2 photos" of Charleston, and Bell now associates Charleston with her childhood past and Talland House (VB/L, 422). "I often think it's not unlike family life in my mother's home in the summer holiday" (Spalding, *Bell*, 255).

In the first month of 1932 Woolf was again thinking about death. Writing to Ottoline Morrell, Woolf describes the characters in *The Waves* as "ghosts" and remarks that "real people have ghosts" (*L*, 5:6). Lytton Strachey's death that month was "like having the globe of the future perpetually smashed . . . a sense of something spent, gone: that is to me so intolerable . . . one knows now how irremediable" (*D*, 4:64–65). In a letter to Lytton's sister Pippa, Woolf places Lytton's death into a chain of family memories, "thinking of Lytton and Thoby and how Lytton came to me when Thoby died" (*L*, 5:8). Again, "the loss of Lytton seems to get harder and harder to bear" (12).

Lytton's death made Woolf think about her own. In February she records in her diary, "what is the point of it—life . . . suddenly becomes thin, indifferent. Lytton is dead" (*D*, 4:74). Again it is photography that reconstitutes the continuity of life for Woolf. Thanking Ottoline Morrell for sending photographs of Woolf and Lytton (fig. 61), Woolf declares, "I am very glad to have the photograph of Lytton—how exactly it brings him back! . . . I am aghast at the futility of life" (*L*, 5:16). In a second letter to Morrell, Woolf rhapsodizes, "how tremendously vivid Lytton becomes in them—one can hear him speak" (18). Woolf had been delighted when Dora Carrington sent photographs (fig. 57). "I loved those little pictures, darling Carrington. How it seizes upon one, the longing for Lytton, when one sees them" (28).

The Woolfs carefully placed Carrington's photographs into Monk's House Album 4, out of chronological sequence, making the memory of Lytton a vivid personal memento mori. The suicide of Carrington immediately after Lytton's death meant that, for Woolf, "she kept so much of Lytton that her death makes his loss more complete" (*L*, 5:34). Writing to Ethel Smyth a few weeks later, Woolf felt "hemmed in and depressed and haunted by poor Carrington" (38). Woolf's diary entry describing her last visit to Carrington, the day before Carrington shot herself, is an unusually exhaustive account, full of exact descriptions of the rooms and garden and clothes, gestures and behavior. Woolf's writing, like a camera, controls appearances, denying death, by means of precise narrative as if to frame the event. In August Goldie Dickinson dies, and Woolf feels "in the midst of some vast operation . . . of being capable of dying . . . at night L. & I talked of death" (*D*, 4:120). Woolf pleads with Roger Fry, "how I hate my friends dying! Please live to be a thousand" (Fry died only two years later) (*L*, 5:87). Fainting at Rodmell, Woolf thinks "a little, of dying suddenly" but is able to recover because "I am going in to be photographed" (*D*, 4:121).

The photographs that the Woolfs took of each other on that day are double portraits in which each body has great presence (fig. 147). The photographs focus on the upper body and head, giving maximum attention to the faces. Both Virginia and Leonard stare directly at the camera (a powerful gaze) and also off-frame as if in intelligent contemplation. The use of space gives each sitter a strong physicality like a double biography. But when another of Leonard's photographs of Virginia is used as the frontispiece of Winifred Holtby's study of Woolf (similar to fig. 148), instead of the Lenare photograph (fig. 69) that Virginia preferred, Woolf feels "my privacy is invaded . . . ugliness revealed" and she dreams of death (*D*, 4:124). The dream of death occurs because the photograph has been torn from its context—the photo album—and therefore from the Woolfs' meaning process. To prize the photograph from the context of an album is a violence, the death of the image's meaning. It is as if the transposition of the photograph into an uncongenial setting (Woolf disparaged Holtby's book) unconsciously triggers traumatic dreams. In November, finishing her essay on Leslie Stephen for the *Times*, Woolf immediately suffers anxiety: "I lay in bed reasoning that I could not come smash. Death I defy you, &c. But it was a terrific effort" (129).

The next year, 1933, John Galsworthy dies, "that stark man lies dead," and so does Lady Cecil, of whom Woolf writes to Ethel, "do you die as I do and lie in the grave and then rise and see people like ghosts? And all my friends are dead" (*L*, 5:164). Disassociating, Woolf is "amused to be dead—one of those ghosts that people talk of respectfully: rather a dignified position: you can't speak ill of the dead" (178). As I have argued elsewhere, the portraits that the Woolfs took of Ethel carry mnemonic traces. Details such as the flower, chair, and positions echo Woolf's favorite photograph taken by Vanessa at St. Ives in 1892, of Virginia together with her mother and father. Again the Woolfs allow Ethel to dominate the space of the photograph in a stylized series of positions (fig. 134). The room at Monk's House is a limited and personal geography giving Ethel a solid presence reinforced by the use of clear lighting, framing, and repetition, as in the Woolfs' other portraiture.

Creating pictures, whether these are fictional or photographic, is the Woolfs' constant defense against the pain of death. On their subsequent Italian holiday, Woolf changes the place of her burial yet again to "be buried, if bones can walk" at Monte Oliveto (*L*, 5:185). The Italian journey was also a journey into Woolf's past as she remembers the holiday in Venice and Florence in 1904 immediately after Stephen's death. Staying in Lerici (fig. 152), Woolf sits "by an open window, by a balcony, by the bay in which Shelley was drowned," and immediately fictionalizes the scene in a visual frame: "describe the hills, the tall pink yellow white houses" (*L*, 5:186). Returning through France and reading that "Lady Cynthia Mosley is dead," Woolf displaces the event visually, "picture the scene; wonder at death" (*D*, 4:160). There was always the danger that fiction would flood into life. "I have just killed Mrs P." (She was writing *The Pargiters*) and found that "these little scenes embroil one, just as in life" (173). *The Pargiters* was the history of Woolf's family and included memories of her childhood and life in London. She originally planned to group the years in *The Pargiters* in sequences that would, coincidentally, omit the years of key deaths (1906, Thoby's death) and key photographs (the 1892 photograph).

At the Rothschilds' engagement party in October 1933, Woolf experienced a dread of death. "Candles were lit, and I chose mine, a green one, and it was the first to die, which means . . . I shall be the first to wear a winding sheet" (*L*, 5:241). But it was the successive deaths of friends that she found more traumatic. Walking through Leicester Square, she read of the "Death of noted Novelist" Stella Benson, who had "sat on the terrace with me at Rodmell . . . how mournful the afternoon seems . . . there seems to be some sort of reproach to me in her death . . . why not my name on the posters?" (*D*, 4:192). Woolf had placed Benson's photograph (fig. 130) into Monk's House Album 3 in 1931.

What is at stake in all of these observations of Woolf is that photographs and fictional scenes are defenses against her instinctual turn to death. As Freud argues, such "object-cathexes" are "self-preservative" (Freud, 97). The year 1934 began with the death of Leonard's sister Clara. George Duckworth's death, following Woolf's completion of the sexual molestation scene in *The Pargiters*, was accompanied by Woolf's "usual incongruous shades of feeling" (*D*, 4:211). But most traumatic of all was the unexpected death of Roger Fry in September, having "the substance gone out of everything" (242). Fry's death immediately reminds Woolf of her mother's death. "I remember turning aside at mother's bed . . . she's pretending, I said: aged 13" (242). At Fry's funeral in Golder's Green Crematorium, Woolf "laid my hand on" Desmond MacCarthy's (fig. 158) shoulder "& said dont die yet. Nor you either he said" (243). Fry's funeral brought "a fear of death," and she imagined, "do you find that is one of the effects of a shock—that pictures come up and up and up, without bidding or much control? I could almost see Roger" (*L*, 5:334). Visualizations gave Woolf "the exalted sense of being above time & death" (*D*, 4:245). Like her letters from the Acropolis, her letters about Fry's death replicate the emotional tone she adopted when writing about her father's death in 1904.

Ann and Judith Stephen, Woolf's nieces, came to stay with the Woolfs in Rodmell that month, and Woolf can immediately "see this through Roger's eyes" (*D*, 4:244). Photographing the Stephen sisters (fig. 163), the Woolfs make use of the same portraiture dynamic. Again there is an extreme close-up gaze, clear lighting, and each sitter has a very strong presence. The photographs witness the stability of each sitter. They are highly intentional, carefully framed portraits in which the girls have an omniscient authority, engaging directly with the camera. The photographs create a sense of agency and corporeality in the context of Fry's recent death. Woolf's last diary entry for 1934 is a visual scene of death. "One's own death—think of lying there alone, looking at it . . . And Roger dead" (*D*, 4:267).

It is relevant that Bell and Woolf's great-aunt Julia Margaret Cameron (fig. 25), like Woolf, suffered from mood swings typified by bipolar personality traits. In a fascinating account of Cameron's photographs and "eccentricity," Kirsten Hoving argues that Cameron's photographs of women (but not of men) are of depressive women, as if Cameron were constructing a "kind of pre-Freudian typological approach to reflect despair" as a kind of vehicle for expressing her own states of mind (Hoving, 53). But although Cameron may have shared Woolf's behaviors—for example, Cameron's "letter-writing may also have been a form of manic activity," compounded, like Woolf's, by numerous ampersands—the Woolfs' and Bell's photographs of women are not depressive female images (49). According to Hoving, Cameron photographs women sitters without perspective or three-dimensional space, as if the external world is dark and blank. Bell and the Woolfs, on the other hand, place women sitters close to the camera in strong poses and full light, including sharp details of background objects.

The Woolfs' photographs are ambient props against the social and personal instabilities of the 1930s. Woolf progressively displaces her instinctual fears of death and fears of the symbolic father by what Freud termed the aesthetic ideal. For the Woolfs this involved the continual creation of visual scenes in which the camera operators live imaginatively close to their sitters as if in a "third space." For example, the Woolfs in their photographs increasingly displace the gap between themselves and their friends by a marked lack of foreground space (fig. 163). There is no amateur caesura between photographer and subject. The early 1930s were years of instability and death, but 1934 ended with a positive view. "My Lodge is demolished; the new house in process of building in the orchard. There will be open doors in front; & a view right over to Caburn," and Woolf looked forward to "a show of Man Ray's photographs in Bedford Sq . . . Man Ray says will I come & be photographed—on Tuesday 3.30" (fig. 165) for what has become an iconic Woolf photograph (*D*, 4:263–264).

Bell's Cassis photographs, taken at the end of the 1930s, also represent some of her finest portraits, particularly the close-up portrait of Duncan Grant (fig. 195). Like a sequence of stills of privileged moments of French bucolic life, the photographs were an expressive resource for Bell after Julian's death. "My views of France are now such as would satisfy the most rabid patriot, I should think. Really the character and beauty and variety as we drove through impressed me even more than ever . . . you should have seen me and Duncan, or rather Duncan [fig. 196], very dapper" (VB/L, 452).

THE AFFECTIVE RELATIONS among Bell's and the Woolfs' photographs, visual memories, and multiple experiences of death (whether real or imagined) in the early 1930s are an important feature of that decade. But throughout their lives Bell and the Woolfs use photographs as a route into these nondepictable relations, creating images of friends almost as a mnemonic device, a scaffolding against the void. Family photographs are semiotic and personal objects in that they contain signifiers representing absent and present emotions, and personal in that subjects share a conversational past. At a general level, Bell's and the Woolfs' photographs engage in a process of *deixis* that psychologists active in photo analysis describe as a "conversational remembering with photographs" (Edwards and Middleton, 9). Photo analysis is a method of using photography to increase self-awareness in groups or individuals. For example, photo analysts who analyze conversations between mothers and children that were triggered by photographs find mediated memories. Mothers reconstructed the past in photographic *deixis* in order to explain the past to themselves and to their children.

Photo albums are not Orwellian "memory holes" into which the past, like paper in *Nineteen Eighty-four*, completely disappears. Taking photographs of friends and mounting photographs into repetitive sequences in photo albums are a technology of memory; the activities perform important memory work in constituting and consolidating friendships and familial identities (Hirsch). If, as Roland Barthes suggests, the photographic image simultaneously records absence and presence, then to double up each photograph, as the Woolfs so frequently do, and Bell does with her constant enlargements, doubles the that-has-been essence of each photograph as if to defy death. While professional photography enabled some modernist visual cultures, including architecture, to appear to transcend time and history, a sociopsychic mnemonic shapes Bell's and the Woolfs' photo albums and sense of time. The albums are horizontal narratives of family life and social events, but shot through with family memories and inscriptions. Photography, and the compilation of many albums, allowed Bell and the Woolfs to activate memories in a social landscape of Bloomsbury life. Photo albums, as visual diaries, are not equivalent to autobiographies but similarly re-present lives in dialogic discursive patterns. Photography, even if improvised and provisional, was another way of telling their life stories in which the albums become a fully expressive "heterotopic" third space—a thick, dense "imagined community." Photo albums negotiate our pasts aesthetically, by telling visual stories of rememberance. Virginia Woolf and Vanessa Bell's albums may be the marginalia of modernism but were also a modernism of their own, and collective and unique snapshots of Bloomsbury.

PART TWO

The Photographs

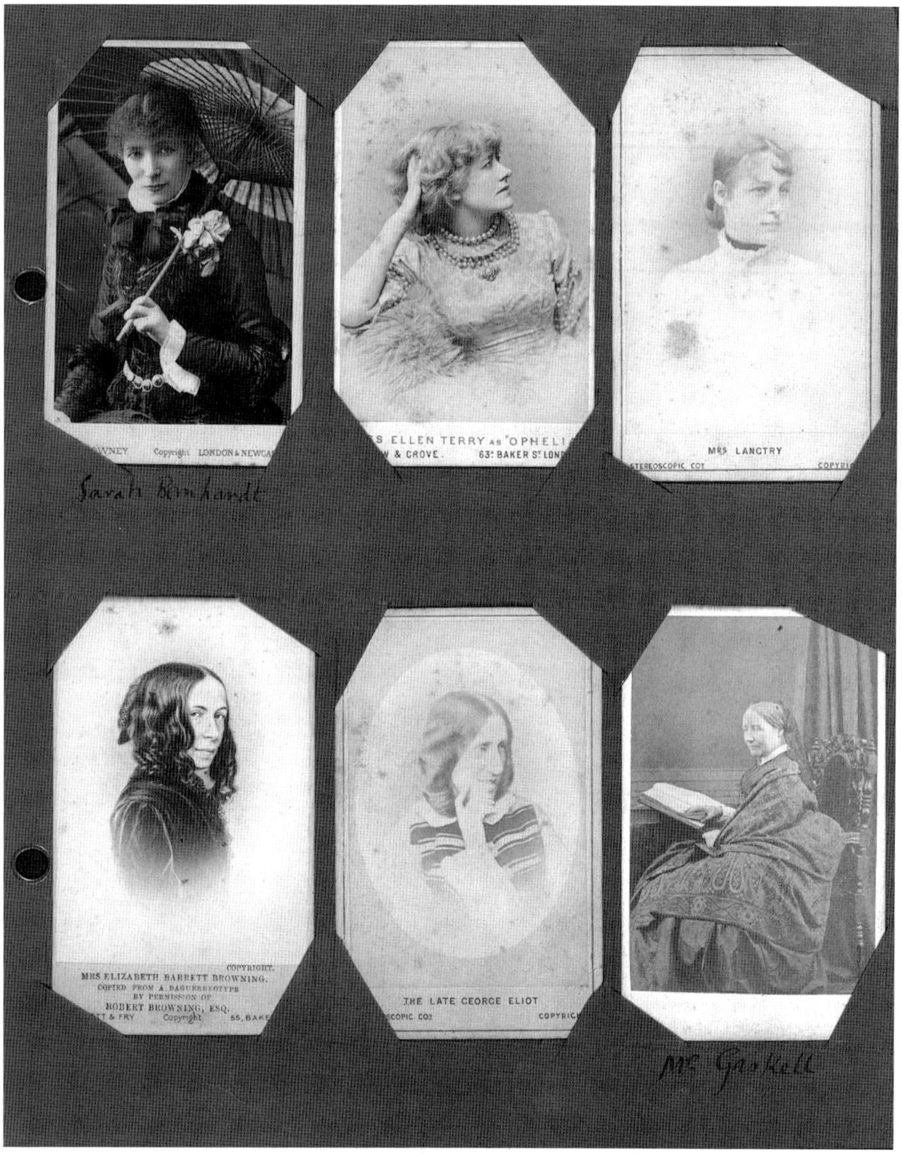

1. Cartes-de-visite: Sarah Bernhardt, Ellen Terry, Mrs. Langtry, Elizabeth Barrett Browning, George Eliot, Mrs. Gaskell. Box 1 Album, p. 4. Reprinted by permission of the Harvard Theatre Collection, the Houghton Library. "How easy it is to fill in the picture with set pieces . . . Ellen Terry dressed as a boy; Garibaldi in his red shirt" (SK, 87).

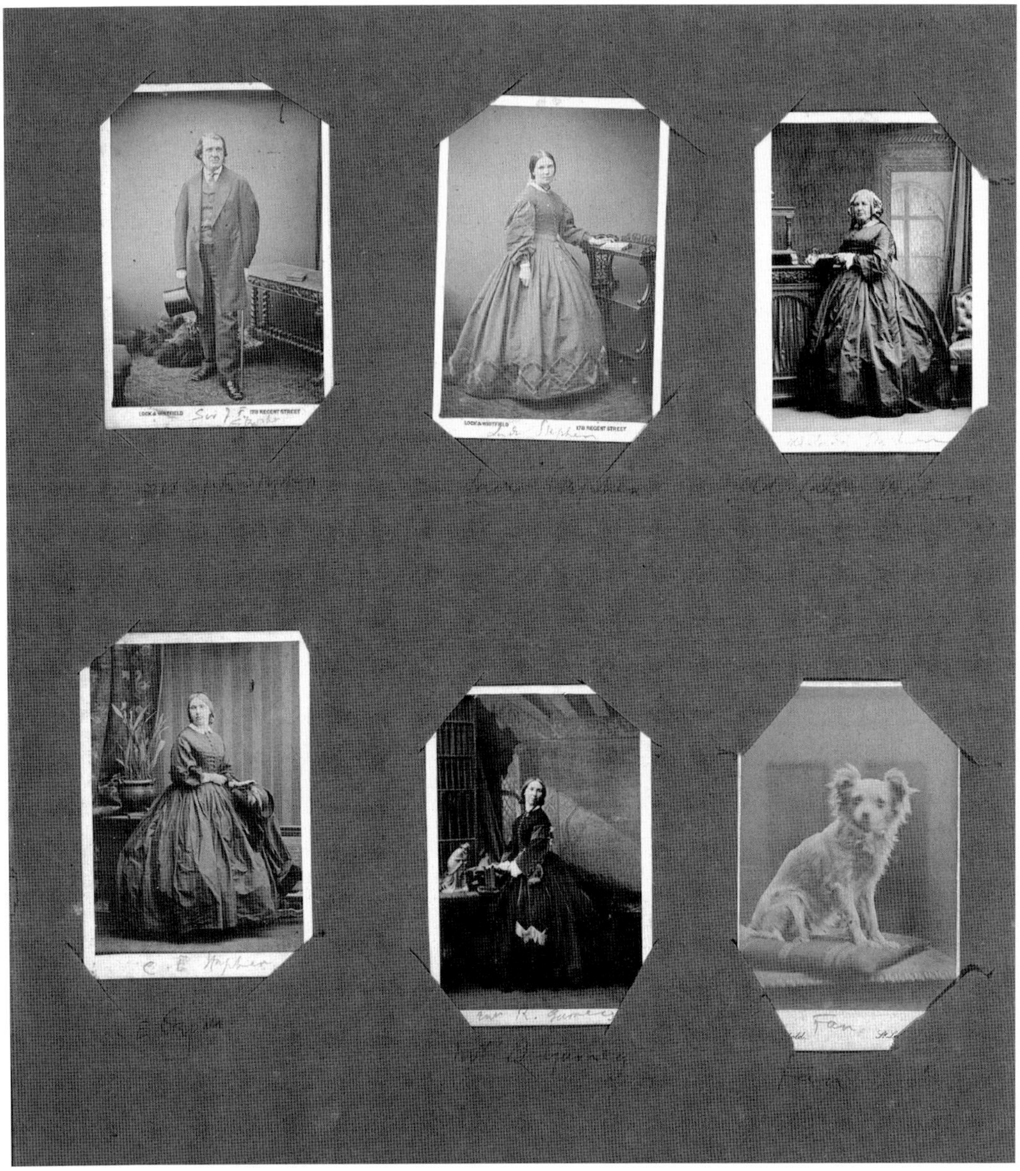

2. Cartes-de-visite: Sir J. Stephen, Lady Stephen, Old Lady Stephen, C. E. Stephen, Mrs. R. Gurney. Fan marked on rear, "April 1879 Stella." Monk's House Album 1, p. 8. Reprinted by permission of the Harvard Theatre Collection, the Houghton Library. I am "a social festivity snob. Any group of people if they are well dressed, and socially sparkling and unfamiliar will do the trick" (AS, 188).

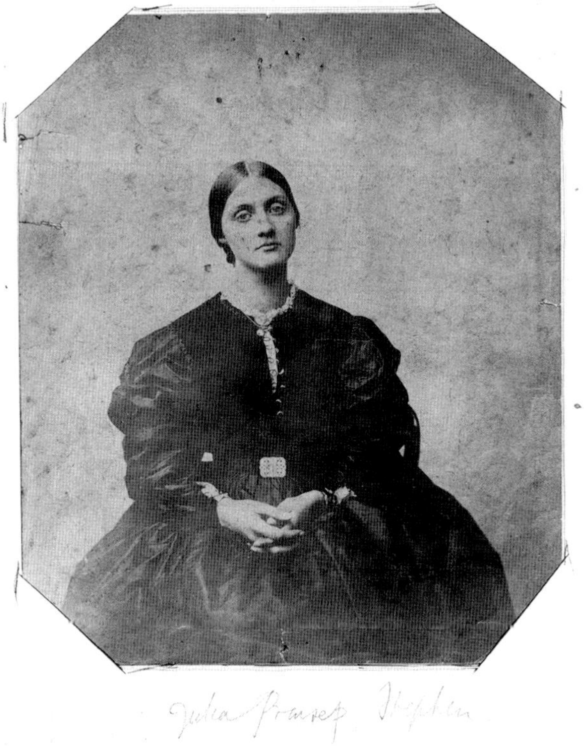

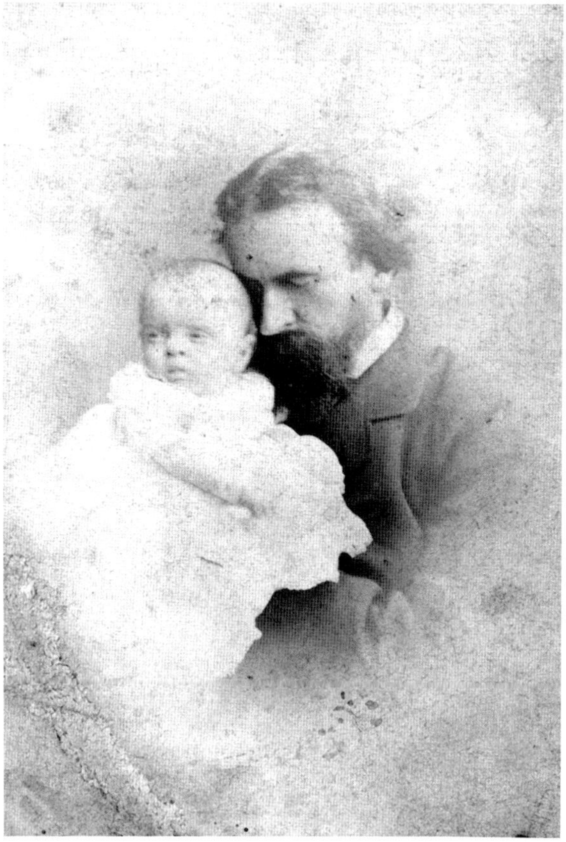

3. (LEFT) Julia Prinsep Stephen, ca. 1863–1865. Monk's House Album 3, p. 1. Reprinted by permission of the Harvard Theatre Collection, the Houghton Library. "'central' gets closest to the general feeling I had of living so completely in her atmosphere" (SK, 83).

4. (RIGHT) Leslie Stephen with Laura Stephen, ca. 1870. Monk's House Album 1, p. 51. Reprinted by permission of the Harvard Theatre Collection, the Houghton Library. "asking her [Julia] advice about a governess for Laura, she followed him to the door and said 'I will try to be a good wife to you'" (SK, 91).

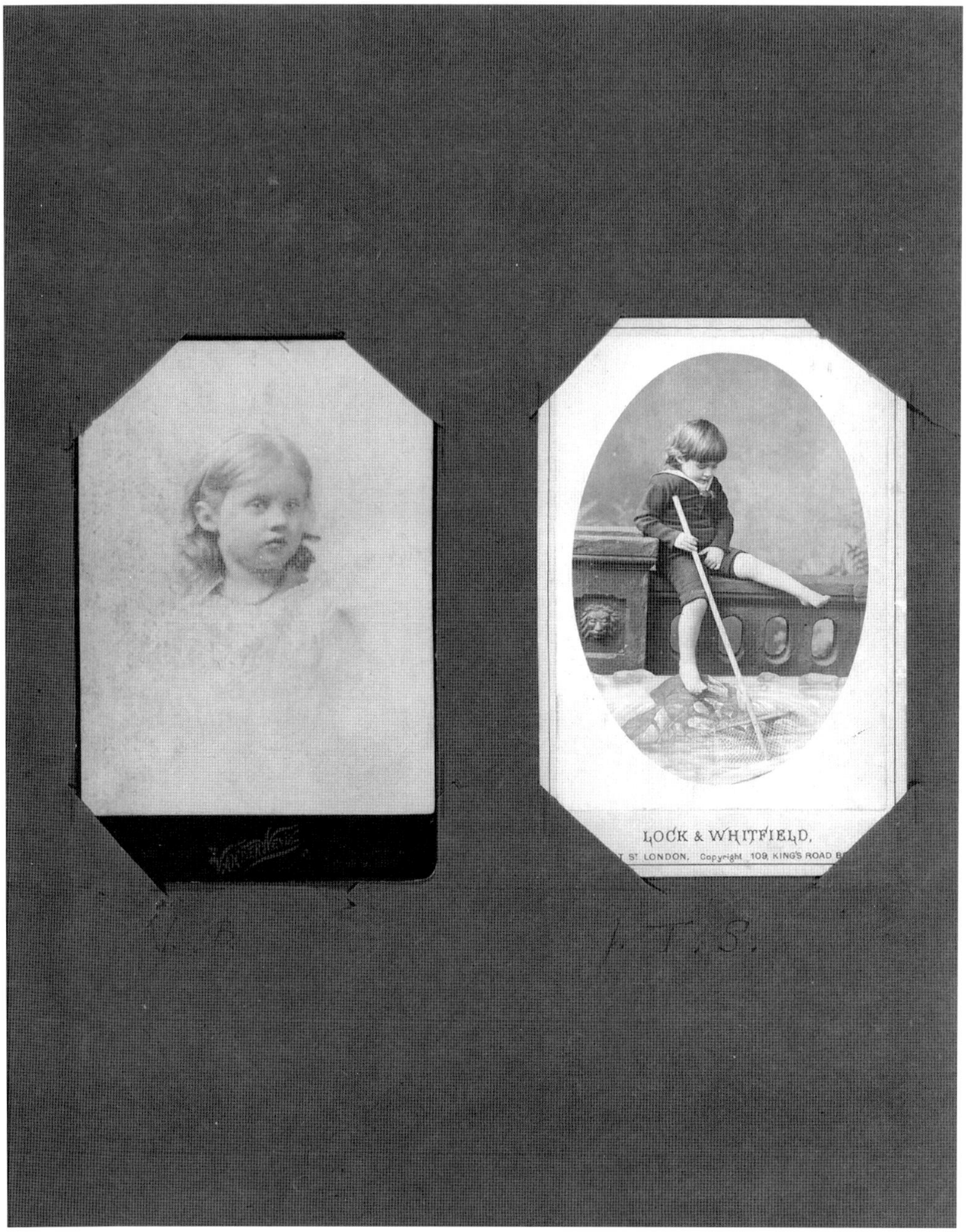

5. Vanessa and Thoby Stephen, ca. 1883. Photographers: Lock and Whitfield (Thoby), van de Weyde (Vanessa). Monk's House Album 1, p. 14. Reprinted by permission of the Harvard Theatre Collection, the Houghton Library. "He was a clumsy little boy, very fat, bursting through his Norfolk jacket . . . Napoleonic" (SK, 107).

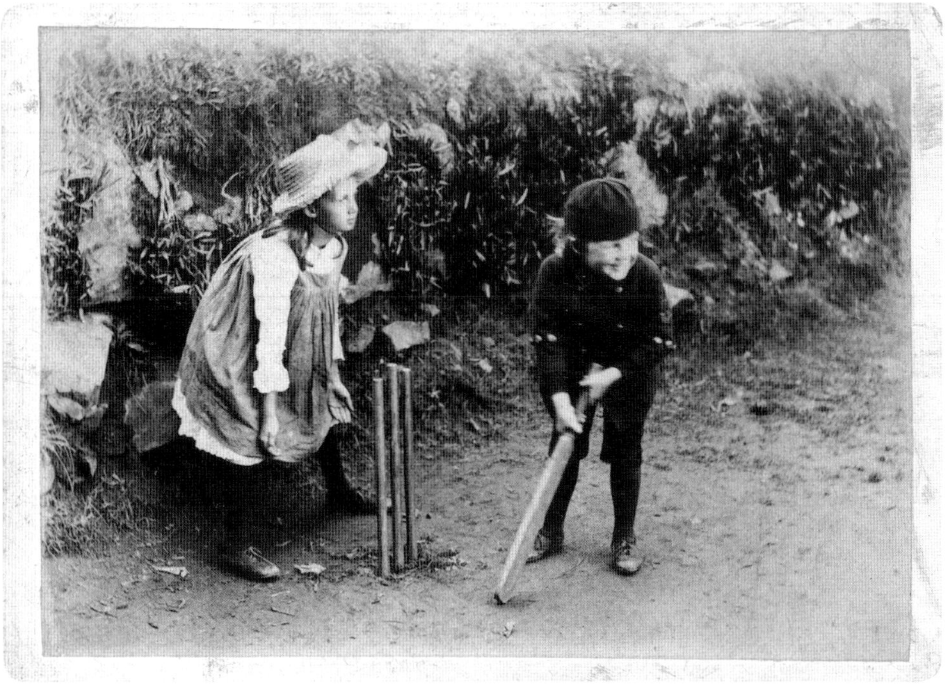

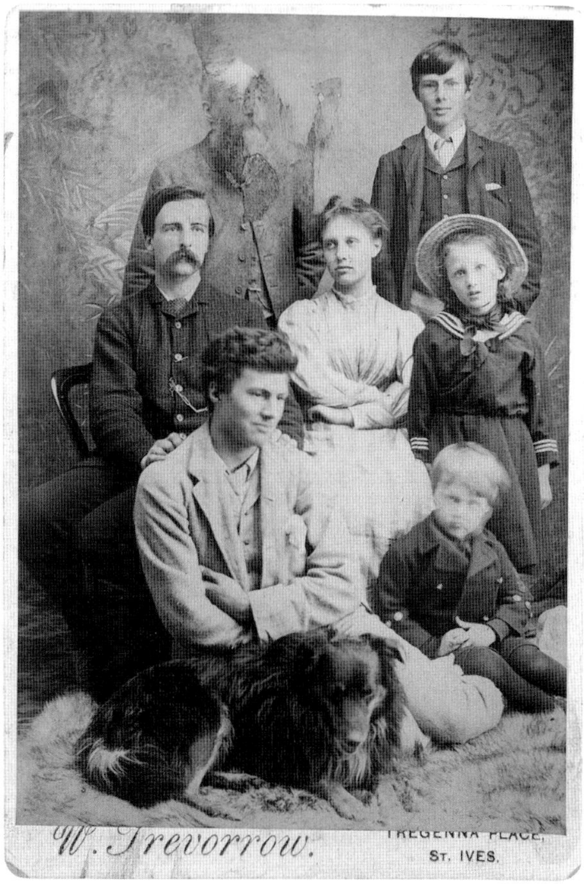

6. (ABOVE) Virginia and Adrian Stephen. St. Ives, ca. 1886–1888. Brown envelope. Reprinted by permission of the Harvard Theatre Collection, the Houghton Library. "what was called tomboys; that is, we played cricket, scrambled over rocks" (SK, 68).

7. (RIGHT) *Back row:* Mr. Wolstoneholme, Gerald Duckworth; *center row:* Arthur Hart, Stella Duckworth, Virginia Stephen; *front row:* George Duckworth, Adrian Stephen. St. Ives, ca. 1889. Photographer: Wm. Trevorrow. Box 4, folder 1 of 2. There is an incomplete version in Bell's Album 1, p. 15. Reprinted by permission of the Harvard Theatre Collection, the Houghton Library. "In the foreground there were of course people; and these people were very like characters in Dickens . . . Mr. Wolstoneholme . . . when he ate plum tart, he spurted the juice through his nose" (SK,73).

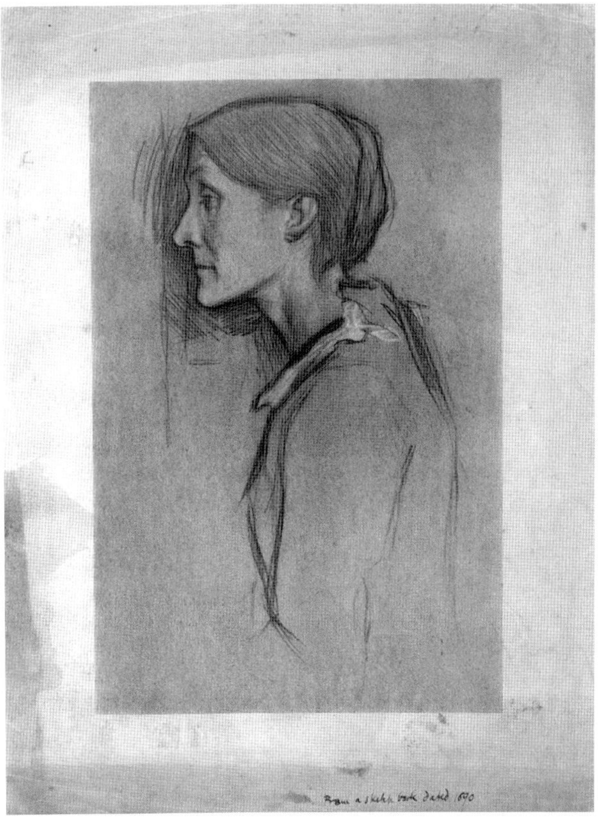

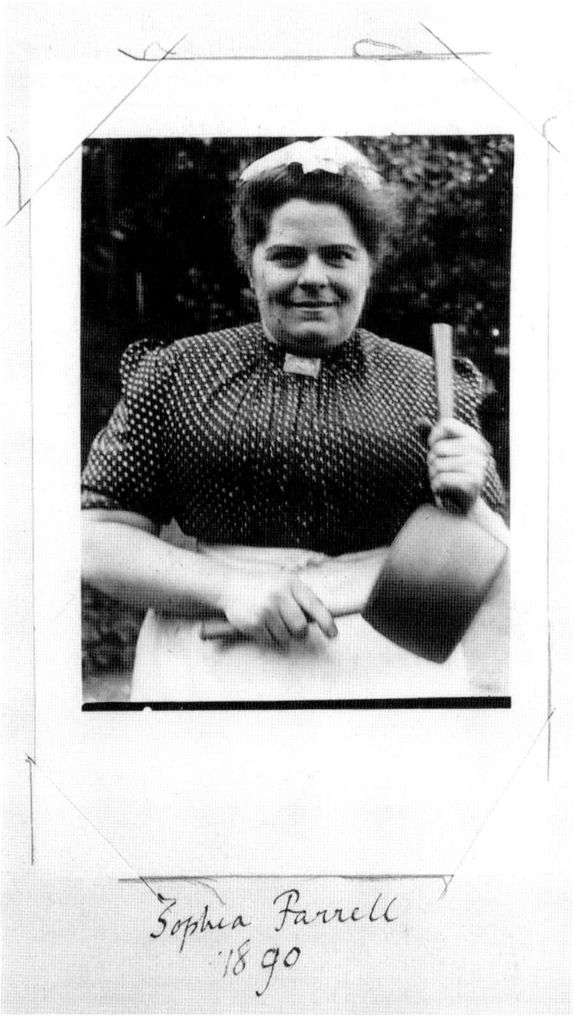

8. Julia Stephen sketch by Sir Wm. Rothenstein, 1890. Large white folder.
Reprinted by permission of the Harvard Theatre Collection, the Houghton Library.
"When the drawing was done she looked at it, then handed it in silence to her daughter . . . the consternation was general" (Rothenstein in Gillespie and Steele, xv).

9. Sophia Farrell, 1890. Monk's House Album 4, p. 18.
Reprinted by permission of the Harvard Theatre Collection, the Houghton Library.
"Her room is hung with photographs. Her mind is like a family album. You turn up Uncle George you turn up Aunt Maria. She has a story about each of them" (Woolf in Lee, 49).

10. (RIGHT) Julia, Leslie, and Virginia Stephen. The library at Talland House, 1892. Photographer: Vanessa Stephen. Monk's House Album 3, p. 2. Reprinted by permission of the Harvard Theatre Collection, the Houghton Library. "Talland House . . . nothing we had as children was quite so important to us" (SK, 109–110).

11. (BELOW) Adrian, Thoby, Vanessa, and Virginia Stephen. "Look Out Point," St. Ives, ca. 1892. Copy of a page from Stella Duckworth's album. Box 4, folder A. Reprinted by permission of the Harvard Theatre Collection, the Houghton Library. "It had, when we came there, a perfect view—right across the Bay to Godrevy Lighthouse" (SK, 111).

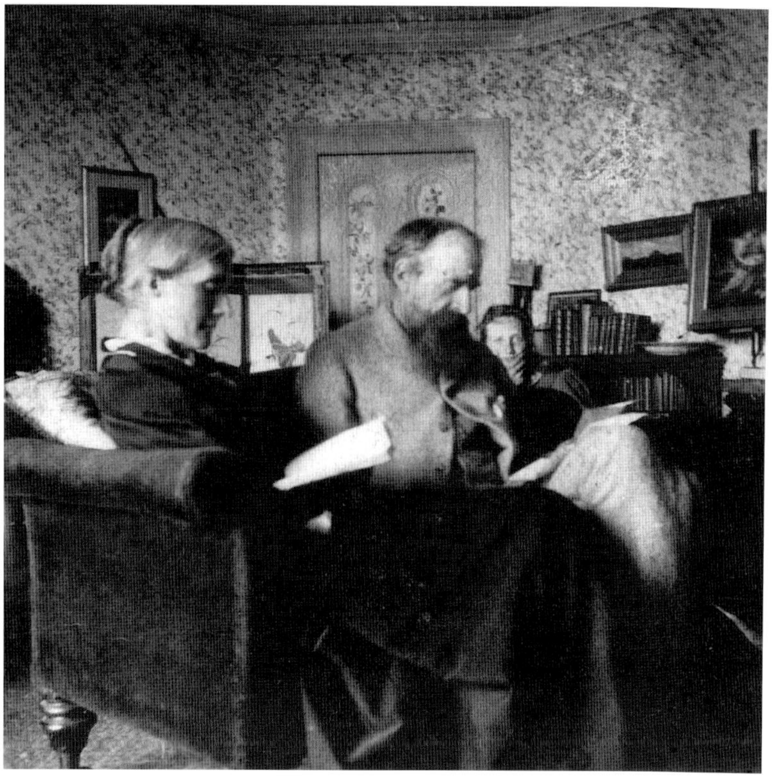

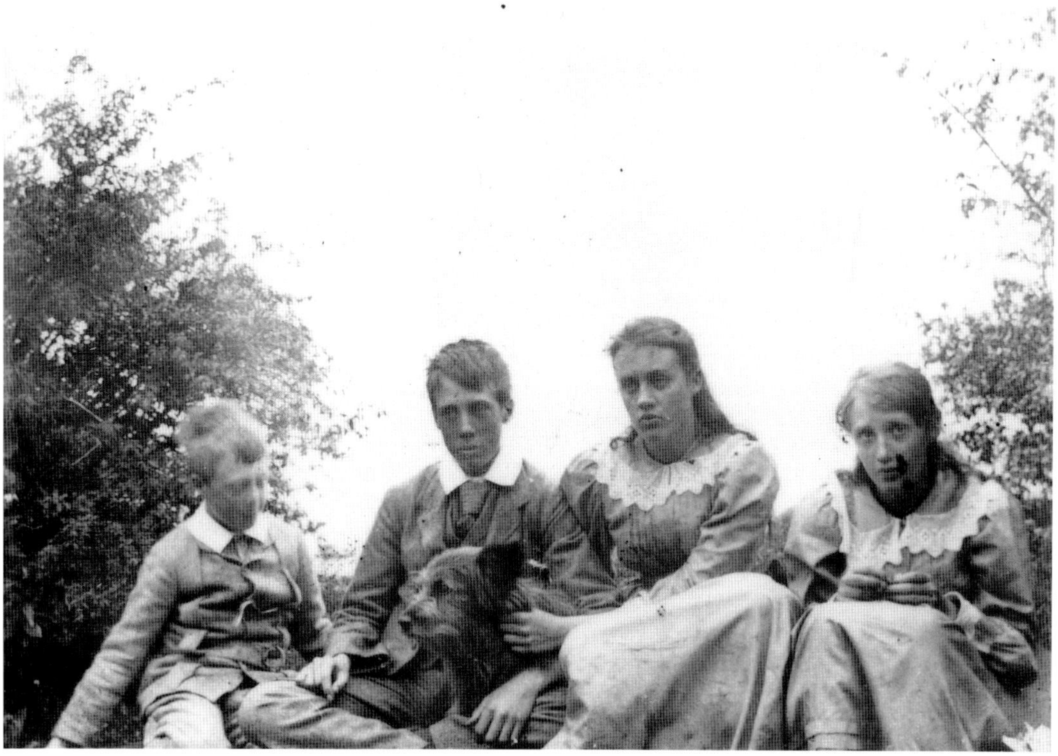

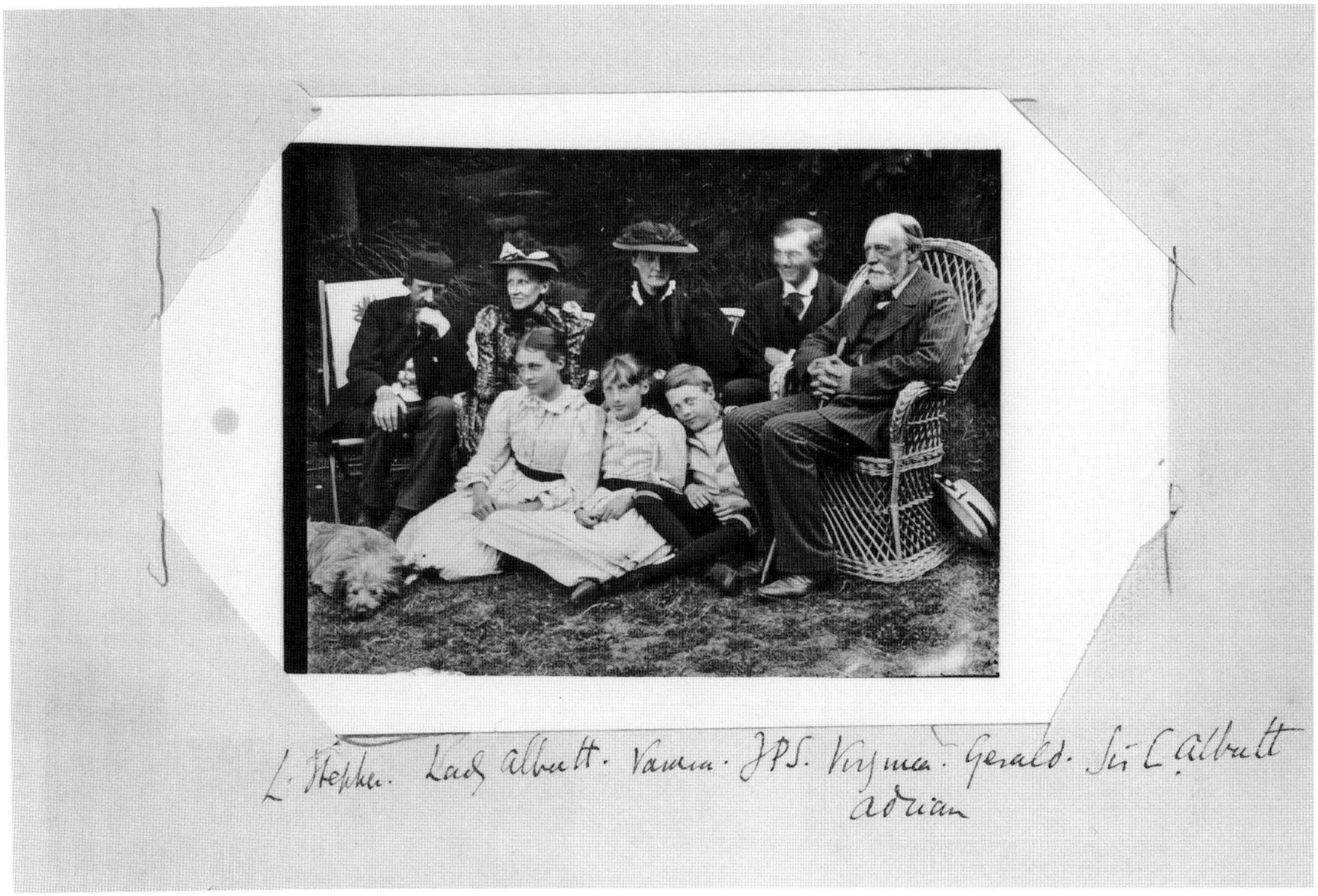

12. *Front row:* Vanessa, Virginia, Adrian, Stephen; *back row:* Sir Leslie Stephen, Lady Albutt, Mrs. Stephen, Gerald Duckworth, Sir Clifford Albutt. St. Ives, ca. 1892. Monk's House Album 5, p. 6. Reprinted by permission of the Harvard Theatre Collection, the Houghton Library. "entirely a grown-up affair—receiving friends. We never had friends to stay with us" (SK, 111).

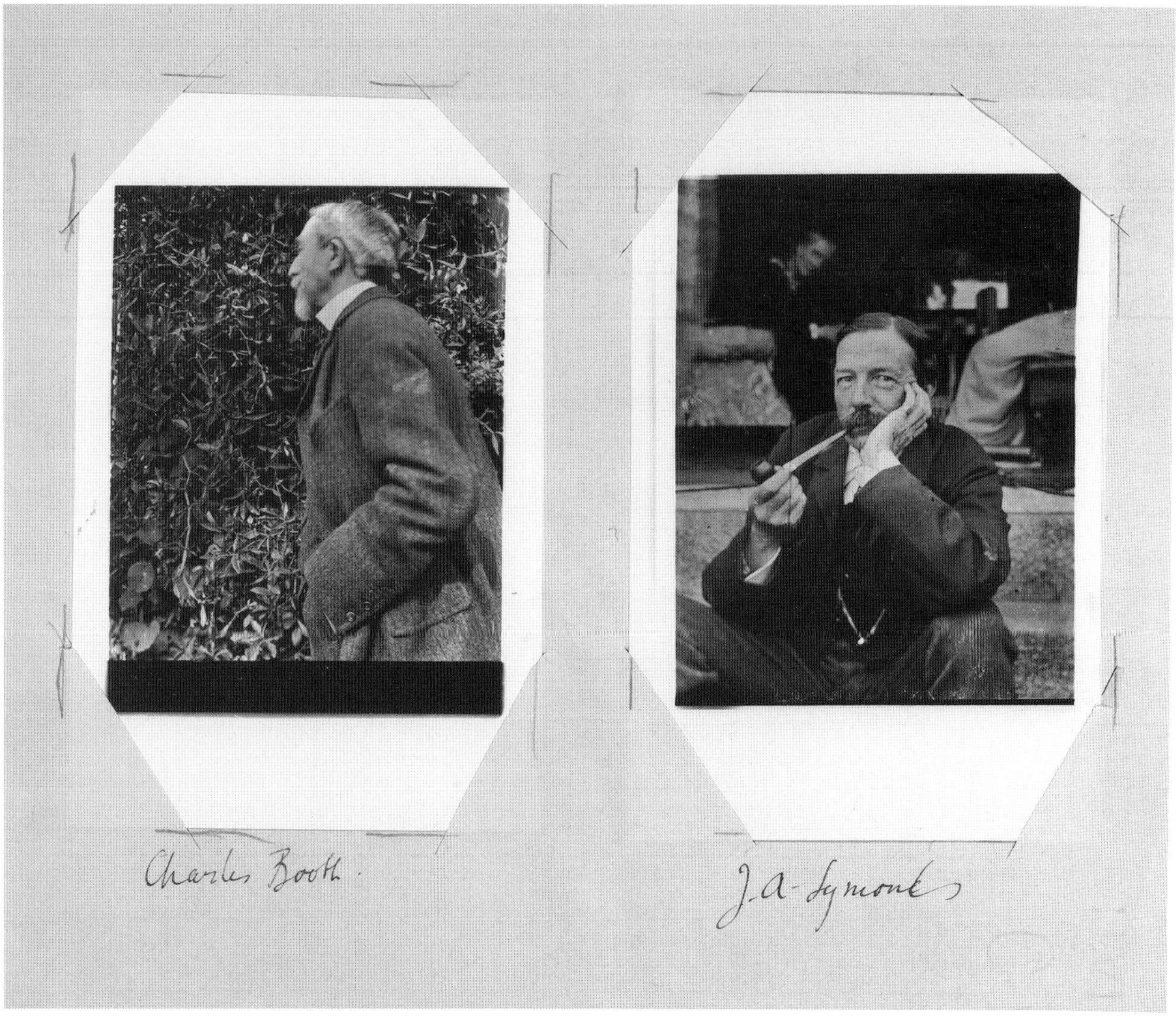

13. Charles Booth; J. A. Symonds, and Julia in rear. Talland House, ca. 1892. Monk's House Album 5, p. 7. Reprinted by permission of the Harvard Theatre Collection, the Houghton Library. "I remember looking down at J. A. Symonds from the landing at Talland House; and noting his nerve-drawn white face" (SK, 136).

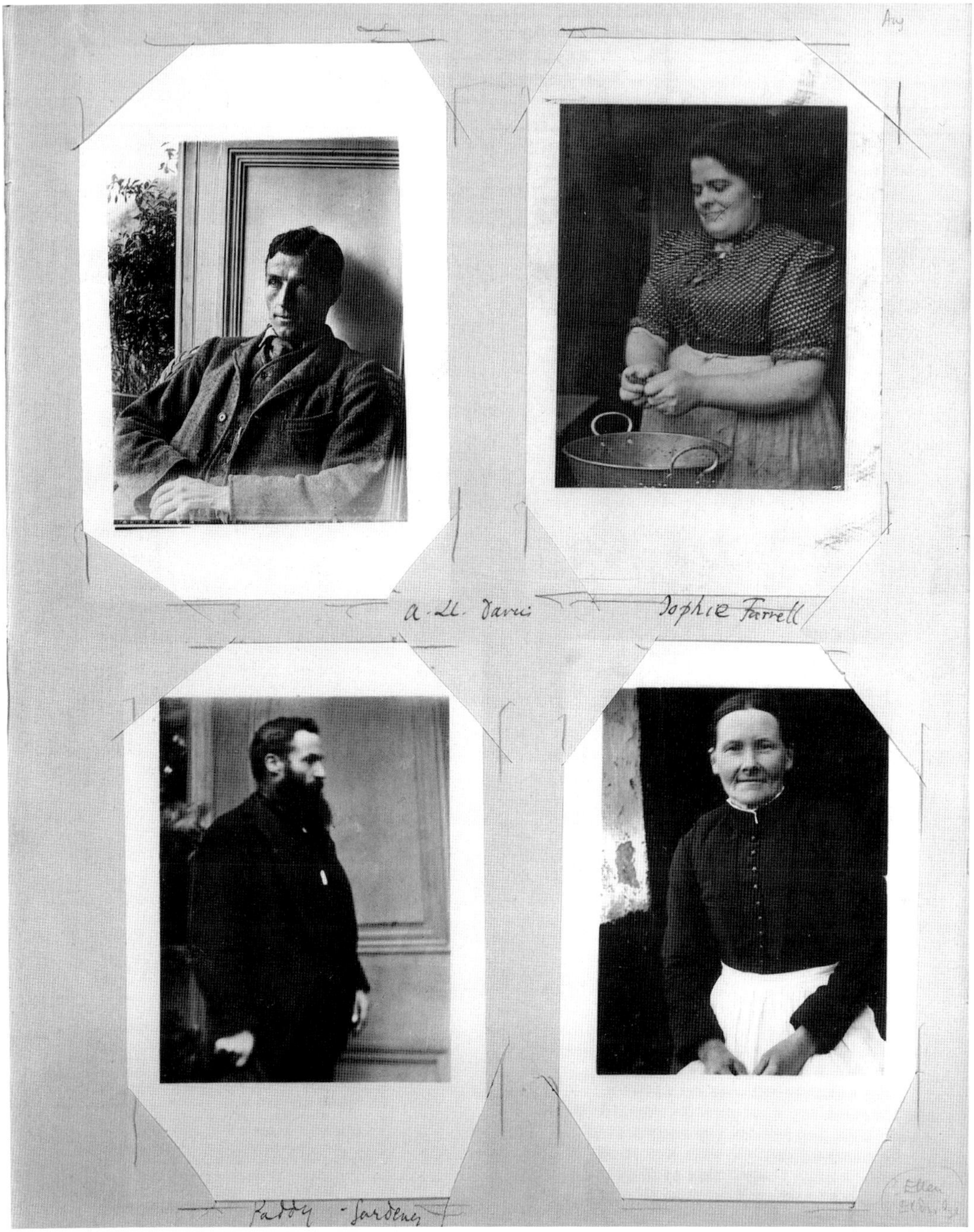

14. A. Ll. Davies (barrister whose son was the model for Peter Pan); Sophie Farrell; Paddy; Ellen Eldridge. St. Ives, ca. 1892. Photographer: Gerald Duckworth. Monk's House Album 5, p. 8. Reprinted by permission of the Harvard Theatre Collection, the Houghton Library.

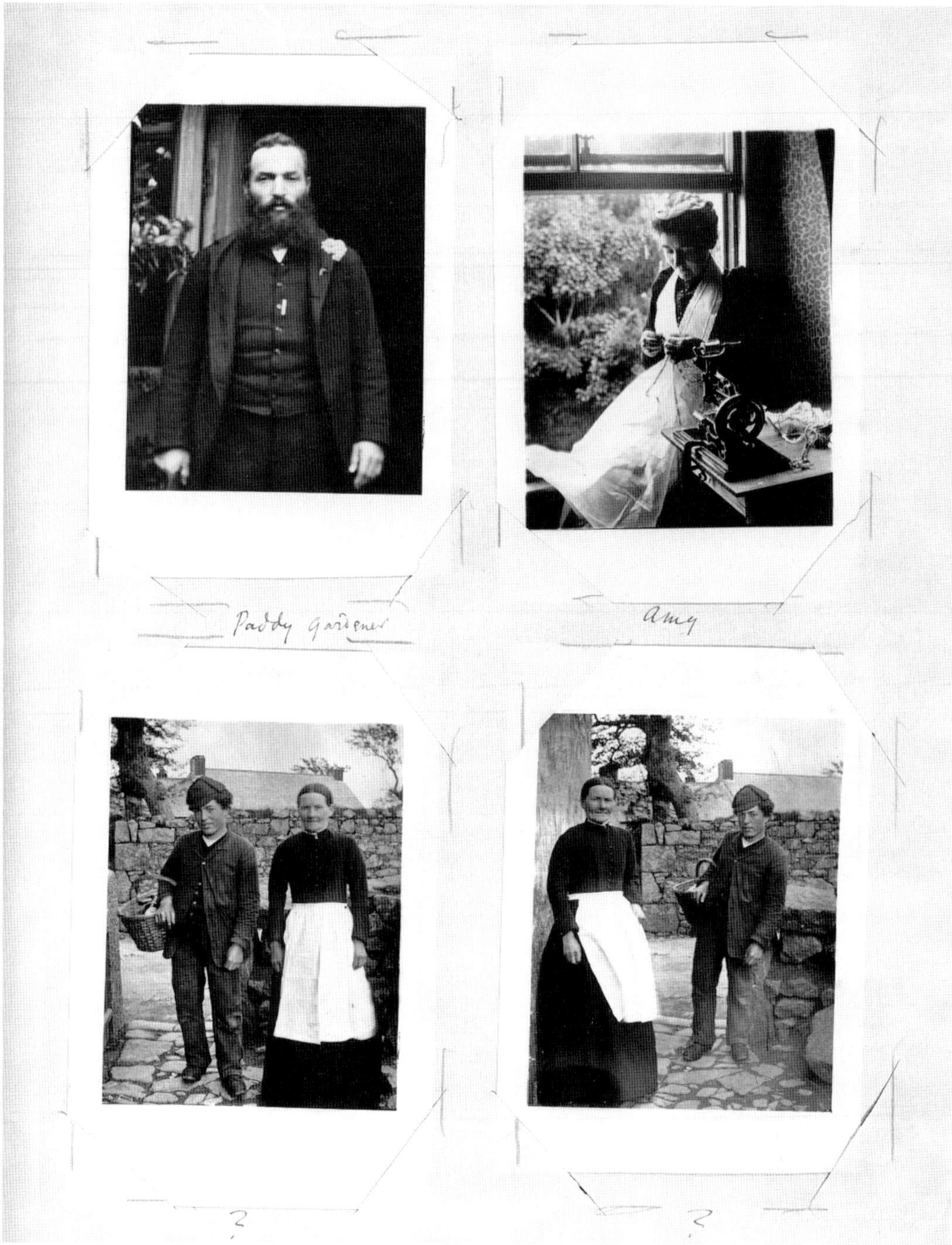

15. Paddy; Amy Norris; Ellen Eldridge and delivery boy. St. Ives, ca. 1892. Photographer: Gerald Duckworth. Monk's House Album 5, p. 10. Reprinted by permission of the Harvard Theatre Collection, the Houghton Library.

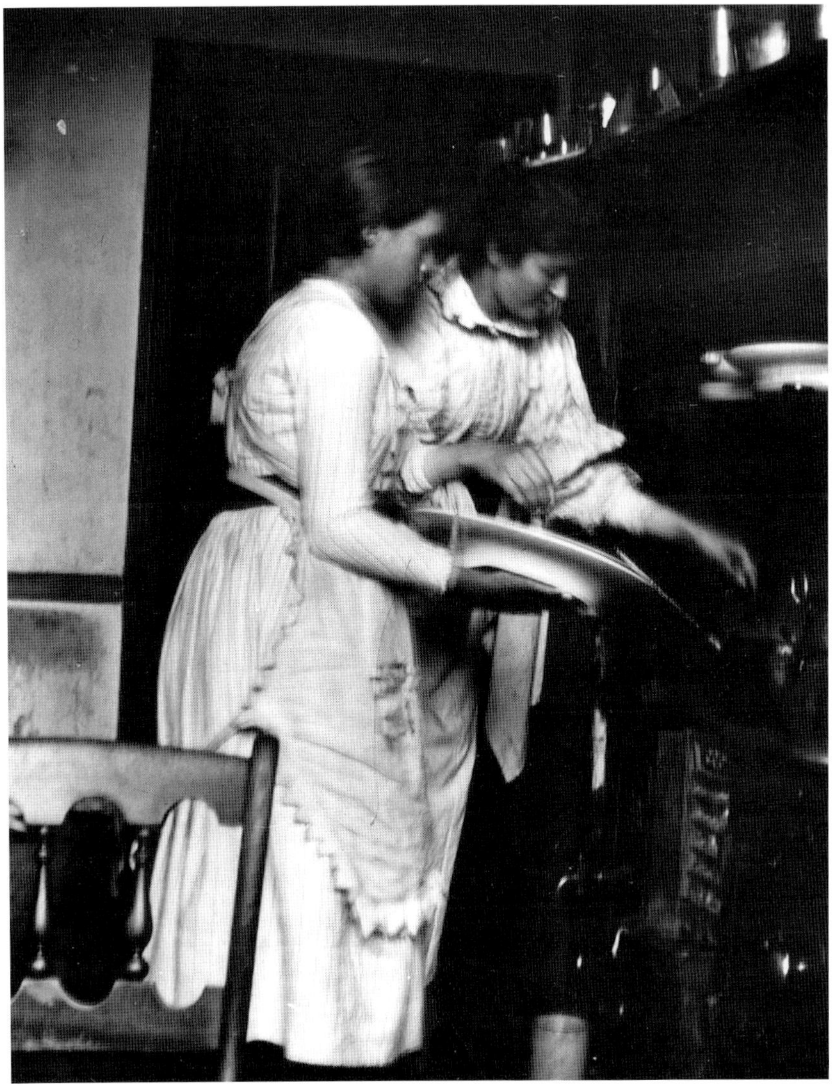

16. Vanessa Stephen and Lisa Stillman. Kitchen, Talland House, ca. 1892. Monk's House Album 5, p. 4. Reprinted by permission of the Harvard Theatre Collection, the Houghton Library.

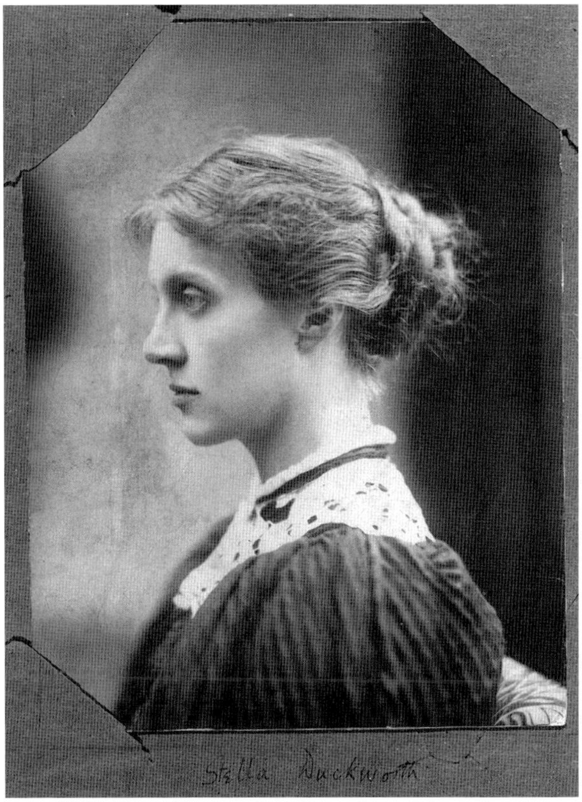

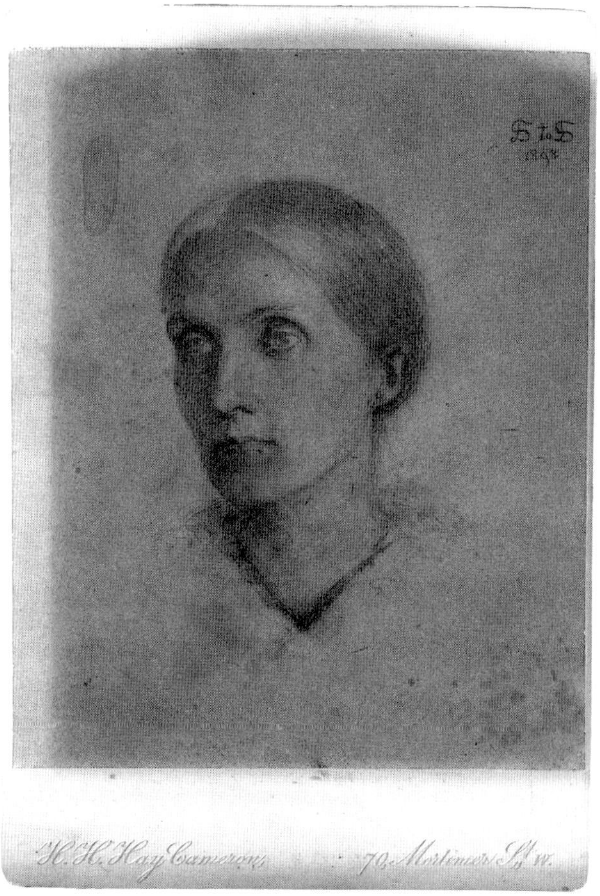

17. (LEFT) Stella Duckworth, Rome. Monk's House Album 1, p. 50. Reprinted by permission of the Harvard Theatre Collection, the Houghton Library. "She was beautiful, more beautiful than her pictures show" (R, 42).

18. (RIGHT) Julia Stephen. Drawing by Lisa Stillman? On 1893 photograph by H. H. H. Cameron. Large white folder. Reprinted by permission of the Harvard Theatre Collection, the Houghton Library. "father found a letter from Phil Burne Jones asking for Lisa's picture—Nessa and I, after much consultation, decided to take it in a hansom" (*EJ*, 29).

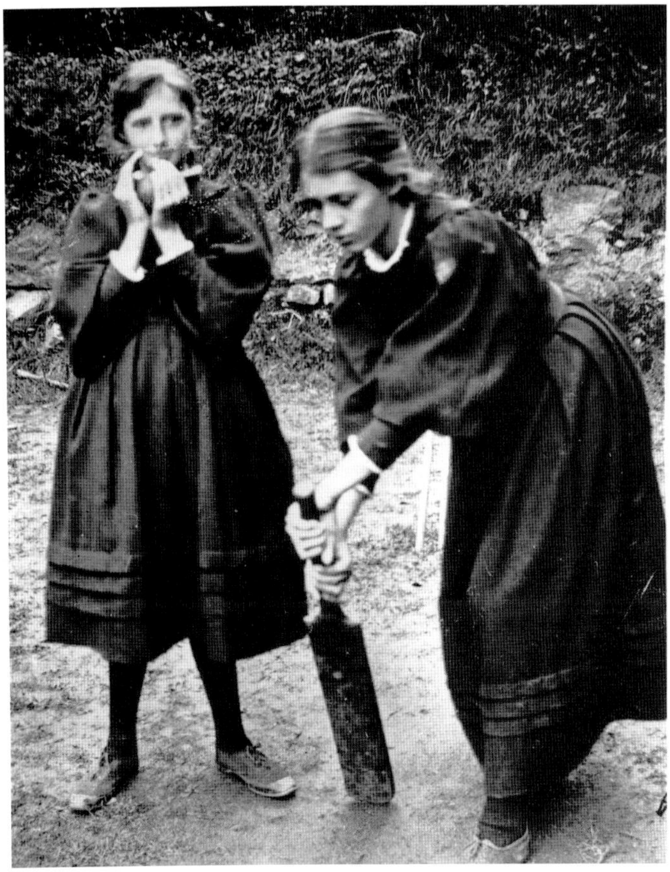

19. (LEFT) Virginia and Vanessa Stephen. St. Ives, ca. 1893–1894. Box 2, folder 4. Reprinted by permission of the Harvard Theatre Collection, the Houghton Library. "[Vanessa] played cricket better for the same reasons [honesty] with her straight forward stroke" (R, 31).

20. (BELOW) *Back row:* Gerald Duckworth, Virginia, Thoby, Vanessa Stephen, George Duckworth; *front row:* Adrian, Julia, Leslie Stephen. Alenhoe, Wimbledon, ca. 1894. Box 2, folder 9. Reprinted by permission of the Harvard Theatre Collection, the Houghton Library. "A woman of forty with seven children . . . and an eighth, Laura, an idiot . . . and a husband . . . dependent on her" (SK, 83).

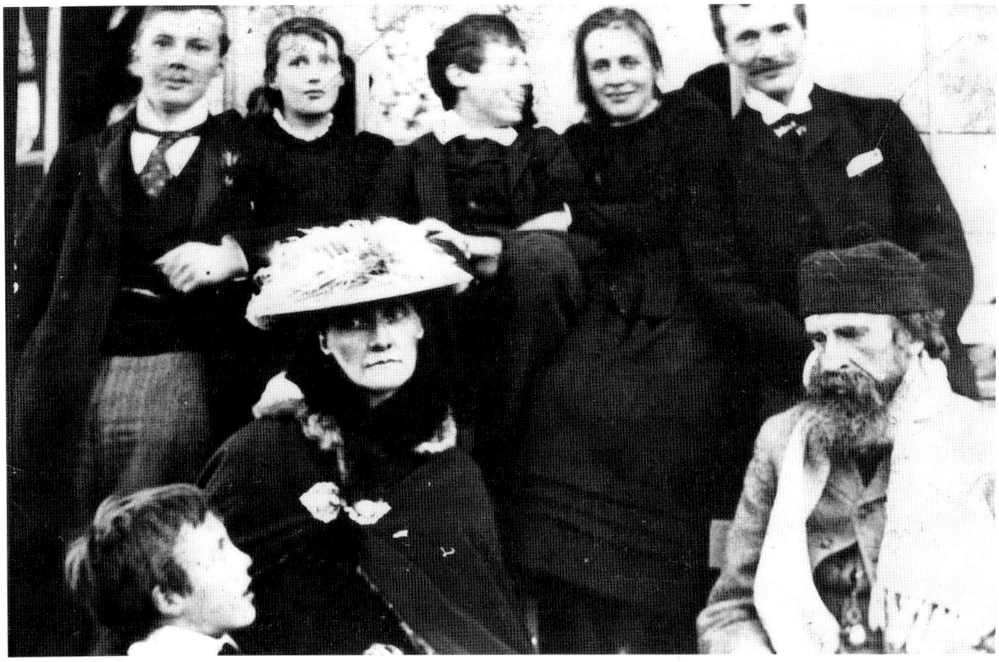

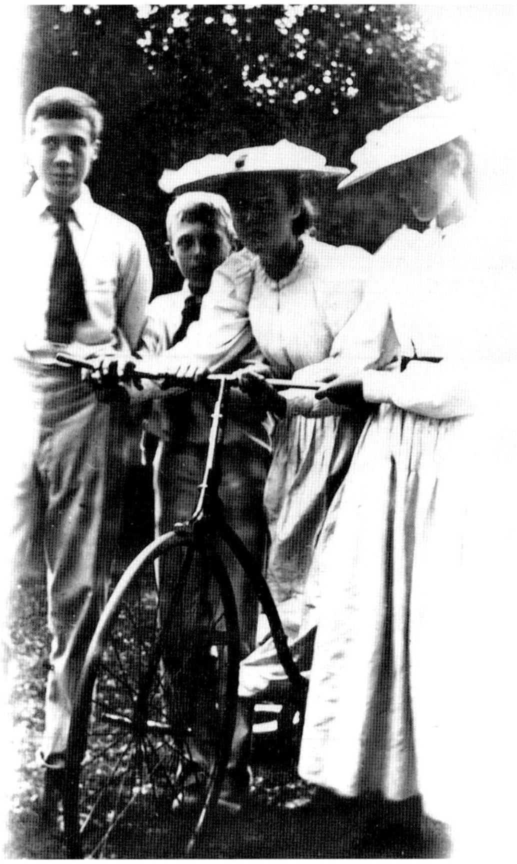

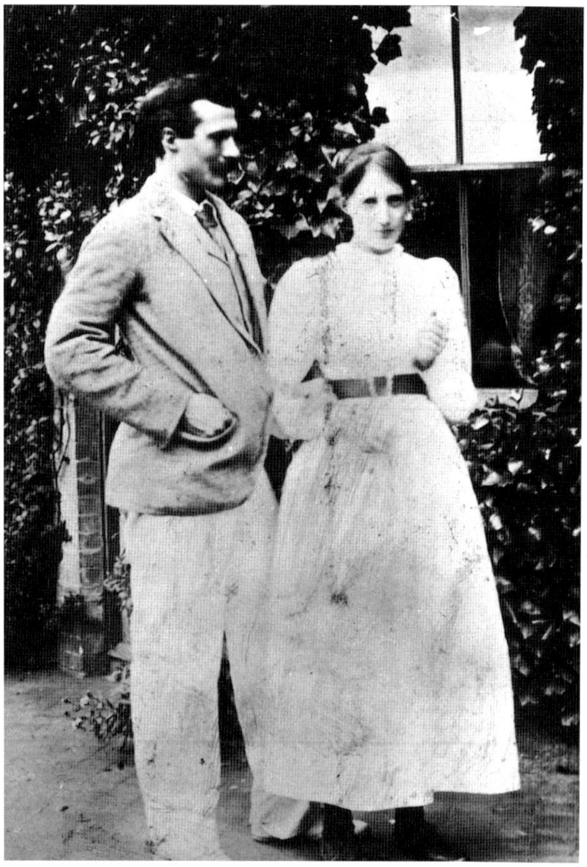

21. (TOP LEFT) Thoby, Adrian, Vanessa, and Virginia Stephen. St. Ives, ca. 1894. Box 2, folder 9. Reprinted by permission of the Harvard Theatre Collection, the Houghton Library. "I want to think of St. Ives . . . butterflies; birds; mud; horses" (SK, 117).

22. (TOP RIGHT) Virginia Stephen and George Duckworth. Freshwater, ca. 1895? Monk's House Album 5 (envelope in album). Reprinted by permission of the Harvard Theatre Collection, the Houghton Library.

23. (RIGHT) Virginia Stephen. Date and photographer unknown. Brown envelope in loose photographs. Reprinted by permission of the Harvard Theatre Collection, the Houghton Library.

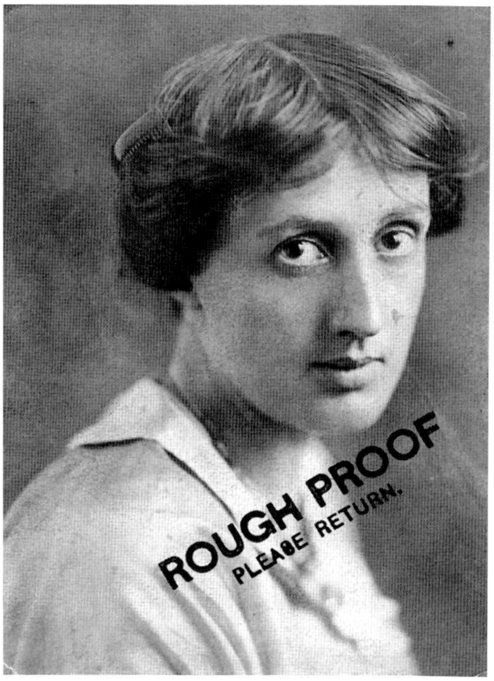

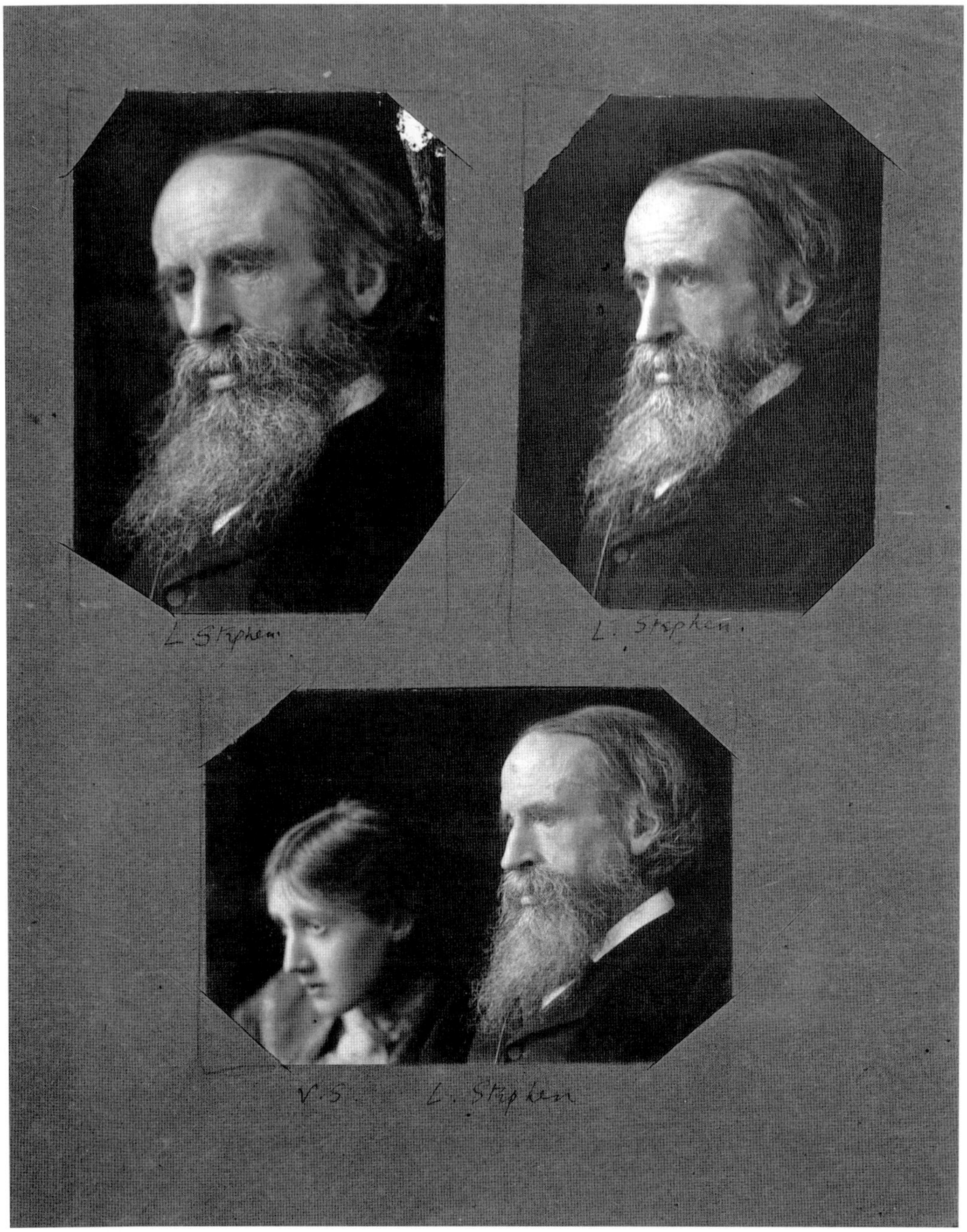

24. Leslie and Virginia Stephen, December 1902.
Photographer: G. Beresford. Monk's House Album 1, p. 60. Reprinted by permission of the Harvard Theatre Collection, the Houghton Library.

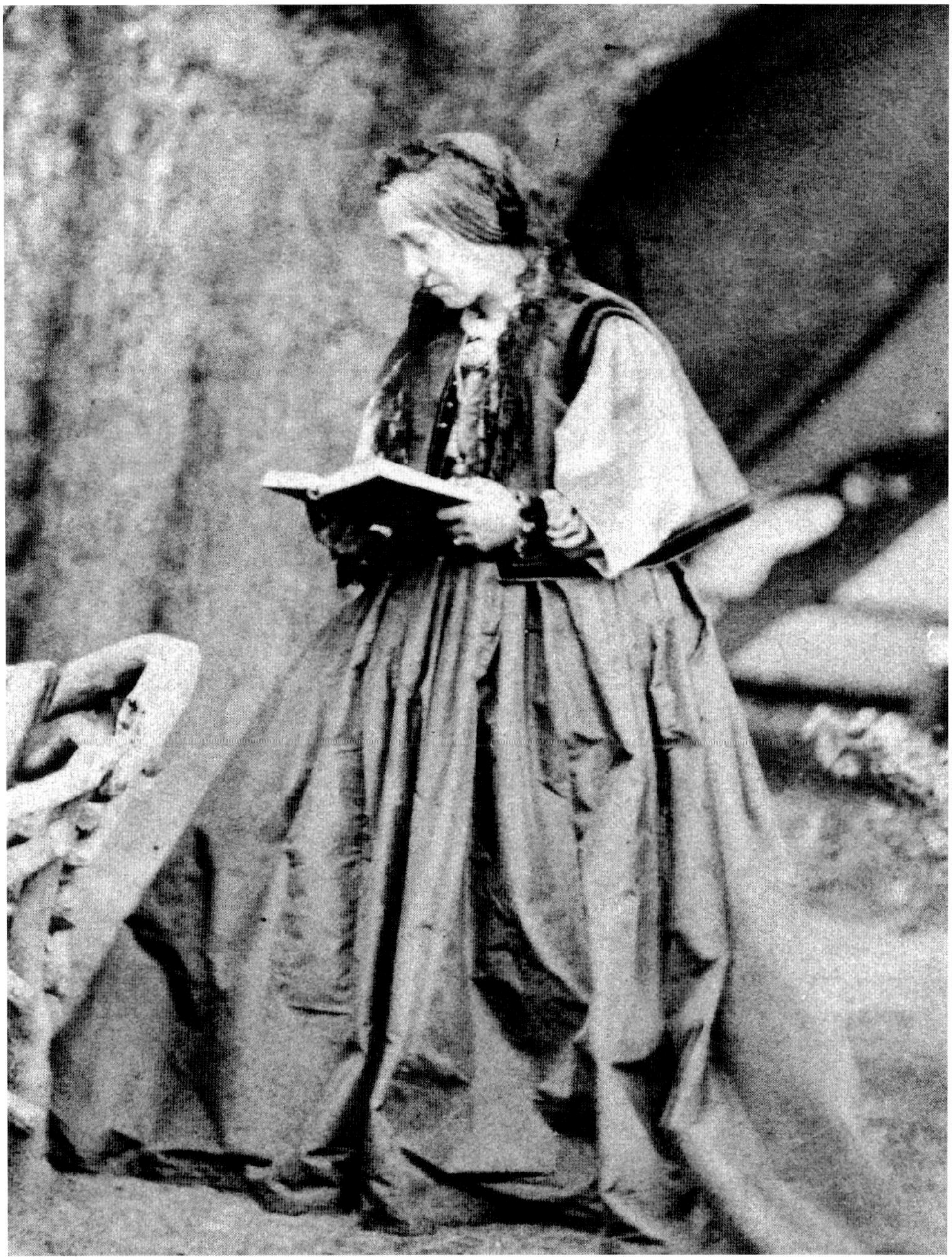

VANESSA BELL ALBUMS

25. Julia Margaret Cameron, ca. 1870? Photographer: H. H. H. Cameron. Bell Album 1, p. 6 AE25. Copyright Tate, London, 2004.

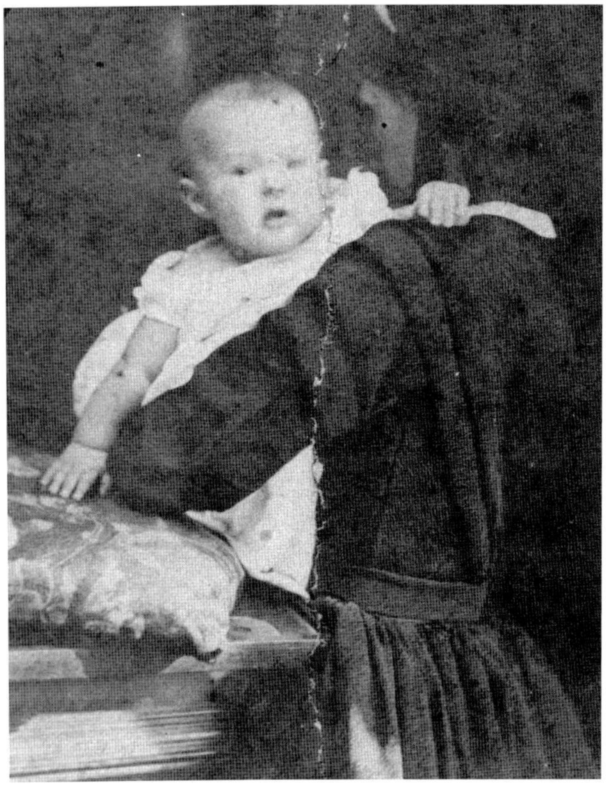

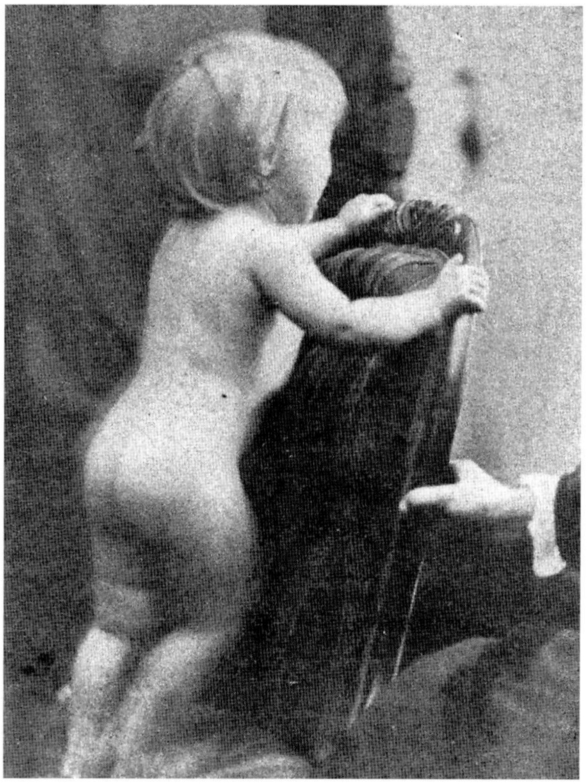

26. (LEFT) Gerald and Julia Duckworth, ca. 1870? Photographer: A & G Taylor. Bell Album 1, p. 2 AE5. Copyright Tate, London, 2004. "my darling had to pass through the valley of the shadow of death" (L. Stephen, 39–40).

27. (RIGHT) Gerald Duckworth, ca. 1871? Photographer: A. & G. Taylor. Bell Album 1, p. 5 AE17. Copyright Tate, London, 2004. "we feel equal to allowing the spoilt children to put their feet . . . if it will give any pleasure to the over indulgent mother who is racked with pain" (Mrs. L. Stephen, 2).

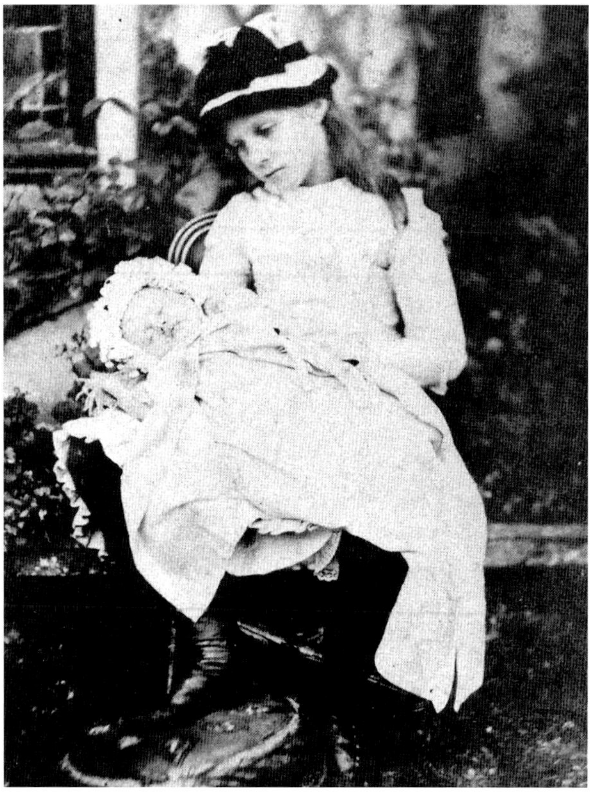

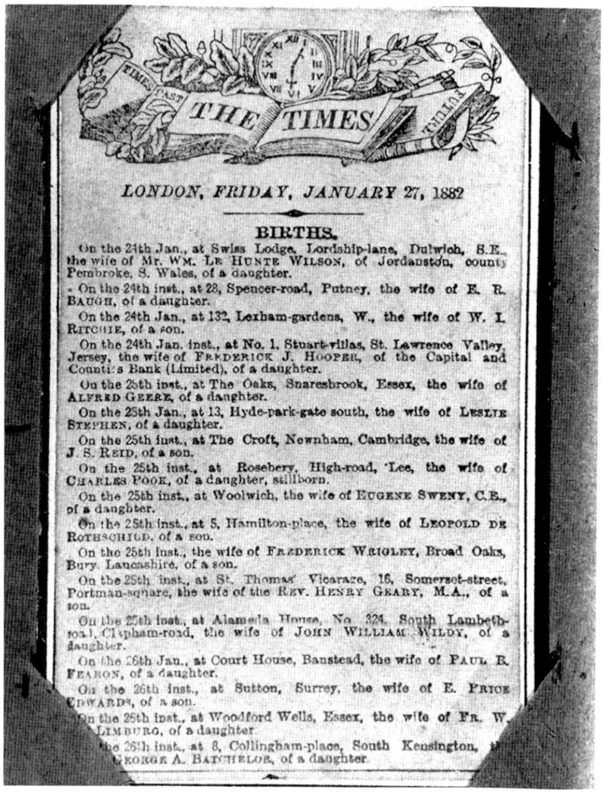

THE TIMES

LONDON, FRIDAY, JANUARY 27, 1882

BIRTHS.

On the 24th Jan., at Swiss Lodge, Lordship-lane, Dulwich, S.E., the wife of Mr. Wm. Le Hunte Wilson, of Jordanston, county Pembroke, S. Wales, of a daughter.

On the 24th inst., at 28, Spencer-road, Putney, the wife of E. R. Baugh, of a daughter.

On the 24th Jan., at 132, Lexham-gardens, W., the wife of W. I. Ritchie, of a son.

On the 24th Jan. inst., at No. 1, Stuart-villas, St. Lawrence Valley, Jersey, the wife of Frederick J. Hooper, of the Capital and Counties Bank (Limited), of a daughter.

On the 25th inst., at The Oaks, Snaresbrook, Essex, the wife of Alfred Geere, of a daughter.

On the 25th Jan., at 13, Hyde-park-gate south, the wife of Leslie Stephen, of a daughter.

On the 25th inst., at The Croft, Newnham, Cambridge, the wife of J. S. Reid, of a son.

On the 25th inst., at Rosebery, High-road, Lee, the wife of Charles Pook, of a daughter, stillborn.

On the 25th inst., at Woolwich, the wife of Eugene Sweny, C.E., of a daughter.

On the 25th inst., at 5, Hamilton-place, the wife of Leopold de Rothschild, of a son.

On the 25th inst., the wife of Frederick Wrigley, Broad Oaks, Bury, Lancashire, of a son.

On the 25th inst., at St. Thomas' Vicarage, 16, Somerset-street, Portman-square, the wife of the Rev. Henry Geary, M.A., of a son.

On the 25th inst., at Alameda House, No. 324, South Lambeth-road, Clapham-road, the wife of John William Wildy, of a daughter.

On the 26th Jan., at Court House, Banstead, the wife of Paul B. Fearon, of a daughter.

On the 26th inst., at Sutton, Surrey, the wife of E. Price Edwards, of a son.

On the 26th inst., at Woodford Wells, Essex, the wife of Fr. W. Limburg, of a daughter.

the 26th inst., at 8, Collingham-place, South Kensington, the wife of George A. Batchelor, of a daughter.

28. (LEFT) Stella Duckworth with Vanessa Stephen. Hyde Park Gate, 1879. Bell Album 1, p. 6 AE22. Copyright Tate, London, 2004. "a pale silent child [Stella] sensitive; modest; uncomplaining; adoring her mother, thinking only how she could help her" (SK, 96).

29. (RIGHT) Photograph from the *Times*, January 27, 1882, with Virginia's birth announcement. Bell Album, 1, p. 14 AF6. Copyright Tate, London, 2004.

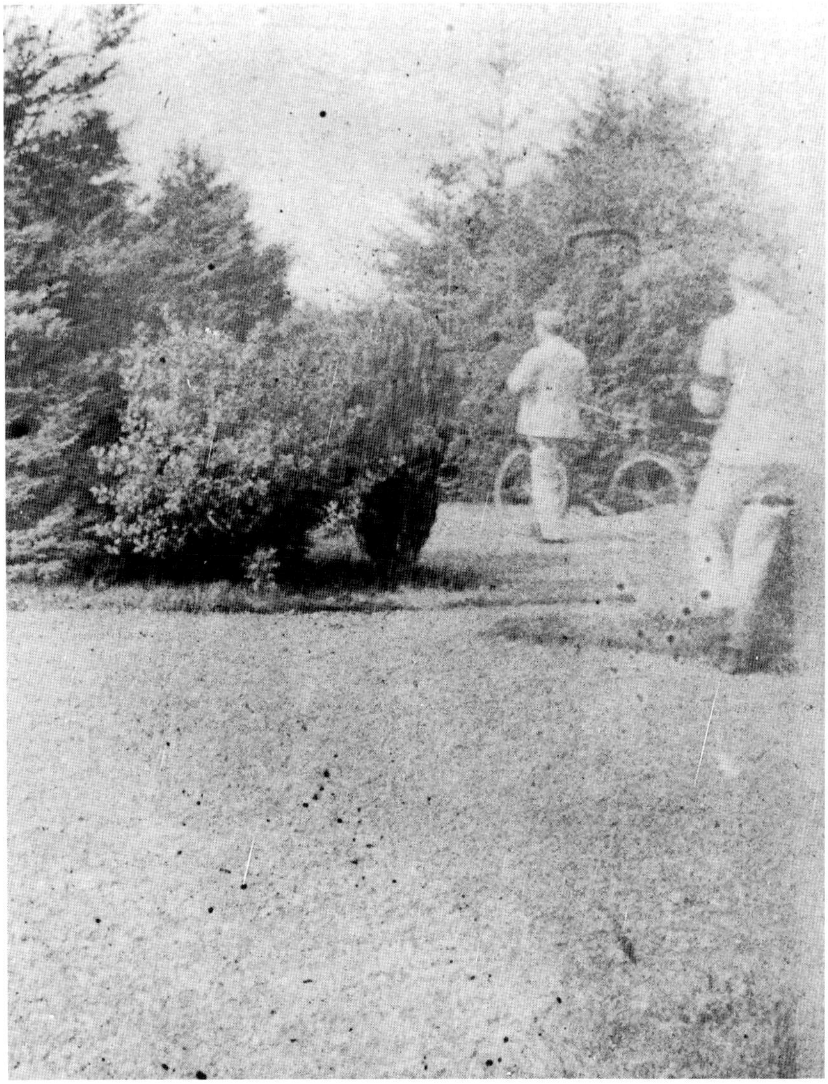

30. Thoby Stephen and Arthur Conan Doyle, "Kodaking Dr. Conan Doyle." Hindhead, 1896.
Bell Album 1A, p. 5 AI48. Copyright Tate, London, 2004. Conan Doyle was an accomplished photographer.
By 1896, flat-folding and "daylight" Kodaks and focusing lenses were available in England.
Conan Doyle built Undershaw House, near Hindhead.

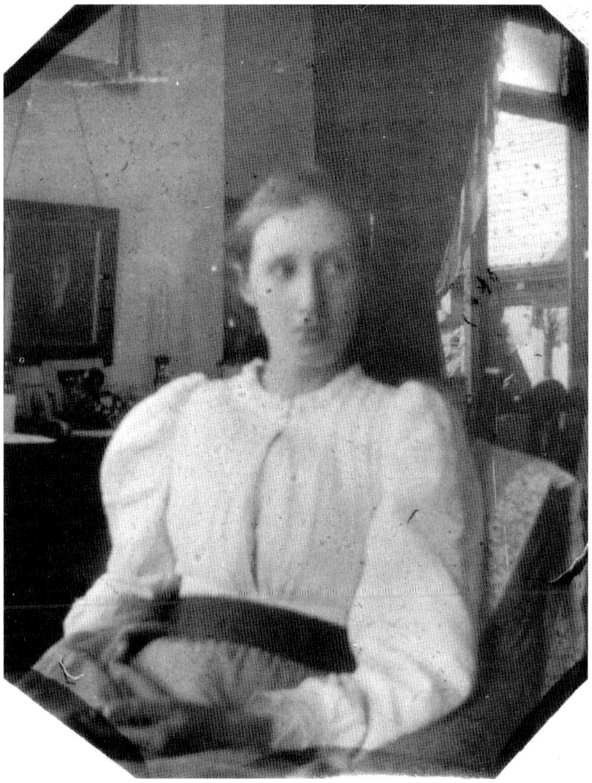
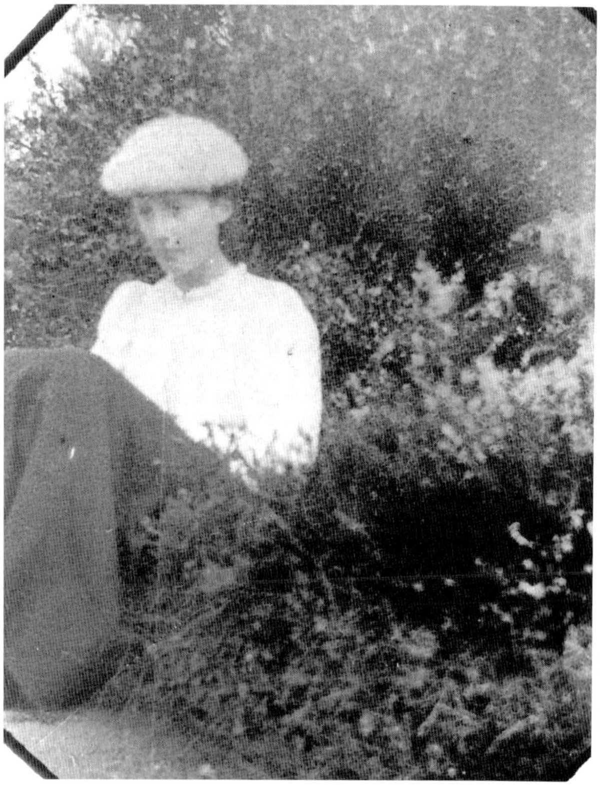

31. (LEFT) Virginia Stephen, Hindhead, 1896. Bell Album 1A, p. 3 AI35.
Copyright Tate, London, 2004. Photograph in rear is *My Niece Julia* by Julia Margaret Cameron, April 1867?

32. (RIGHT) Virginia Stephen, Hindhead, August 1896? Bell Album 1A, p. 8 AJ13.
Copyright Tate, London, 2004.

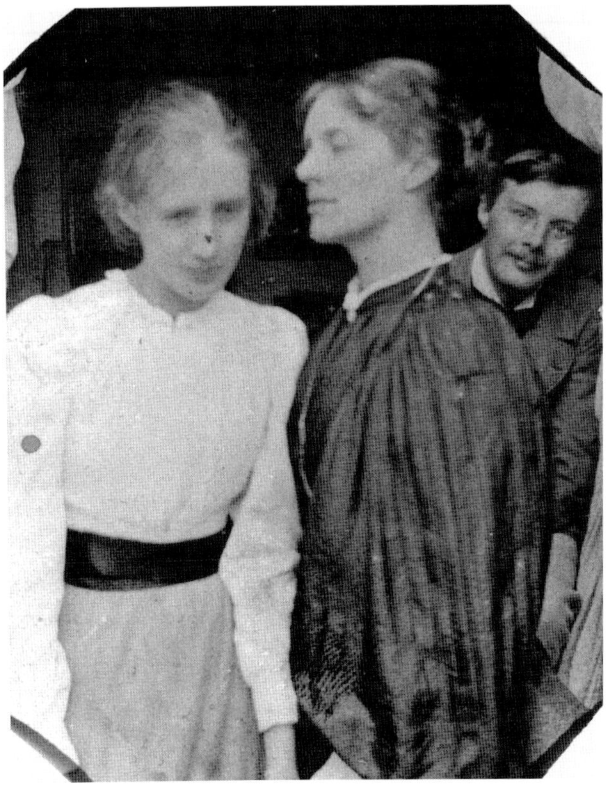

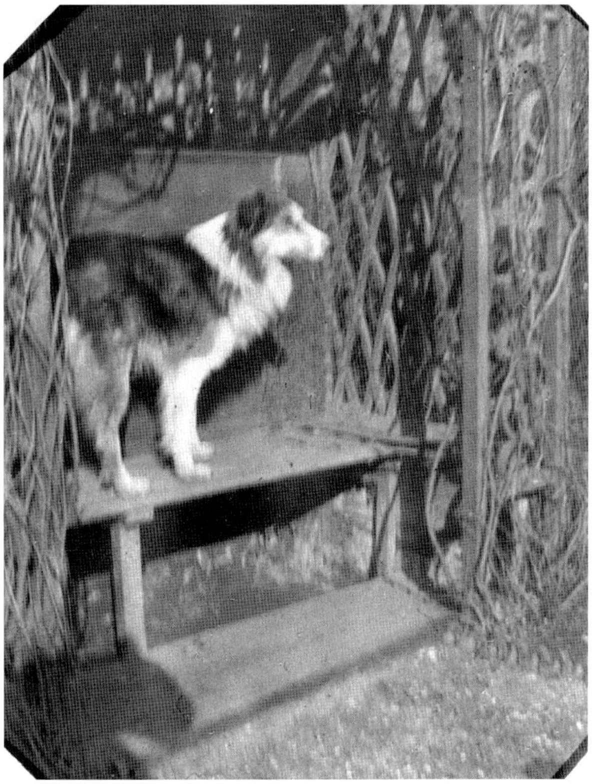

33. (LEFT) Virginia Stephen, Stella and Gerald Duckworth. Hindhead, August 1896. Bell Album 1A, p. 6 AJ6. Copyright Tate, London, 2004. "the night at Hindhead . . . saw Stella and Jack . . . she came and told us she was engaged; and I whispered 'Did mother know?' and she murmured, 'Yes'" (SK, 100–101).

34. (RIGHT) Simon, February 1897. Bell Album 1A, p. 13 AJ45. Copyright Tate, London, 2004. "We photographed Simon 6 times—on the chair with a coat and pipe, and lying on the ground . . . after tea, Nessa and I developed in the night nursery" (*EJ*, 35). Simon belonged to Arthur Studd, the painter.

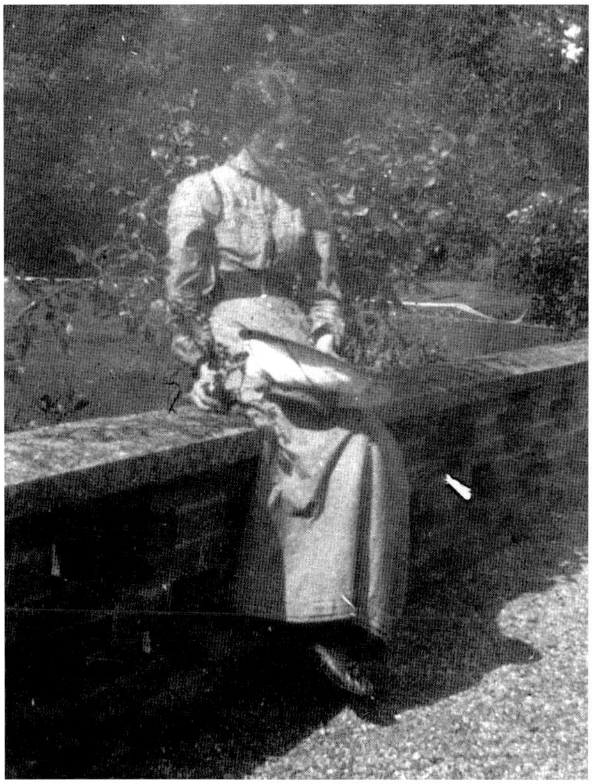

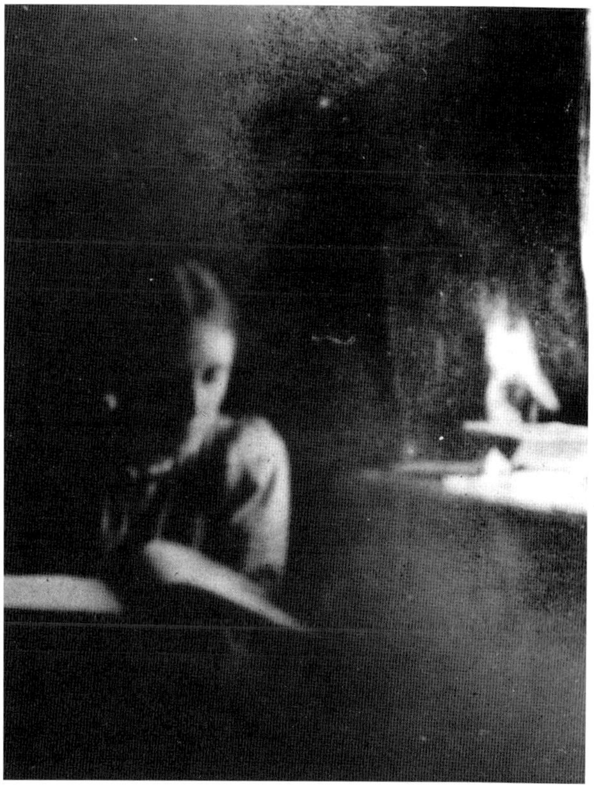

35. (LEFT) Virginia Stephen, Warboys, 1899. Bell Album 1A, p. 41 AM8. Copyright Tate, London, 2004. "This is a photograph which you have not seen. I think it somewhat like an ancient beast of my acquaintance" (*L*, 1:29).

36. (RIGHT) Virginia Stephen, 1900. Bell Album 1A, p. 59 AN31. Copyright Tate, London, 2004. "the sight of the large yellow page [Hakluyt] entranced me" (*D*, 3: 271).

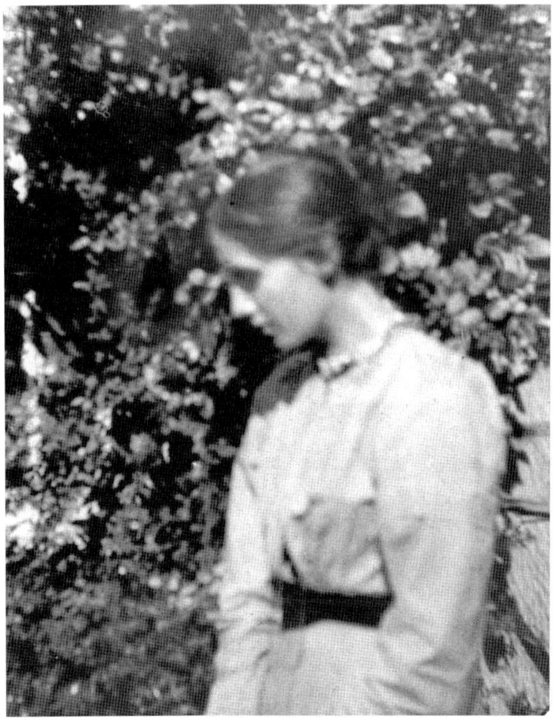

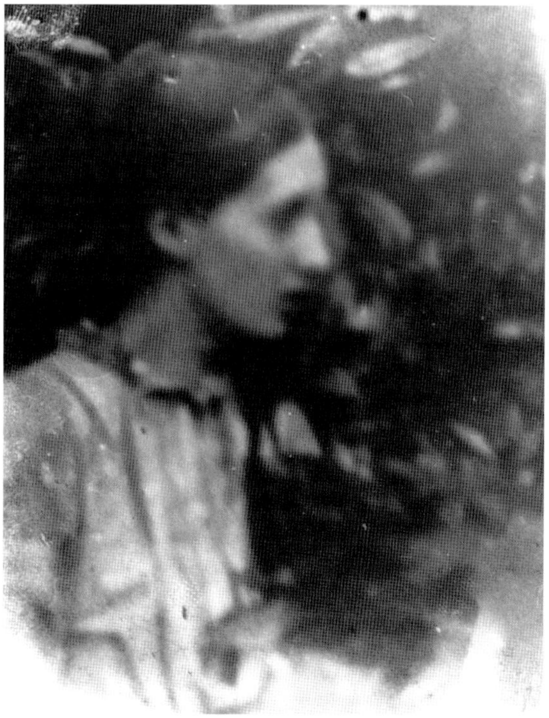

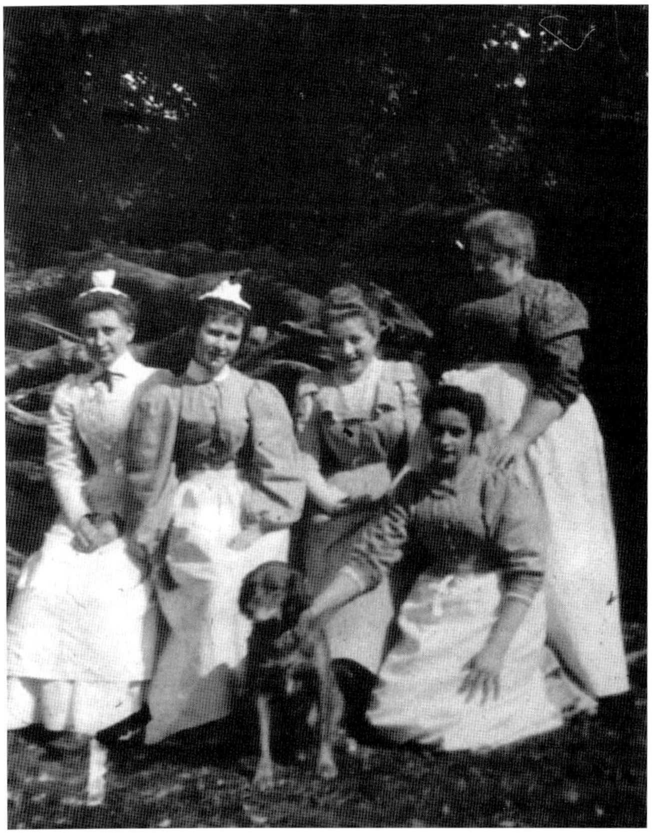

37. (TOP LEFT) Virginia Stephen, Fritham, ca. 1900? Bell Album 1A, p. 62 AN39. Copyright Tate, London, 2004. "I have a Pony and a respectable trap all to myself—the others ride and cycle all day—and in this I drive solitary miles and miles" (*L*, 1:36).

38. (LEFT) Ellen, Annie, Louisa, Sophie, and Maud kneeling with Lassie. Fritham, 1900. Bell Album 1A, p. 70 AP11. Copyright Tate, London, 2004. "We returned on the 17th from Fritham, Lyndhurst. The place was delicious" (L. Stephen, 108).

39. (TOP RIGHT) Virginia Stephen, Fritham, ca. 1900? Bell Album 1A, p. 57 AN25. Copyright Tate, London, 2004.

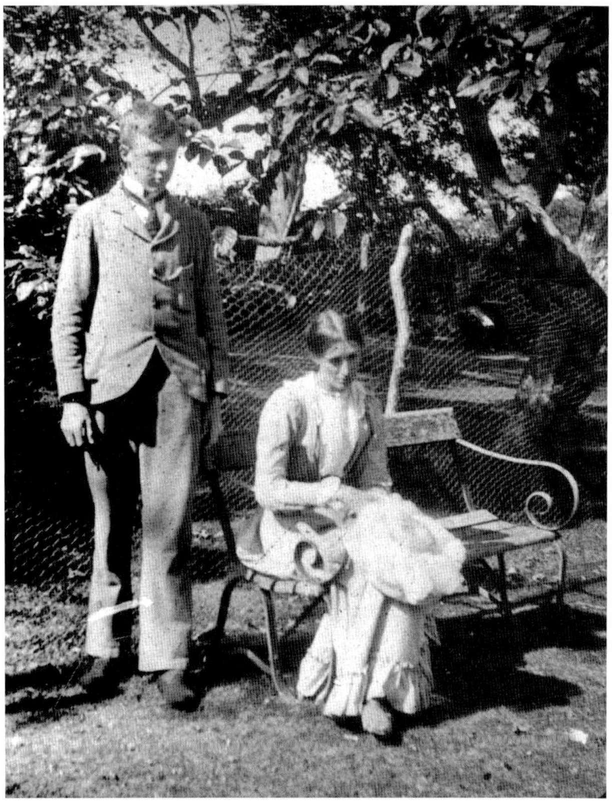

40. (TOP) Adrian and Virginia Stephen, Fritham, 1900. Bell Album 1A, p. 70 AP10. Copyright Tate, London, 2004. "We were the most incompatible of people. We drove each other perpetually into frenzies of irritation or into the depths of gloom" (OB, 171).

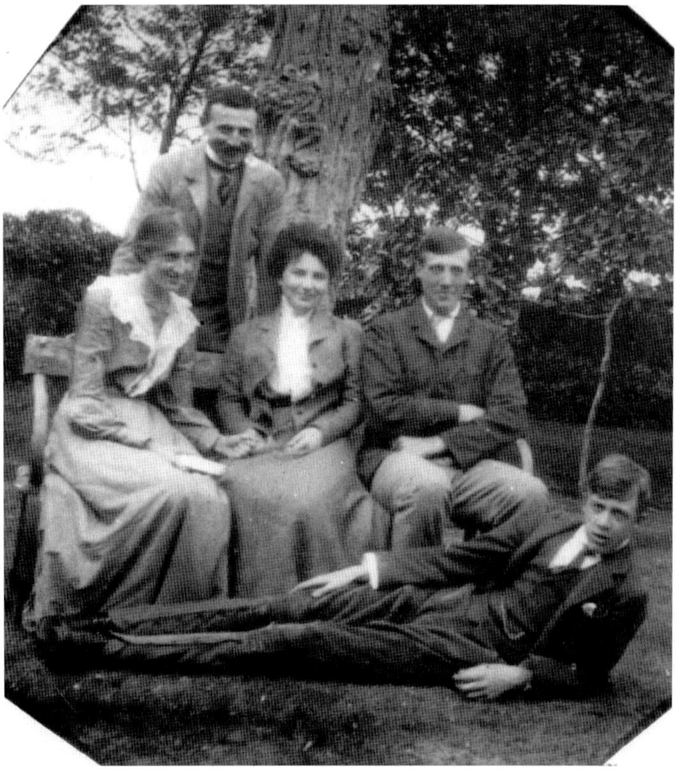

41. (BOTTOM) *Standing*: Principe Filippo Corsini; *seated*: Virginia Stephen, Principessa Rezia Corsini née Rasponi (on honeymoon), Thoby and Adrian Stephen. Fritham, 1901. Bell Album 1A, p. 74 AP23. Copyright Tate, London, 2004. "Father has begun to say 'We must talk about what you are to read at Fritham' . . . Father wants . . . Sophocles, only it is in seven volumes" (*L*, 1:42).

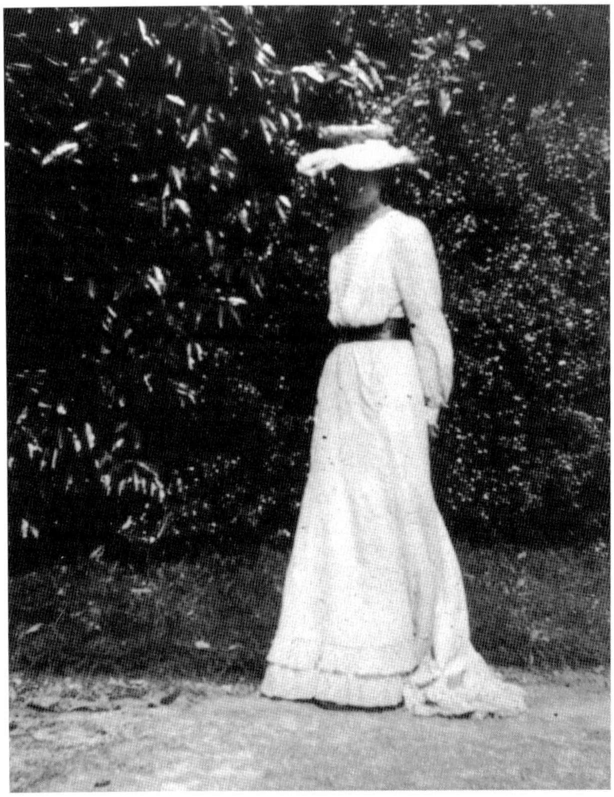

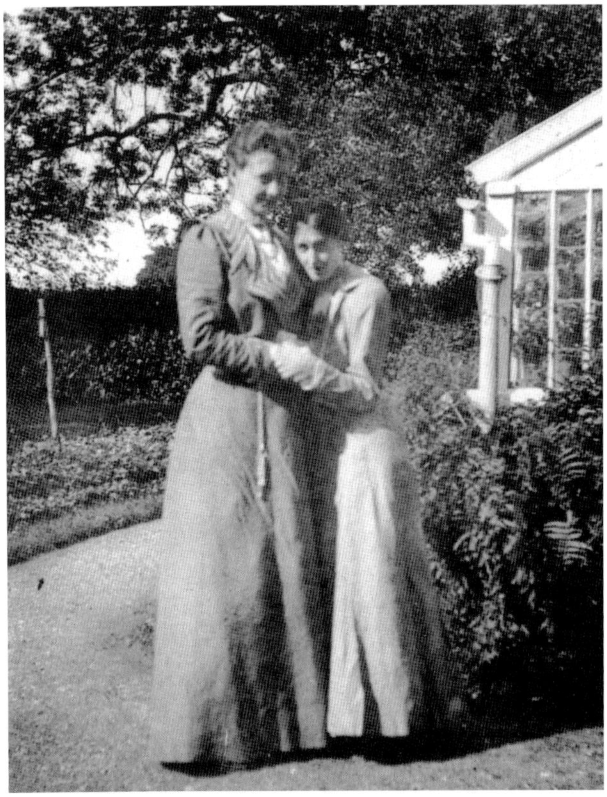

42. (TOP) Virginia Stephen, Fritham, 1902. Bell Album 1A, p. 90 AQ 28. Copyright Tate, London, 2004. "This place where we are staying is a *sham* country cottage . . . I haven't talked to an educated woman (except the cook) for a fortnight" (*L*, 1:50).

43. (BOTTOM) Violet Dickinson with Virginia Stephen. Fritham, 1902. Bell Album 1A, p. 92 AQ 38. Copyright Tate, London, 2004. "If you are very kind to me, and spoil me thoroughly, and behave in every way tenderly you shall have one [photograph] when you come here" (*L*, 1:53).

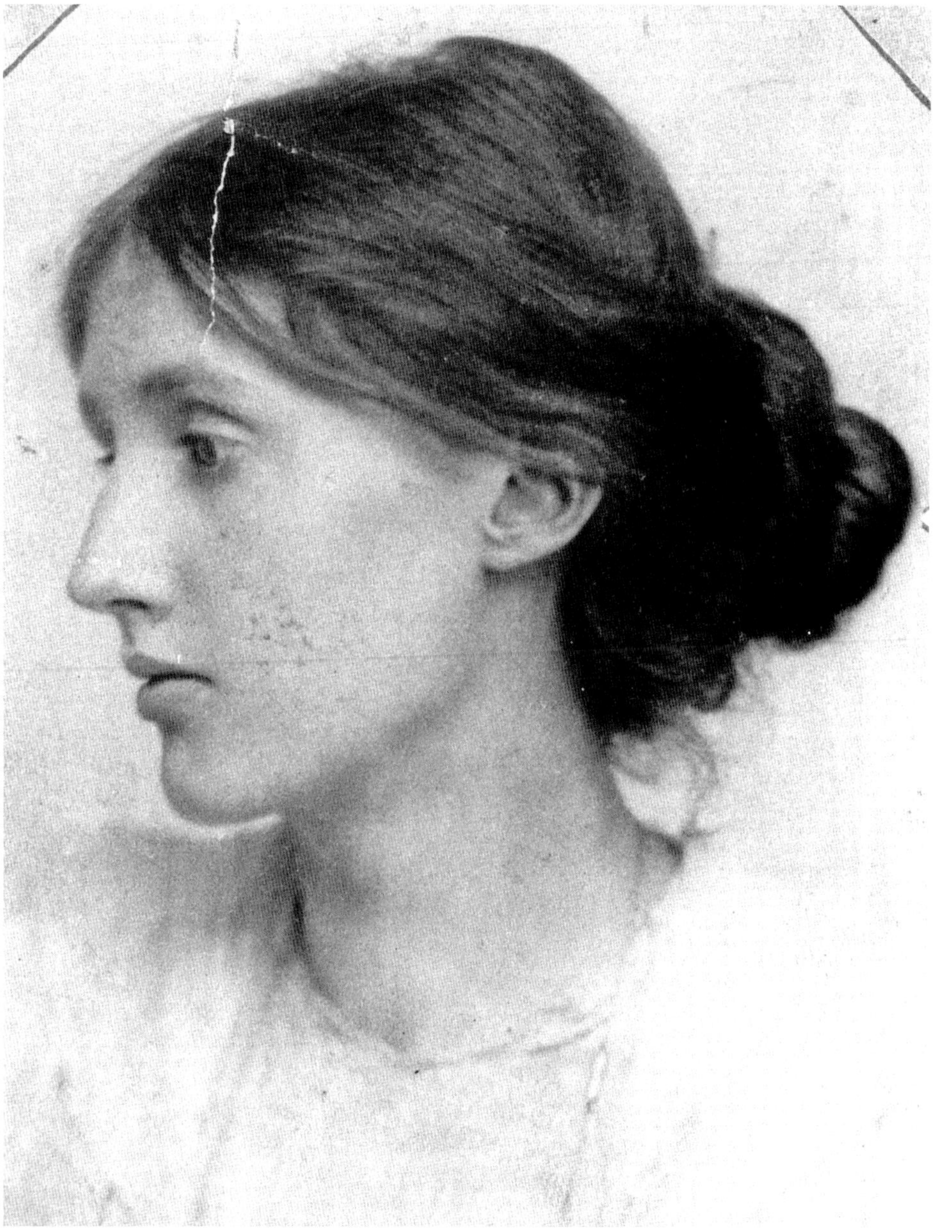

44. Virginia Stephen, July 1902. Photographer: G. Beresford. Platinum print. Bell Album 1, p. 27 AF48. Copyright Tate, London, 2004.

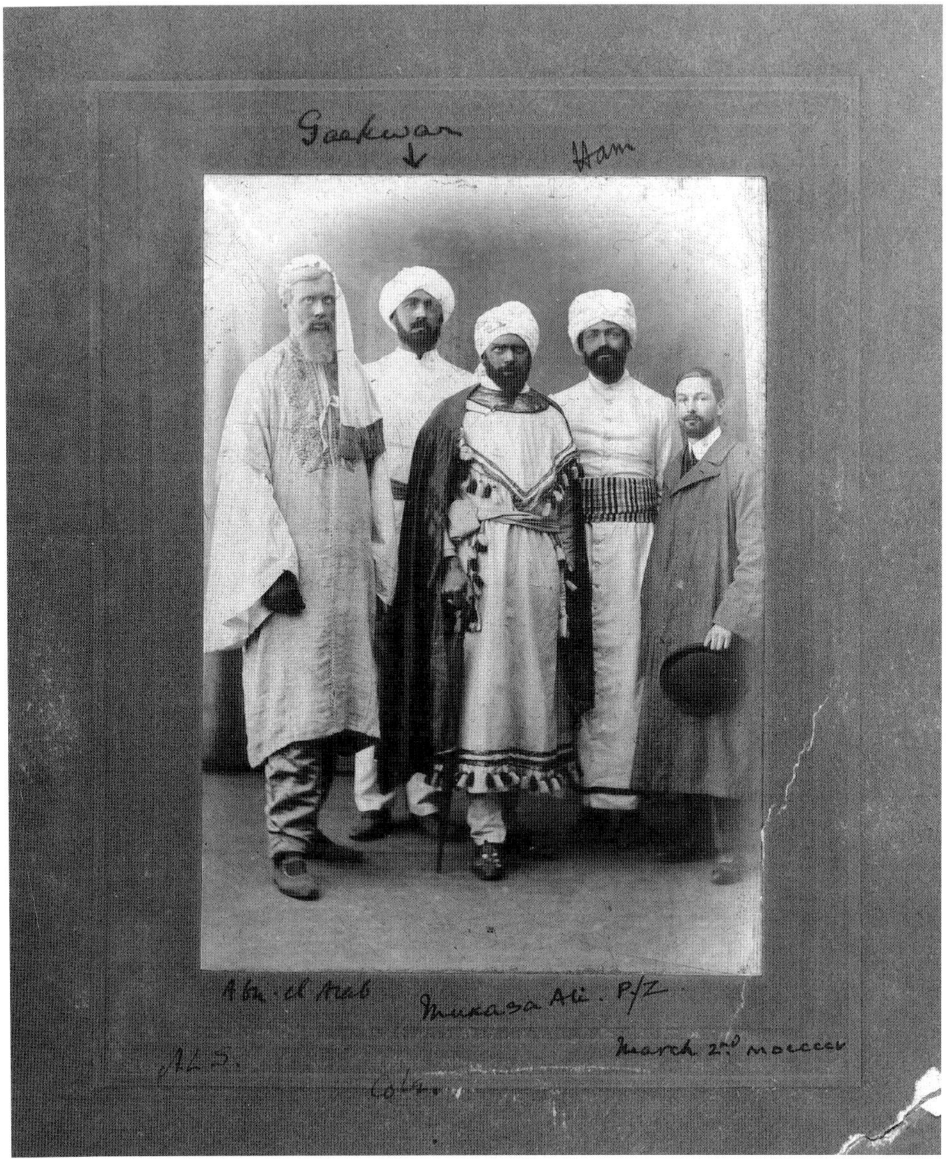

45. *Left to right:* Adrian Stephen, Bowen Colthurst, Horace Cole, Leland Buxton, "Drummer" Howard. March 1905. Photographer: W. W. Wright. The Zanzibar Hoax, forerunner of the Dreadnought Hoax. Monk's House Album 1, p. 59. Reprinted by permission of the Harvard Theatre Collection, the Houghton Library. "The Sultan of Zanzibar was in England; what could be simpler than to impersonate him and pay a state visit to Cambridge [but] he was not in the least like either of us" (A. Stephen, 24).

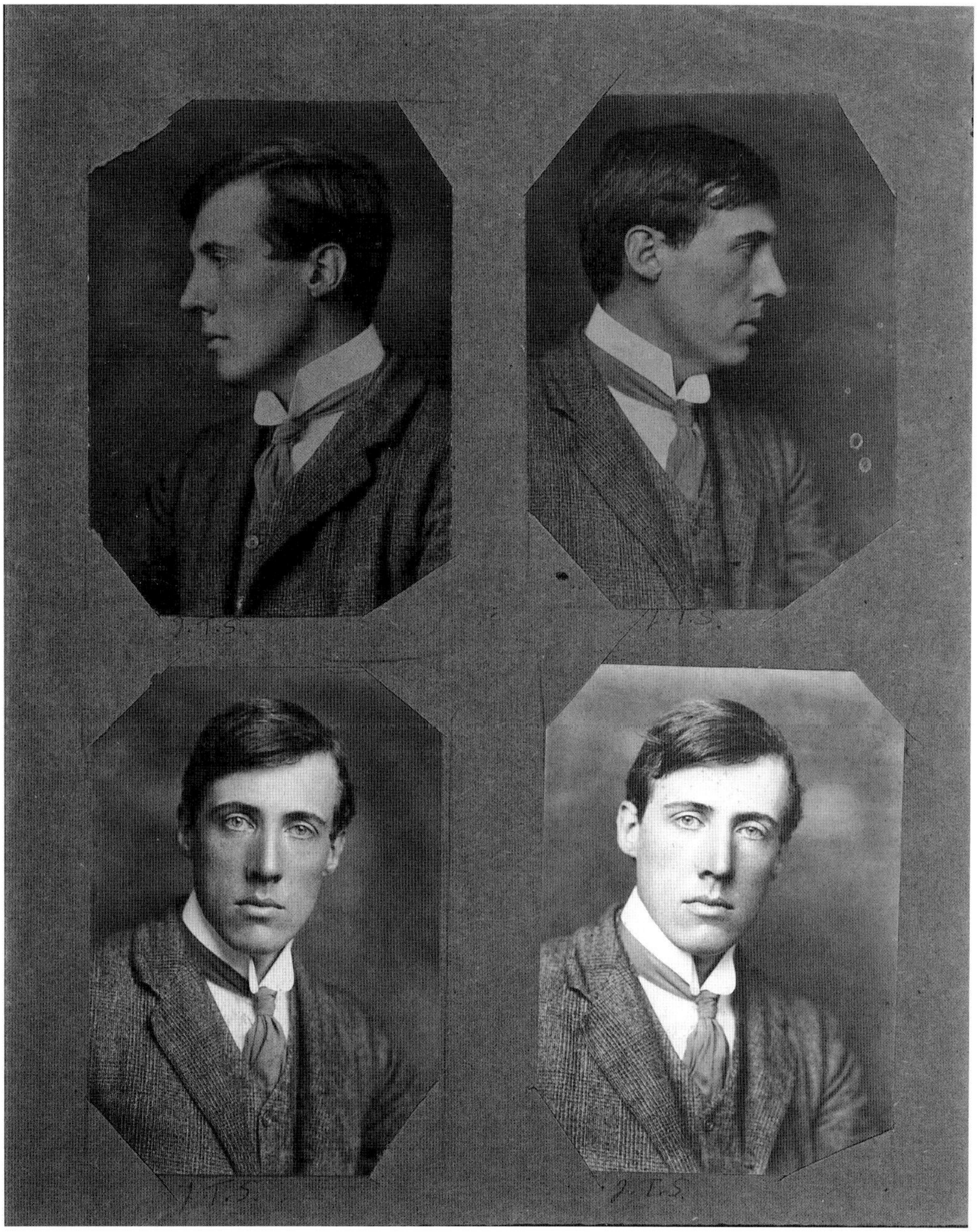

46. Thoby Stephen, August 1906. Photographer: G. Beresford.
Monk's House Album 1, p. 61. Reprinted by permission of the Harvard Theatre Collection, the Houghton Library. "He was taken by Beresford the week he left England [for Greece] they are good—but not very much when you think of him" (L, 1:265).

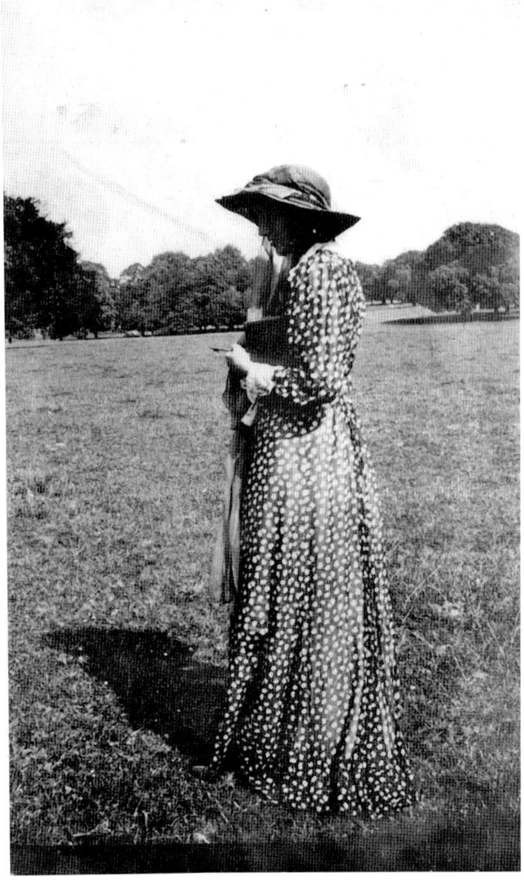

47. (LEFT) Virginia Stephen, Firle Park, 1911. Box 4, folder 1 of 2. Reprinted by permission of the Harvard Theatre Collection, the Houghton Library. "another side of life reveals itself in the country, which I cant help thinking of amazing interest" (*L*, 1:446).

48. (BELOW) Janet Case, Virginia Stephen, and Vanessa Bell. Firle Park, 1911. Box 3, folder 2. Reprinted by permission of the Harvard Theatre Collection, the Houghton Library. "I had an interesting time with Case. She is a woman of great magnanimity" (*L*, 1:471–472).

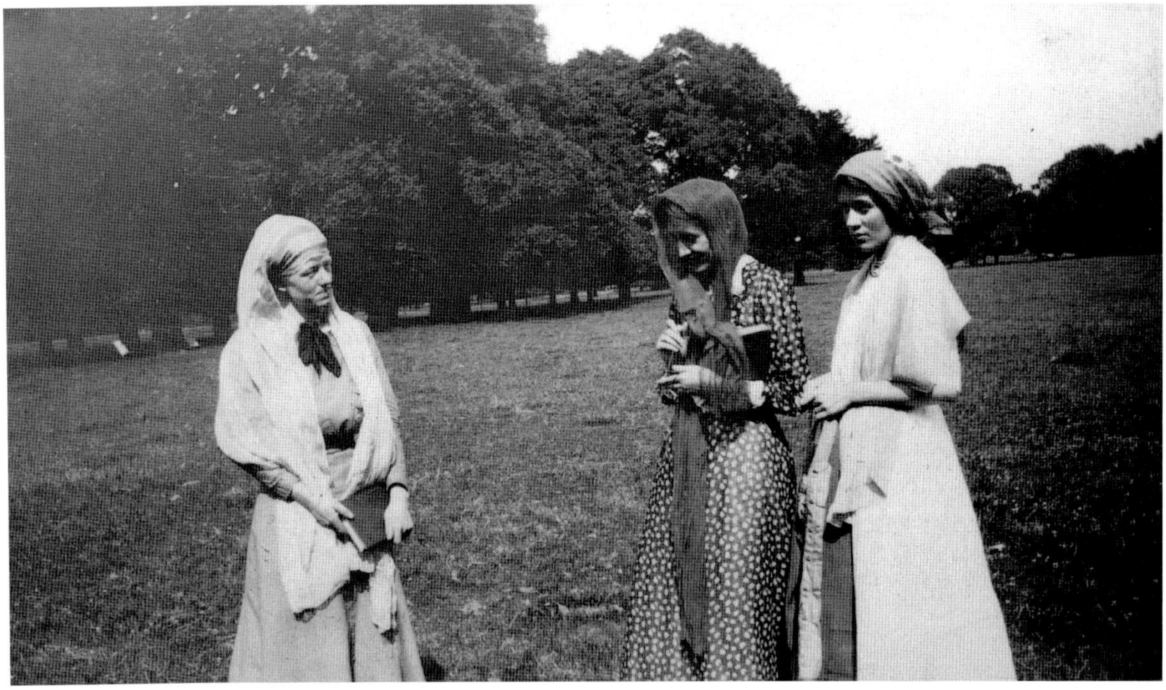

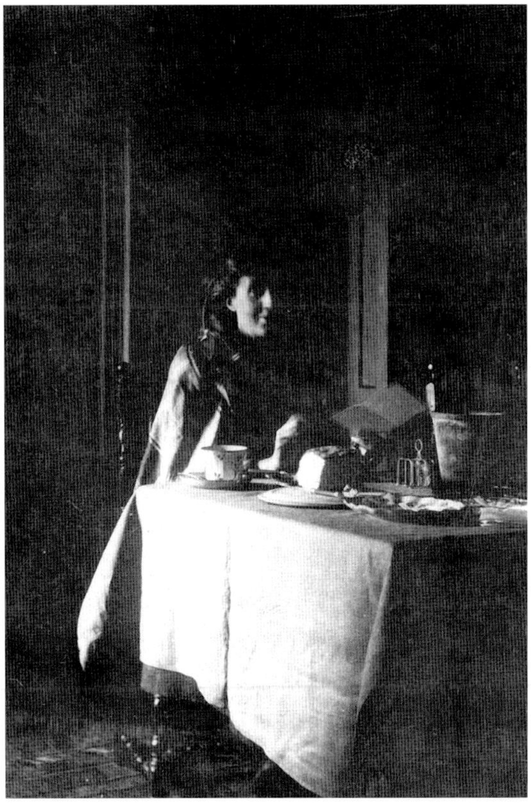

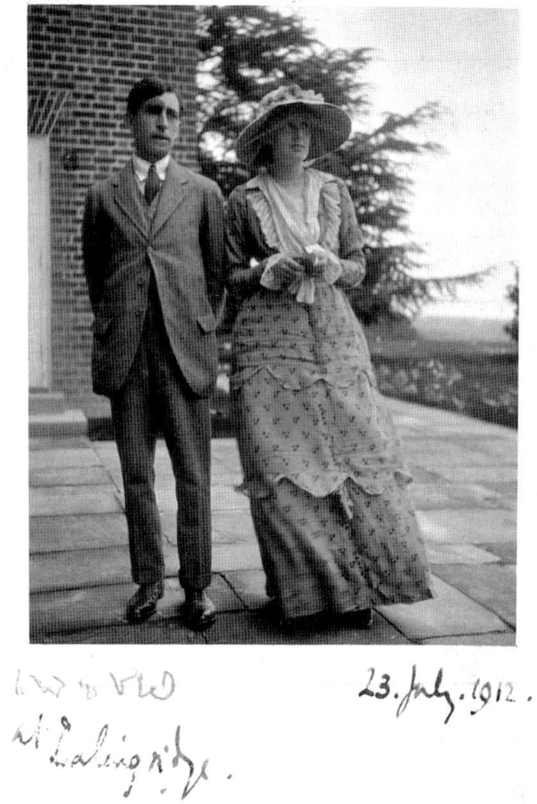

49. (LEFT) Virginia Stephen, Brunswick Square, 1912. Box 4, folder A. Reprinted by permission of the Harvard Theatre Collection, the Houghton Library. "Here is the scheme of the house . . . tea, egg and bacon, toast or roll for breakfast . . . it is hoped that inmates will make a special effort to be punctual" (*L*, 1:484–485).

50. (RIGHT) Leonard Woolf and Virginia Stephen. Dalingridge, July 23, 1912. Photographer: George Duckworth. Box 4, folder A. Reprinted by permission of the Harvard Theatre Collection, the Houghton Library. "I've got a confession to make. I'm going to marry Leonard Wolf [*sic*] He's a penniless Jew. I'm more happy than anyone ever said was possible" (*L*, 1:500).

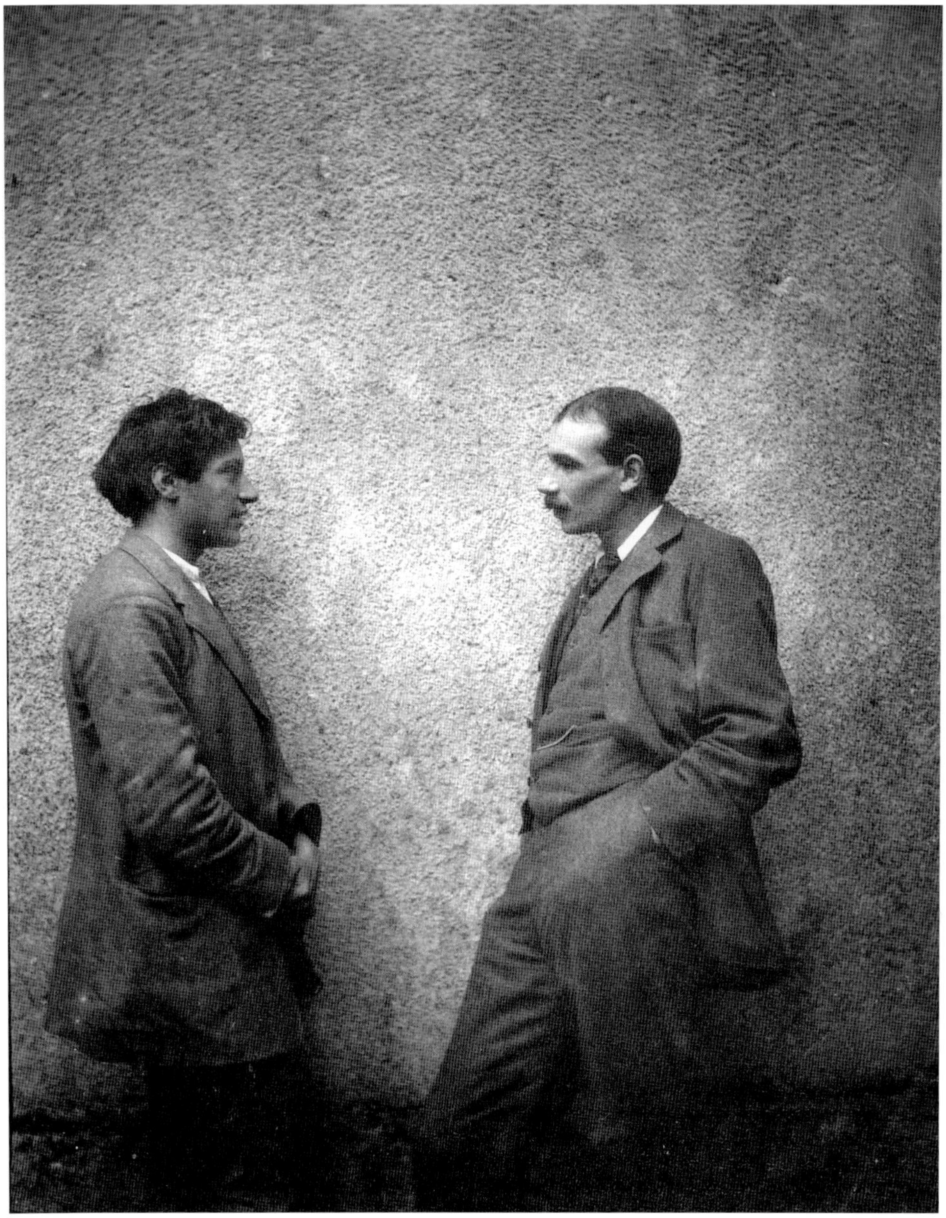

51. Duncan Grant and John Maynard Keynes. Asheham, 1912.
Photographer: Vanessa Bell. Box 4, folder 1 of 2. Reprinted by permission of the Harvard Theatre Collection, the Houghton Library.

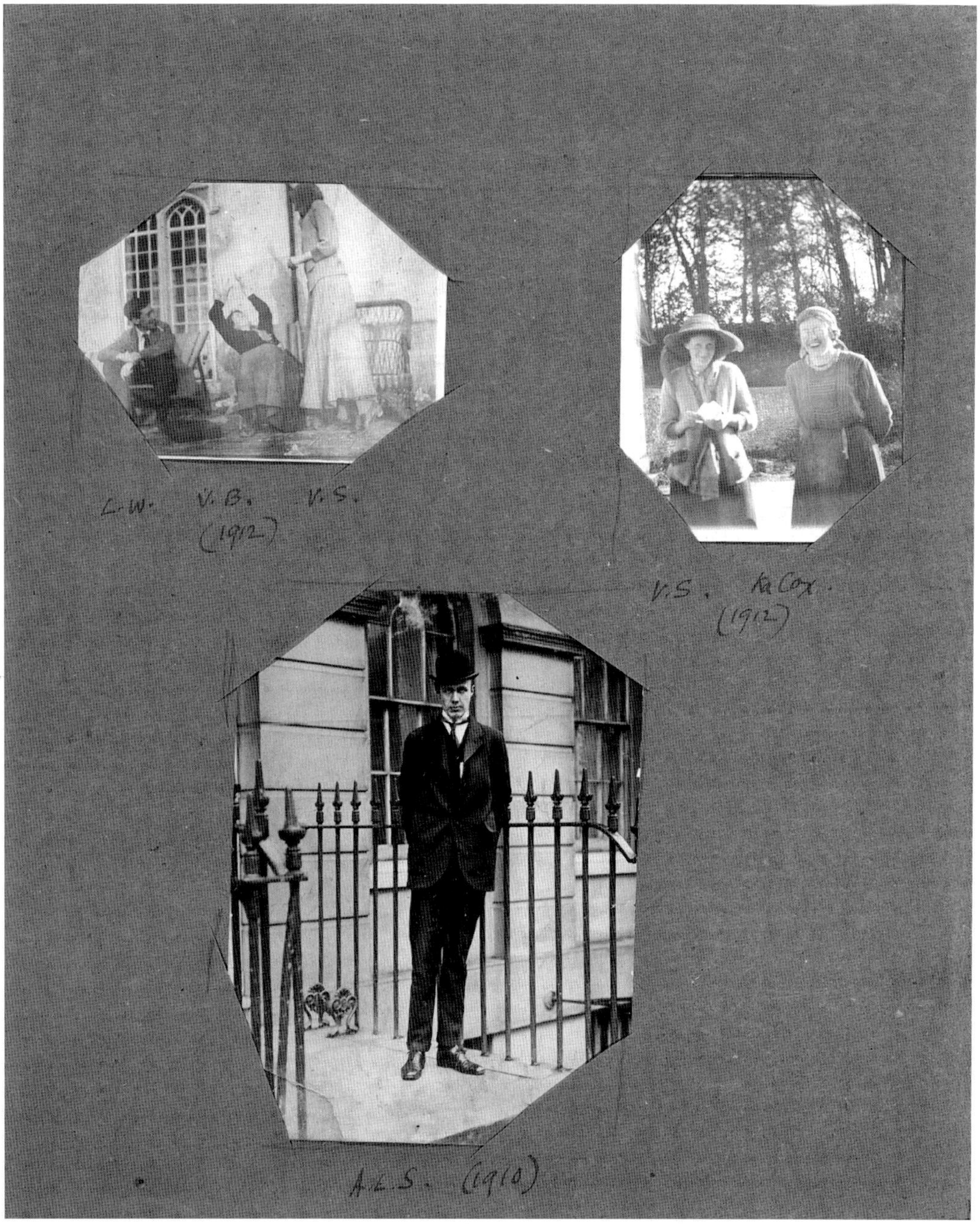

52. Leonard and Virginia Woolf, Vanessa Bell, Asheham, 1912. Virginia Woolf and Ka Cox, 1912. Adrian Stephen, Fitzroy Square, 1910. Monk's House Album 1, p. 69. Reprinted by permission of the Harvard Theatre Collection, the Houghton Library. "Ka and I stitch, gossip, grumble" (L, 2:12).

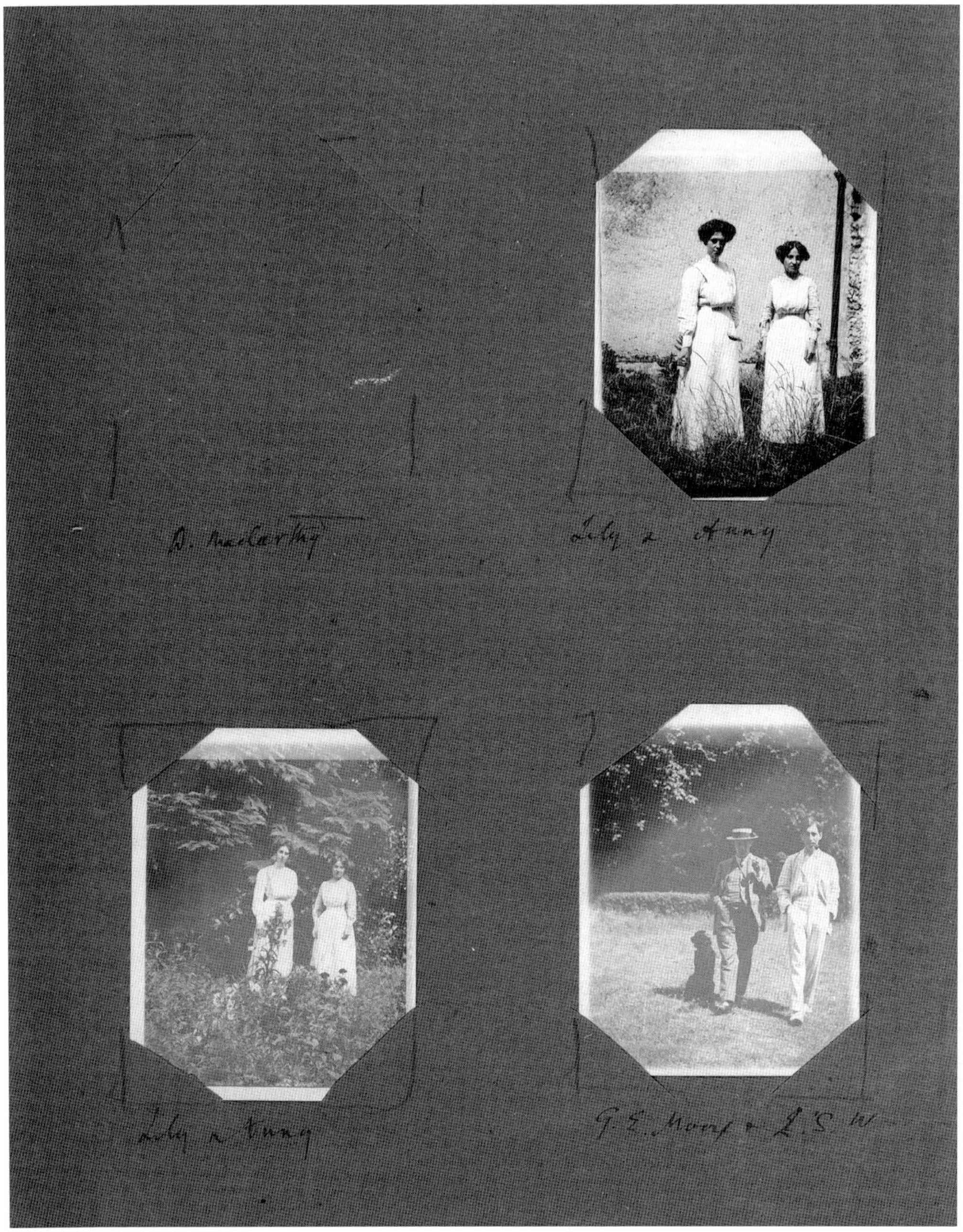

53. Lily and Annie, servants. G. E. Moore and Leonard Woolf, Asheham, July 1914. Monk's House Album 1, p. 66. Reprinted by permission of the Harvard Theatre Collection, the Houghton Library. "Moore sang to us every night. He is quite easy, and much more human than his followers" (*L*, 2:112).

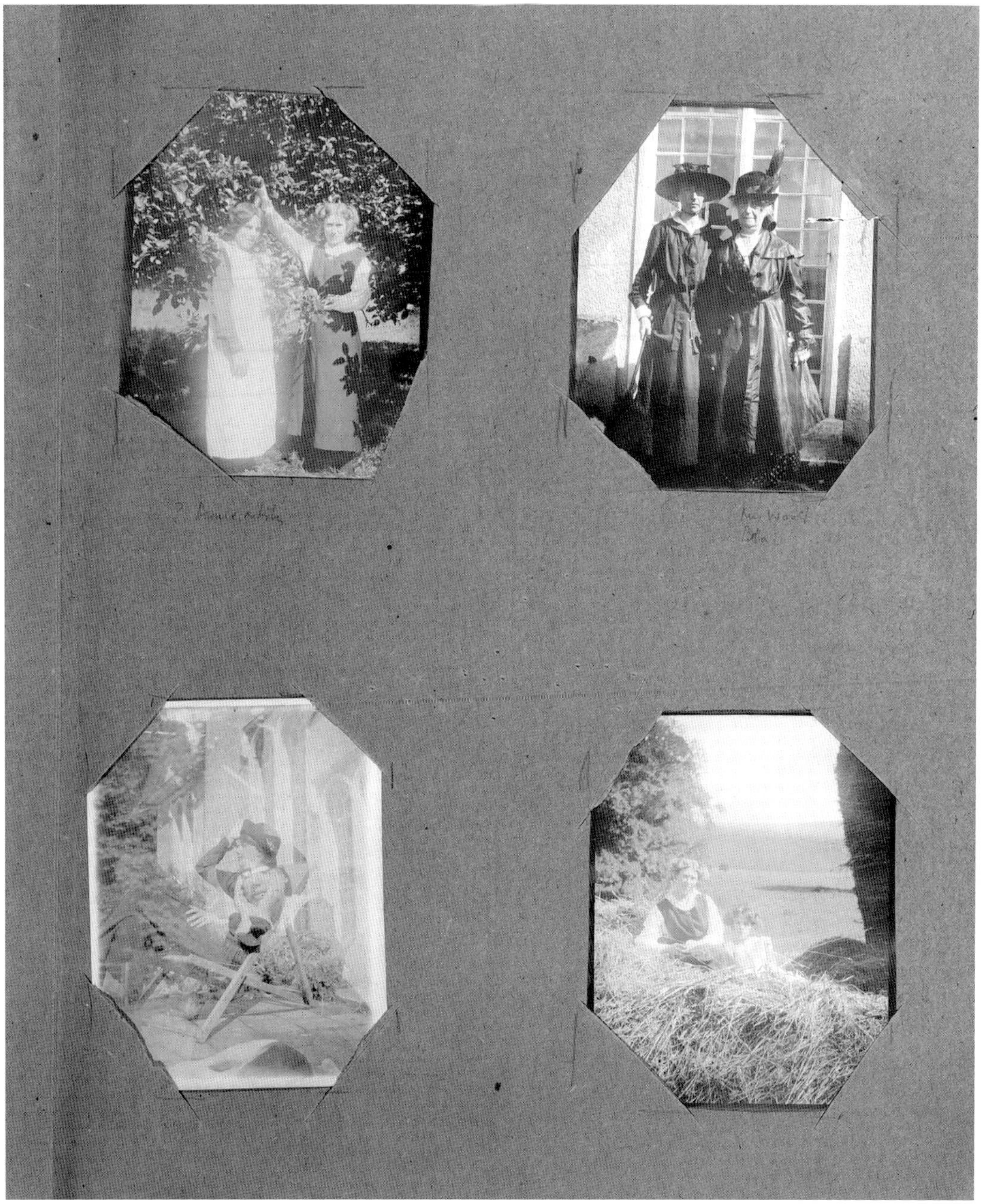

54. Annie and Lily. Mrs. Woolf and Bella, ca. 1915–1917. Virginia Woolf, Asheham, ca. 1915. Monk's House Album 2, p. 5. Reprinted by permission of the Harvard Theatre Collection, the Houghton Library. "the cook is really a great improvement . . . Lily is a real servant in the way of brushing ones clothes" (*L*, 2:44).

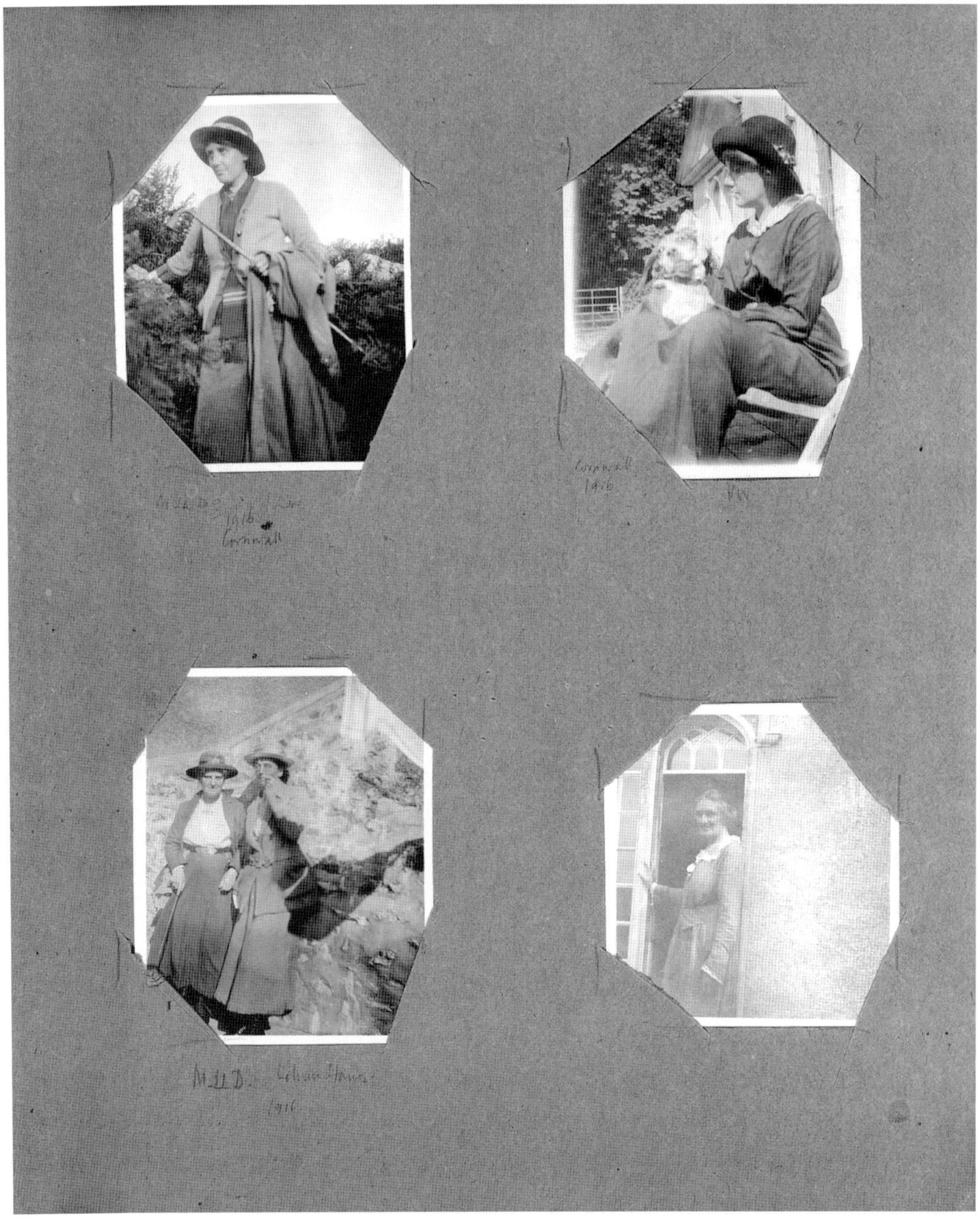

55. Virginia Woolf; Margaret Llewelyn Davies and Lilian Harris. Carbis Bay, Cornwall, 1916. Monk's House Album 2, p. 6. Reprinted by permission of the Harvard Theatre Collection, the Houghton Library. "We are a very funny party. Miss Harris has turned up, Margarets secretary, an old creature of 50, extremely sensible and unselfish, and independent, who smokes a pipe . . . when Margaret gets excited, she calls her 'John,' and Miss Harris calls Margaret 'Jim'" (L, 2:119).

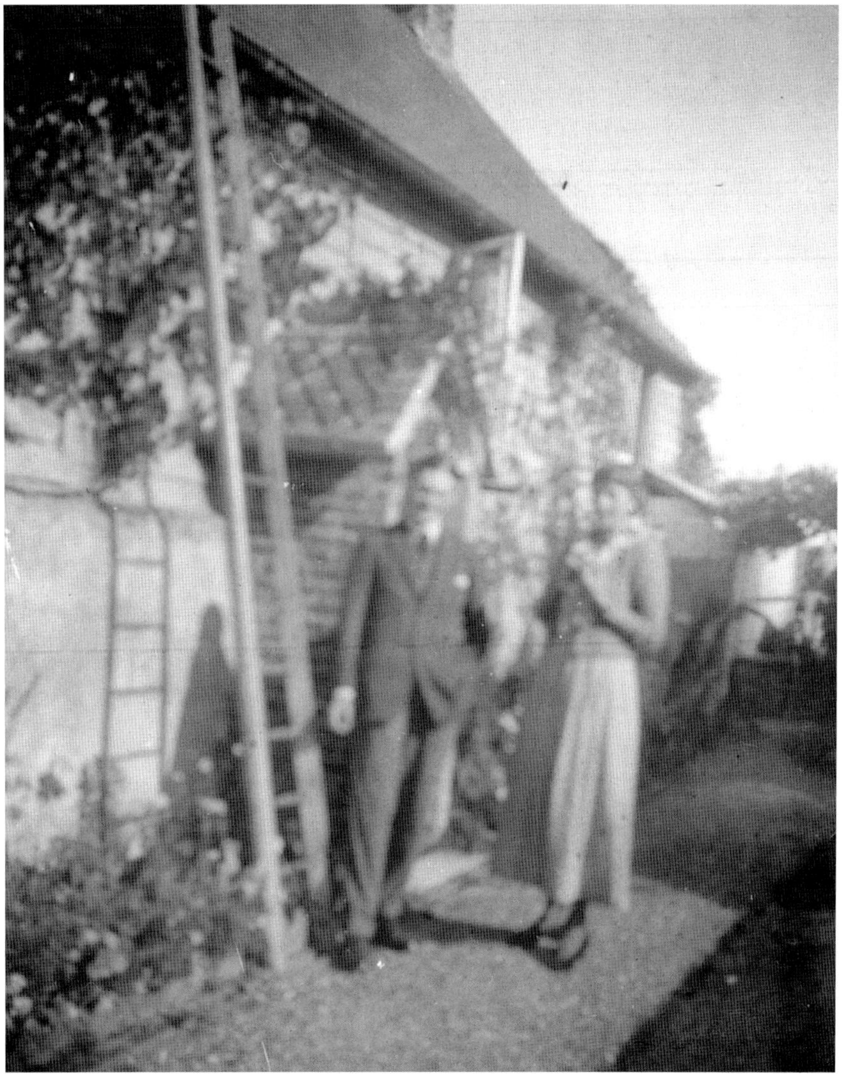

56. T. S. Eliot and Virginia Woolf, Monk's House, ca. 1920s? Monk's House Album 2, p. 16. Reprinted by permission of the Harvard Theatre Collection, the Houghton Library. "The odd thing about Eliot is that his eyes are lively & youthful when the cast of his face & the shape of his sentences is formal & even heavy" (D, 2:67).

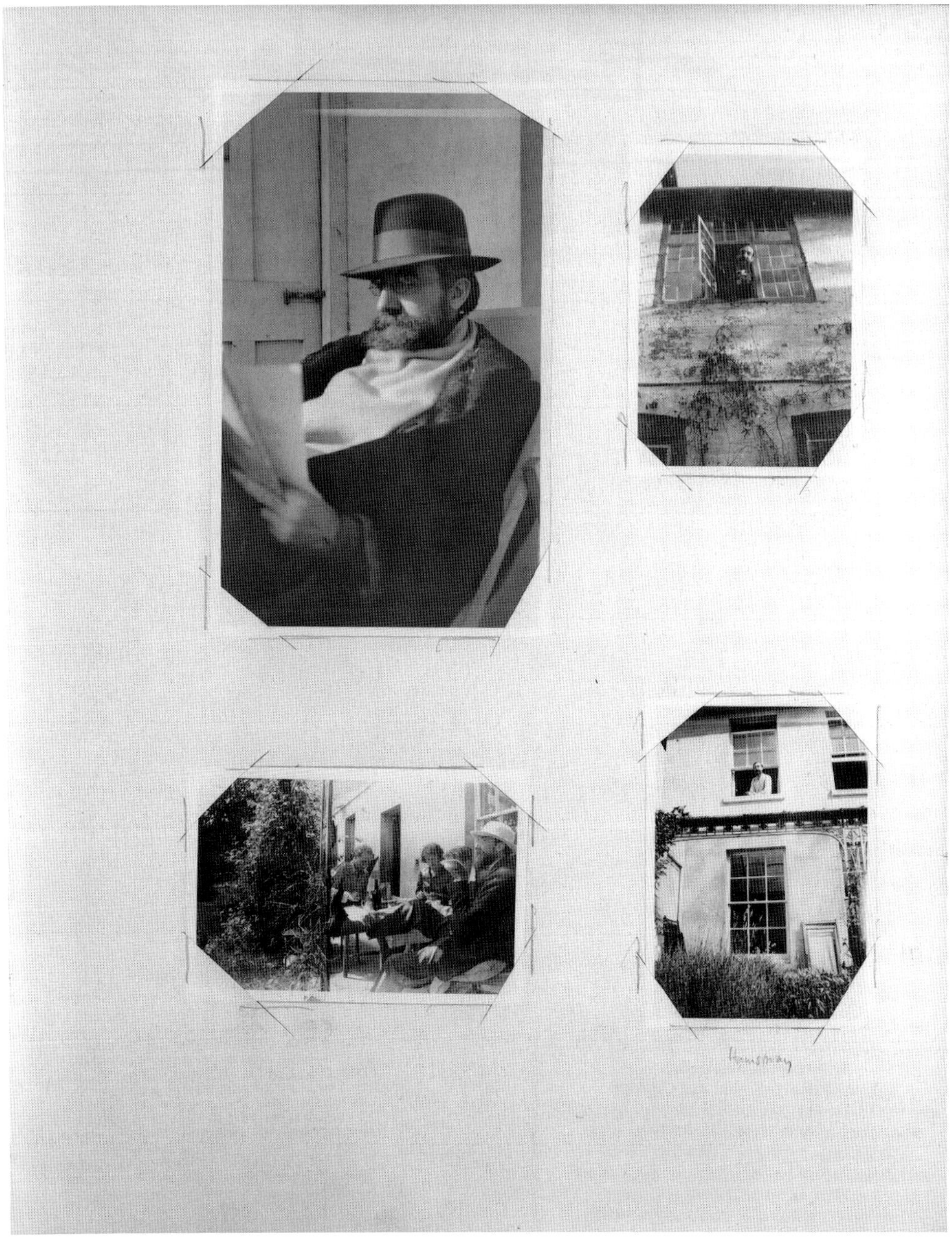

57. Lytton Strachey; Ralph Partridge, Dora Carrington, Lytton Strachey; Ham Spray. 1920s. Monk's House Album 4, p. 5. Reprinted by permission of the Harvard Theatre Collection, the Houghton Library. "Lytton this morning, very affable and easy, and greatly excited, I think, about his house [Ham Spray] which is being drained, and has a studio for Carrington, a workshop for Ralph, and several gigantic beech trees" (*L*, 3:105).

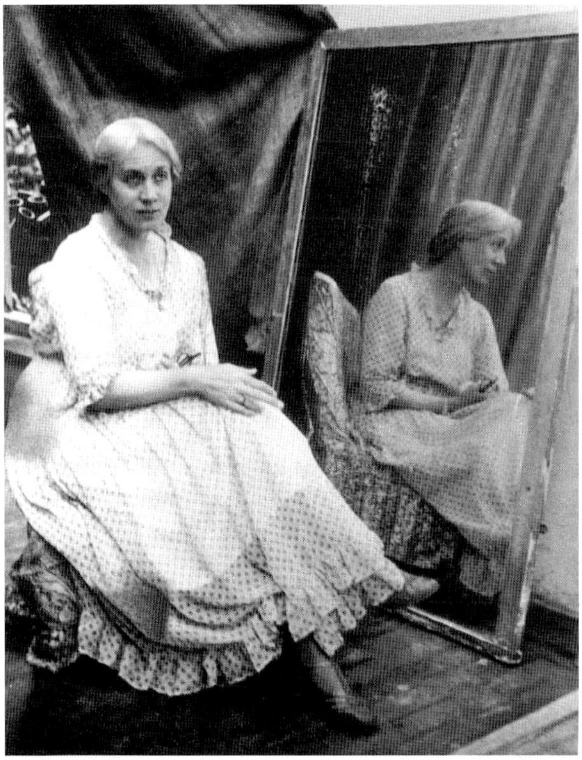

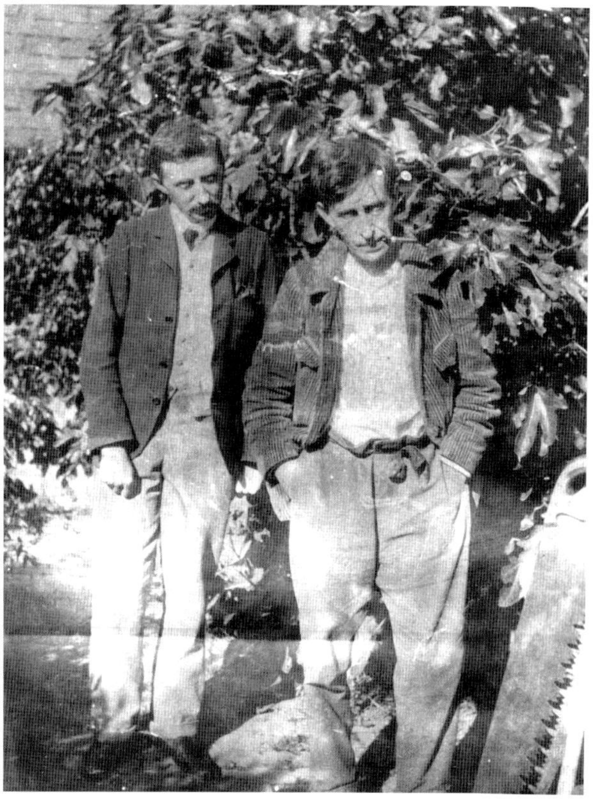

58. (LEFT) Vanessa Bell, 1920s? Photographer: Barbara Bagenal? Box 4, folder 2 of 2. Reprinted by permission of the Harvard Theatre Collection, the Houghton Library. "Barbara at the club today, stunned with the problem of life, thoroughly in for it" (*D*, 2:117).

59. (RIGHT) E. M. Forster and Leonard Woolf. Monk's House, ca. 1922. Monk's House Album 2, p. 24. Reprinted by permission of the Harvard Theatre Collection, the Houghton Library. "Morgan became very familiar; anecdotic; simple, gossiping about friends & humming his little tunes . . . he is happy in his novel [*A Passage to India*]" (*D*, 2:204).

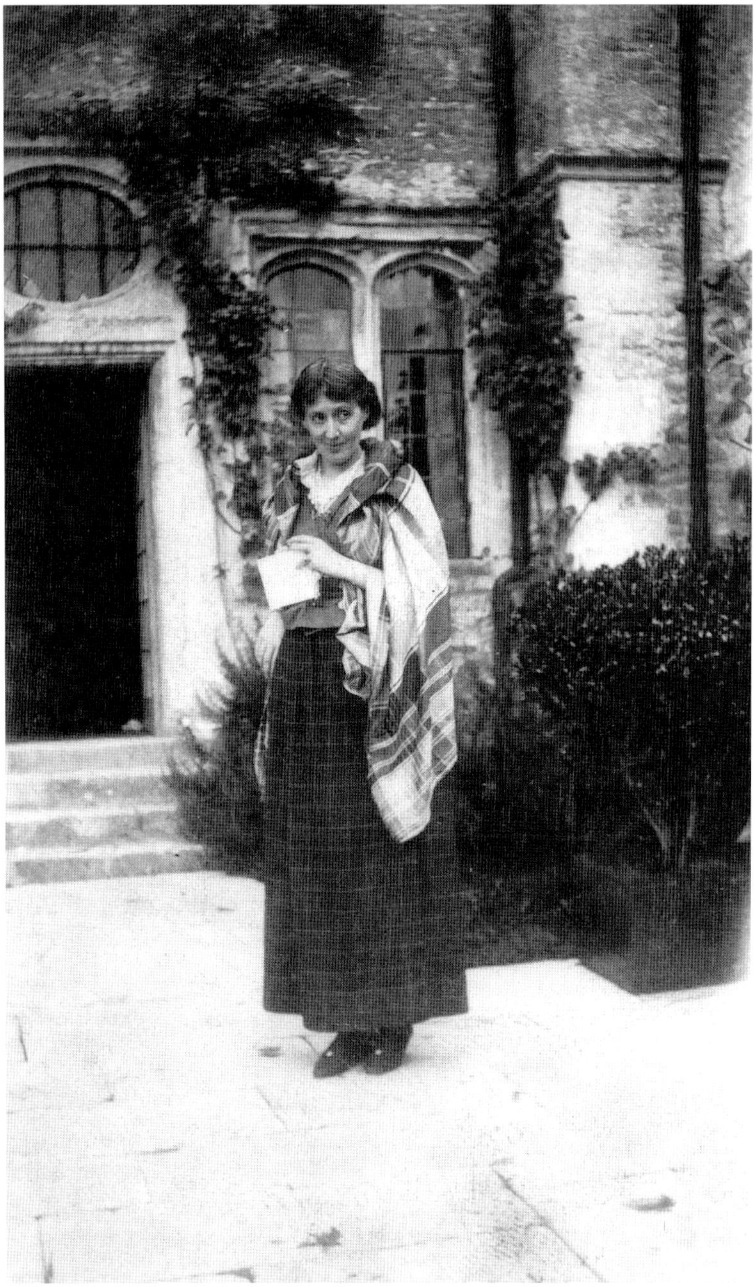

60. Virginia Woolf, Garsington, 1923. Photographer: Lady Ottoline Morrell. Box 3, folder 1. Reprinted by permission of the Harvard Theatre Collection, the Houghton Library. "She worked with a variety of cameras, and was constantly changing them with dealers in London. I think the greatest number of pictures were taken with a Rolliflex" (Julian Morrell Vinogradoff [Ottoline's daughter] in Heilbrun, vii). The Rolliflex twin lens was launched in 1928, after this photograph.

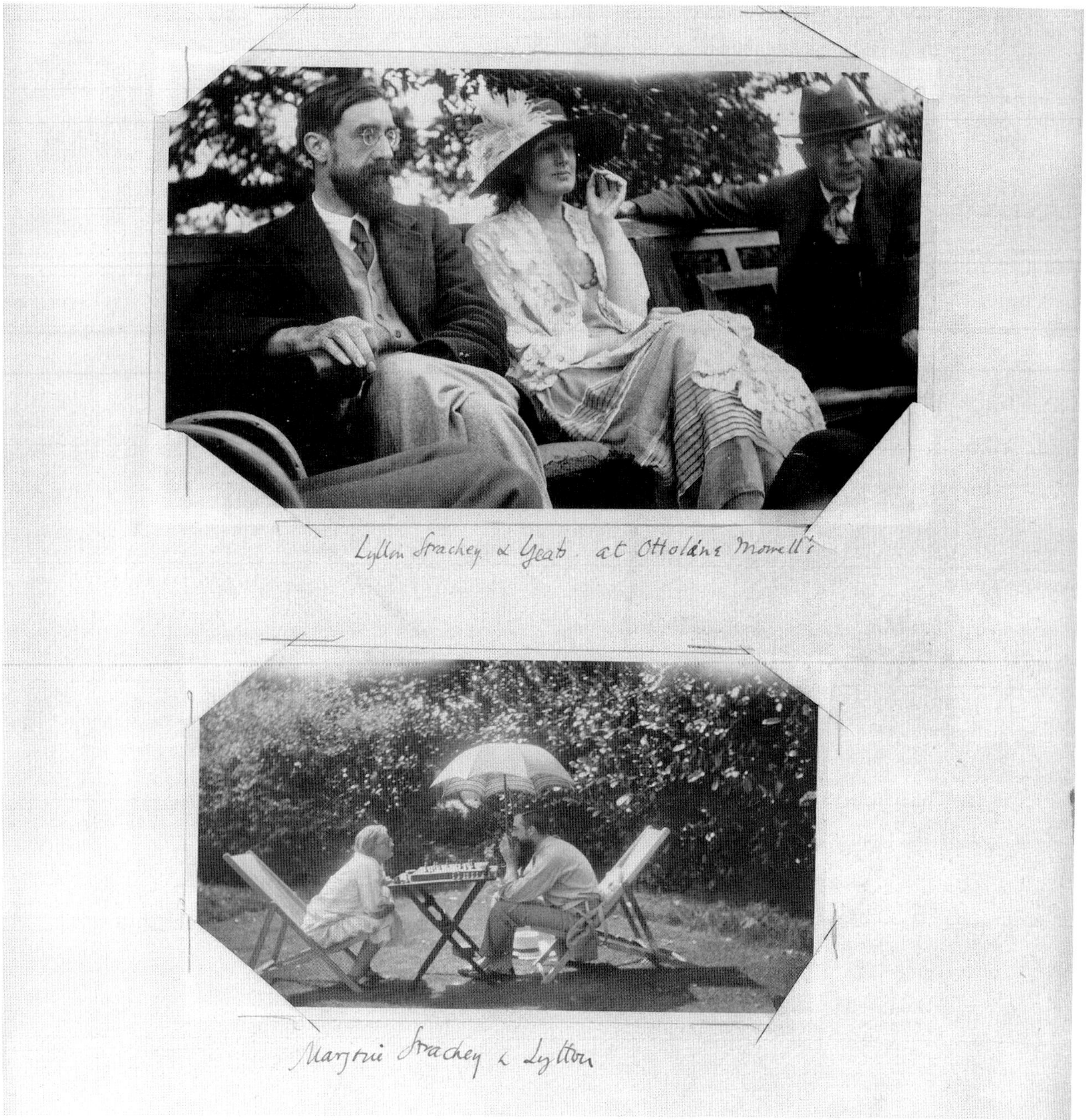

61. Lytton Strachey, Virginia Woolf, and Goldsworthy Lowes "Goldie" Dickinson. Garsington, June 1923. Photographer: Lady Ottoline Morrell. Marjorie and Lytton Strachey, 1930s. Monk's House Album 4, p. 3. Reprinted by permission of the Harvard Theatre Collection, the Houghton Library. "Thank you very much for the photograph which seems to me highly flattering (not of Goldie, I agree) . . . yours come out so much better than the professionals" (*L*, 3:47).

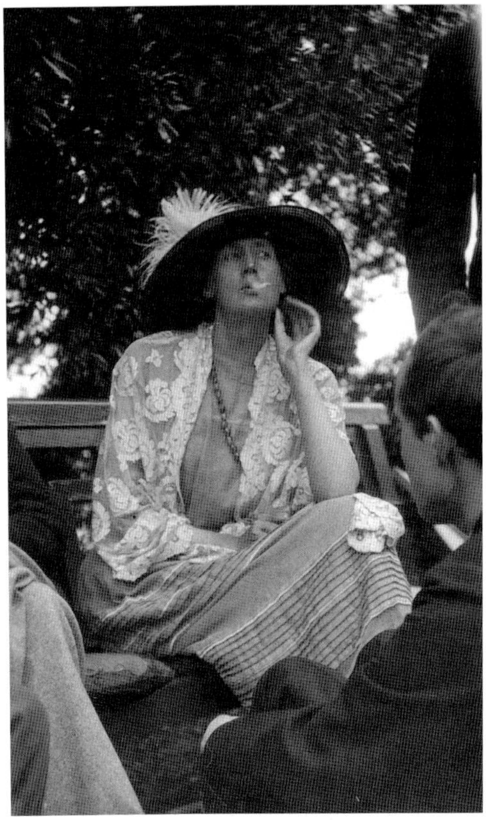

62. (LEFT) Virginia Woolf (and rear of David Cecil's head). Garsington, June 1923. Photographer: Lady Ottoline Morrell. Box 4, unmarked folder. Reprinted by permission of the Harvard Theatre Collection, the Houghton Library. "I see the nervous shoulders, the creative wrists, the unprecedented sculpture of the temples and eye-sockets" (David Cecil in Heilbrun, 73).

63. (BELOW LEFT) Lydia Keynes and Duncan Grant. Studland, 1923. Box 4, folder A. Reprinted by permission of the Harvard Theatre Collection, the Houghton Library. "Lydia has the soul of a squirrel . . . she sits by the hour polishing the sides of her nose with her front paws" (*L*, 3:76).

64. (BELOW RIGHT) Jacques Raverat, ca. 1924? Box 4, folder A. Reprinted by permission of the Harvard Theatre Collection, the Houghton Library. "Have you a snapshot or any photograph of him [Raverat]? I go on making things up to tell him" (*L*, 3:172–173).

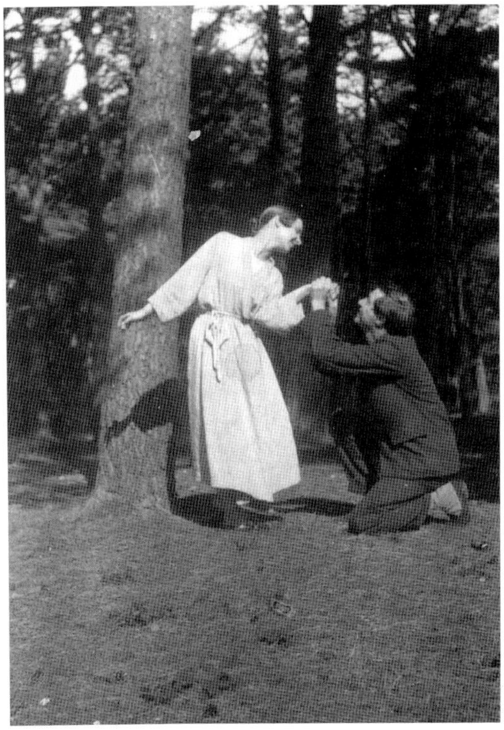

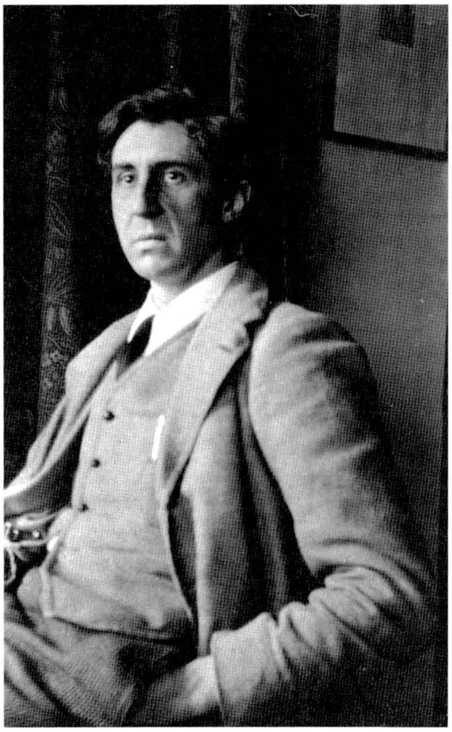

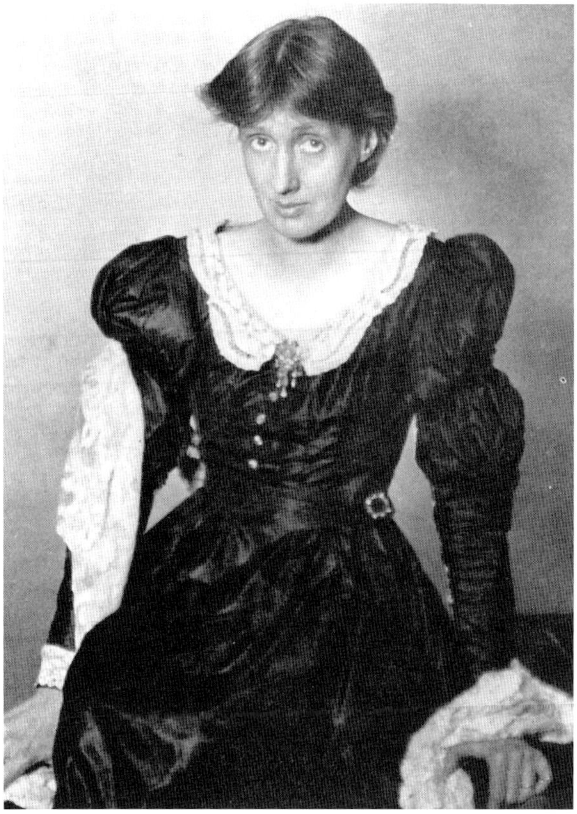

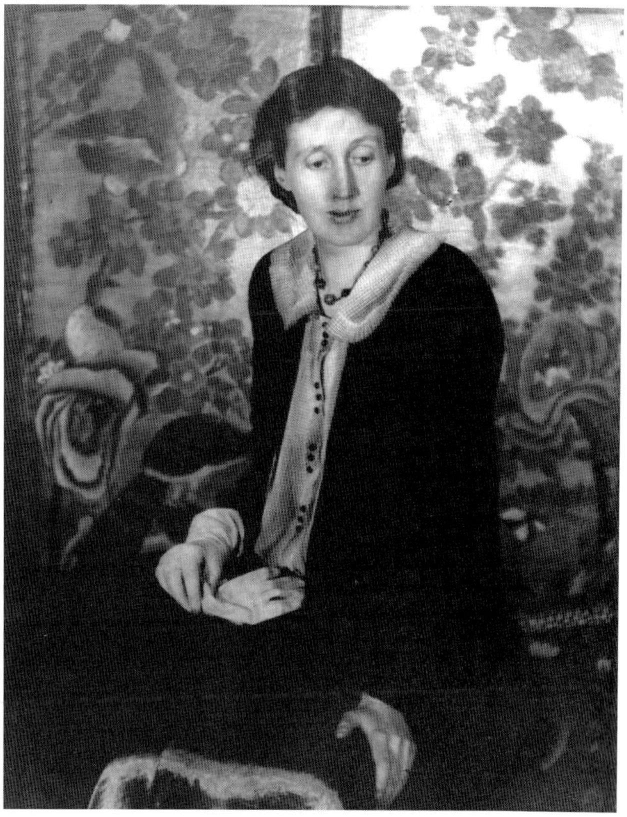

65. (LEFT) Virginia Woolf, 1924. Photographers: Maurice Adams Beck and Helen Macgregor, Marylebone Mews, London, for *Vogue*. Reprinted by permission of the Harvard Theatre Collection, the Houghton Library. Virginia is wearing her mother's dress.

66. (RIGHT) Virginia Woolf, April 27, 1925. Photographers: Maurice Adams Beck and Helen Macgregor, Marylebone Mews, London. Box 3. Reprinted by permission of the Harvard Theatre Collection, the Houghton Library. At rear of the house in which Thomas Woolner, sculptor, proposed a sitting and marriage to Julia Jackson. "I have been sitting to Vogue, the Becks that is, in their mews, which Mr Woolner built as his studio, & perhaps it was there that he thought of my mother, whom he wished to marry" (*D*, 3:12).

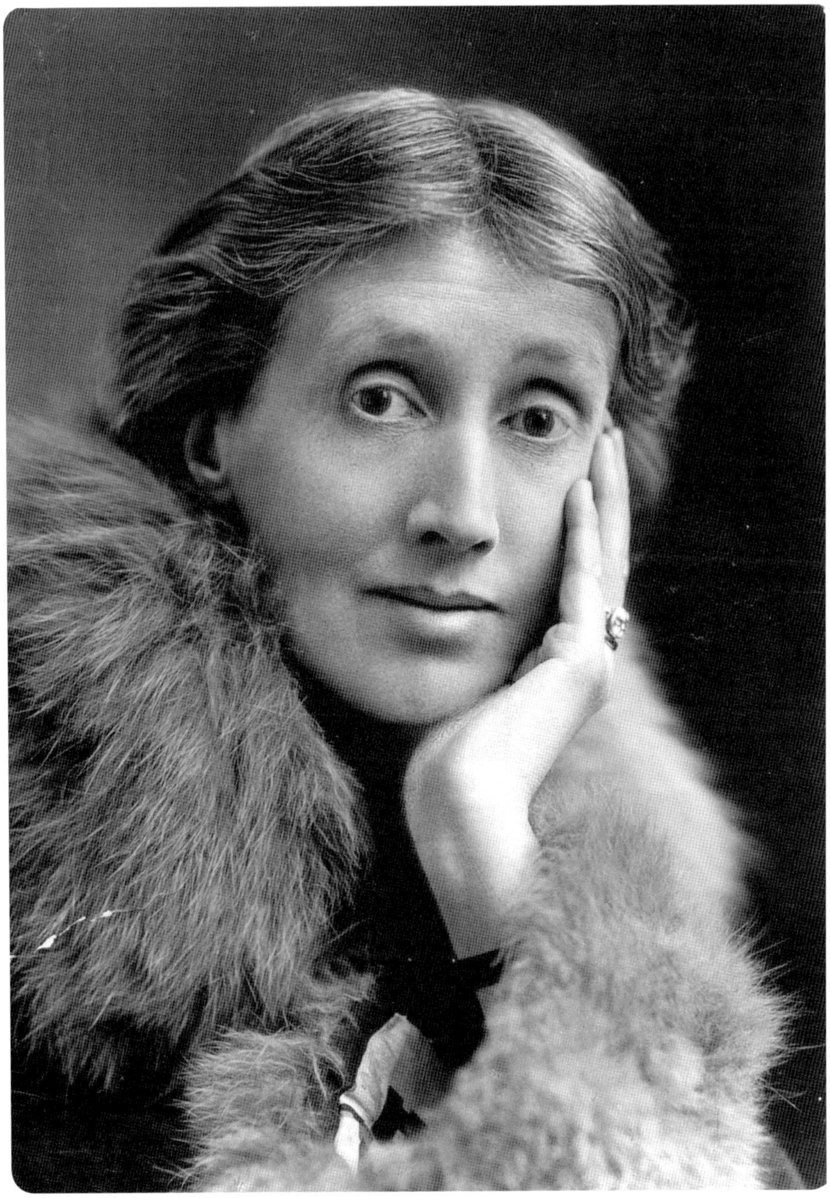

67. (RIGHT) Virginia Woolf, ca. 1927? Box 3, folder 2. Reprinted by permission of the Harvard Theatre Collection, the Houghton Library. "I think, however, I am now almost an established figure—as a writer. They dont laugh at me any longer" (D, 3:137).

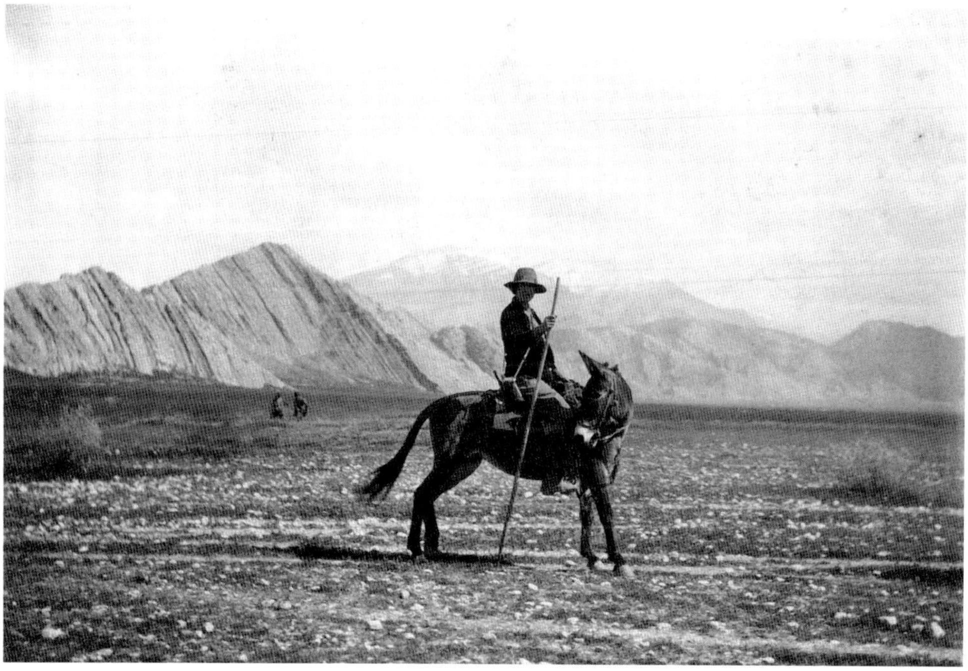

68. (ABOVE) Vita Sackville-West, 1927, on Mouse, her donkey. On the road to Isafahan, Persia. Box 4, folder A. Reprinted by permission of the Harvard Theatre Collection, the Houghton Library. "Now you are nearly at Teheran I make out . . . you are very excited, all in a whirl, like a flock of birds" (*L*, 3:326).

69. (RIGHT) Virginia Woolf, January 1929. Photographer: Lenare. Box 2, folder 3. Reprinted by permission of the Harvard Theatre Collection, the Houghton Library. "I've got some rather nice photographs of Virginia" —Vita thought Virginia looked "mischievous" and "tidy" (*L*, 4:9).

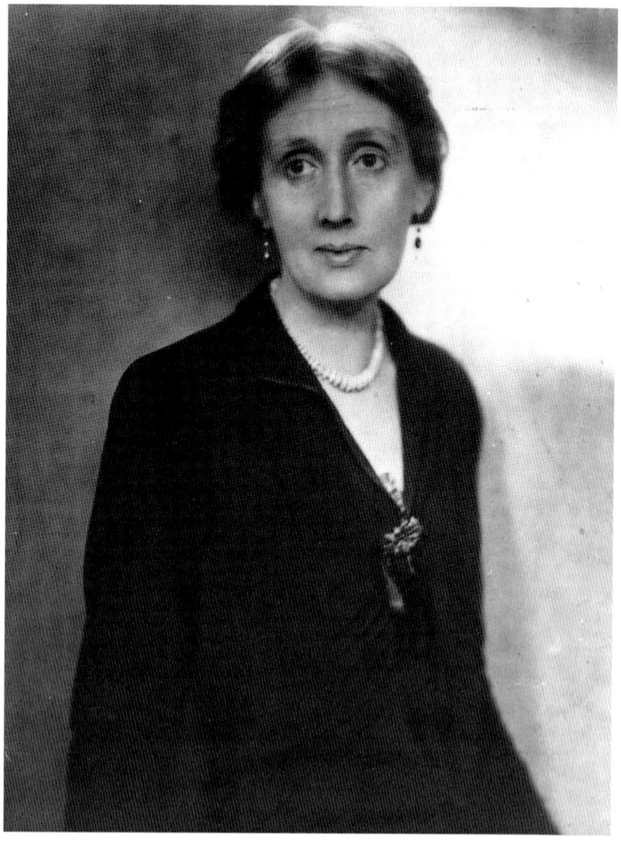

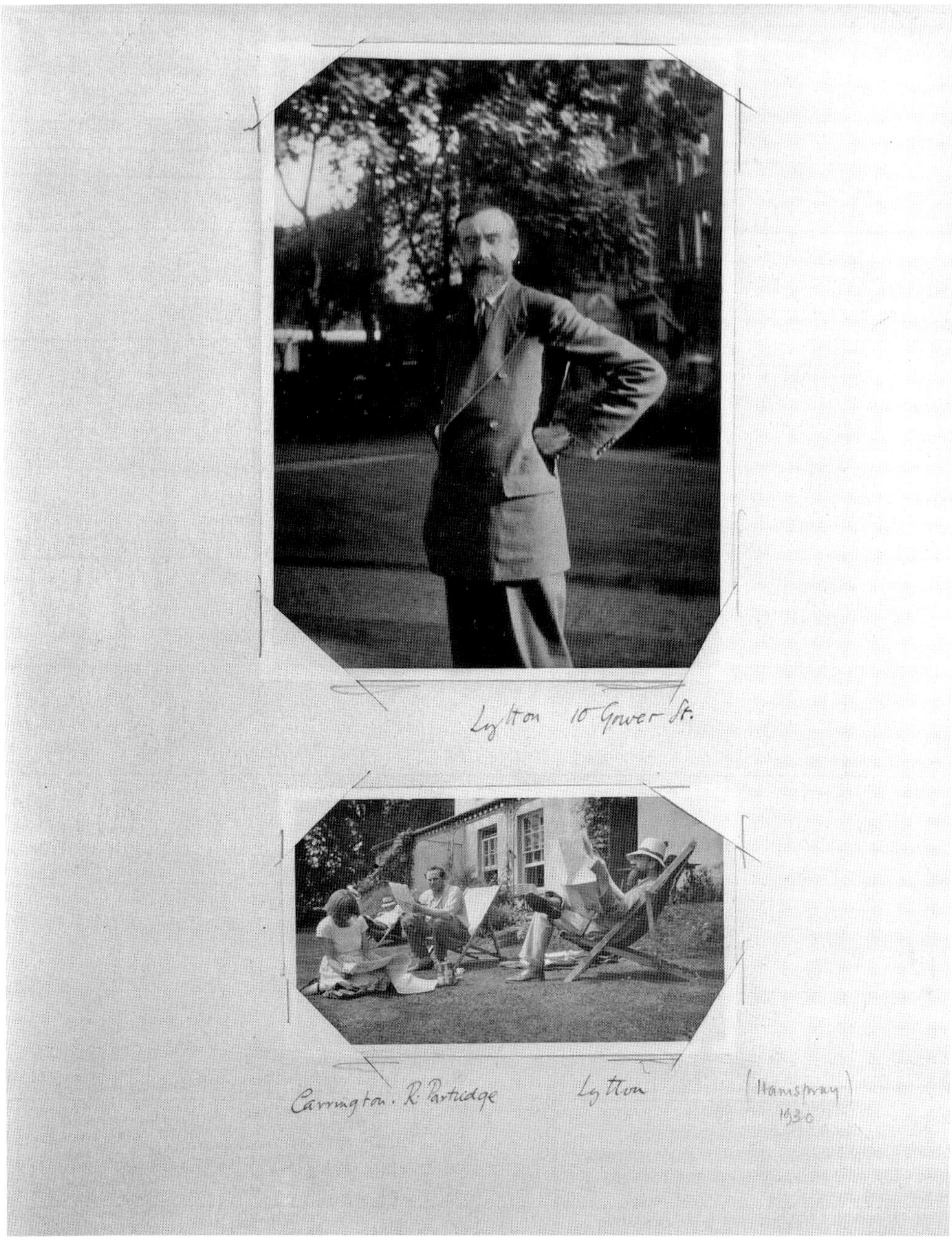

70. Lytton Strachey, 10 Gower Street, 1920s. Photographer: Lady Ottoline Morrell.
Dora Carrington, Ralph Partridge, Lytton Strachey, possibly Saxon Sydney-Turner, dated 1930. Monk's House Album 4, p. 4. Reprinted by permission of the Harvard Theatre Collection, the Houghton Library.
"Lytton tells me that Ottoline has crammed two Garsingtons into one small house, wears pink plush, and is so much of a ruin . . . one can only drop a wreath and heave a sigh" (L, 3:394).

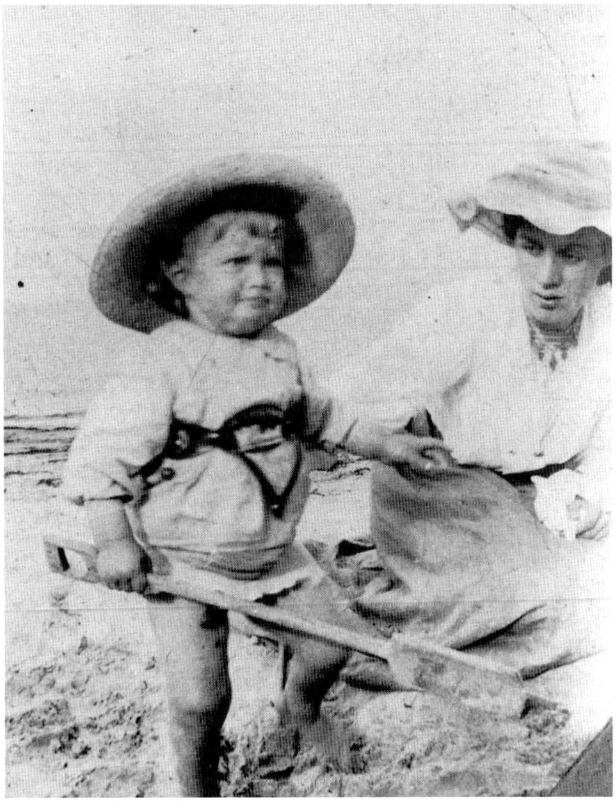

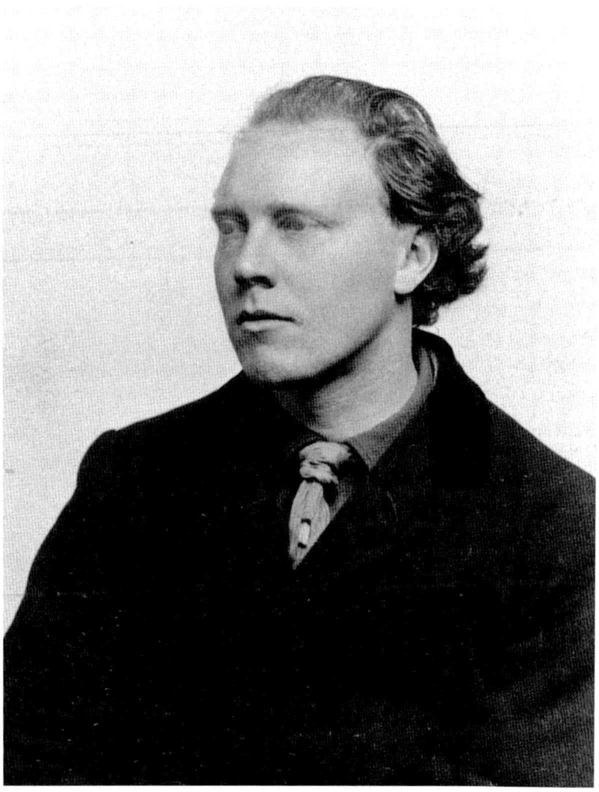

71 (LEFT) Julian and Vanessa Bell, Studland, 1909. Bell Album 1, p. 28 AG2. Copyright Tate, London, 2004. "Julian rushes straight into the sea, and falls flat on his face. Nessa tucks her skirts up, and wades about with him" (*L*, 1:412).

72. (RIGHT) Clive Bell, Blean, 1910. Bell Album 1, p. 31 AG14. Copyright Tate, London, 2004. "I got a fantastic impression that this man Bell was a kind of Sun God—with straw in his hair" (OB, 165).

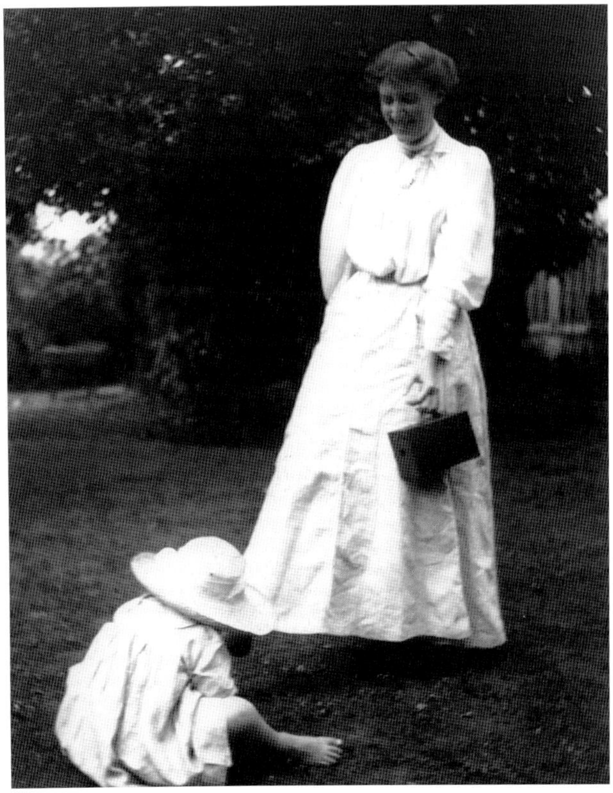

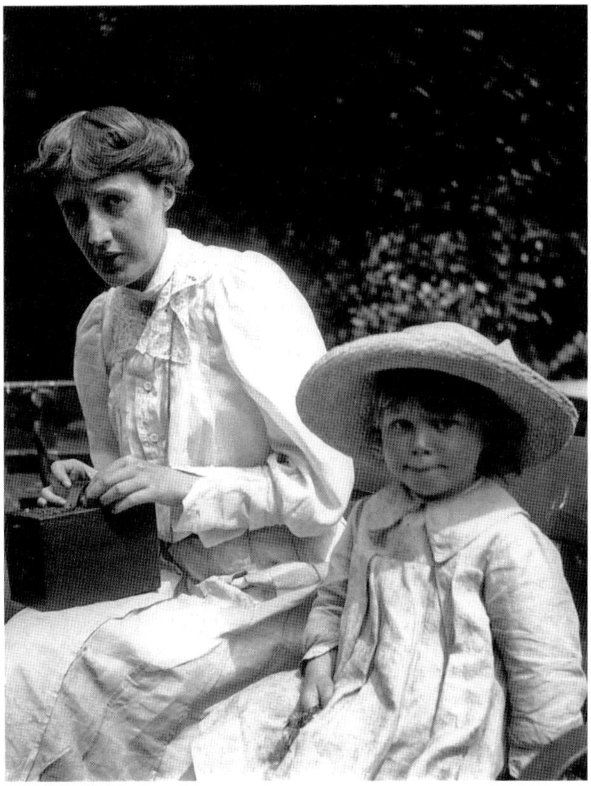

73. (LEFT) Julian Bell and Virginia Stephen (with Frena). Blean, 1910. Bell Album 1, p. 30 X19. Copyright Tate, London, 2004. "Julian has just raised a blush on the face of the parlourmaid by calling his mother a —! When she said 'Hush!' he replied —! Did you ever?" (*L*, 1:428).

74. (RIGHT) Virginia Stephen and Julian Bell. Blean, June 1910. Bell Album 1, p. 32 V19. Copyright Tate, London, 2004.

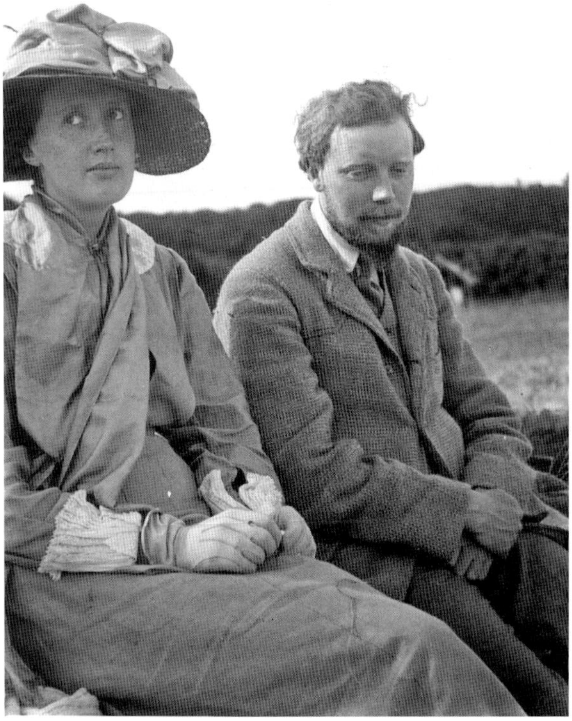 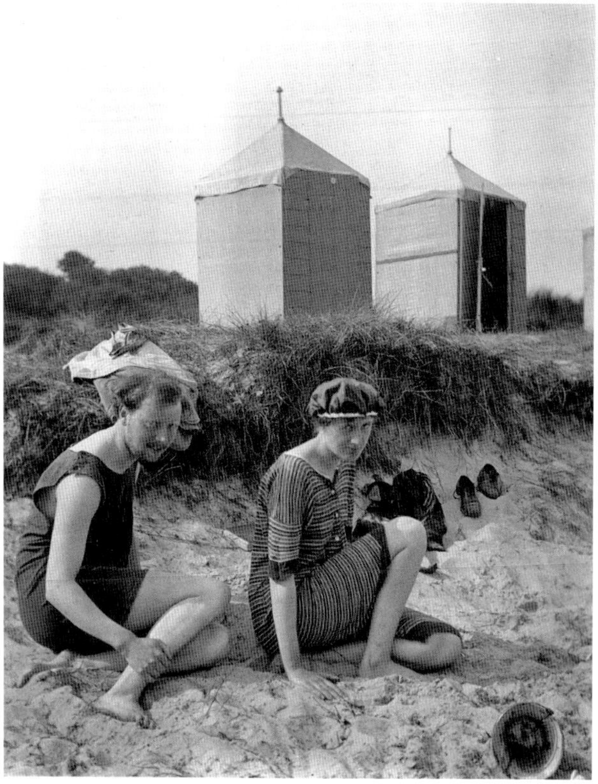

75. (LEFT) Clive Bell and Virginia Stephen. Studland, 1910. Bell Album 1, p. 38 U24. Copyright Tate, London, 2004. "My resolution is to be cautious at Studland, not walking too far, or exciting the emotions . . . will you try not to irritate the beast, for amusement . . . it will be very nice to see you" (*L*, 1:434).

76. (RIGHT) Clive Bell and Virginia Stephen. Studland, 1910. Bell Album 1, p. 40 V12. Copyright Tate, London, 2004. "I hired a gentlemans or ladies—it was bisexual —a bathing dress, and swam far out . . . a drifting sea anemone" (*L*, 1:412).

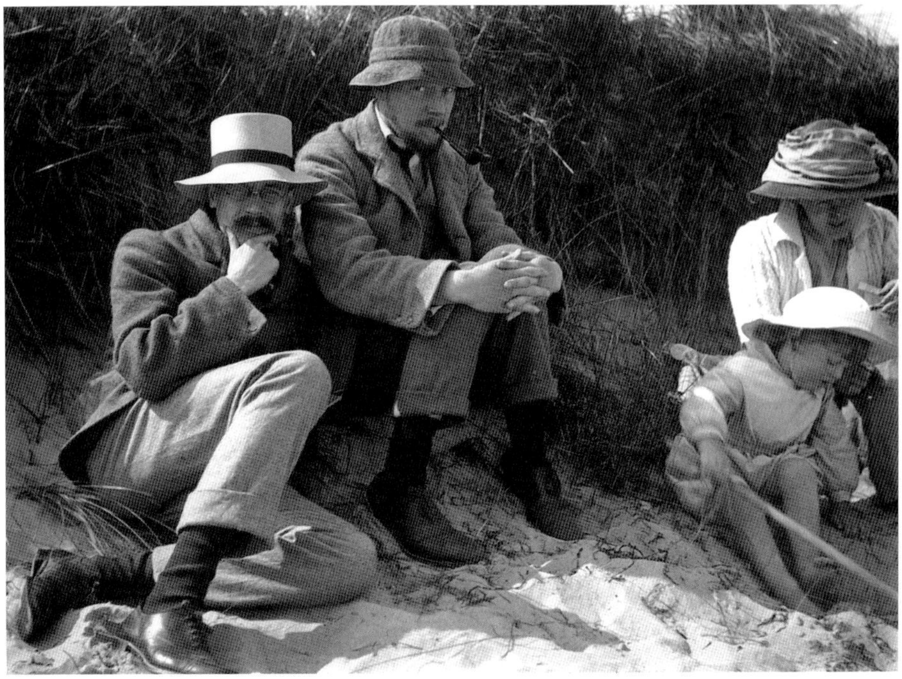

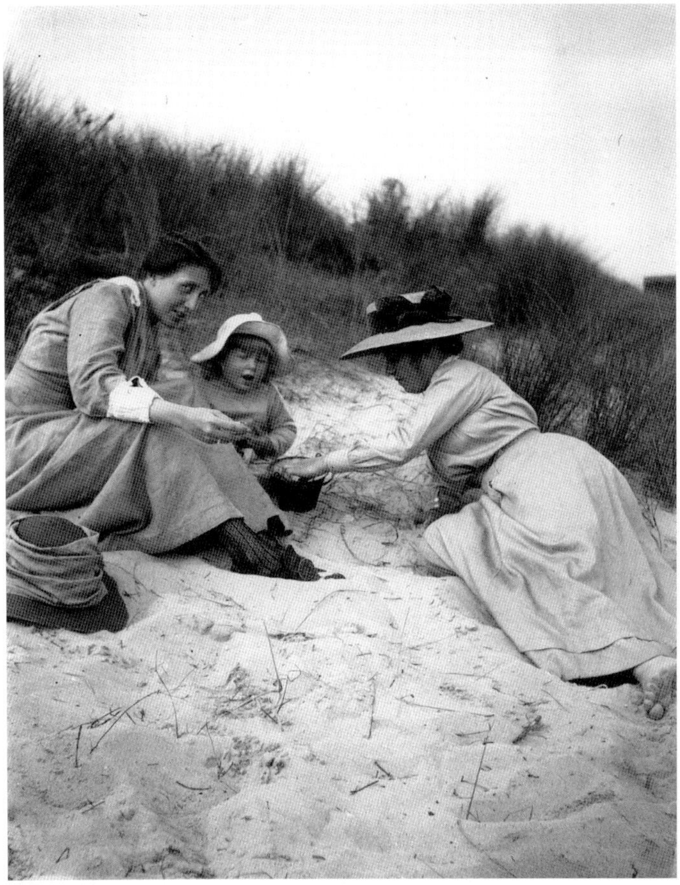

77. (ABOVE) Saxon Sydney-Turner, Clive Bell, Julian Bell, and Virginia Stephen. Studland, 1910. Bell Album 1, p. 39 U25. Copyright Tate, London, 2004.

78. (LEFT) Virginia Stephen, Julian Bell, and Mabel. Studland, 1910. Bell Album 1, p. 38 U22. Copyright Tate, London, 2004. "Julian told a visitor who admired Quentin's [red] hair that if Mabel would only brush it, his hair would become that colour too!" (VB/L, 123).

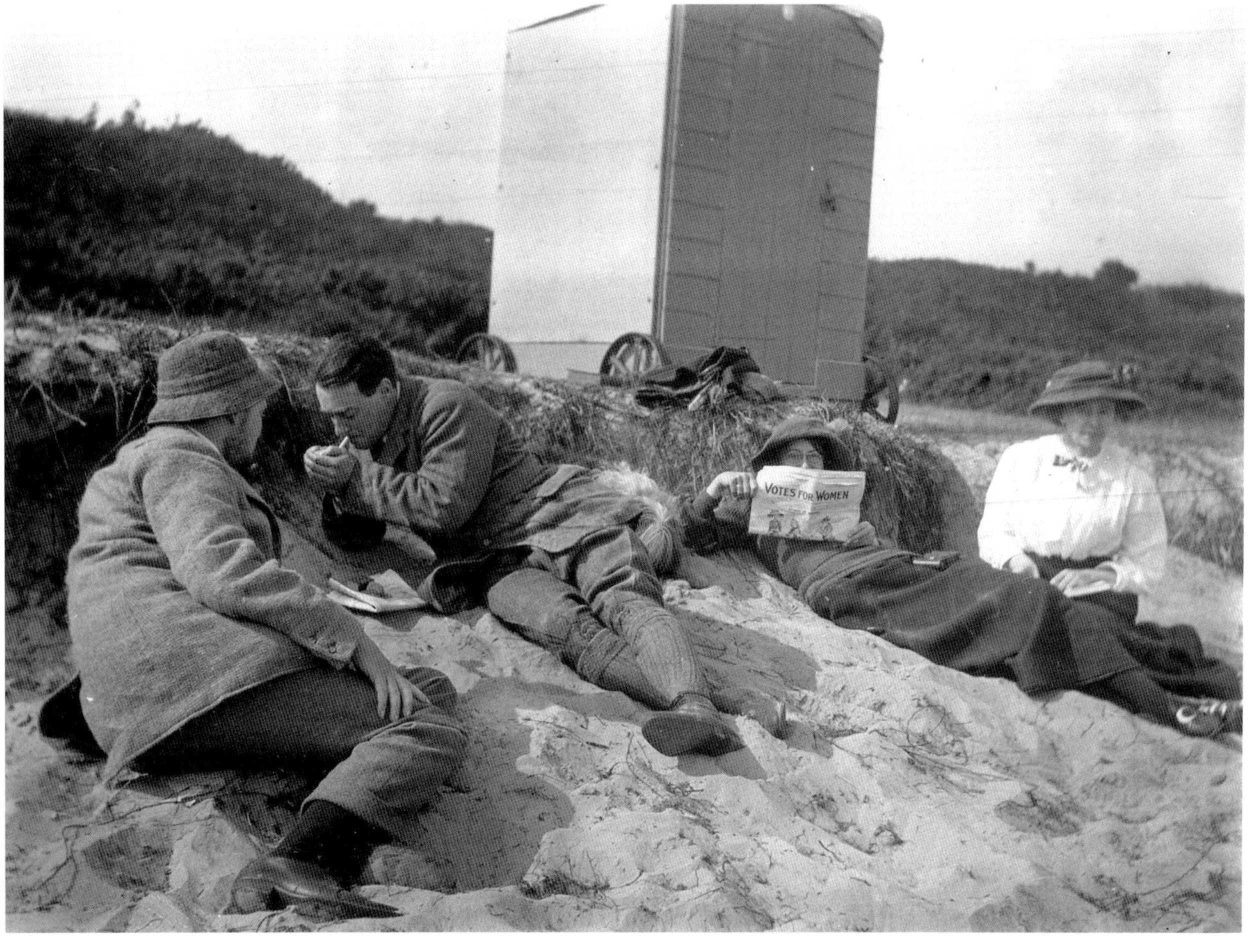

79. Clive Bell, Desmond MacCarthy, Marjorie Strachey (holding *Votes for Women*), and Virginia Stephen. Studland, 1910. Bell Album 1, p. 39 AA9. Copyright Tate, London, 2004. "I hope to work on Women every morning at Studland" (L, 1:434).

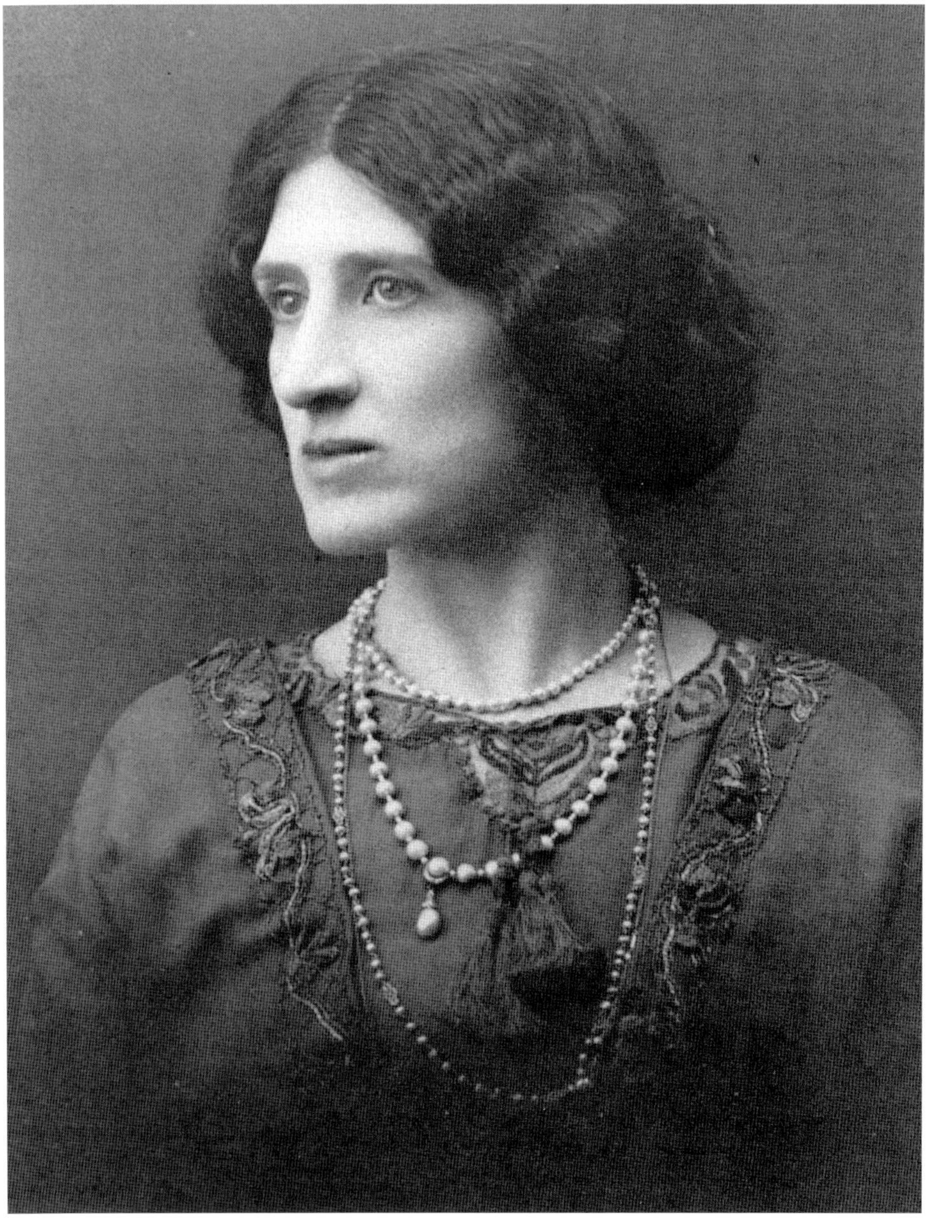

80. Ottoline Morrell, Studland, 1910. Bell Album 1, p. 41 AG18.
Copyright Tate, London, 2004. "Lady Ottoline . . . a fine work in the late renaissance style; the brow and eyes magnificent, the chin perhaps restored" (OB, 177–178).

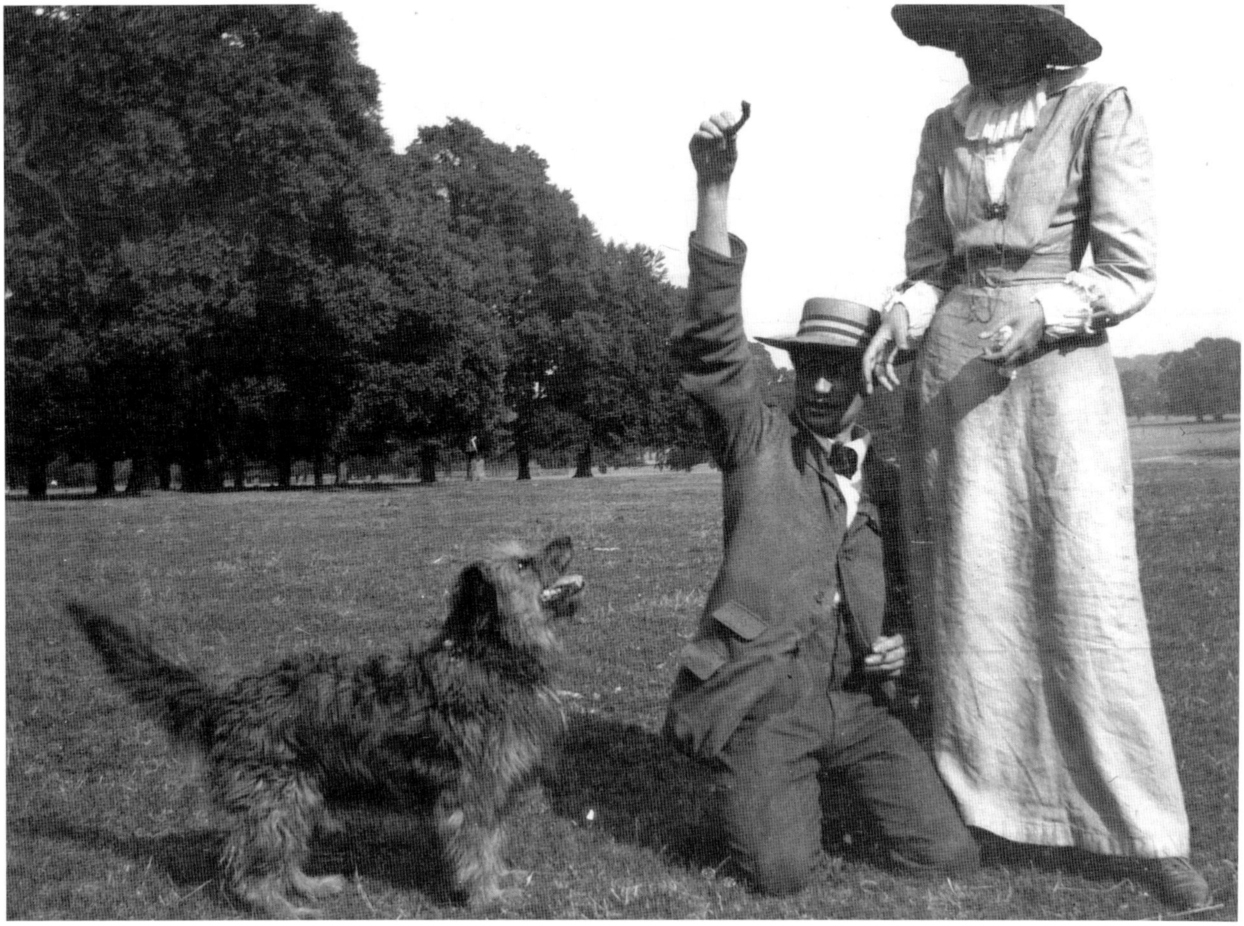

81. Gurth, Duncan Grant, and Virginia Stephen. Firle, 1911. AD1. Copyright Tate, London, 2004. "To be intimate with Virginia Stephen in those days . . . no one so beautiful and so fierce would give offence except to the very stupid" (Grant, *V. Woolf*, 101).

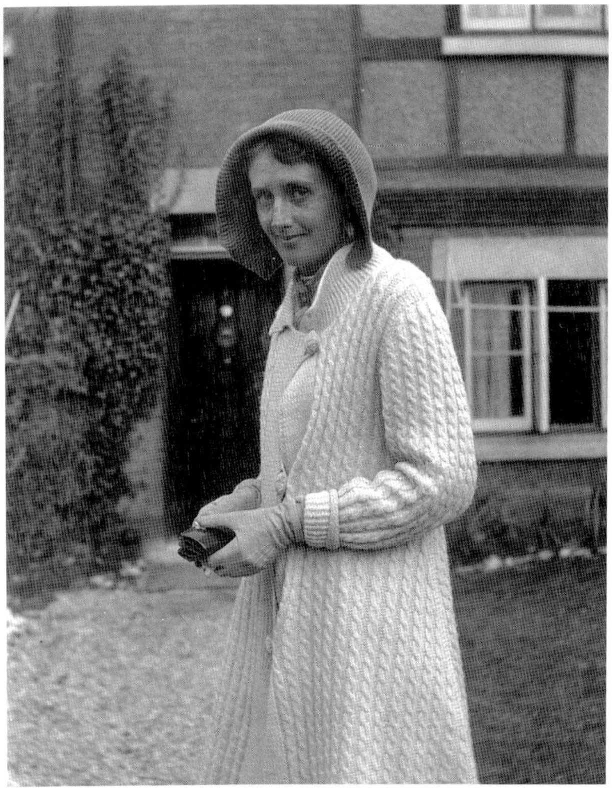

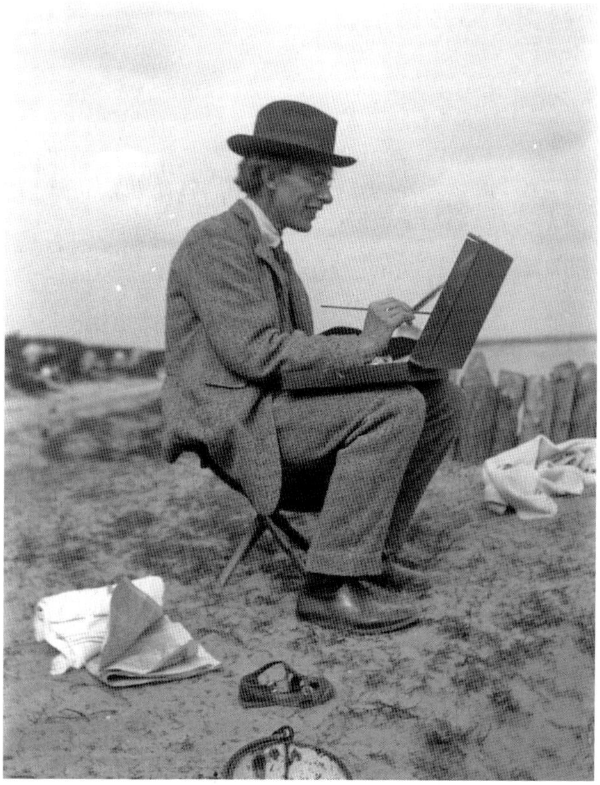

82. (LEFT) Virginia Stephen, Studland, 1911. Bell Album 2, p. 1 B23.
Copyright Tate, London, 2004.

83. (RIGHT) Roger Fry, Studland, 1911. Q29.
Copyright Tate, London, 2004. "You *are* beautiful, both you and your character and your whole view of life" (VB/L, 105).

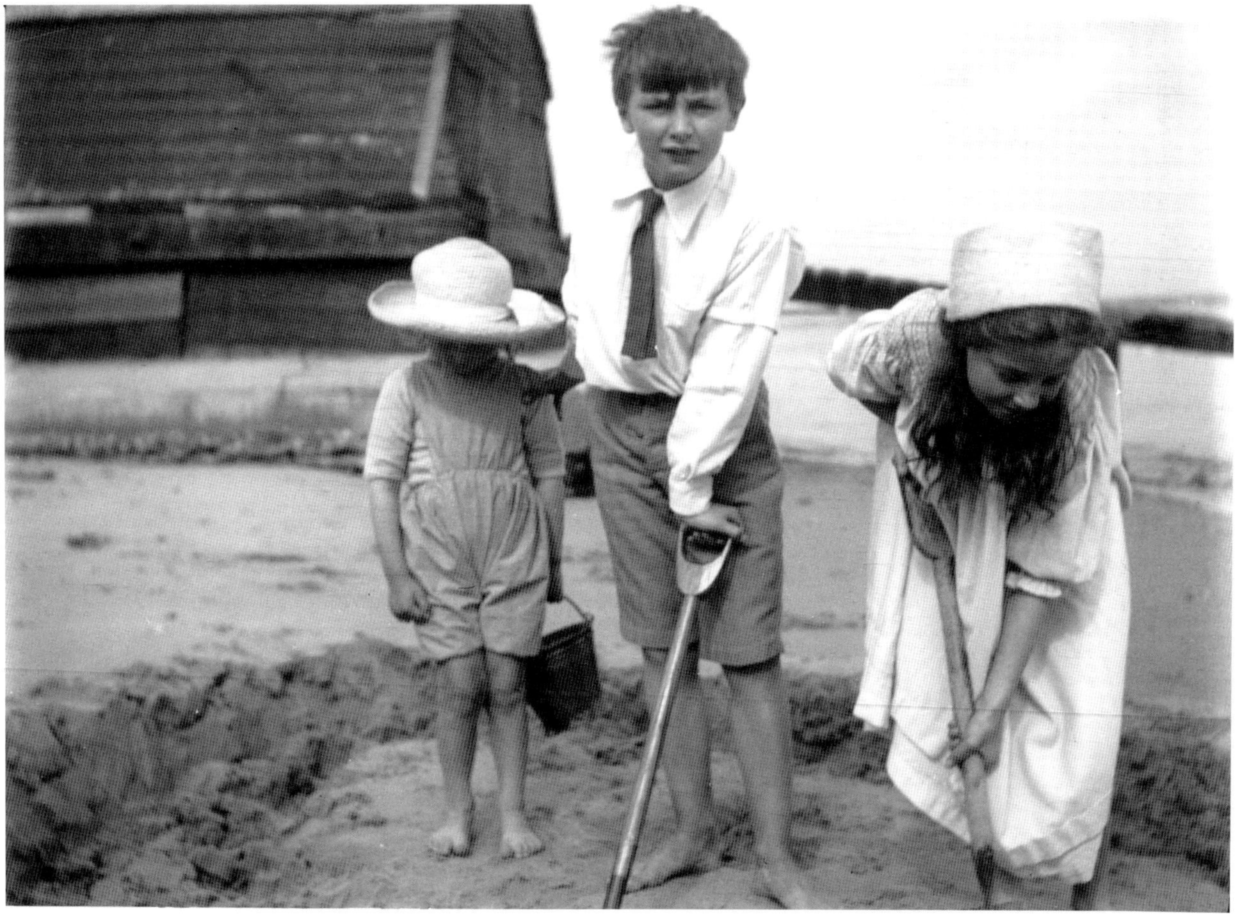

84. Julian Bell, Julian and Pamela Fry. Studland, 1911. Bell Album 2, p. 2 Z42. Copyright Tate, London, 2004. "I have written to Studland. By the way, if you could get rooms for most of you, we shall have one room at any rate in our house that you could use . . . I know the shape of all of you pretty well now" (VB/L, 100–101).

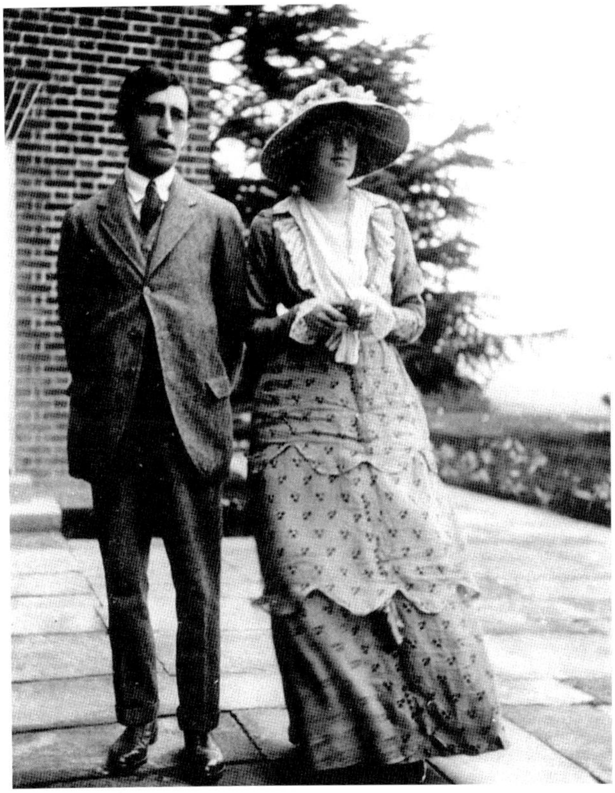

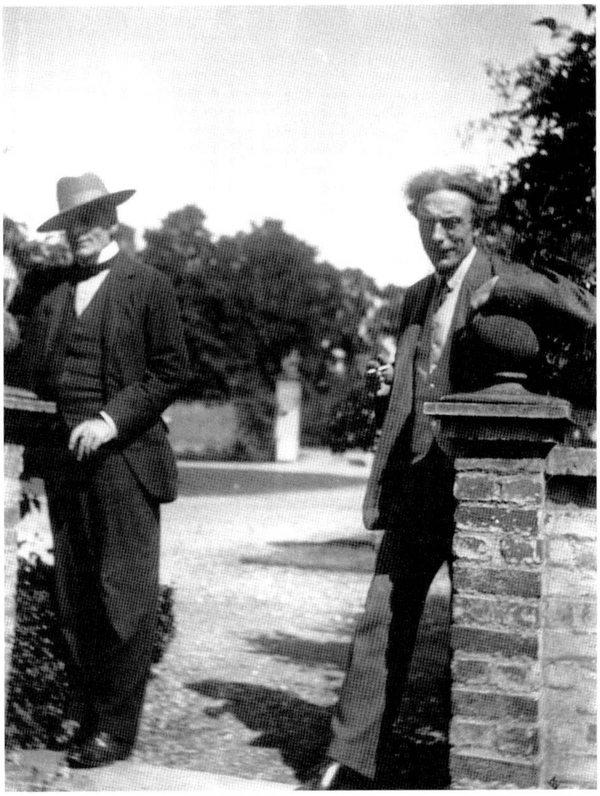

85. (LEFT) Leonard Woolf and Virginia Stephen. Dalingridge Place, July 23, 1912. Photographer: George Duckworth. Bell Album 2, p. 18 AG49. Copyright Tate, London, 2004. "I think Leonard one of the most remarkable and charming people I know. I am looking forward very much to having him for a brother-in-law" (VB/L, 117).

86. (RIGHT) Walter Sickert and Roger Fry. Newington, 1913. Bell Album 2, p. 28 U20. Copyright Tate, London, 2004. "Clive said he couldn't stand Newington [home of Nan Hudson and Ethel Sands] I was a little alarmed at their excessive elegance and 18th century stamp. It isn't what we want even for our minor arts, is it?" (VB/L, 120–121).

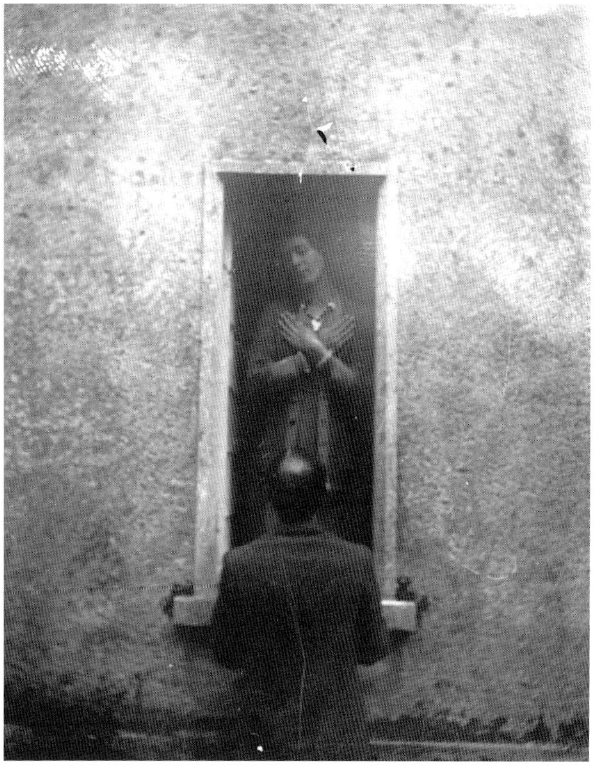

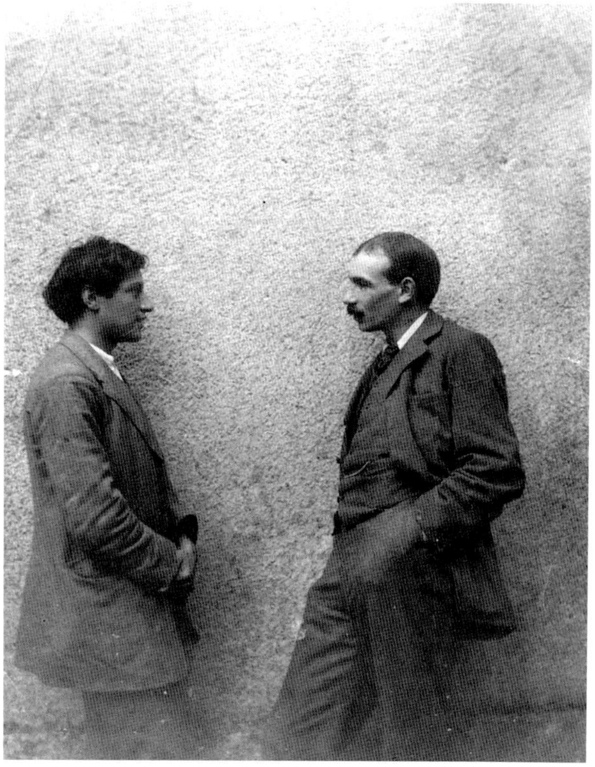

87. (LEFT) Vanessa Bell and John Maynard Keynes. Asheham, 1912. Bell Album 2, p. 11 AC 28. Copyright Tate, London, 2004. "It is very damp and grey at Asheham" (VB/L, 124).

88. (RIGHT) Duncan Grant and John Maynard Keynes. Asheham, 1912. Bell Album 2, p. 22 AH1. Copyright Tate, London, 2004.

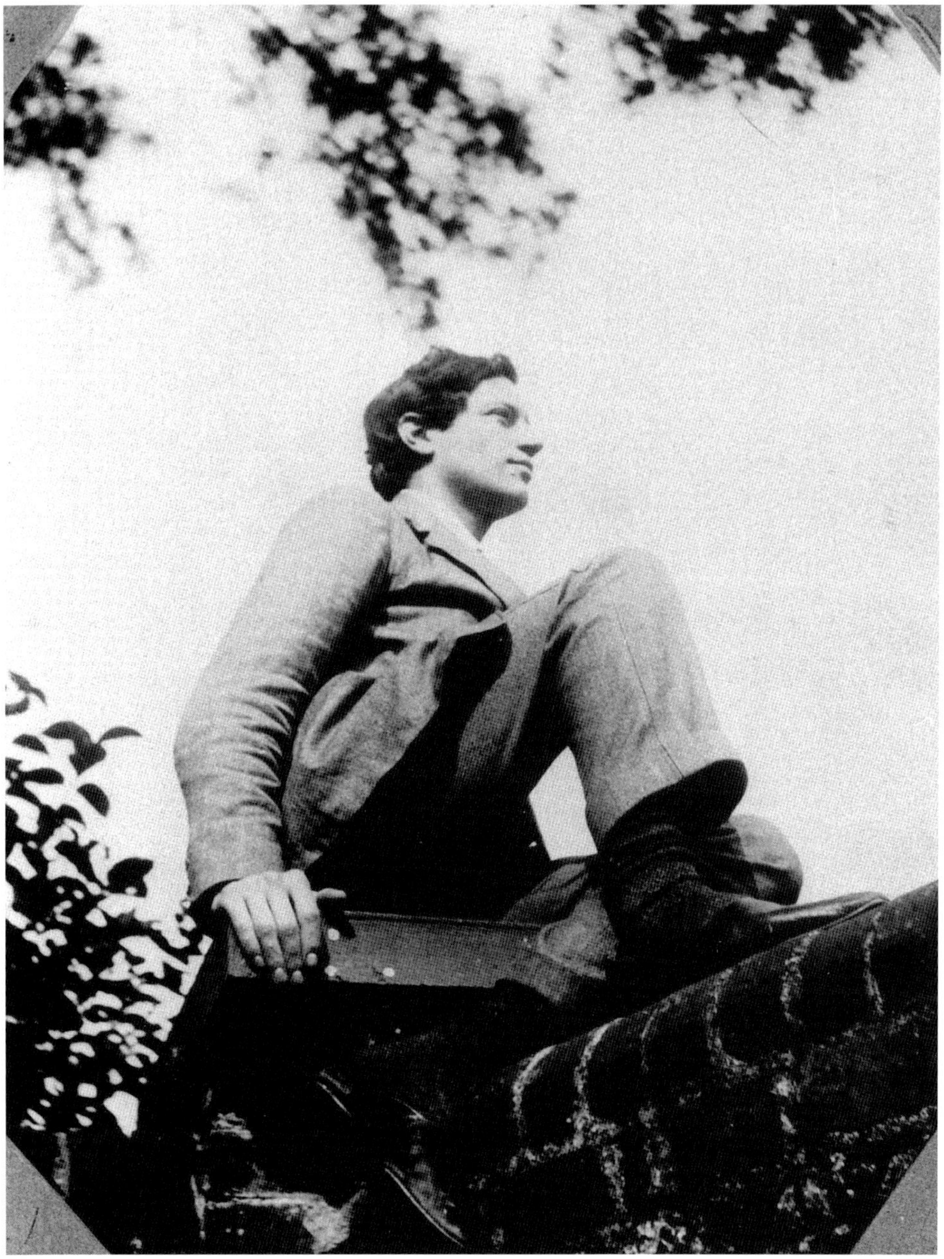

89. Duncan Grant, Asheham, 1912. Bell Album 2, p. 14 AG43. Copyright Tate, London, 2004. "I find that I am not now much impeded by working with Duncan, although of course I always think why didn't I see it like that?" (Bell in Shone, *Portraits,* 78 and 81).

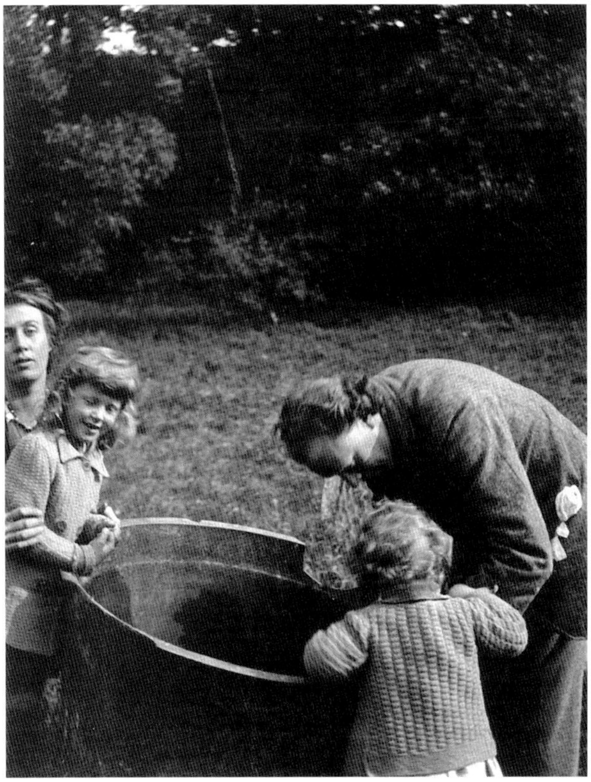 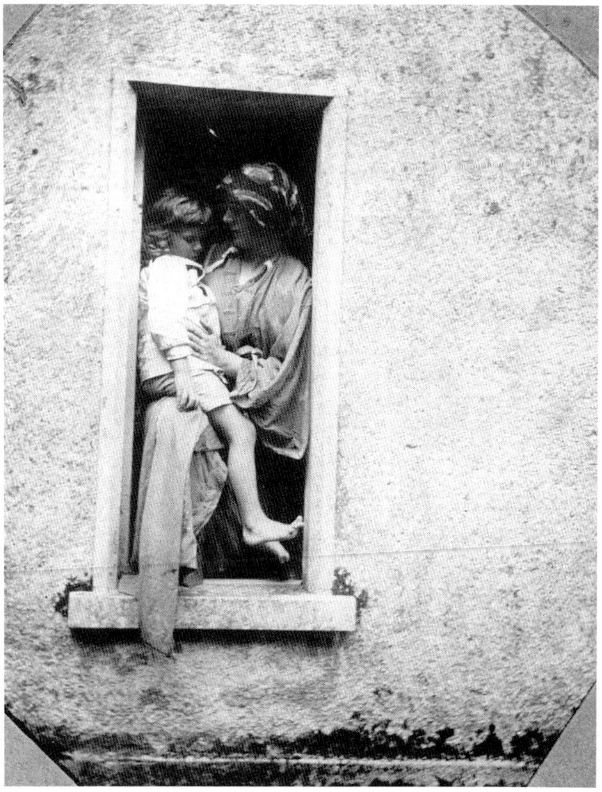

90. (LEFT) Vanessa, Julian, Clive, and Quentin Bell. Asheham, 1913. Bell Album 2, p. 24 X30.Copyright Tate, London, 2004. "The front lawn is used as a playground by the children and is not changed" (VB/L, 127).

91. (RIGHT) Vanessa and Julian Bell. Asheham, 1912. Bell Album 2, p. 15 AG44. Copyright Tate, London, 2004. "Vanessa was, I think, usually more beautiful than Virginia . . . Vanessa in her thirties had something of the physical splendour which Adonis must have seen when the goddess suddenly stood before him" (*BA*, 27).

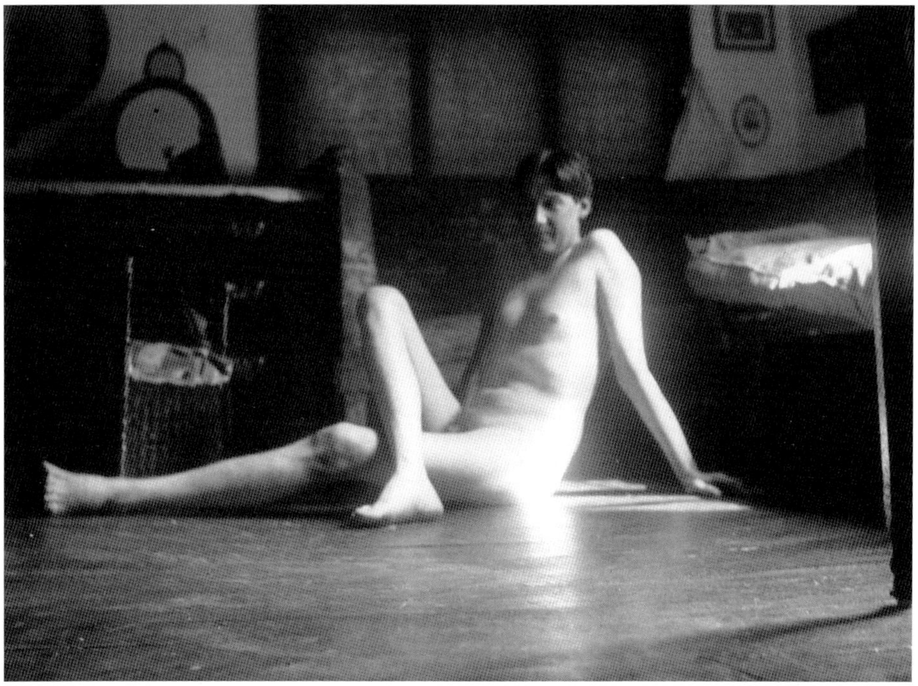

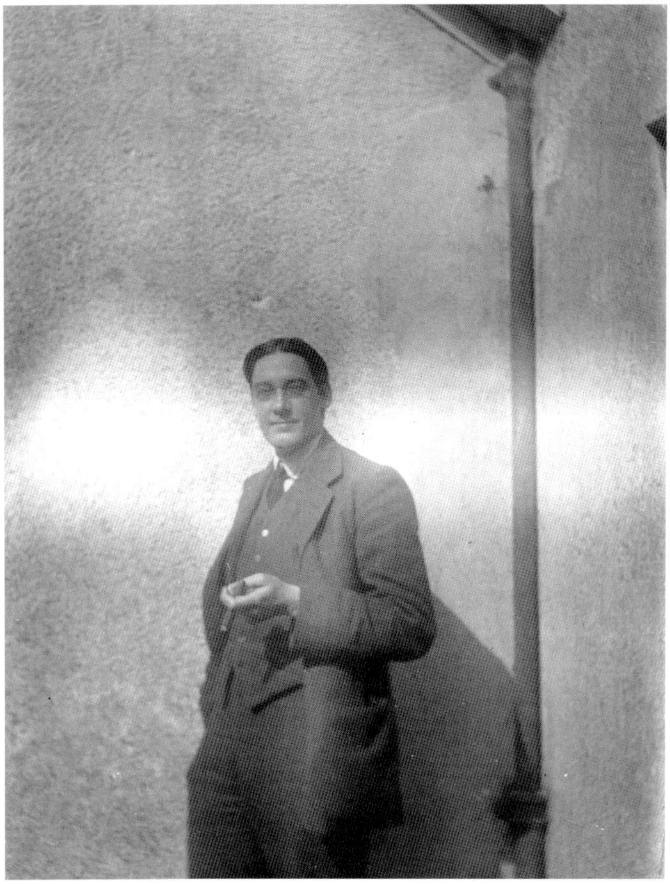

92. (ABOVE) Oliver Strachey, Asheham, 1912. Bell Album 2, p. 16 U19. Copyright Tate, London, 2004. "It is the most gorgeous September day . . . indoors with the windows shut sit Oliver Strachey and Norton in the thick of an aesthetic discussion" (VB/L, 127).

93. (LEFT) Oliver Strachey, Asheham, 1912. AD10. Copyright Tate, London, 2004.

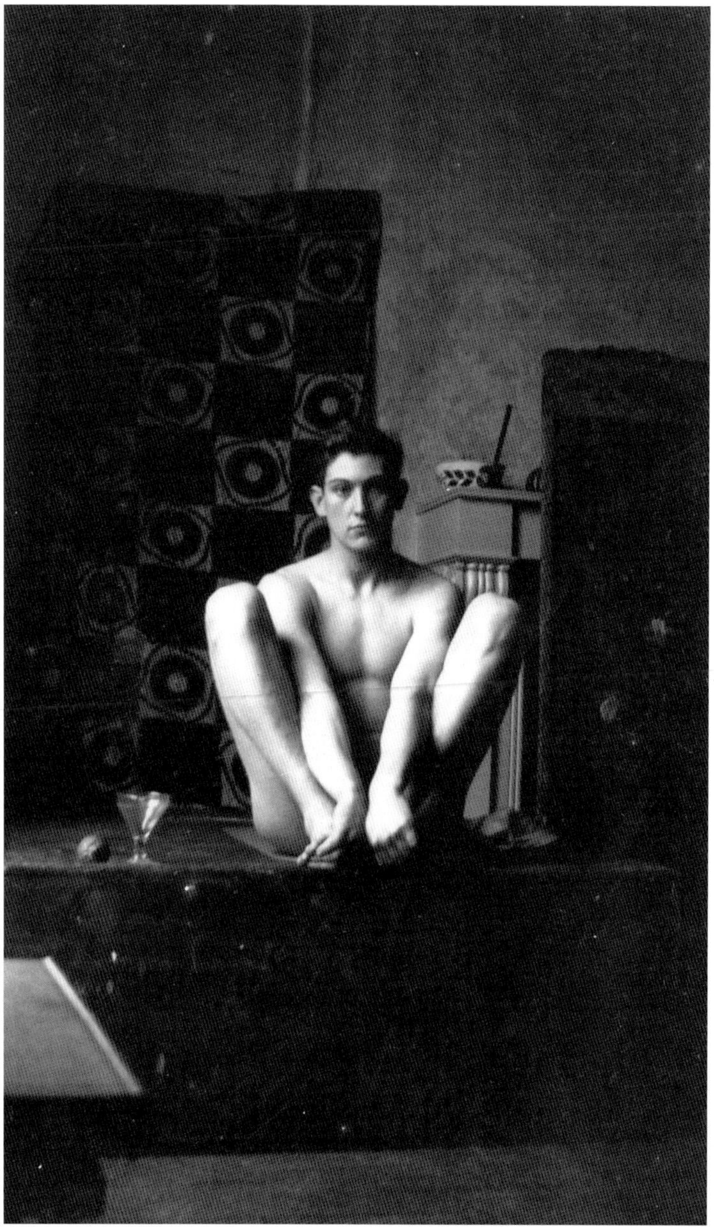

94. George Mallory, the Everest climber, 38 Brunswick Square, ca. 1912. AD12. Copyright Tate, London, 2004. "With good looks in the Botticelli style . . . with the build of an ideal athlete unspoilt by over development of any part" (Sir Geoffrey Keynes in Shone, *Portraits*, 256).

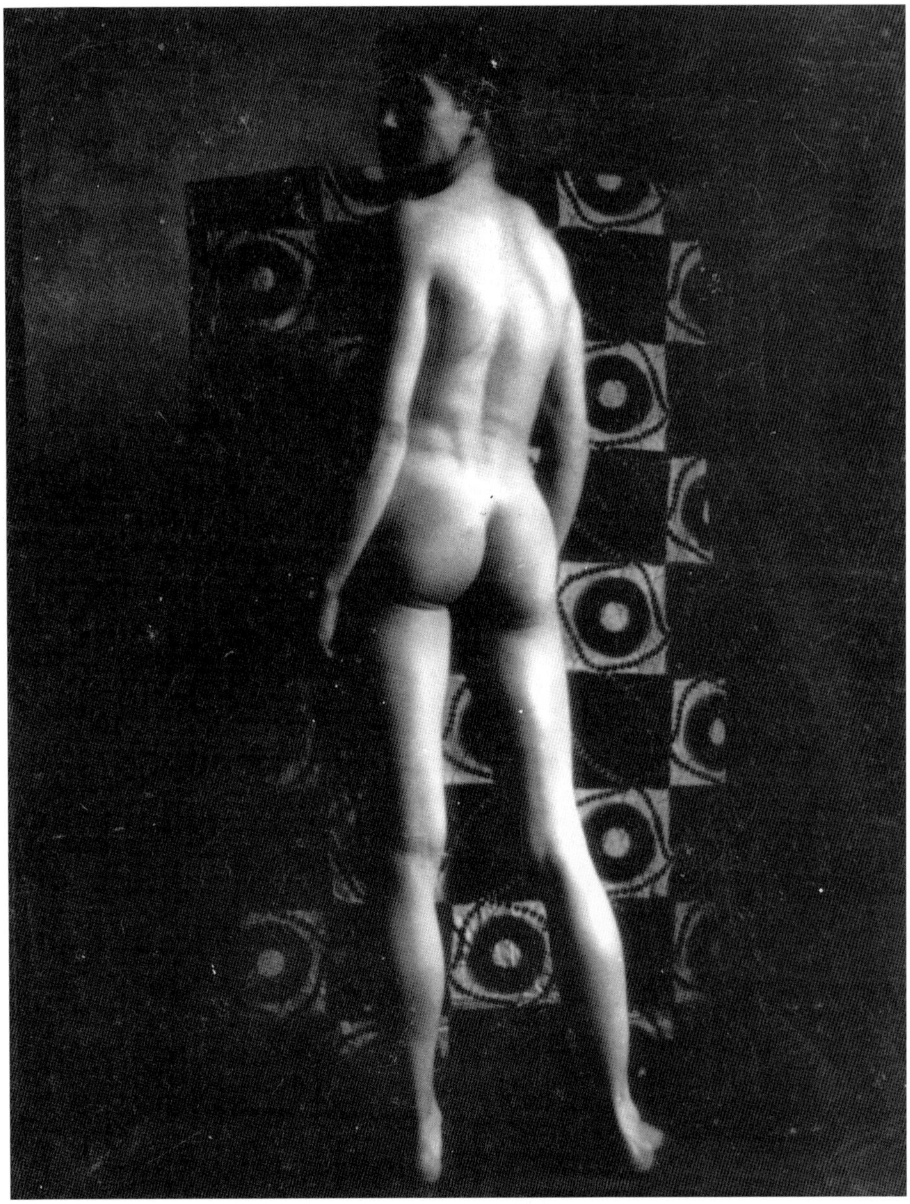

95. George Mallory, 38 Brunswick Square, ca. 1912 (Grant's portrait, *George Mallory*, NPG, is 1912). AD24. Copyright Tate, London, 2004.

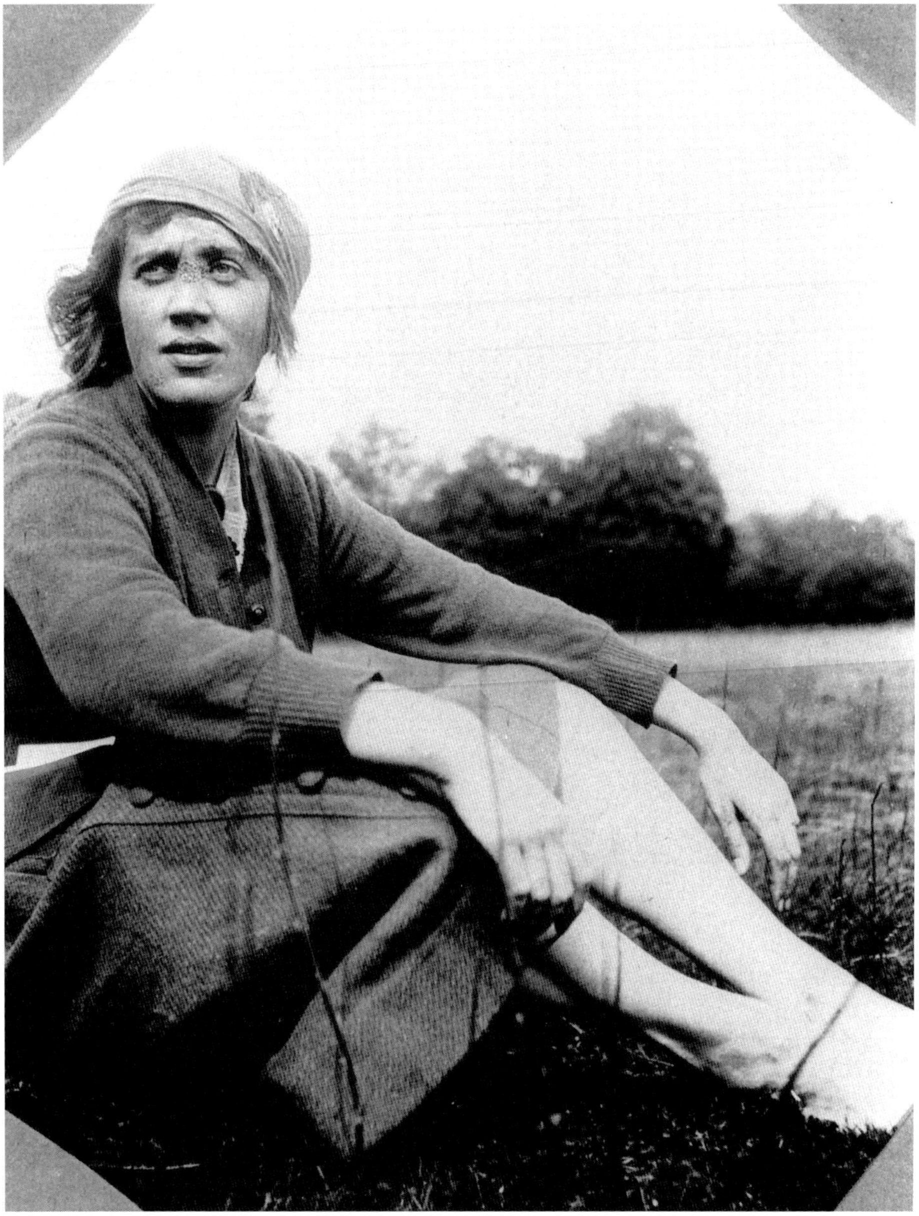

96. Vanessa Bell, Brandon Camp, August 1913. Bell Album 2, p. 30 AH7. Copyright Tate, London, 2004. "Today luckily has been lovely again . . . and I am sitting over the fire keeping watch on a wonderful stew R. [Roger Fry] has made with a chicken, bacon, potatoes, a touch of apple, mint, etc.!" (VB/L, 140).

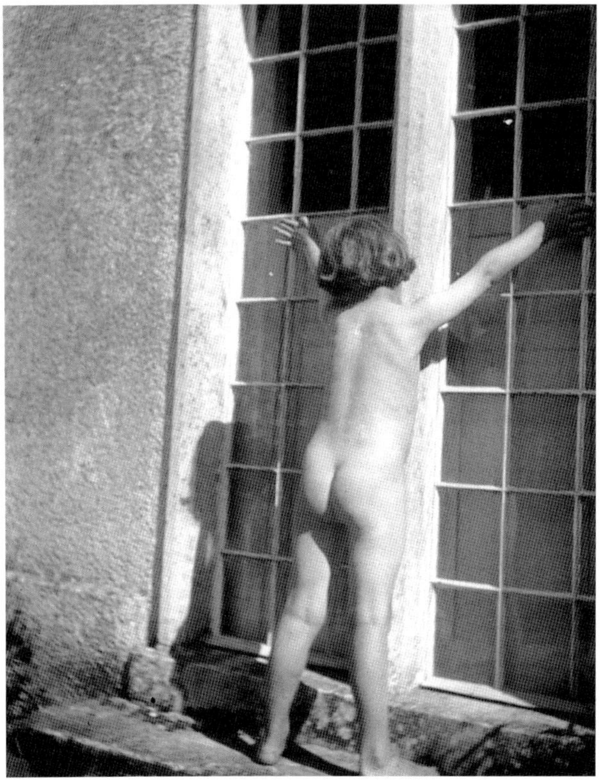

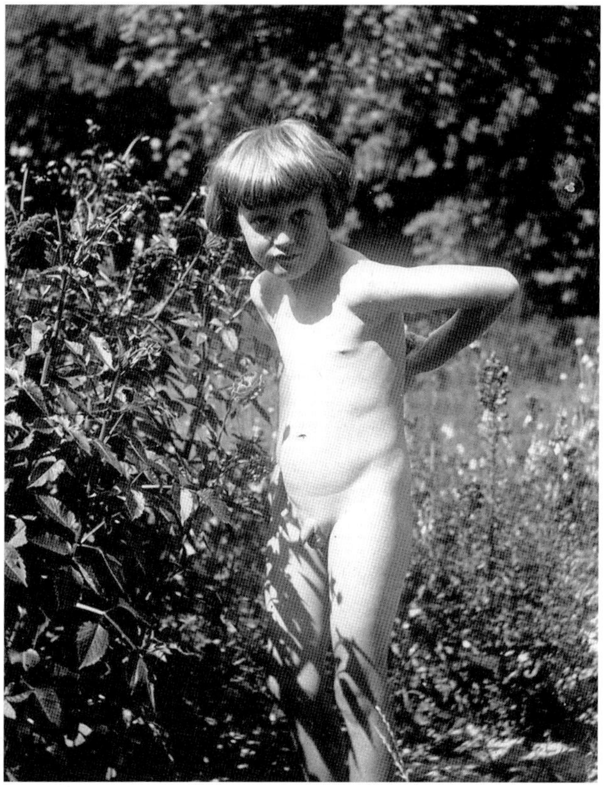

97. (LEFT) Julian Bell, Asheham, 1913. Bell Album 2, p. 37 H46. Copyright Tate, London, 2004. "I often look at a picture . . . without seeing in the least what the things are . . . I got quite a strong emotion from the forms and colours" (VB/L, 133).

98. (RIGHT) Julian Bell, Asheham, 1913. X42. Copyright Tate, London, 2004. "The children are very good and have games of their own most of the time" (VB/L, 234).

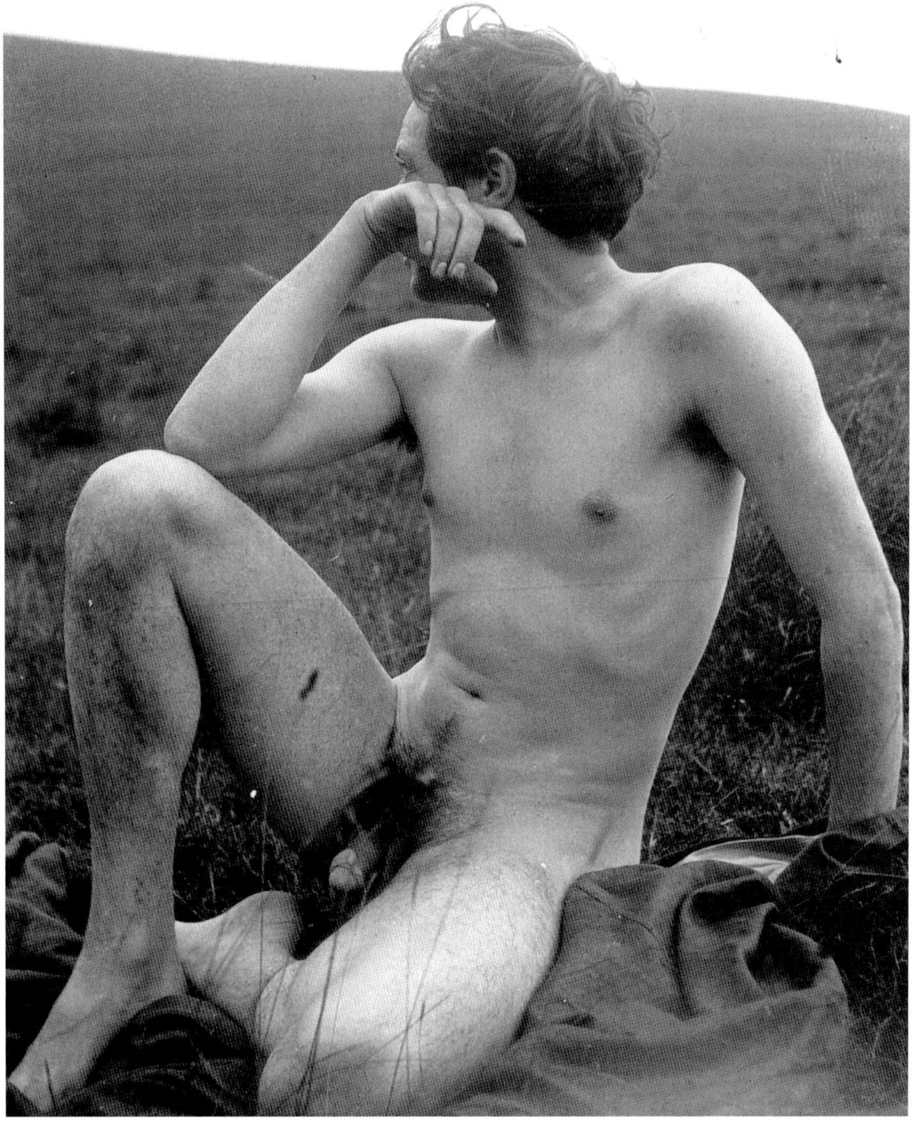

99. Duncan Grant, Asheham, ca. 1912–1914. AD11. Copyright Tate, London, 2004. "Duncan was deeply sensuous, his passions chiefly physical and uncomplicated, and, like Vanessa, he was without shame" (Spalding, *Bell*, 119).

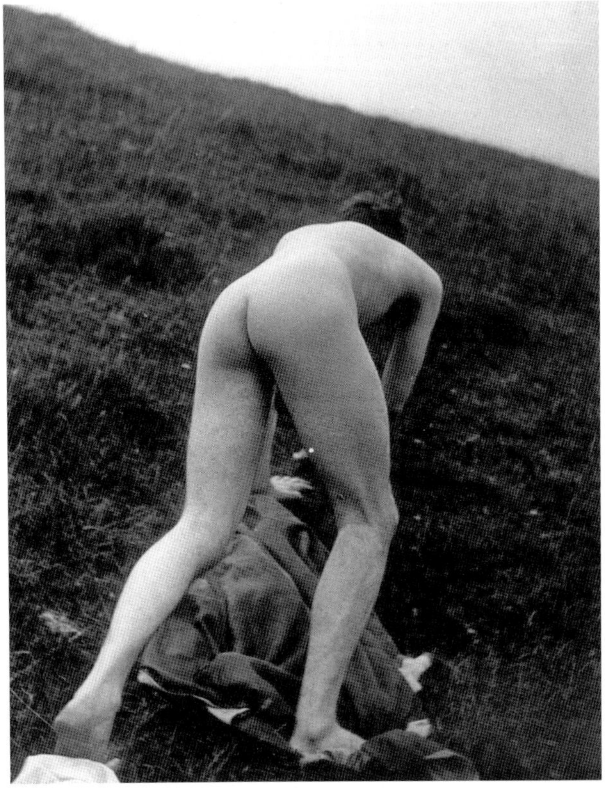

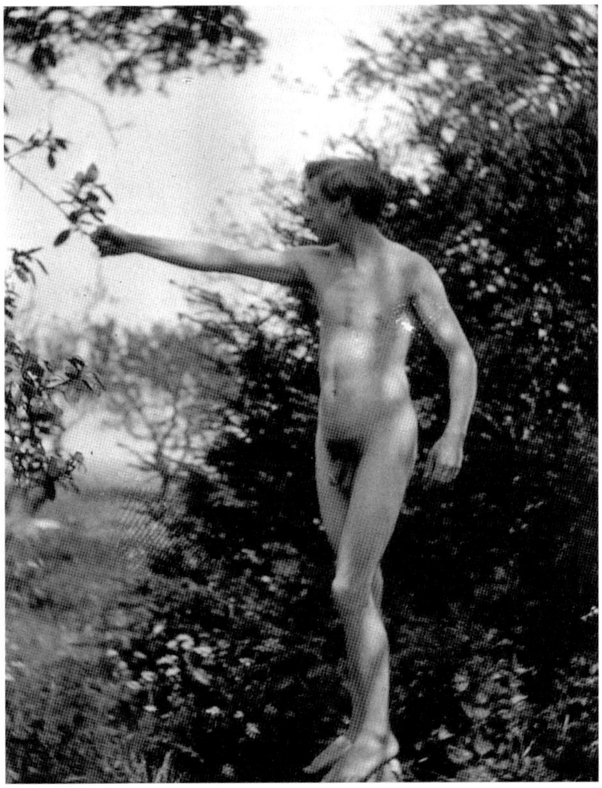

100. (LEFT) Duncan Grant, Asheham, ca. 1912–1914. AD18.
Copyright Tate, London, 2004.

101. (RIGHT) Duncan Grant, Charleston, ca. 1912–1914. H17.
Copyright Tate, London, 2004.

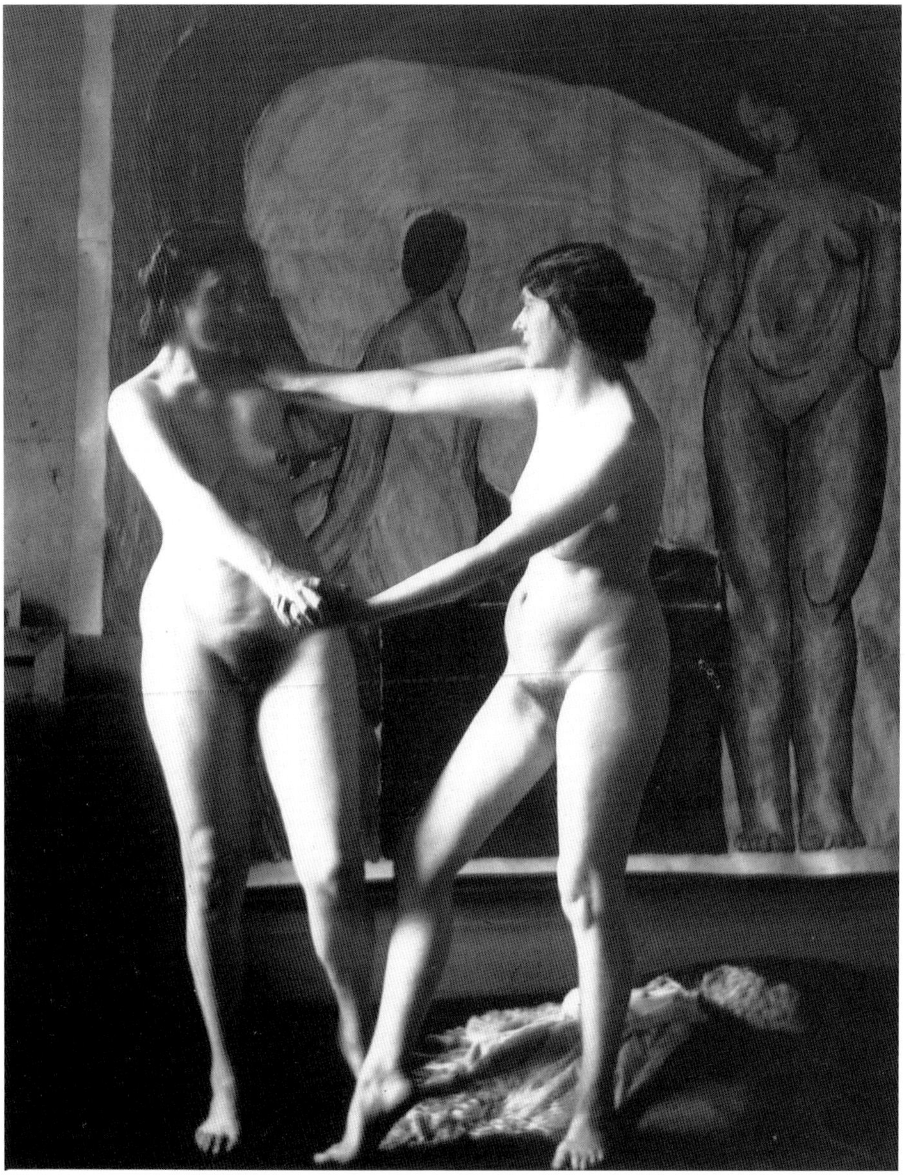

102. Vanessa Bell and Molly MacCarthy, 46 Gordon Square, 1913. AD27.
Copyright Tate, London, 2004. The rear painting is preparatory work for Bell's *Design for Overmantel* (1913); Bell's and MacCarthy's position is similar to that in Grant's *Dancers* (1912). "Grant was fascinated by the theme of a ring of dancers" (Turnbaugh, *Grant and Bloomsbury,* 121).

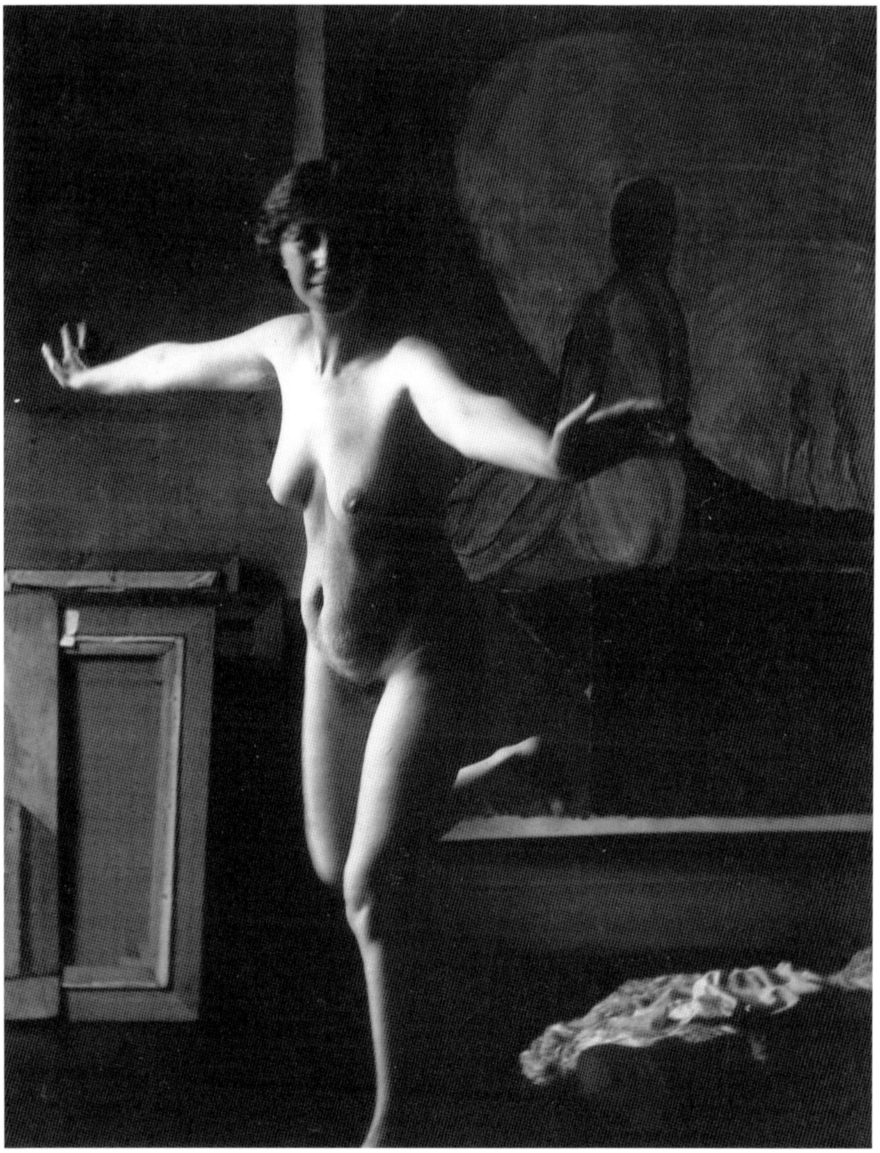

103. Molly MacCarthy, 46 Gordon Square, 1913. AD5. Copyright Tate, London, 2004.
"That devil Marjorie . . . the fact is she's so much afraid of saying the wrong thing if she says anything about Art that she has to invent" (VB/L, 153).

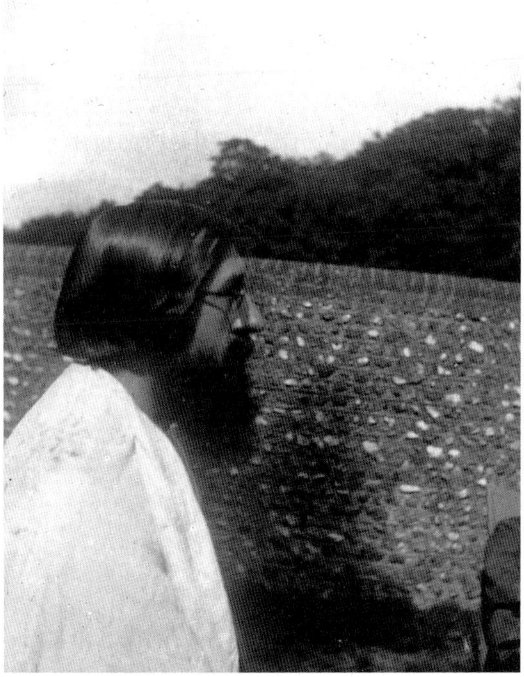

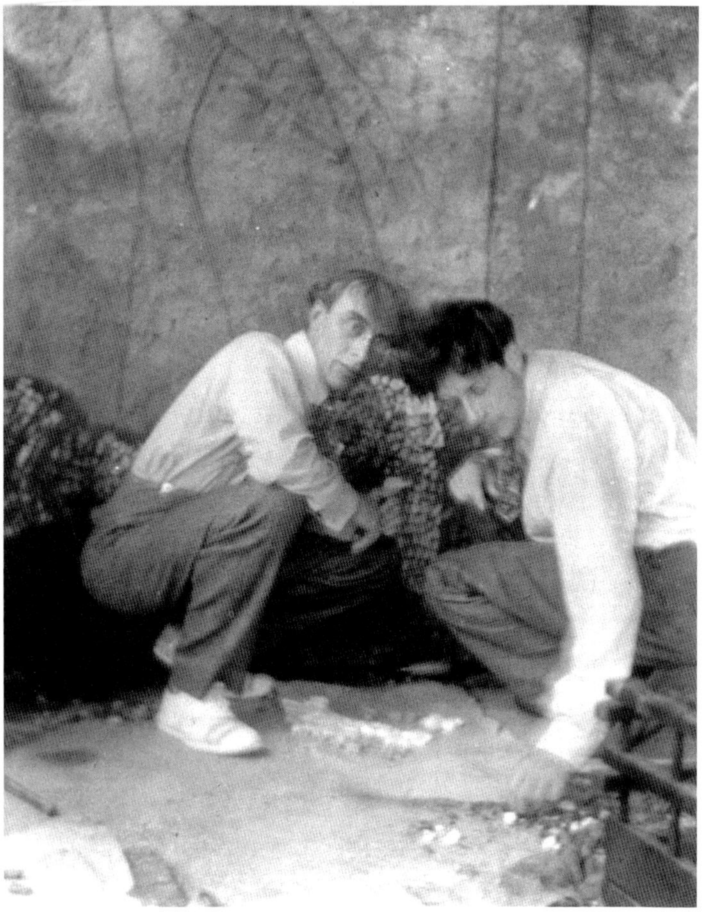

104. (TOP) Lytton Strachey, Asheham, 1913. Bell Album 3, p. 2 U30. Copyright Tate, London, 2004. "He [Lytton] was exotic, extreme in every way—Thoby described him—so long, so thin that his thigh was no thicker than Thoby's arm" (OB, 166).

105. (BOTTOM) Roger Fry and Duncan Grant, Durbins, April 1914, Q36. Copyright Tate, London, 2004. "In good weather they worked on a mosaic . . . its subject was a doubles match at badminton" (Reed, 46).

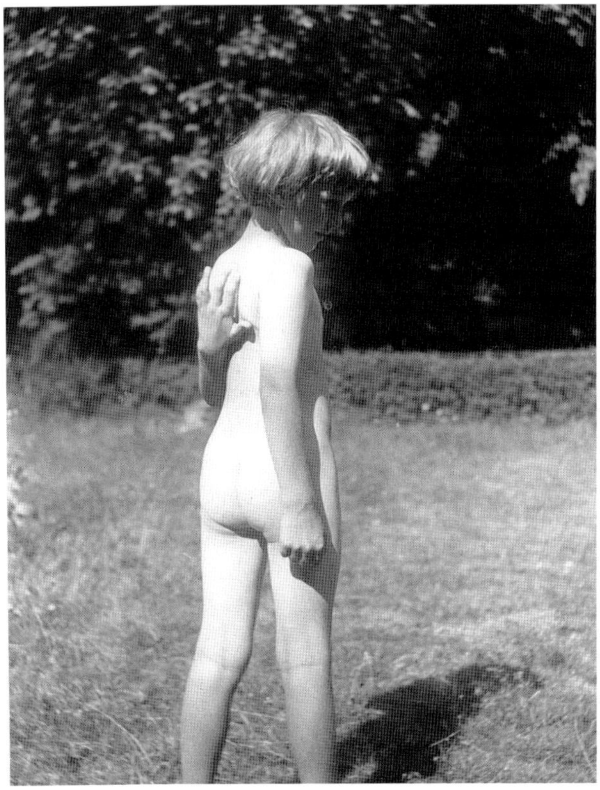

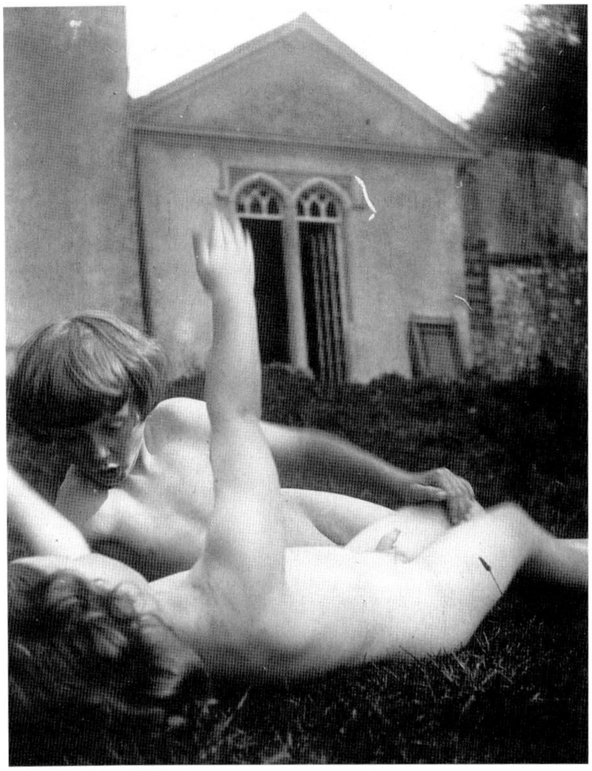

106. (TOP) Julian Bell, Asheham, 1914. Bell Album 3, p. 11 X40. Copyright Tate, London, 2004.

107. (BOTTOM) Quentin and Julian Bell, Asheham, 1914. Bell Album 3, p. 12 U16. Copyright Tate, London, 2004.

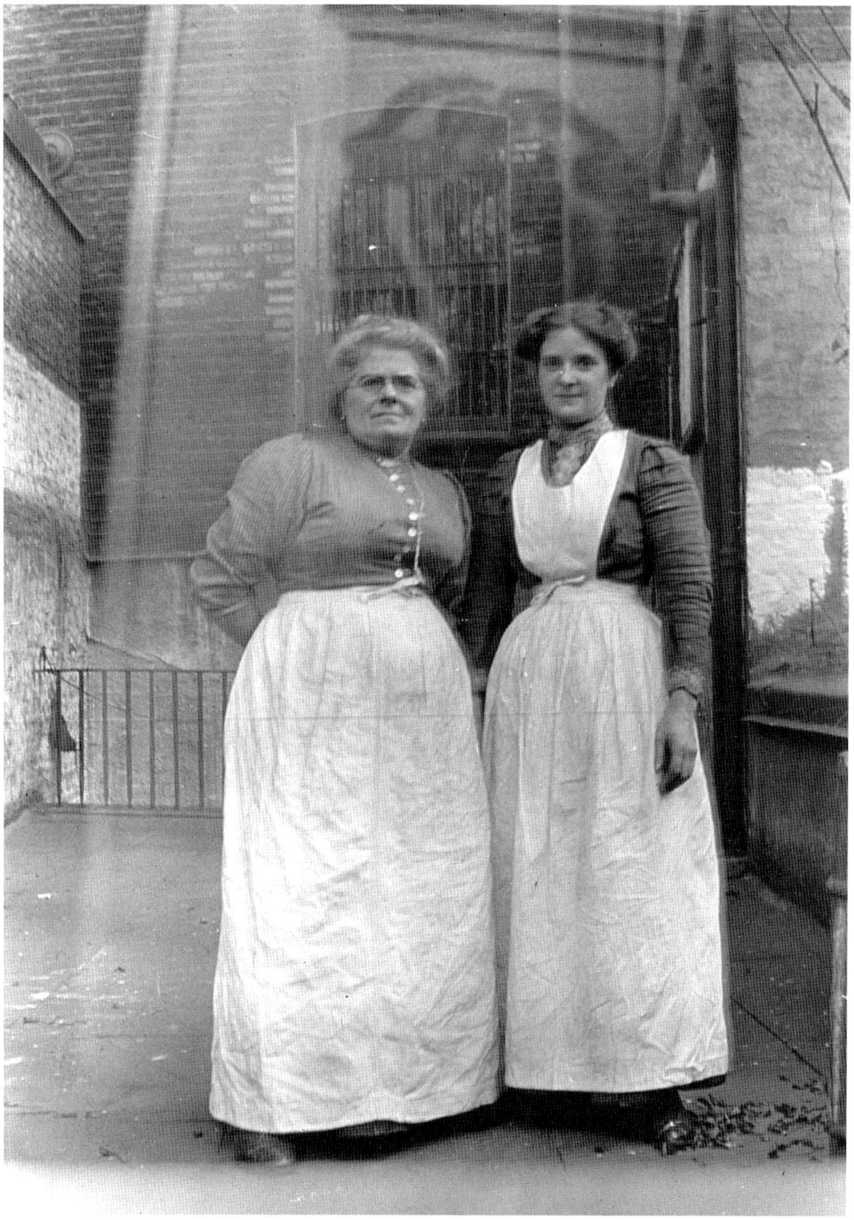

108. Sophie Farrell and Maud, 38 Brunswick Square, 1914. Bell Album 4, p. 1 G33. Copyright Tate, London, 2004. Duncan Grant's studio was at the rear; "[Matisse's] *Dance 1* was a model for the Brunswick Square mural" (Reed, 97). "A long talk with Sophy . . . she thinks you eat better when you are helped, and don't have to cut your own helpings . . . Miss Geenia doesn't like to be bothered with those things" (VB/L, 125–126).

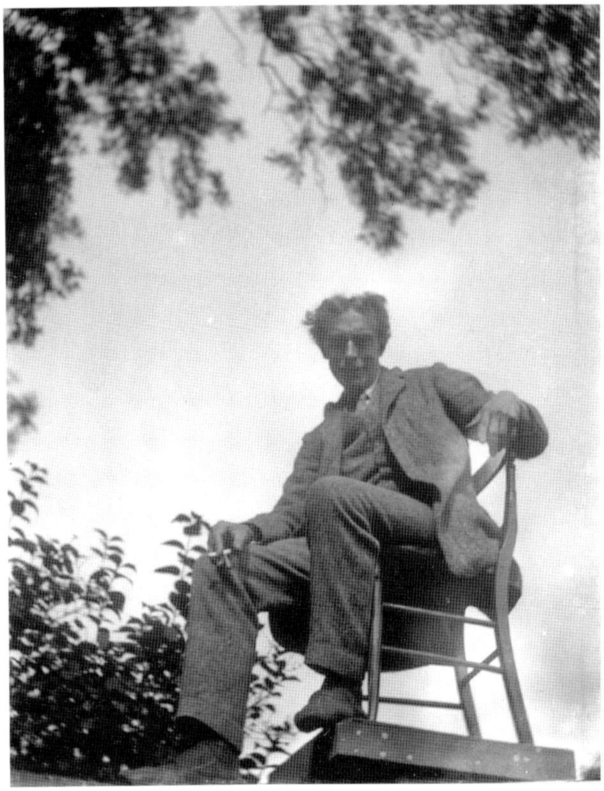

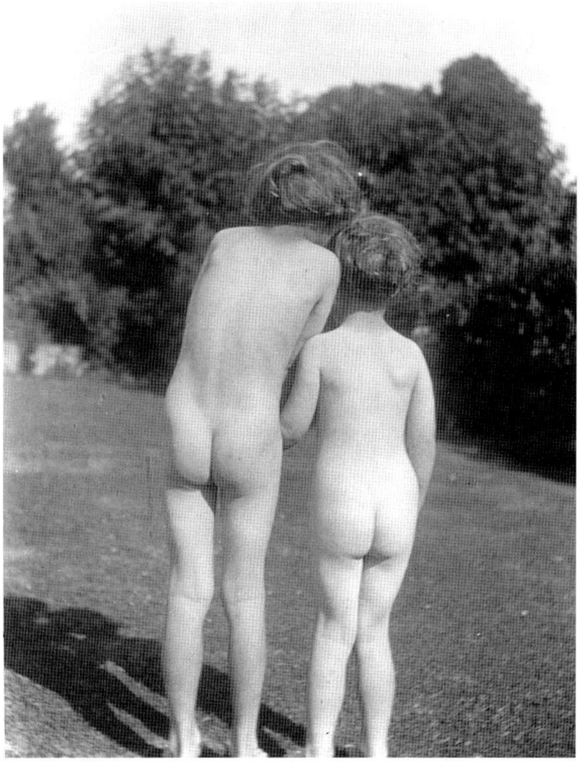

109. (LEFT) Roger Fry, Guilaford, 1914. Bell Album 3, p. 9 Q31. Copyright Tate, London, 2004. "There is too much in us both that the other really wants" (VB/L, 171).

110. (RIGHT) Julian and Quentin Bell, Bosham, ca. 1915. AB6. Copyright Tate, London, 2004. "I see a good deal of the children in a very nice and easy way" (VB/L, 188).

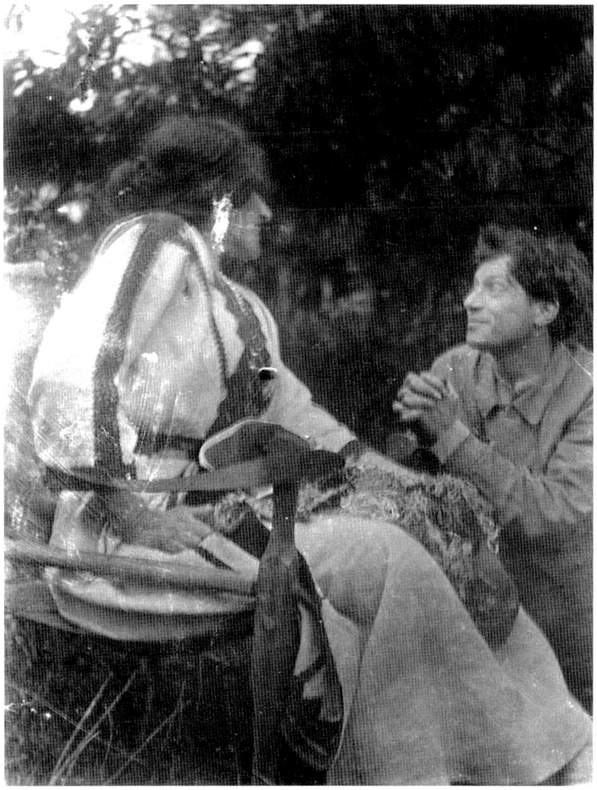

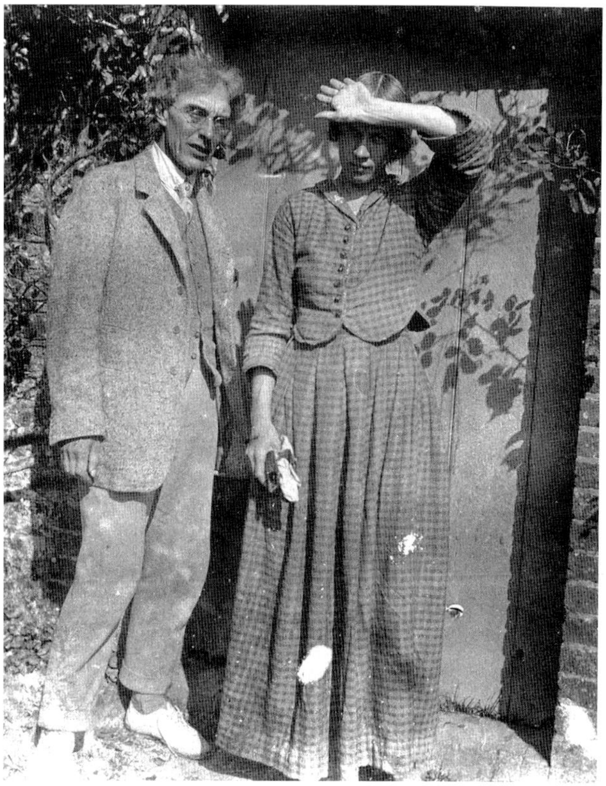

111. Ottoline Morrell and Duncan Grant, Wissett Lodge, August 1916. T42. Copyright Tate, London, 2004. "She [Ottoline] delighted in fairs and music halls and slapstick comedy" (David Cecil in Heilbrun, 10).

112. Roger Fry and Vanessa Bell, Charleston, ca. 1917. R7. Copyright Tate, London, 2004.

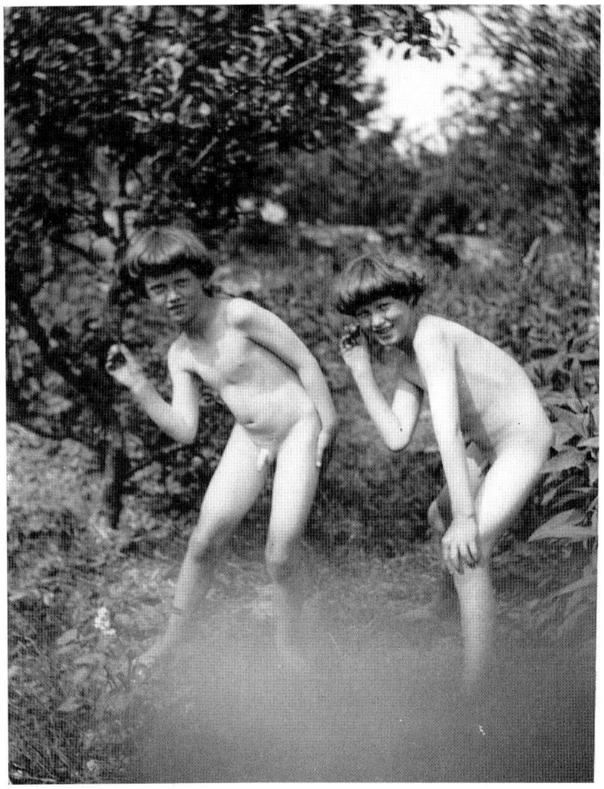

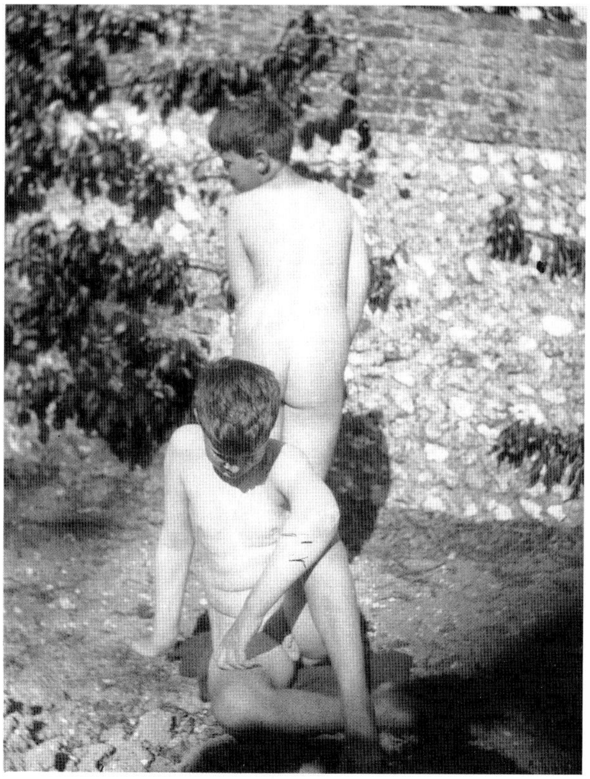

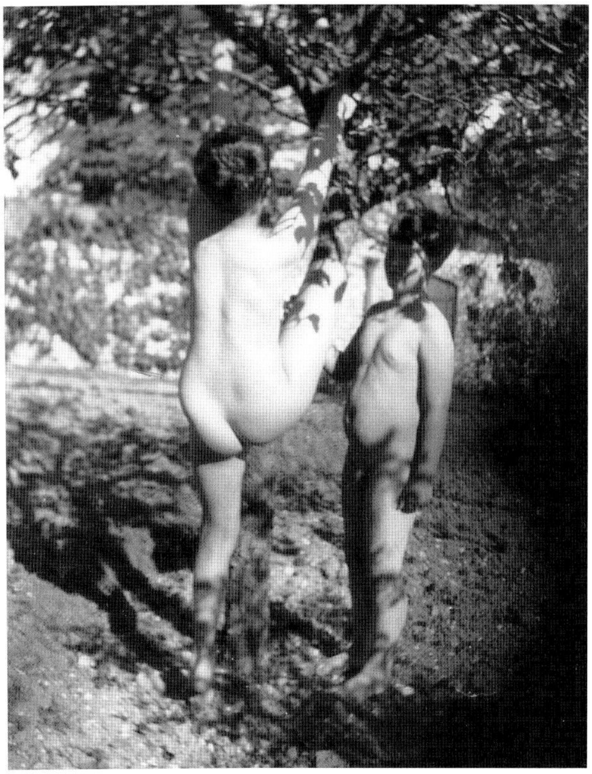

113. (TOP LEFT) Quentin and Julian Bell, Charleston, ca. 1919. H28. Copyright Tate, London, 2004.

114. (TOP RIGHT) Quentin and Julian Bell, Charleston, ca. 1921. Bell Album 4, p. 17 AB34. Copyright Tate, London, 2004. "Nessa presides over the most astonishing ménage; Belgian hares, governesses, children, gardeners, hens, ducks, and painting all the time" (*L*, 2:355).

115. (LEFT) Quentin and Julian Bell, Charleston, 1921. Bell Album 4, p. 18 AB10. Copyright Tate, London, 2004. "A branch blew down off Allison's tree . . . the children of the cottages collect every morning & swing . . . I suppose Julian & Quentin would soon be tired of it" (*D*, 2:129).

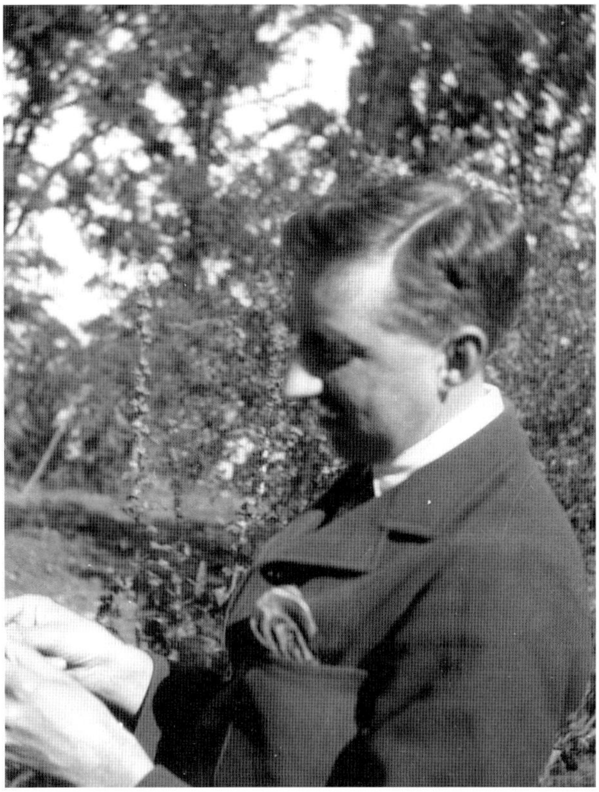

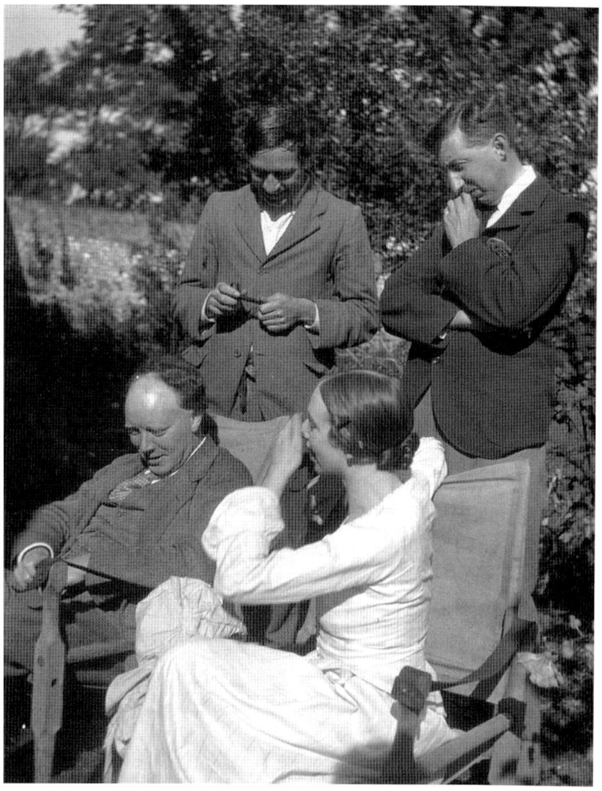

116. (LEFT) E. M. Forster, Charleston, 1923. Bell Album 4, p. 31 B37. Copyright Tate, London, 2004. "We all grow old; grow stocky . . . even Morgan seems to me to be based on some hidden rock. Talking of Proust & Lawrence he said he'd prefer to be Lawrence; but much rather would be himself" (*D*, 2:269).

117. (RIGHT) *Standing*: Duncan Grant, E. M. Forster; *sitting*: Clive Bell, Mary Hutchinson. Charleston, 1923. Bell Album 4, p. 32 A26. Copyright Tate, London, 2004. "Mary . . . a person of singularly little originative power and rather irritates me by being so self-conscious to her finger tips of what every fraction of herself is doing and looking" (VB/L, 280).

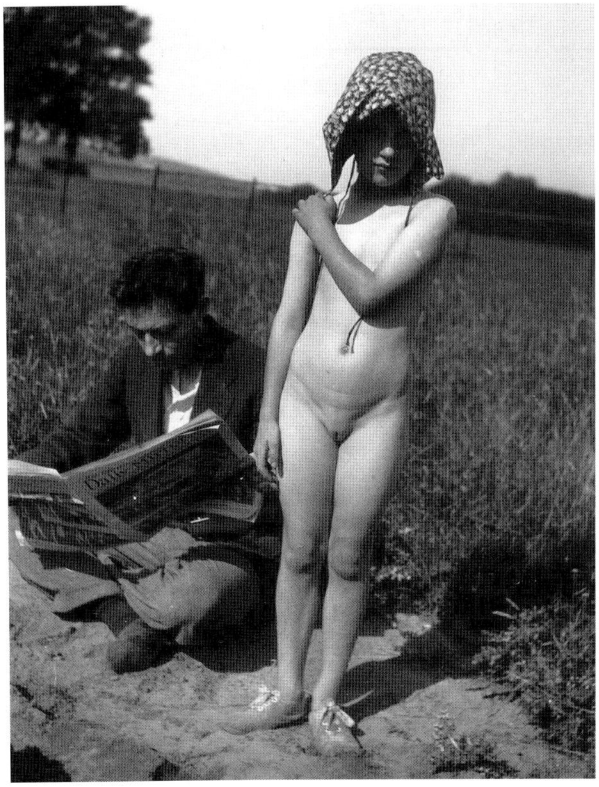

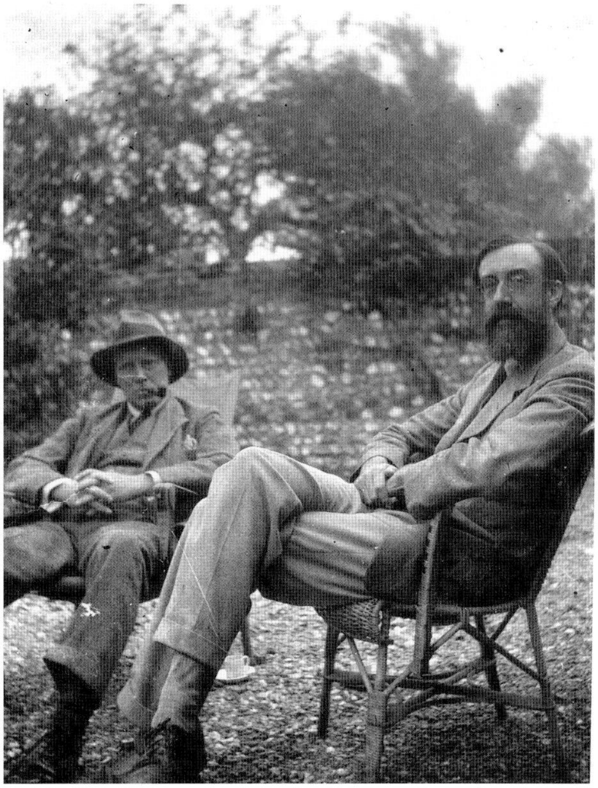

118. (LEFT) Duncan Grant and Angelica Bell. Charleston, ca. 1925. Bell Album 4, p. 51 S34. Copyright Tate, London, 2004. "The *Daily Mirror*, the paper at which Vanessa most often glanced" (Spalding, *Bell*, 140).

119. (RIGHT) Clive Bell and Lytton Strachey. Charleston, 1926. Bell Album 4, p. 61 B6. Copyright Tate, London, 2004.

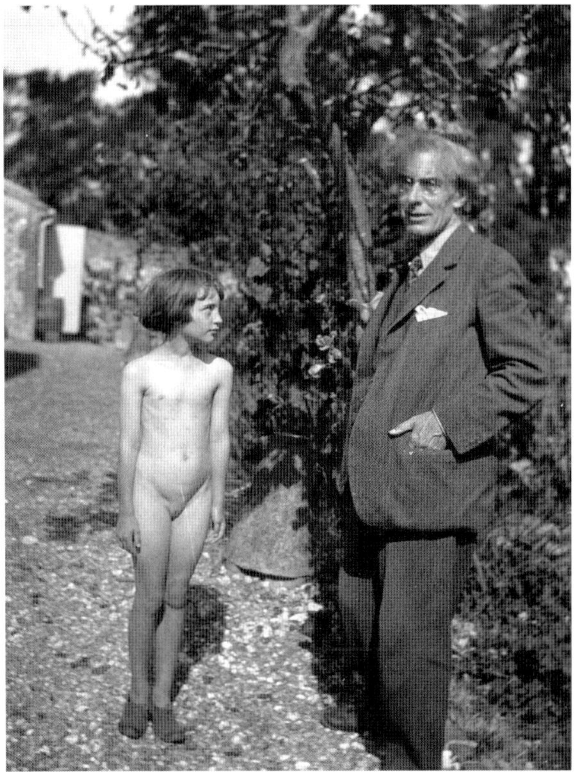

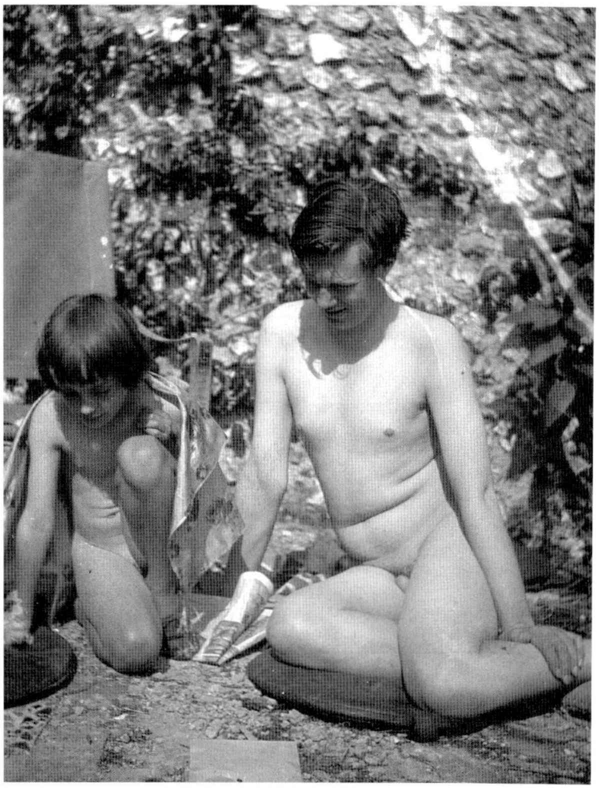

120. (LEFT) Angelica Bell and Roger Fry. Charleston, 1926. Bell Album 4, p. 57 Q47. Copyright Tate, London, 2004. "It really is an almost ideal family based as it is on adultery and mutual forbearance with Clive the deceived husband and me the abandoned lover" (Fry in Spalding, *Bell*, 210).

121. (RIGHT) Angelica and Julian Bell, Charleston, August 1926. C35. Copyright Tate, London, 2004. "The summer dominated by a feeling of washing in boundless warm fresh air—such an August not come my way for years" (*D*, 3: 106).

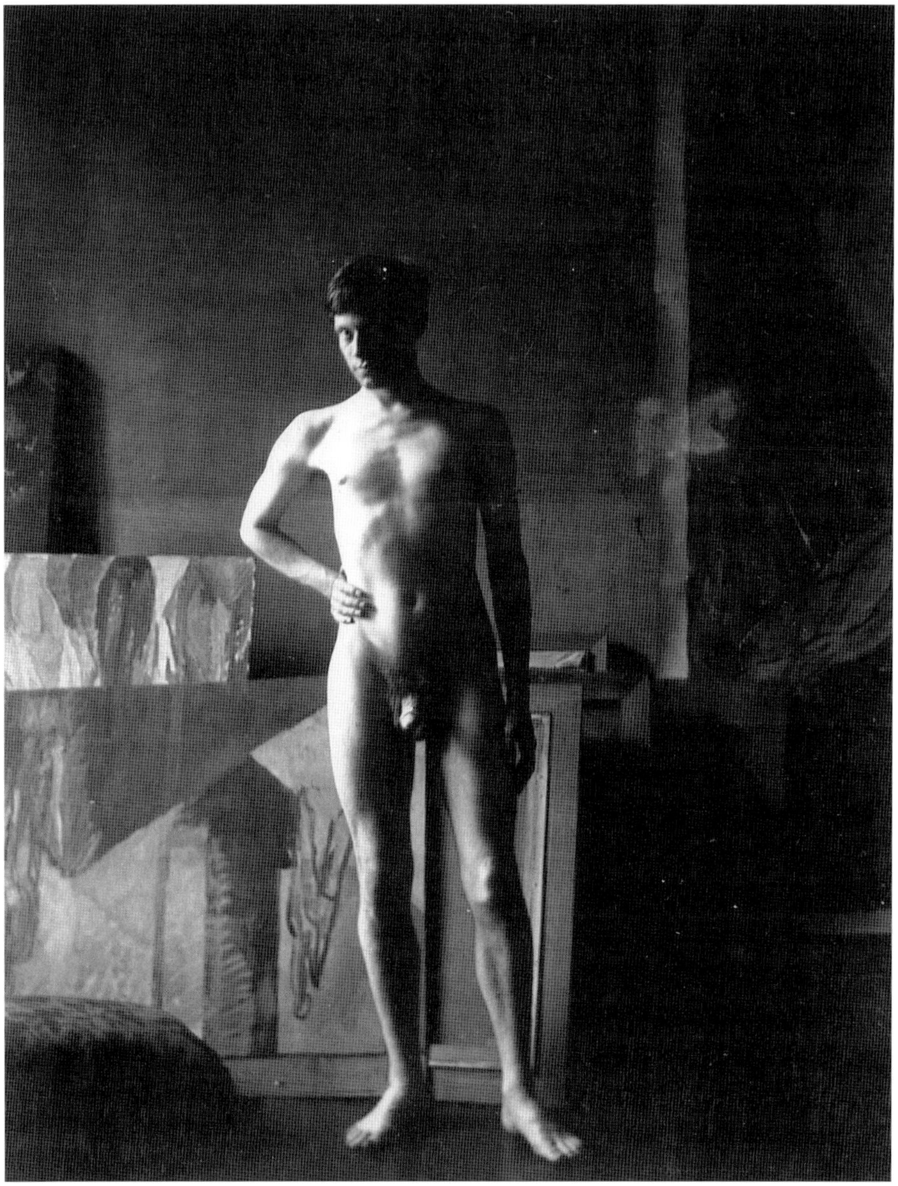

122. Figure and date unknown, 46 Gordon Square. AD6. Copyright Tate, London, 2004. The stance resembles Duncan Grant's *Male Nude* (1920s) and a figure in *The Bathers* (1927).

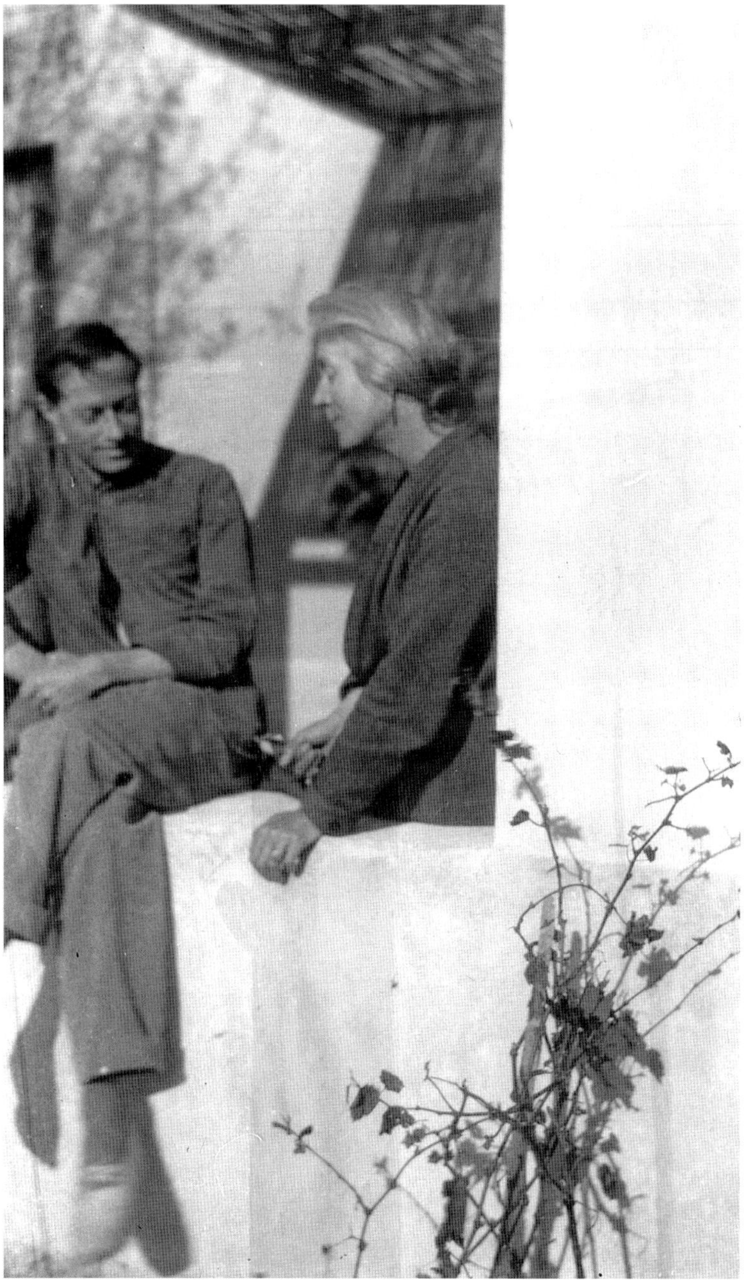

123. Duncan Grant and Vanessa Bell. La Bergère, Cassis, 1928. Q39.
Copyright Tate, London, 2004. "It is incredibly beautiful here now and so hot that one is very glad of shade to sit in. The verandah has been roofed in with canes" (VB/L, 337).

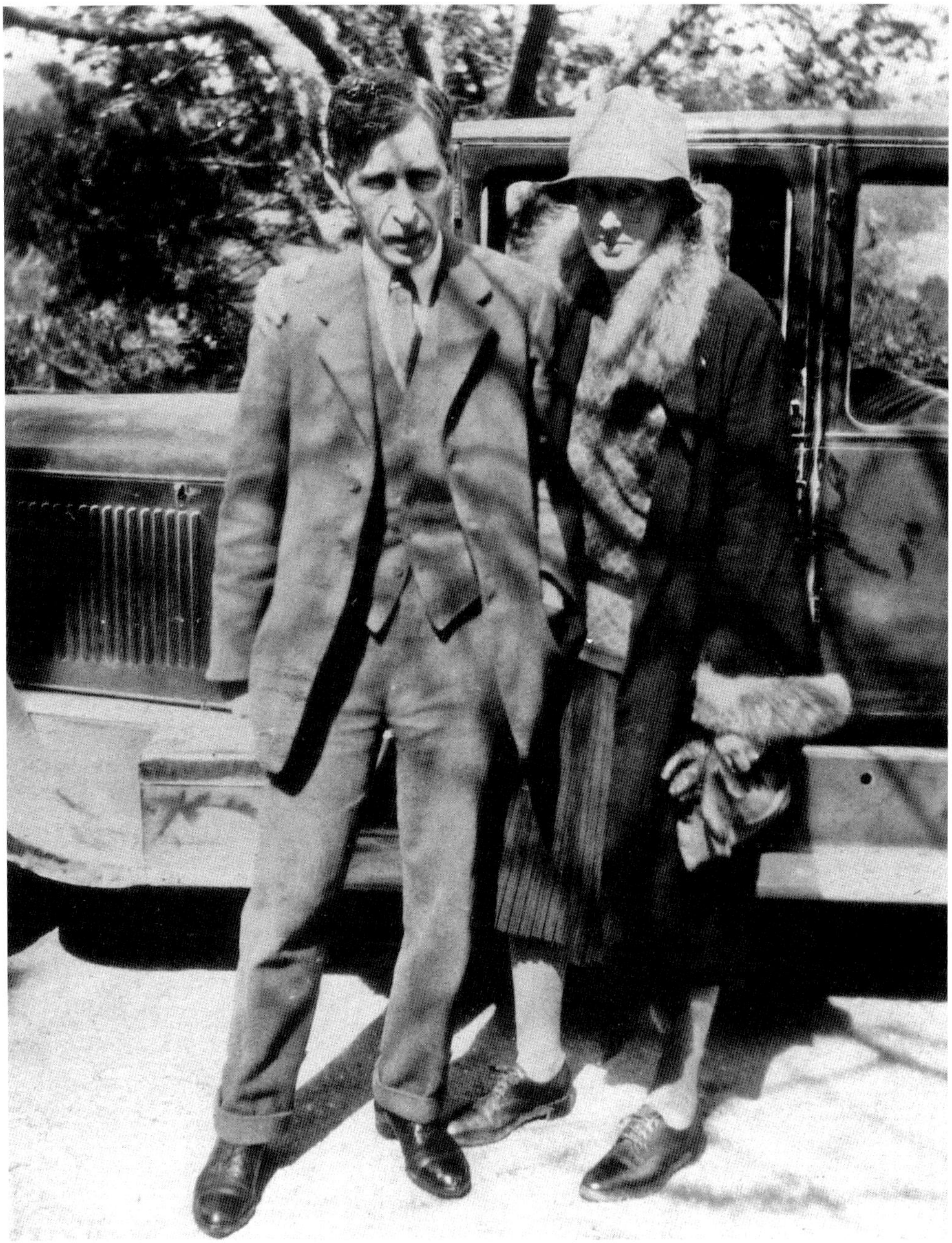

124. Leonard and Virginia Woolf and Singer car. Cassis, 1928. Bell Album 5, p. 5 AH35. Copyright Tate, London, 2004. "We are motoring to Cassis through France at the end of March. The old umbrella [the Singer] is absolutely sublime. . . . Nessa sends me astonishingly indecent details about the Renault. It cant go, she says, because its hermaphrodite" (*L*, 3:464).

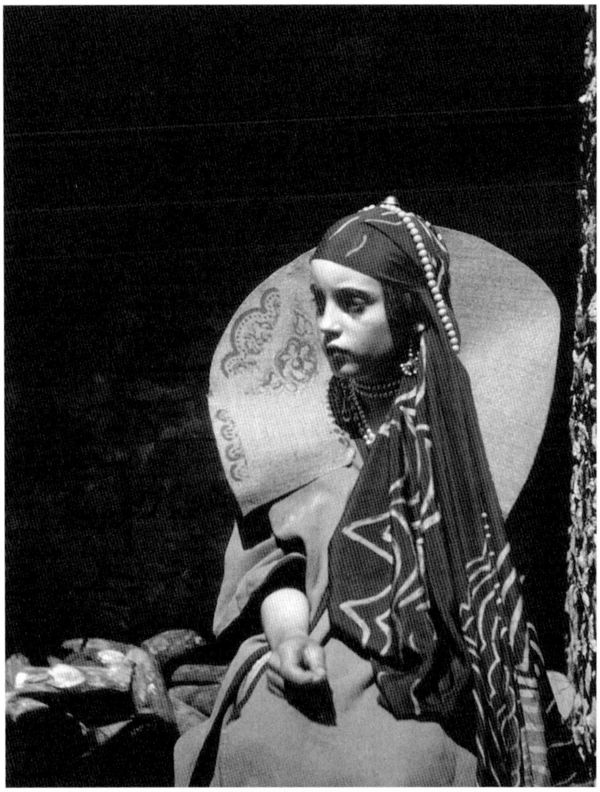

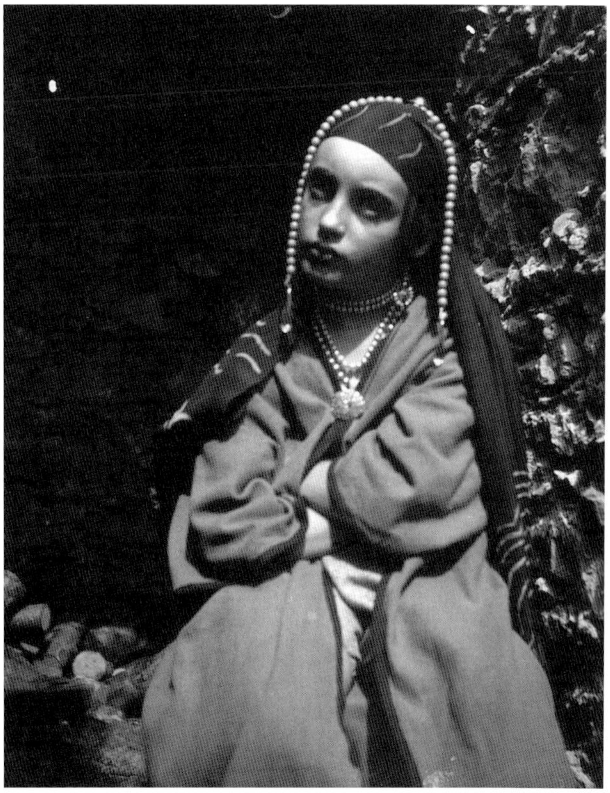

125. (LEFT) Angelica Bell, Cassis, 1928. Bell Album 5, p. 15 AA16. Copyright Tate, London, 2004. Posing for *Orlando* photographs.

126. (RIGHT) Angelica Bell, Cassis, 1928. Bell Album 5, p. 15 AA20. Copyright Tate, London, 2004. "The photographs are most lovely . . . I'm showing them to Vita, who doesn't want to be accused of raping the under age. My God—I shall rape Angelica one of these days" (*L*, 3:497).

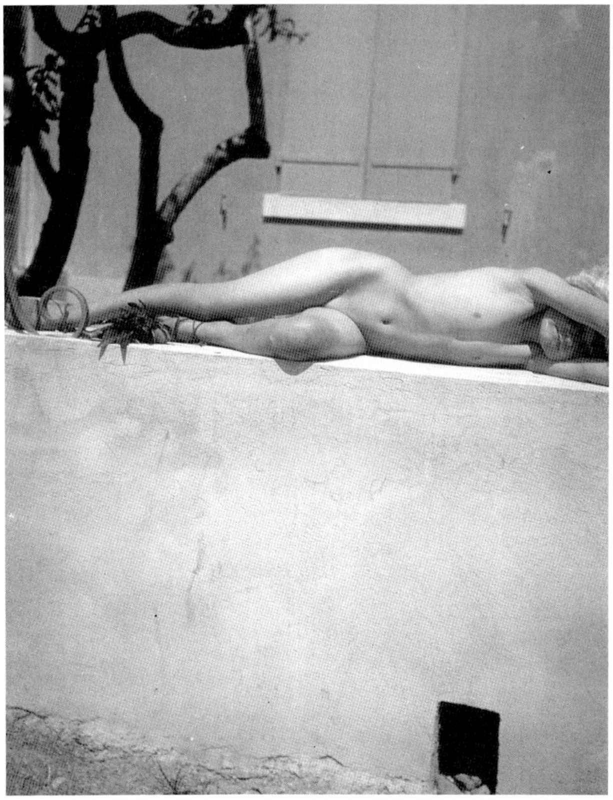

127. (LEFT) Judith Bagenal, Cassis, 1928. Bell Album 5, p. 6 I24. Copyright Tate, London, 2004. "Judith, impervious to all variety of treatment, or so one hopes" (VB/*L*, 333).

128. (BELOW) Francis Birrell, Quentin, Clive, and Julian Bell, Angus Davidson, Angelica Bell, Virginia and Leonard Woolf, and Richard Kennedy. Picnic at High and Over, 1928. Bell Album 5, p. 10 G25. Copyright Tate, London, 2004.

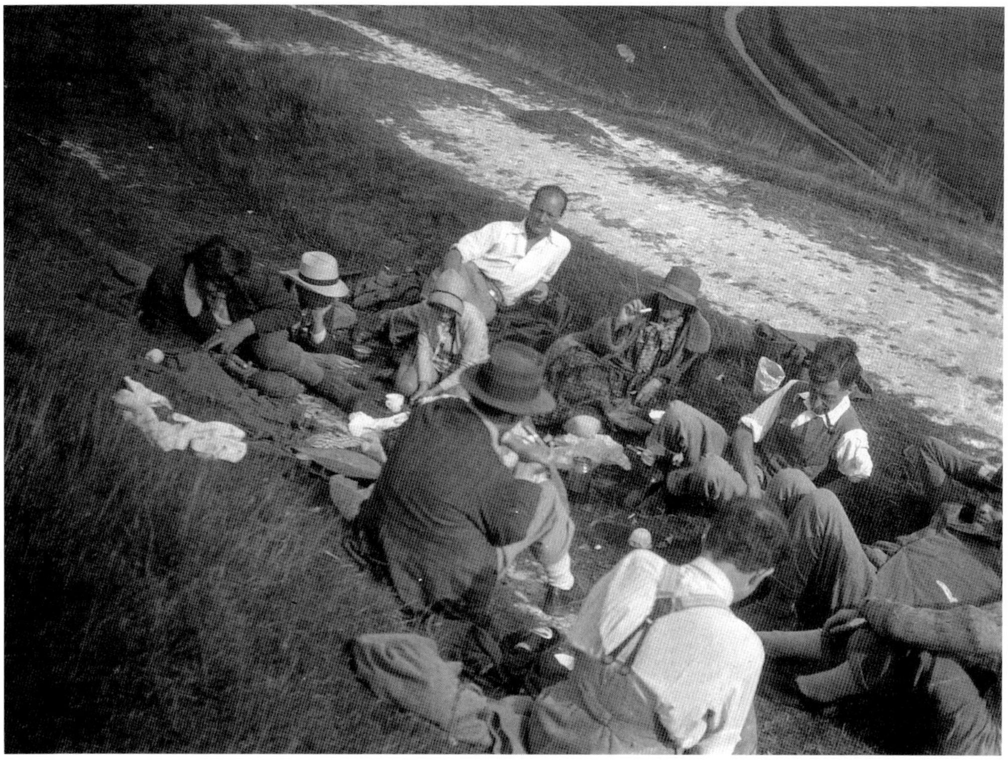

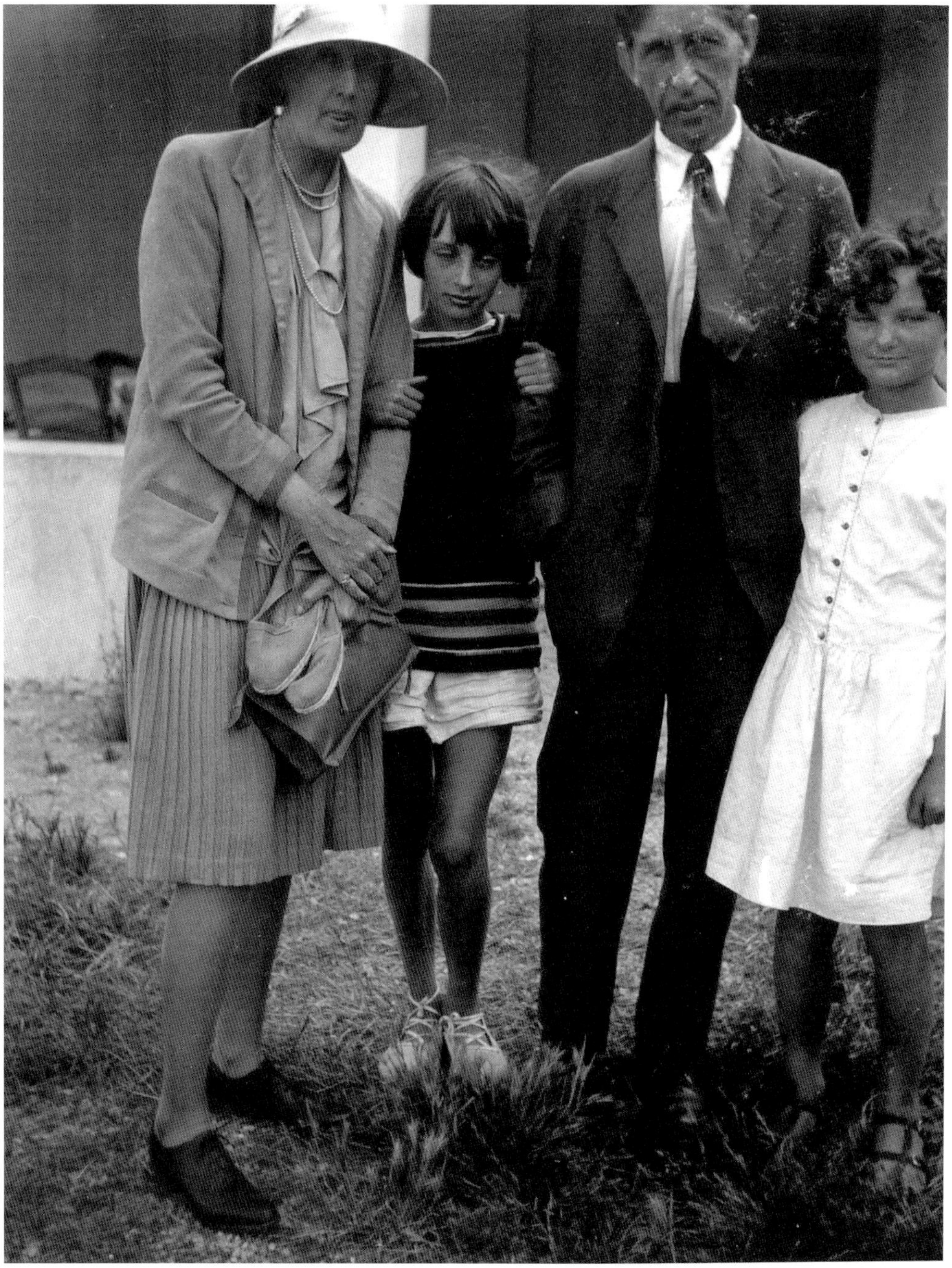

129. Virginia Woolf, Angelica Bell, Leonard Woolf, and Judith Bagenal.
La Bergère, Cassis, 1929. Bell Album 5, p. 19 B32. Copyright Tate, London, 2004. "Nessa's villa is five minutes off, and Leonard and I live up here, on a verandah, and go to her for meals—a delicious life, with a great deal of wine, cheap cigars, conversation" (*L*, 4:65).

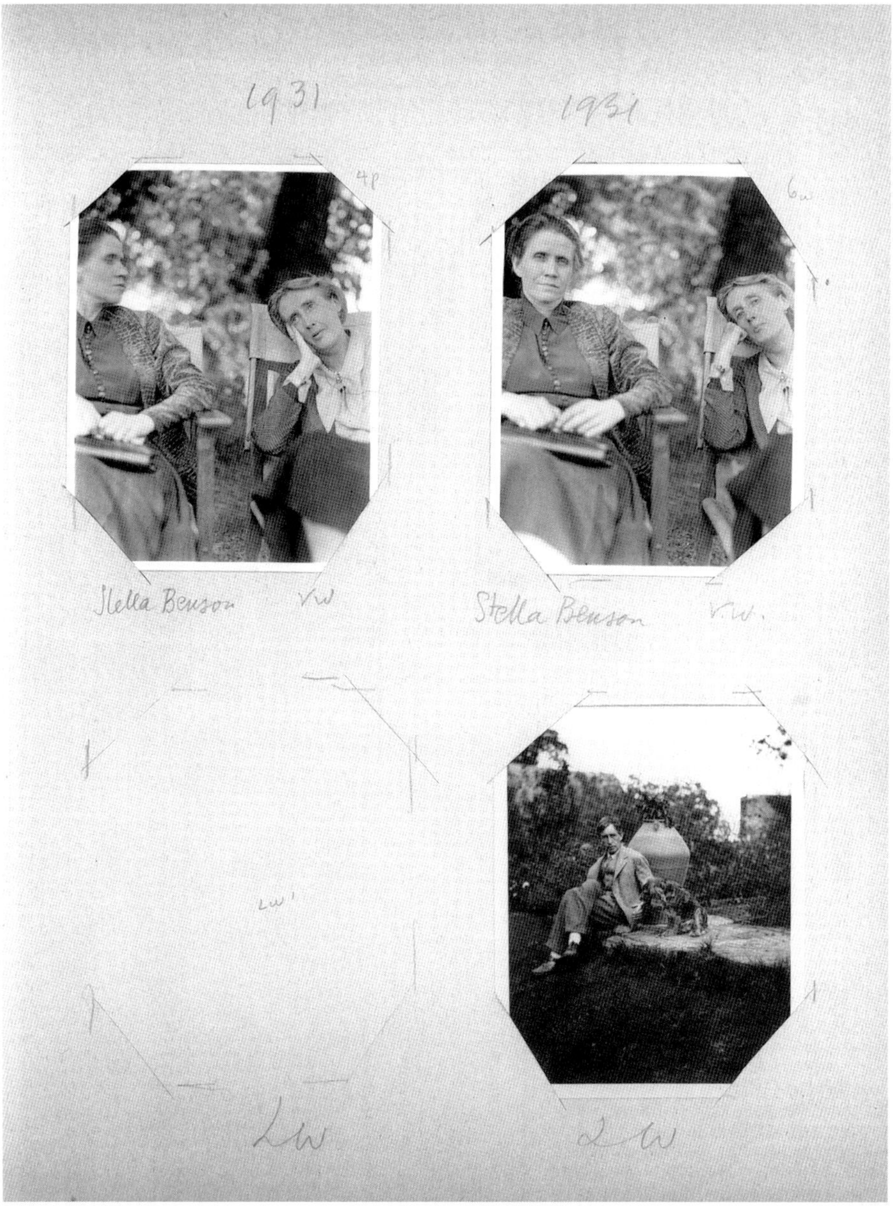

130. Virginia Woolf and Stella Benson, 1931–1932; Leonard Woolf. 1931. Monk's House Album 3, p. 48. Reprinted by permission of the Harvard Theatre Collection, the Houghton Library. "Stella Benson . . . she is a nice woman —bleached like a skull . . . on the other hand I like her very much, and am going, after 20 years to begin to read" (*L*, 5:101–102).

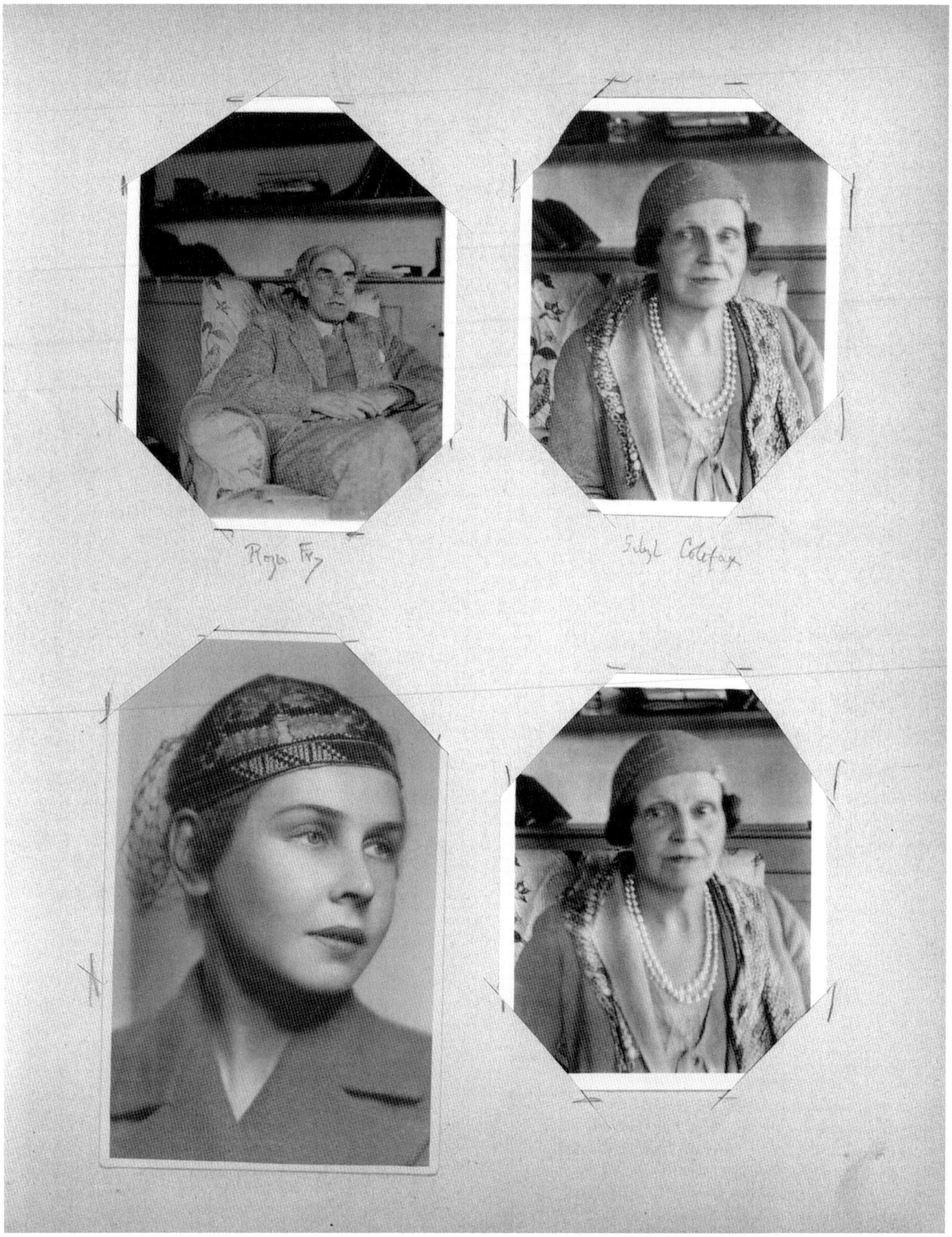

131. Roger Fry; Sibyl Colefax. Lydia Keynes, ca. August 1931. Monk's House Album 3, p. 9. Reprinted by permission of the Harvard Theatre Collection, the Houghton Library. "L. is in the house making his Index & printing the photographs we developed last night. The reason why Colefax is so dull is that she never feels or thinks for herself" (*D*, 4:40).

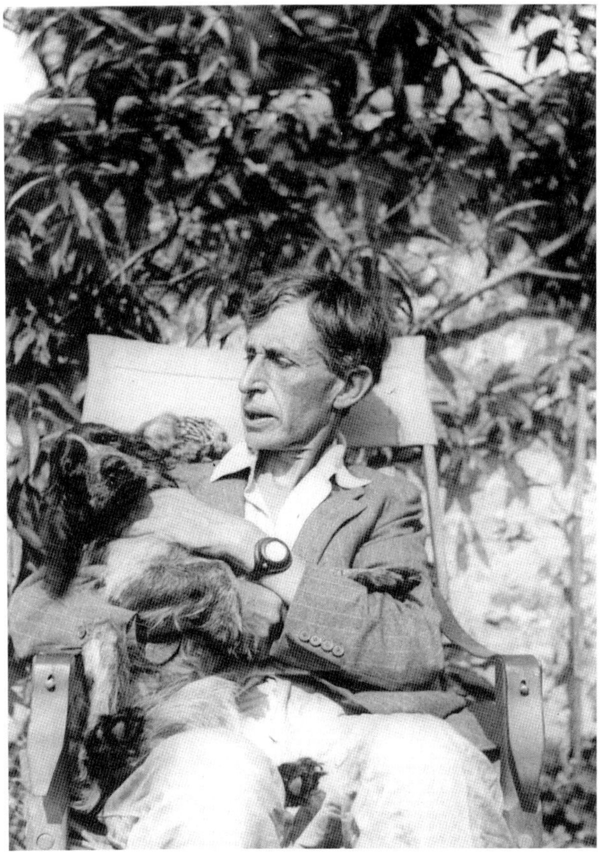

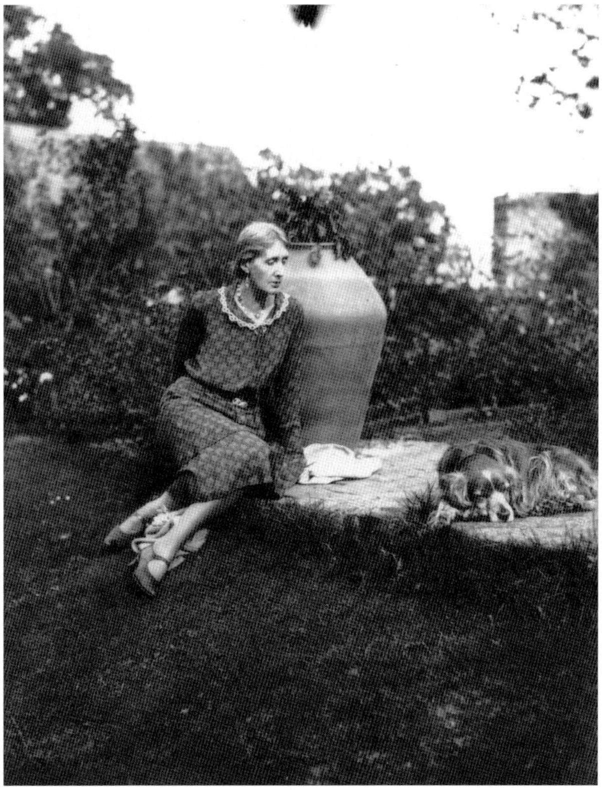

132. (LEFT) Leonard Woolf, ca. August 1931. Box 4, folder A. Reprinted by permission of the Harvard Theatre Collection, the Houghton Library.

133. (RIGHT) Virginia Woolf, August 1931. Box 2, folder 7. Reprinted by permission of the Harvard Theatre Collection, the Houghton Library. "We take photographs which develop in a slope of mist undulating from one end of the film to another" (*L*, 4:365).

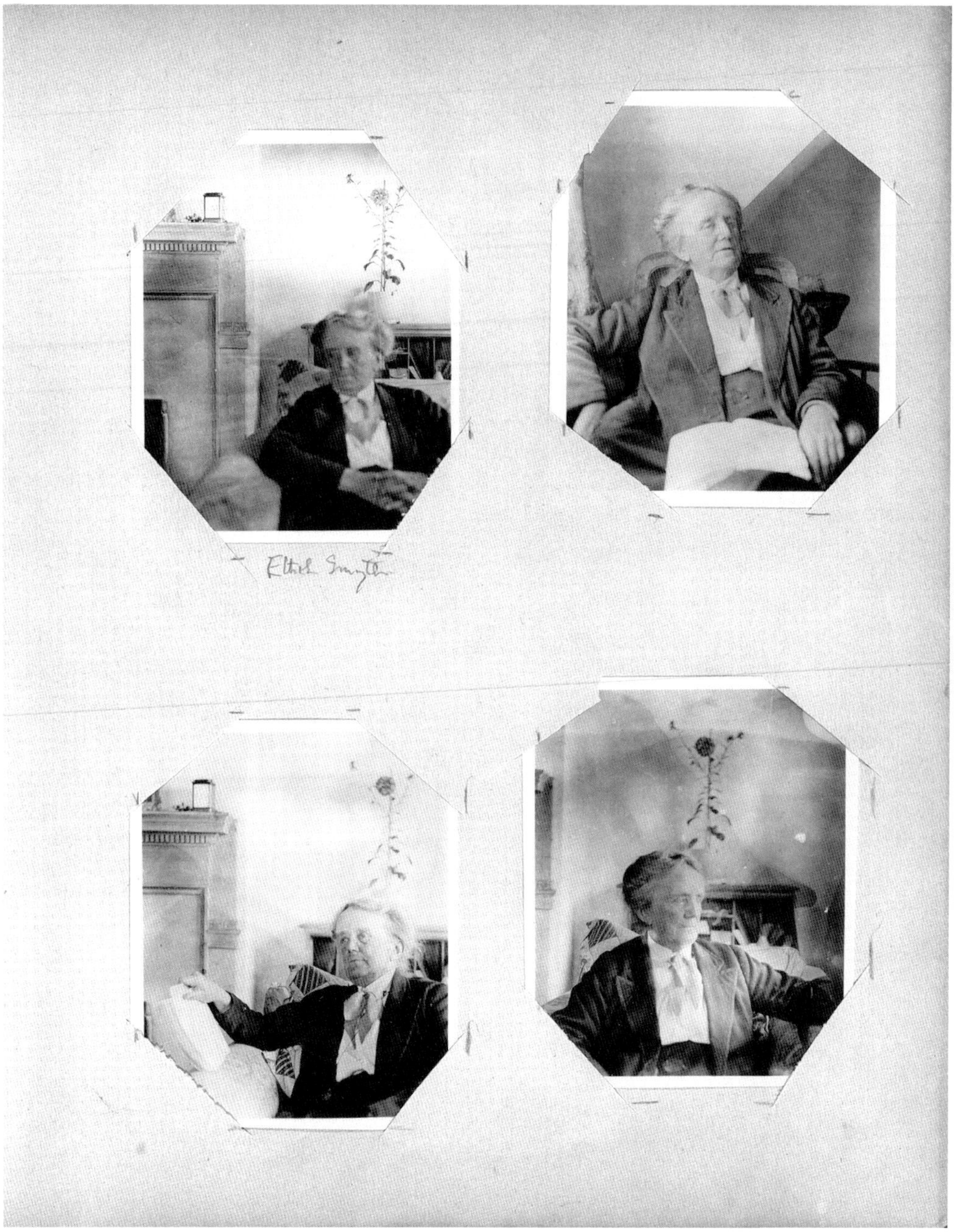

134. Ethel Smyth, August 1931, Monk's House Album 3, p. 12. Reprinted by permission of the Harvard Theatre Collection, the Houghton Library. "Well, here are the prints. What d'you think of them? I think one of them magnificent, but wont say which, as you may hate them all" (*L*, 4:372).

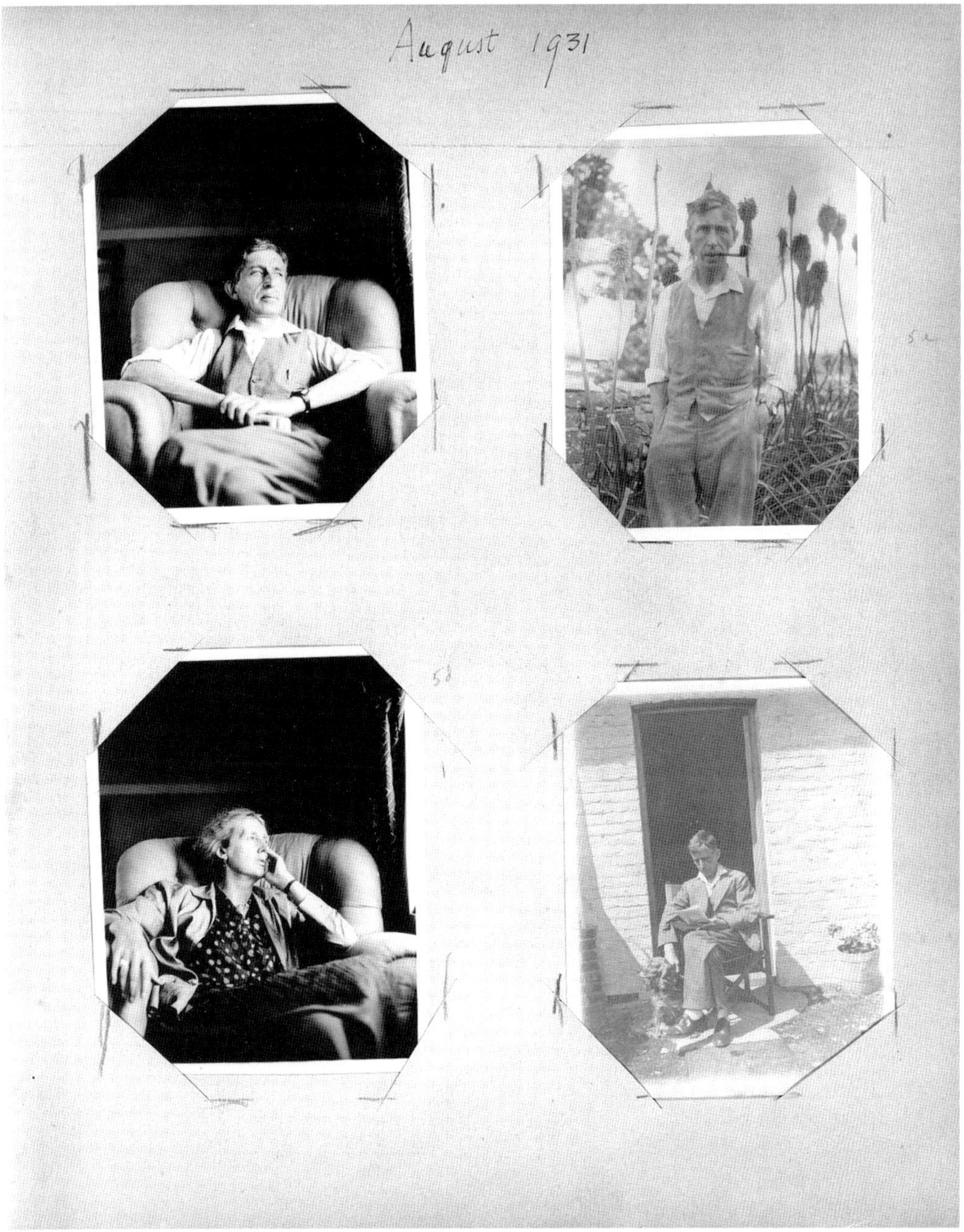

135. Leonard and Virginia Woolf, August 1931. Monk's House Album 3, p. 3. Reprinted by permission of the Harvard Theatre Collection, the Houghton Library. "Out of the profits [from Sackville-West's *All Passion Spent*] I've bought a boat and a camera {Zeiss}. Such are the blessings you shower" (*L*, 4:363).

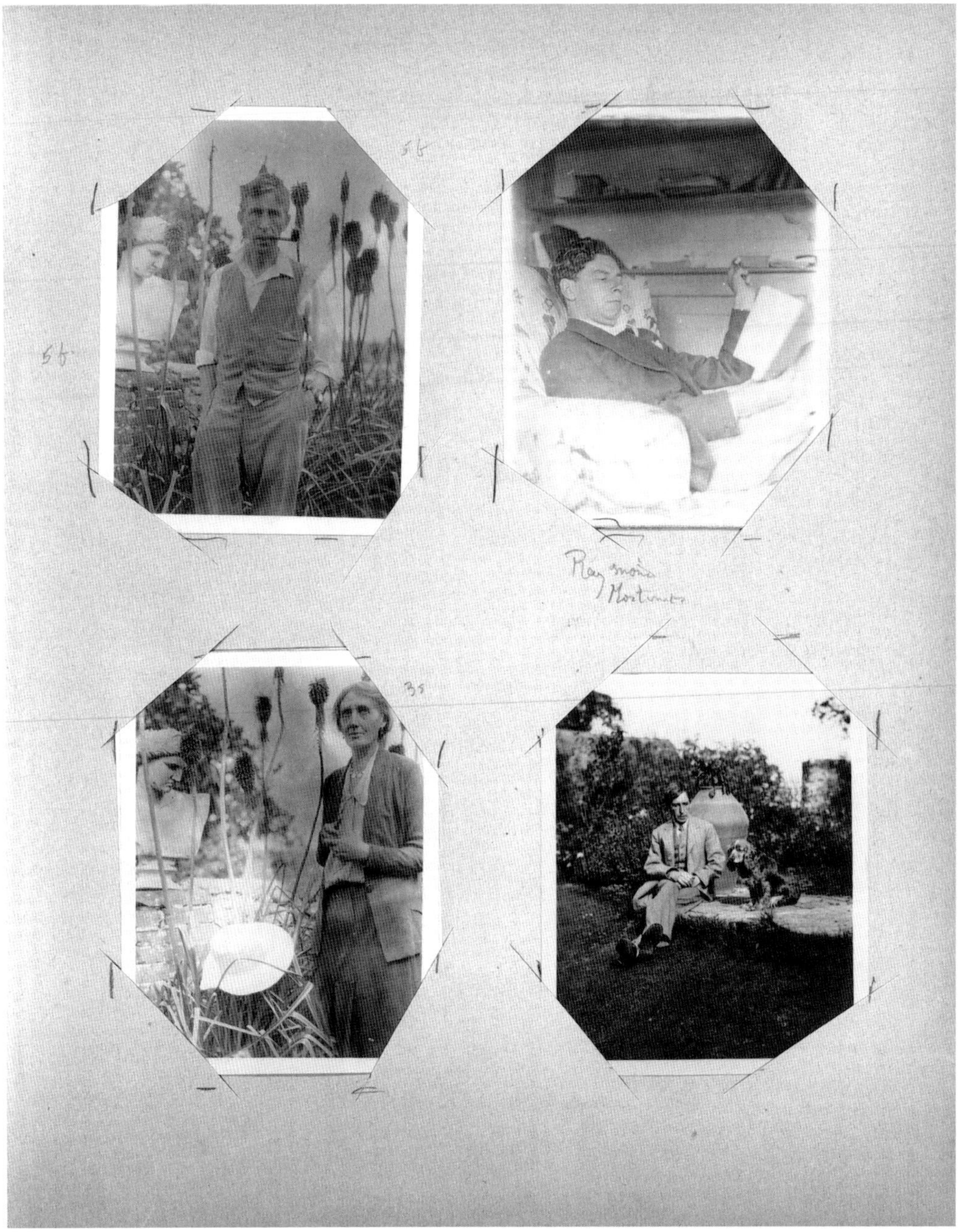

136. Leonard Woolf; Raymond Mortimer; Virginia Woolf. August 1931.
Monk's House Album 3, p. 8. Reprinted by permission of the Harvard Theatre Collection, the Houghton Library. "I've taken some photographs and am now coiled in a desperate grapple with the last pages of that wearysome book [*The Waves*]" (*L*, 4:369).

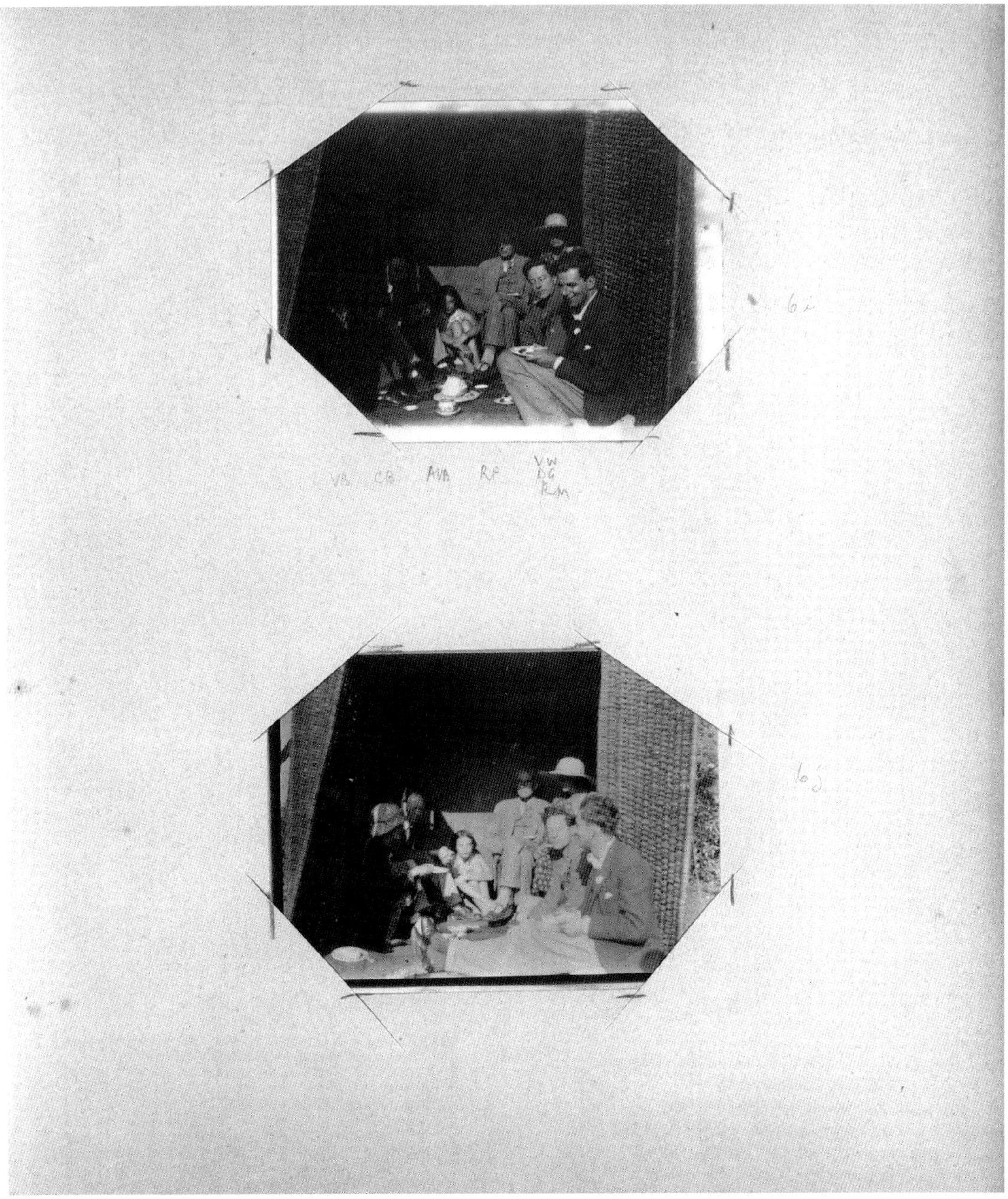

137. Vanessa, Clive, and Angelica Bell, Roger Fry, Virginia Woolf, Duncan Grant, Raymond Mortimer, August 9, 1931. Monk's House Album 3, p. 7. Reprinted by permission of the Harvard Theatre Collection, the Houghton Library. "Photography; developing at night in a cavern hung with red calico—hence many films spoilt; but some are tremendously ugly and very like" (L, 4:367).

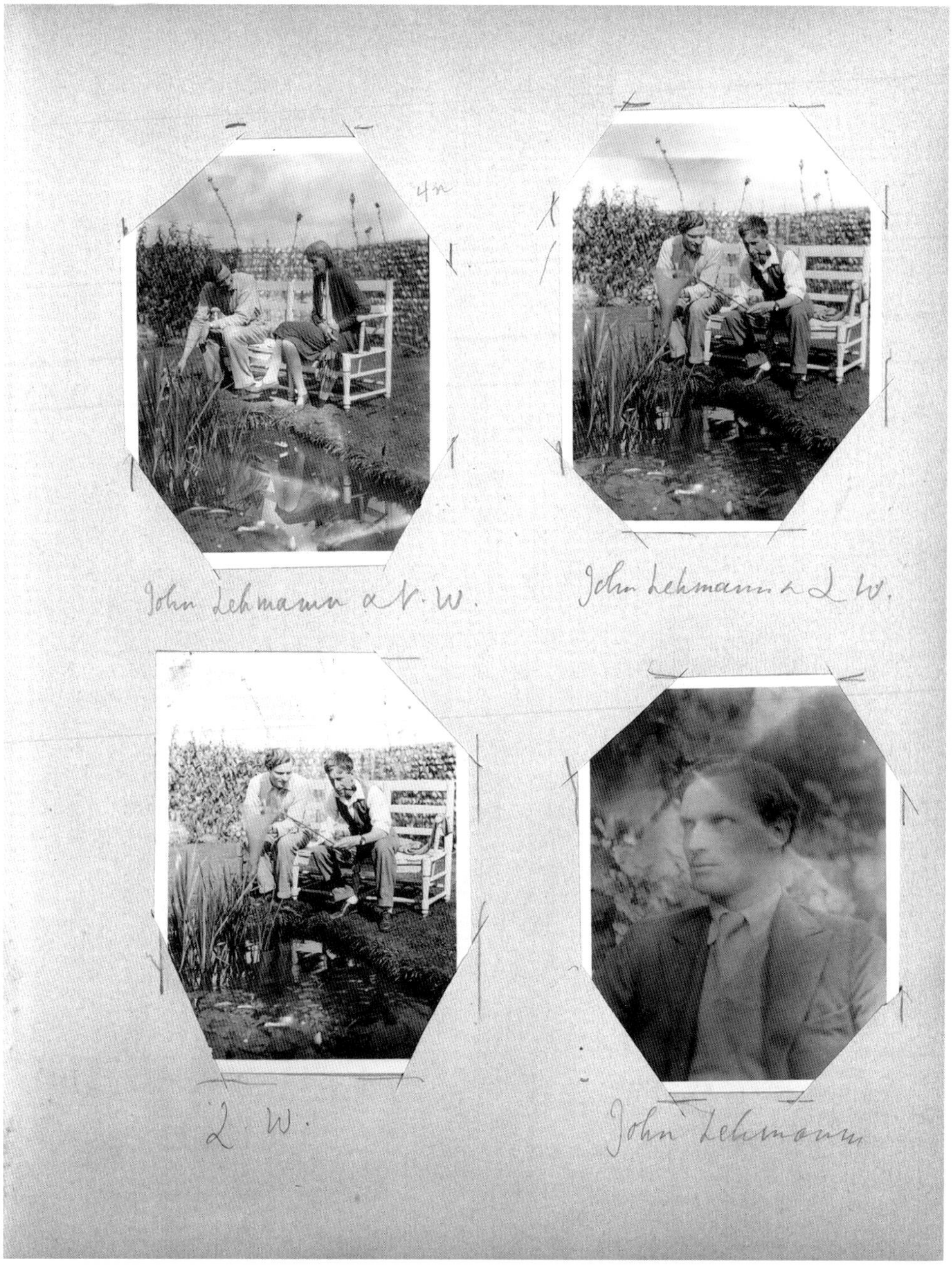

138. John Lehmann, Leonard and Virginia Woolf. September 1931. Monk's House Album 3, p. 15. Reprinted by permission of the Harvard Theatre Collection, the Houghton Library. "We enjoyed having you enormously, though in such a tempest of kittens and photographs. Some of them (the photographs) are good; not your portrait though" (*L*, 4:378).

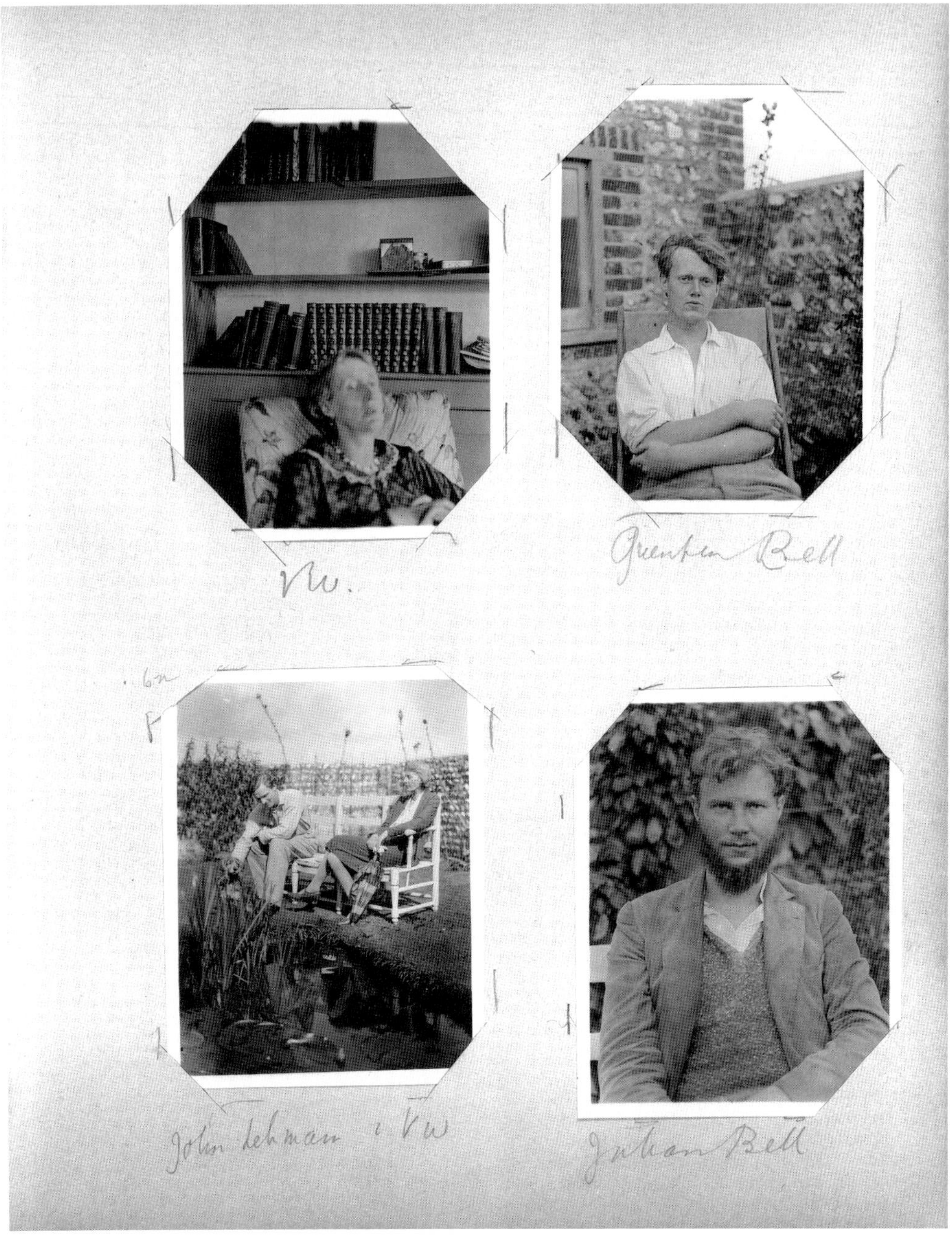

139. Virginia Woolf; Quentin and Julian Bell; John Lehmann. 1931. Monk's House Album 3, p. 16. Reprinted by permission of the Harvard Theatre Collection, the Houghton Library.

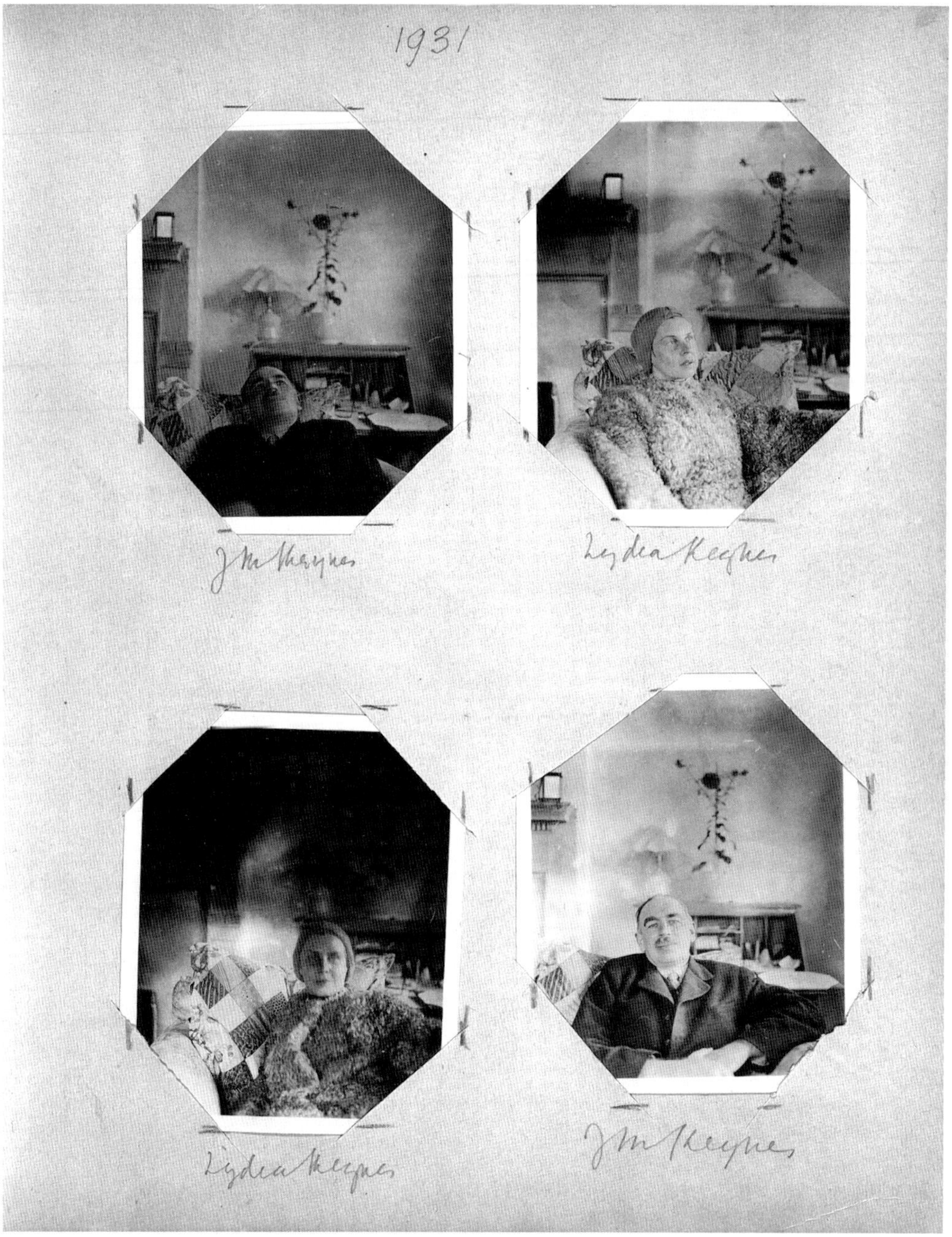

140. John Maynard and Lydia Keynes, December 1931. Monk's House Album 3, p. 13. Reprinted by permission of the Harvard Theatre Collection, the Houghton Library. "[Maynard said] there should be death arranged for couples simultaneously, like himself & Lydia, me & Leonard. But he always supposed he would die before Lydia, & I, I said, before Leonard. Then Lydia & Leonard will marry. They will combine all these dogs. . . . And I kissed Maynard. And they are coming to tea" (*D*, 4:56).

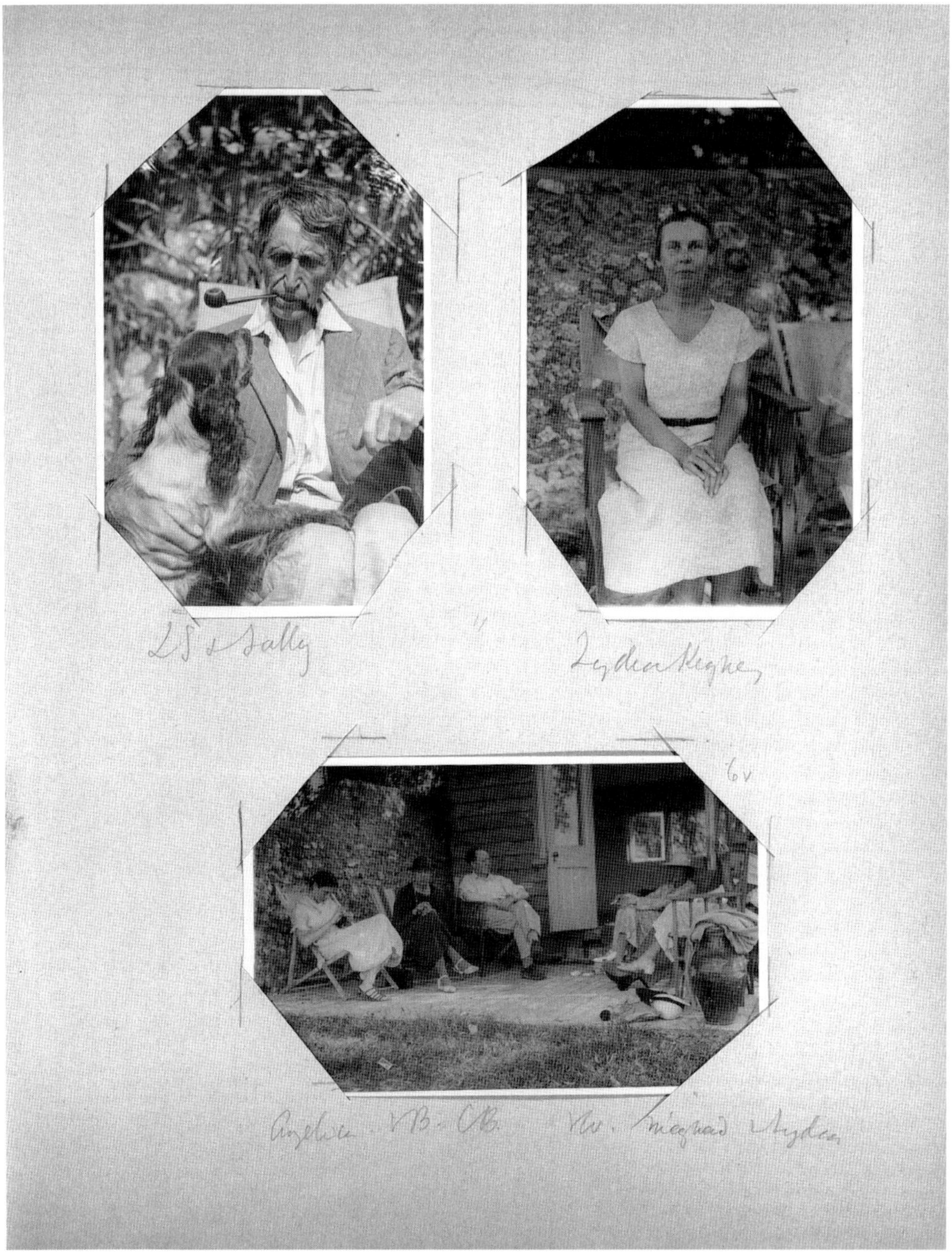

141. Leonard and dog; Lydia Keynes, ca. 1931. Angelica, Vanessa, Clive Bell, Virginia Woolf, Maynard Keynes, August 6, 1935. Monk's House Album 3, p. 63. Reprinted by permission of the Harvard Theatre Collection, the Houghton Library. "By Gods grace we may get 10 or 12 days without visitors . . . the truth is, I like it when people actually come; but I love it when they go" (*D*, 4:179).

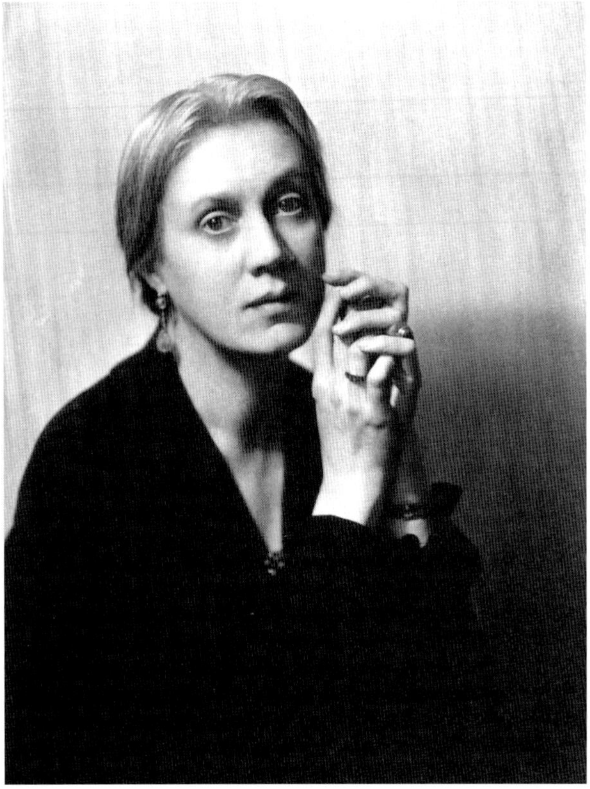

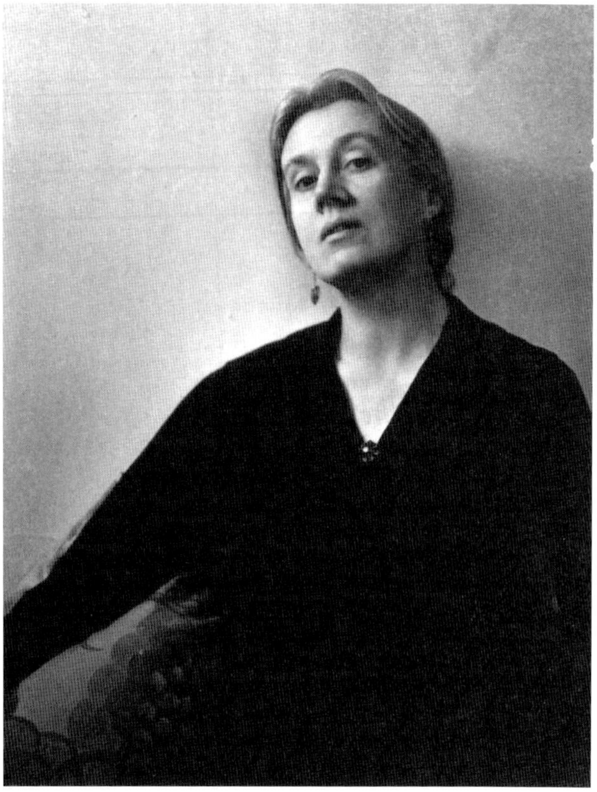

142. (LEFT) Vanessa Bell, March 1932. Photographer: Lettice Ramsey, Mortimer Road, Cambridge. Box 4, folder 2 of 2. Reprinted by permission of the Harvard Theatre Collection, the Houghton Library. "Poor Carrington has killed herself—yesterday . . . we are just off to Cambridge but I thought I had better send you a line" (VB/L, 372–373).

143. (RIGHT) Vanessa Bell, March 1932. Photographer: Lettice Ramsey, Mortimer Road, Cambridge. Box 4, folder 2 of 2. Reprinted by permission of the Harvard Theatre Collection, the Houghton Library.

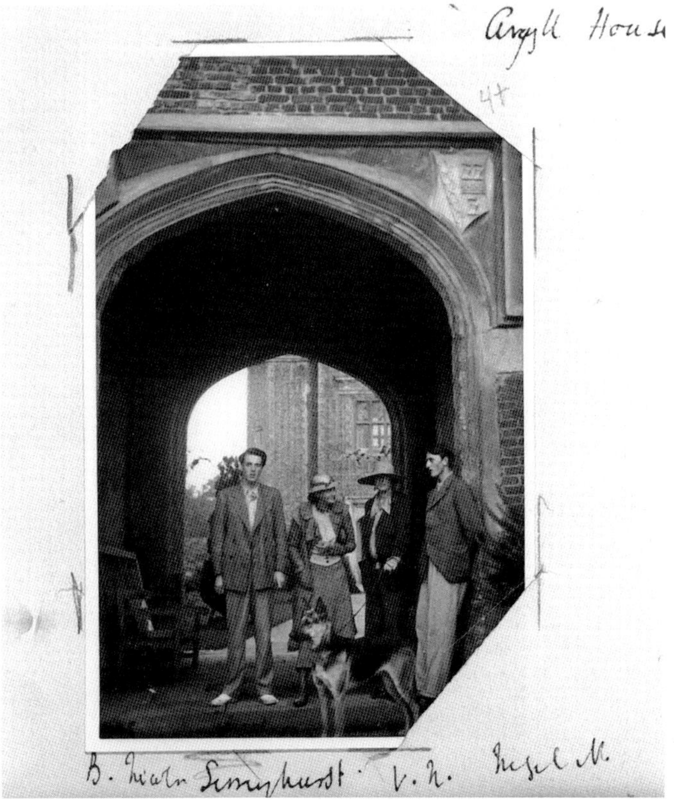

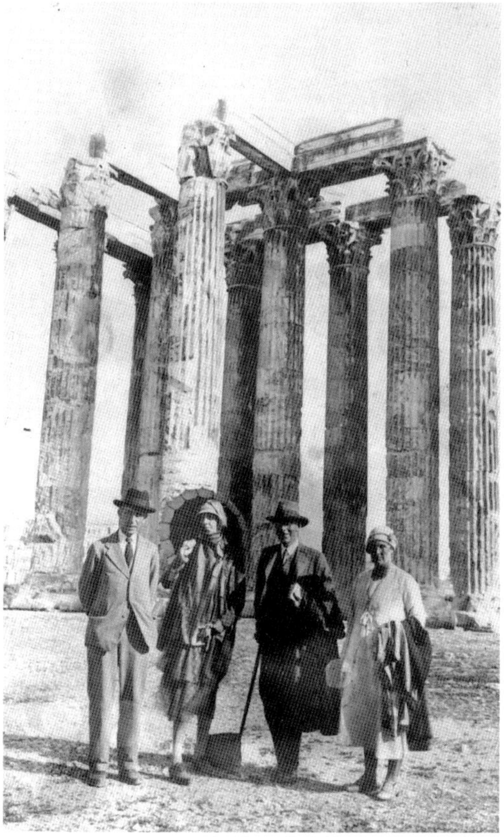

144. (LEFT) Vita Sackville-West, Virginia Woolf, Ben and Nigel Nicolson. Sissinghurst, 1932. Monk's House Album 5, p. 23. Reprinted by permission of the Harvard Theatre Collection, the Houghton Library. Marked Argyll House (Sibyl Colefax's house) because the postcard is from Sibyl? (see Catalogue, "Monk's House Album 5," referencing p. 208) August 14, 1936, Paddington W2, to Leonard. "We went to Sissinghurst . . . Vita in breeches & pink shirt . . . we ate cold salmon & raspberries & cream & little variegated chocolates given by Lady Sackville . . . then climbed Vita's tower" (D, 4:87).

145. (RIGHT) Roger and Margery Fry, Leonard and Virginia Woolf. Acropolis, Greece, May 1932. Monk's House Album 3, p. 19. Reprinted by permission of the Harvard Theatre Collection, the Houghton Library. "Its blazing white in Athens . . . we're now changing into thin clothes and going up to the Acropolis" (L, 5: 51).

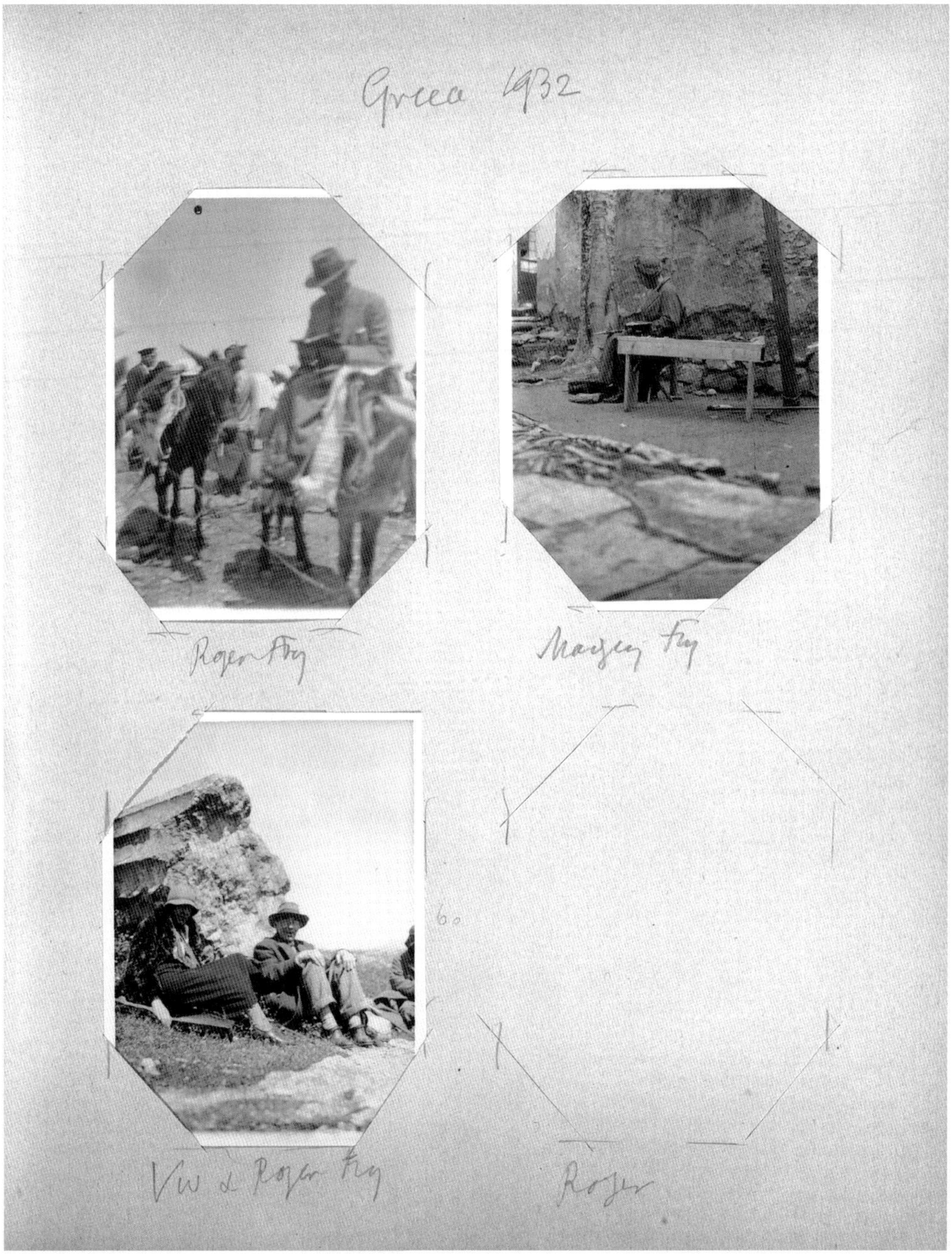

146. Roger and Margery Fry, Virginia Woolf. Greece, May 1932. Monk's House Album 3, p. 20. Reprinted by permission of the Harvard Theatre Collection, the Houghton Library. "For R. & M. were mounted, & very queer they looked, jolting up the hill . . . how happy today was . . . why cant we live for ever like this" (*D*, 4:93).

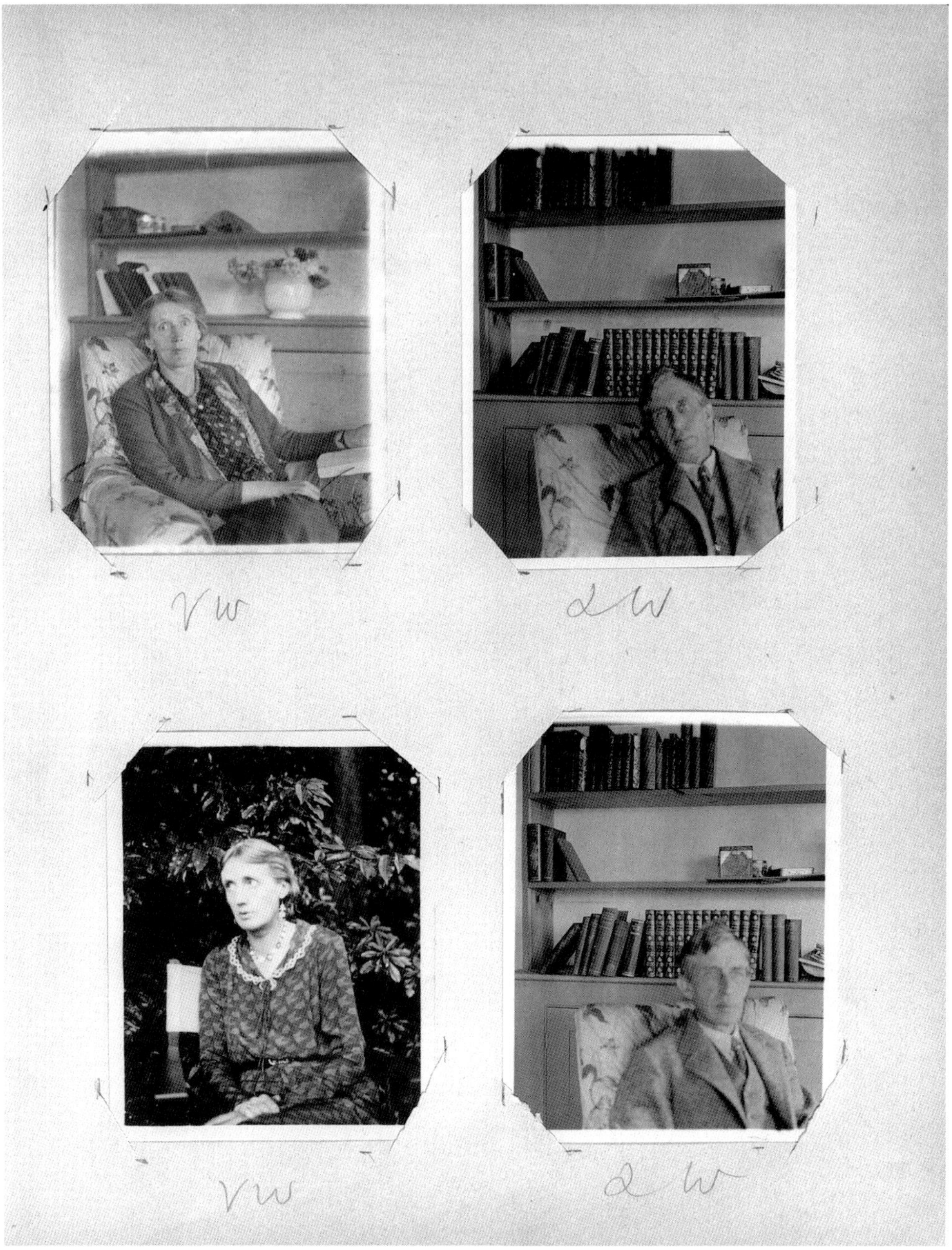

147. Virginia and Leonard Woolf, ca. 1932. Monk's House Album 3, p. 18. Reprinted by permission of the Harvard Theatre Collection, the Houghton Library. "Rodmell . . . with the may tree like a breaking wave outside . . . never a person to be seen, never an interruption: the place to ourselves" (*D*, 4:109).

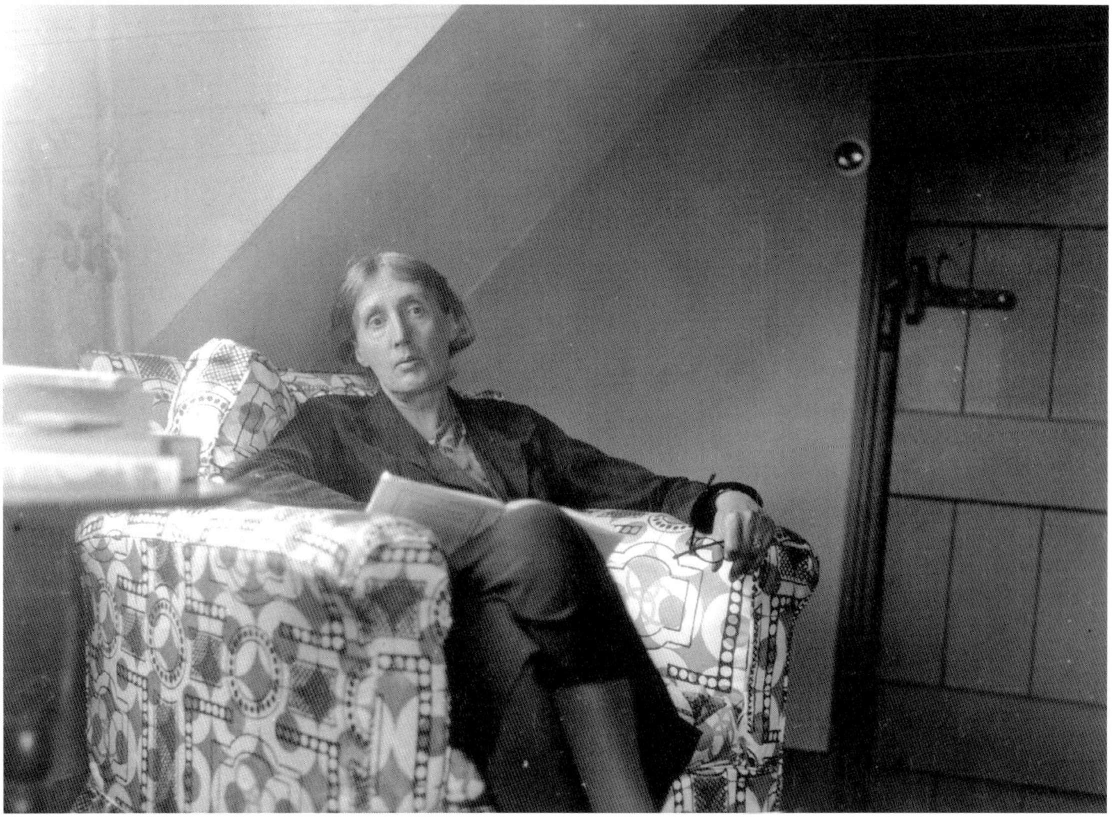

148. Virginia Woolf, Monk's House, August 20, 1932. Box 3, folder 1.
Reprinted by permission of the Harvard Theatre Collection, the Houghton Library.
"Wishart is publishing [as frontispiece of Holtby's *Virginia Woolf*] L's snap shot of me instead of the Lenare photograph & I feel that my privacy is invaded; my legs show; & I am revealed to the world (1,000 at most) as a plain dowdy old woman" (*D*, 4:124). Woolf is clearly writing about this image and not the actual published photograph (taken at the same sitting) in which Woolf's legs are hidden.

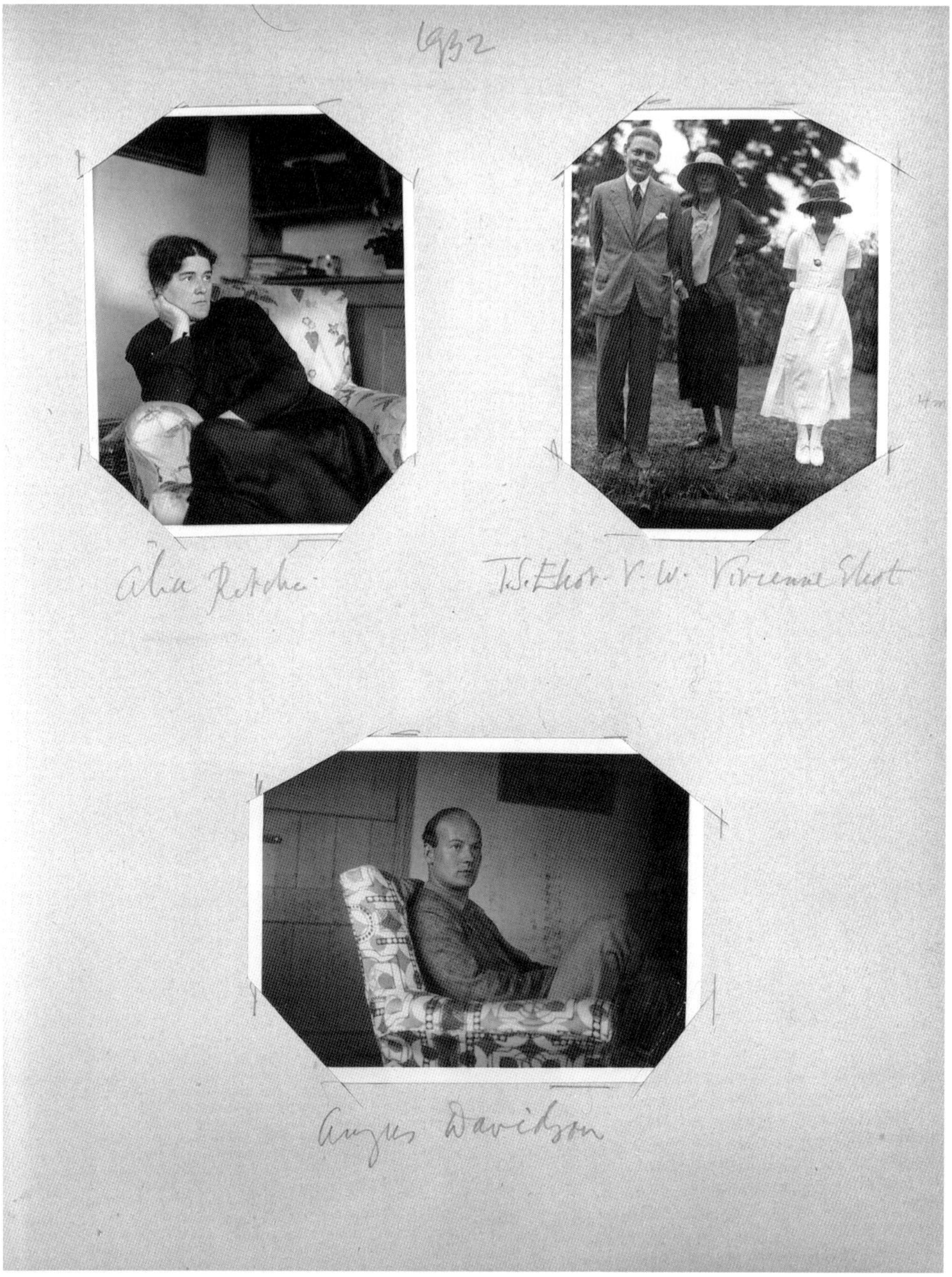

149. Alice Ritchie, August 1932. T. S. and Vivienne Eliot and Virginia Woolf, September 1932. Angus Davidson, September 1932. Monk's House Album 3, p. 29. Reprinted by permission of the Harvard Theatre Collection, the Houghton Library. "Behold Tom & Vivienne . . . she wild as Ophelia—alas no Hamlet would love her, with her powdered spots—in white satin, L. said" (*D*, 4:123).

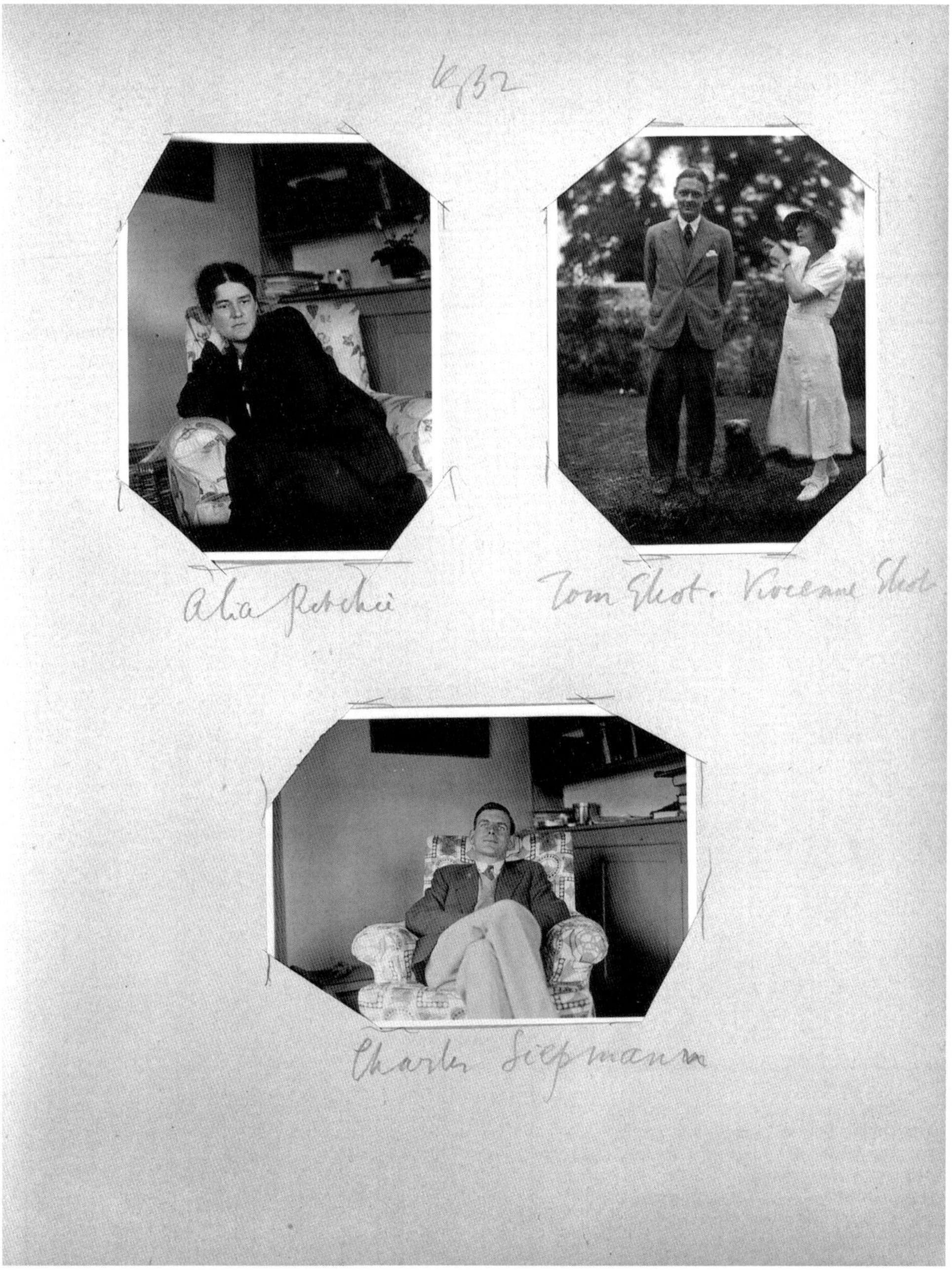

150. Alice Ritchie; T. S. and Vivienne Eliot. Charles Siepmann, September 1932. Monk's House Album 3, p. 30. Reprinted by permission of the Harvard Theatre Collection, the Houghton Library. "I have the Hell of a weekend—two people staying here, one at his own invitation [Siepmann] in order to disburden his soul—a shallow vessel" (*L*, 5: 105).

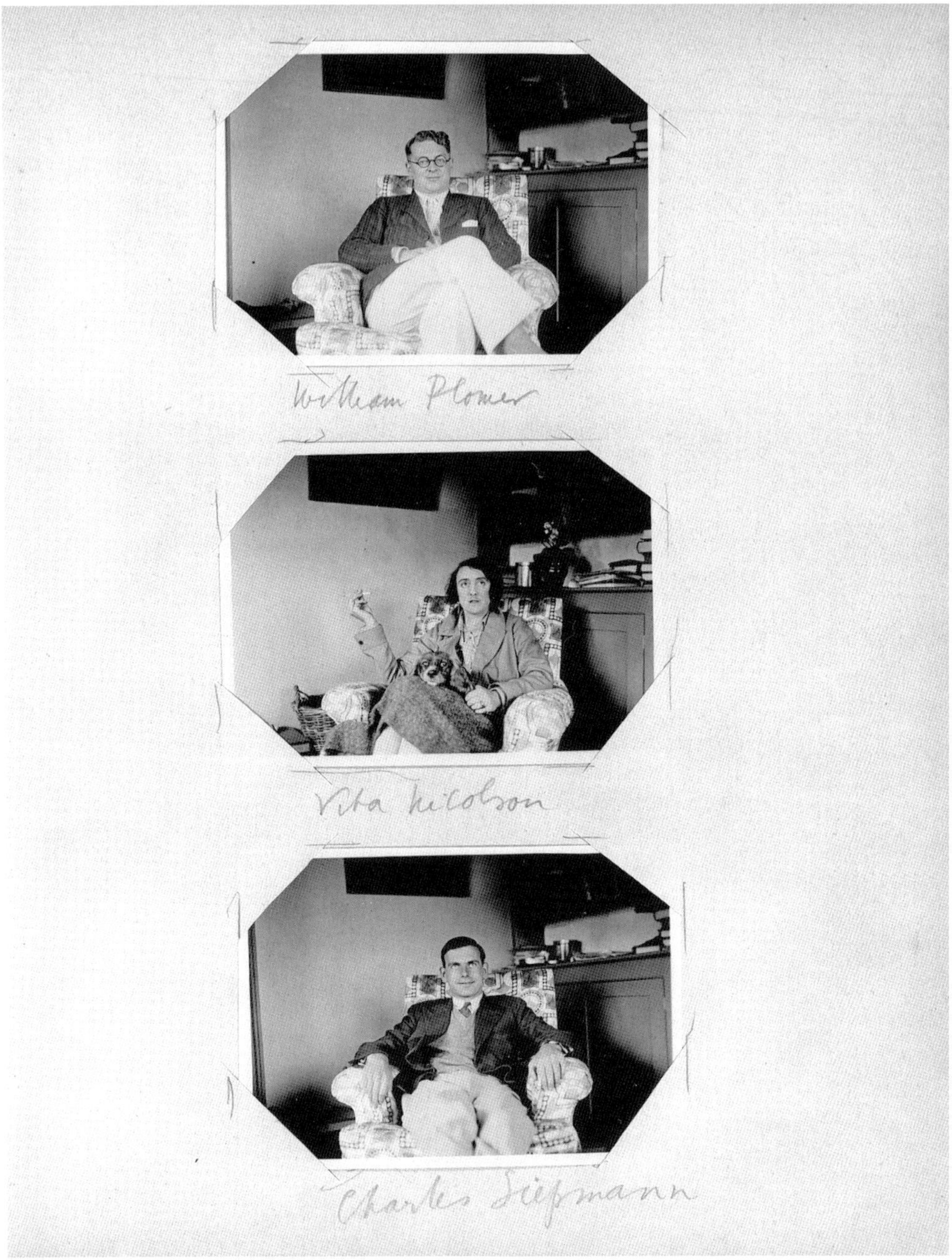

151. William Plomer; Vita Sackville-West (Nicolson); Charles Siepmann. September 1932. Monk's House Album 3, p. 31. Reprinted by permission of the Harvard Theatre Collection, the Houghton Library. "Dear William, We shall like it very much if you would come for the week end next Saturday—17th that is: I rather think Charles Siepman [*sic*] of the B.B.C. is coming . . . all experiences will wait till you come" (L, 5: 103).

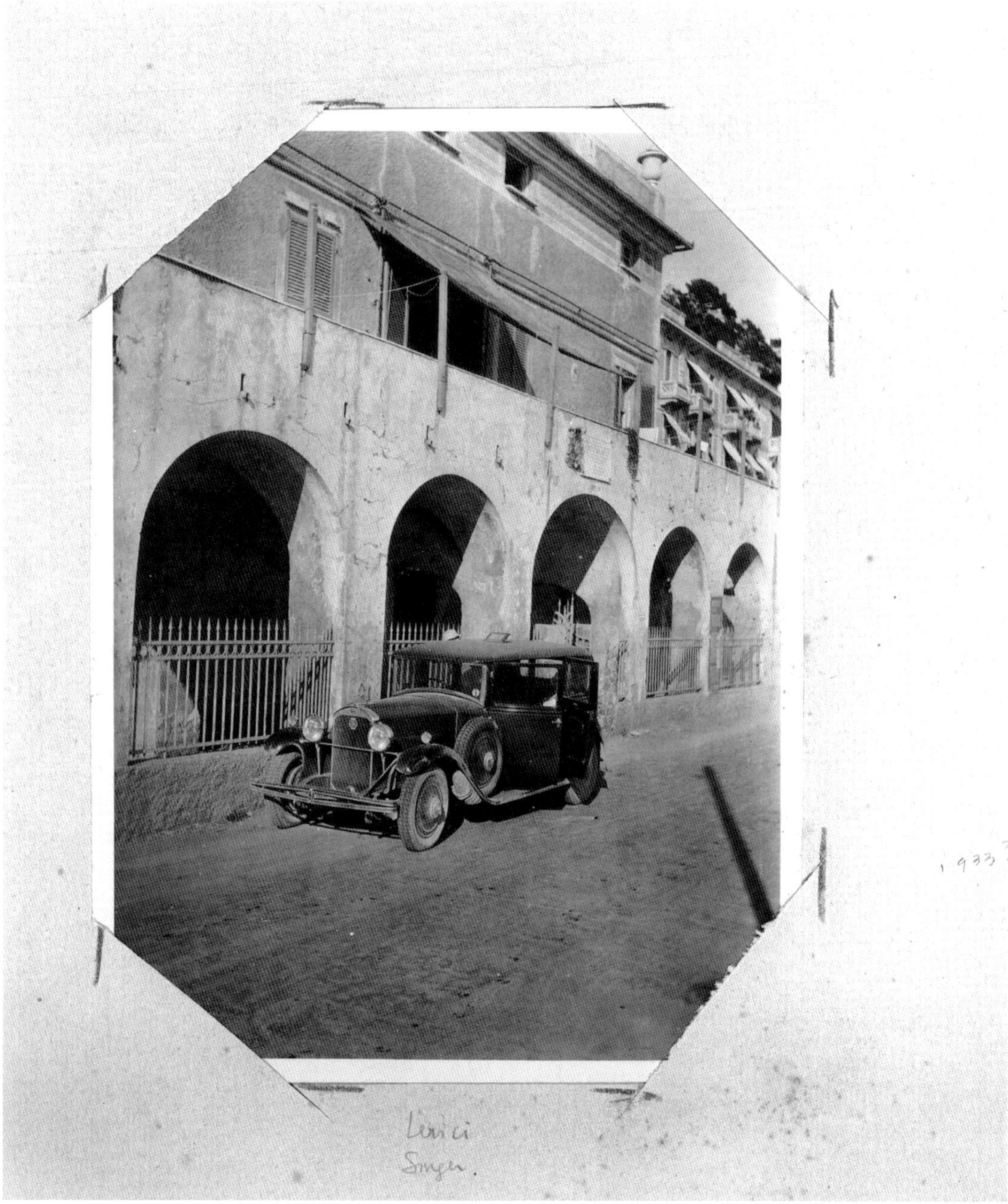

152. "Lerici Singer," Italy, 1933. Monk's House Album 3, p. 6. Reprinted by permission of the Harvard Theatre Collection, the Houghton Library. The trip to Italy was in their new Lanchester. "The little servant girl . . . she had enough mind to envy us the Lanchester . . . Lerici is hot & blue & we had a room with a balcony" (*D*, 4:154 and 158).

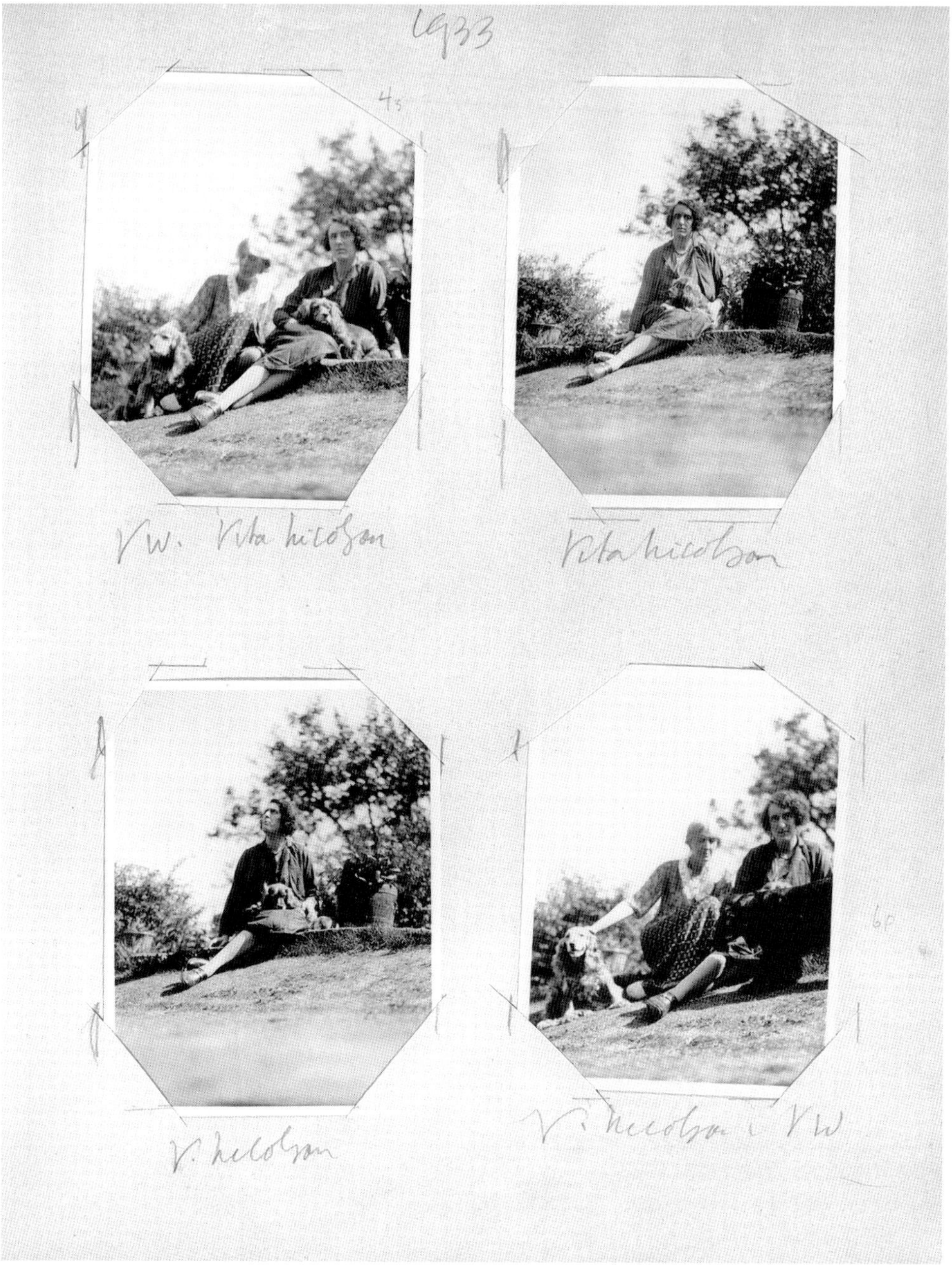

153. Vita Sackville-West (Nicolson) and Virginia Woolf, August 1933. Monk's House Album 3, p. 34. Reprinted by permission of the Harvard Theatre Collection, the Houghton Library. "Yesterday here was hot, baking hot . . . at 6 Vita came . . . stayed the night; we had grouse for dinner; she spent the morning talking to me" (*D*, 4:175–176).

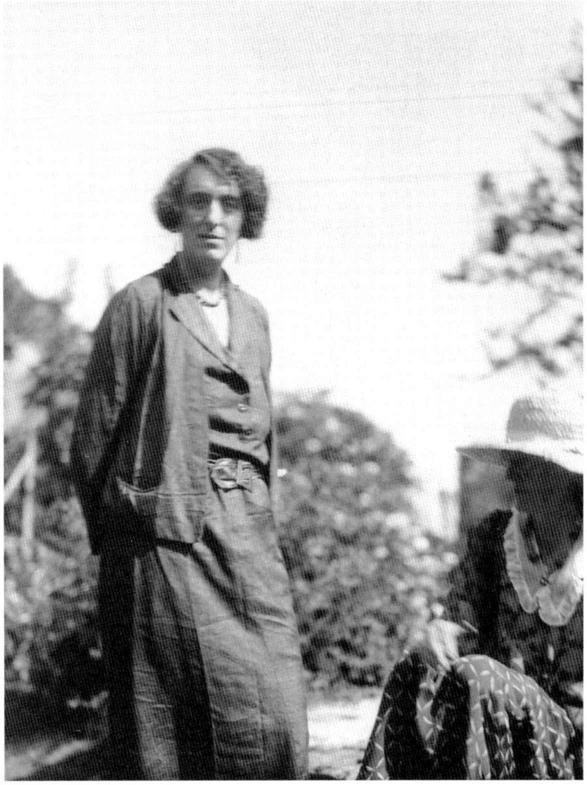

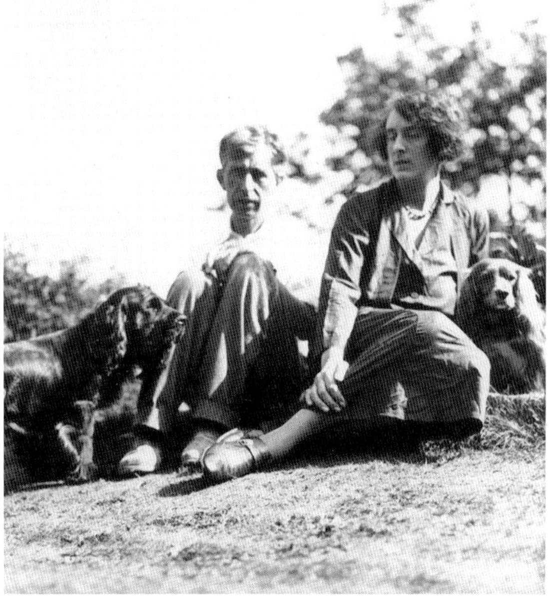

154. (LEFT) Vita Sackville-West (Nicolson) and Virginia Woolf, August 1933. Box 4, folder 4-1. Reprinted by permission of the Harvard Theatre Collection, the Houghton Library. "Her strong masculinity came out in a number of ways . . . she never introduced Harold Nicolson as 'my husband'" (Nigel Nicolson in Heilbrun, 86).

155. (RIGHT) Leonard Woolf and Vita Sackville-West, August 1933. Box 2, folder 1. Reprinted by permission of the Harvard Theatre Collection, the Houghton Library. "Well we are very happy. Life buds & sprouts all round us . . . and Vita lunches" (*D*, 4:193).

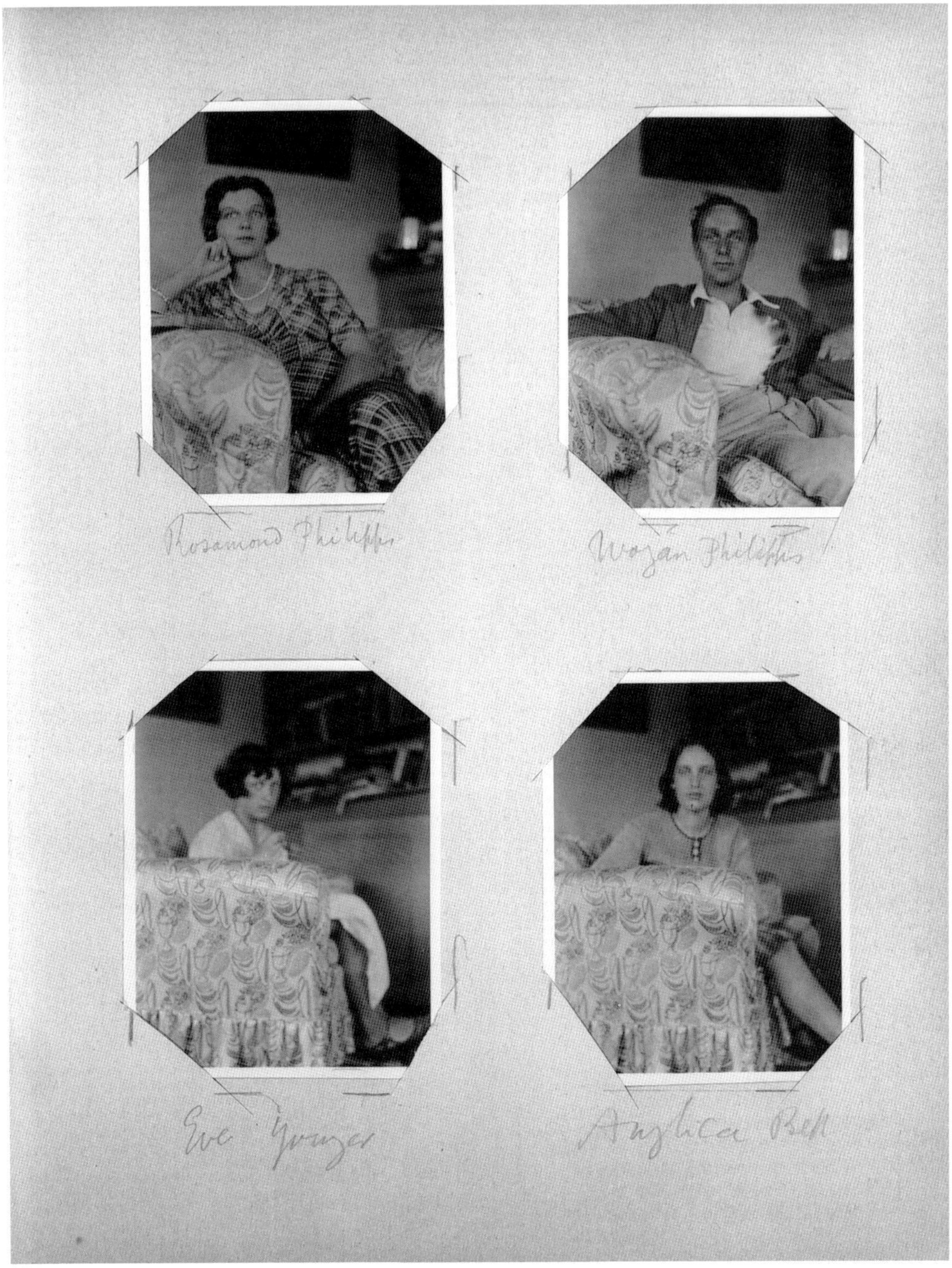

156. Rosamond Philipps (née Lehmann); Wogan Philipps; Eve Younger; Angelica Bell. September 1933. Monk's House Album 3, p. 36. Reprinted by permission of the Harvard Theatre Collection, the Houghton Library. "Eve very pretty; mouse like with her pointed twitching nose" (*D*, 4:342).

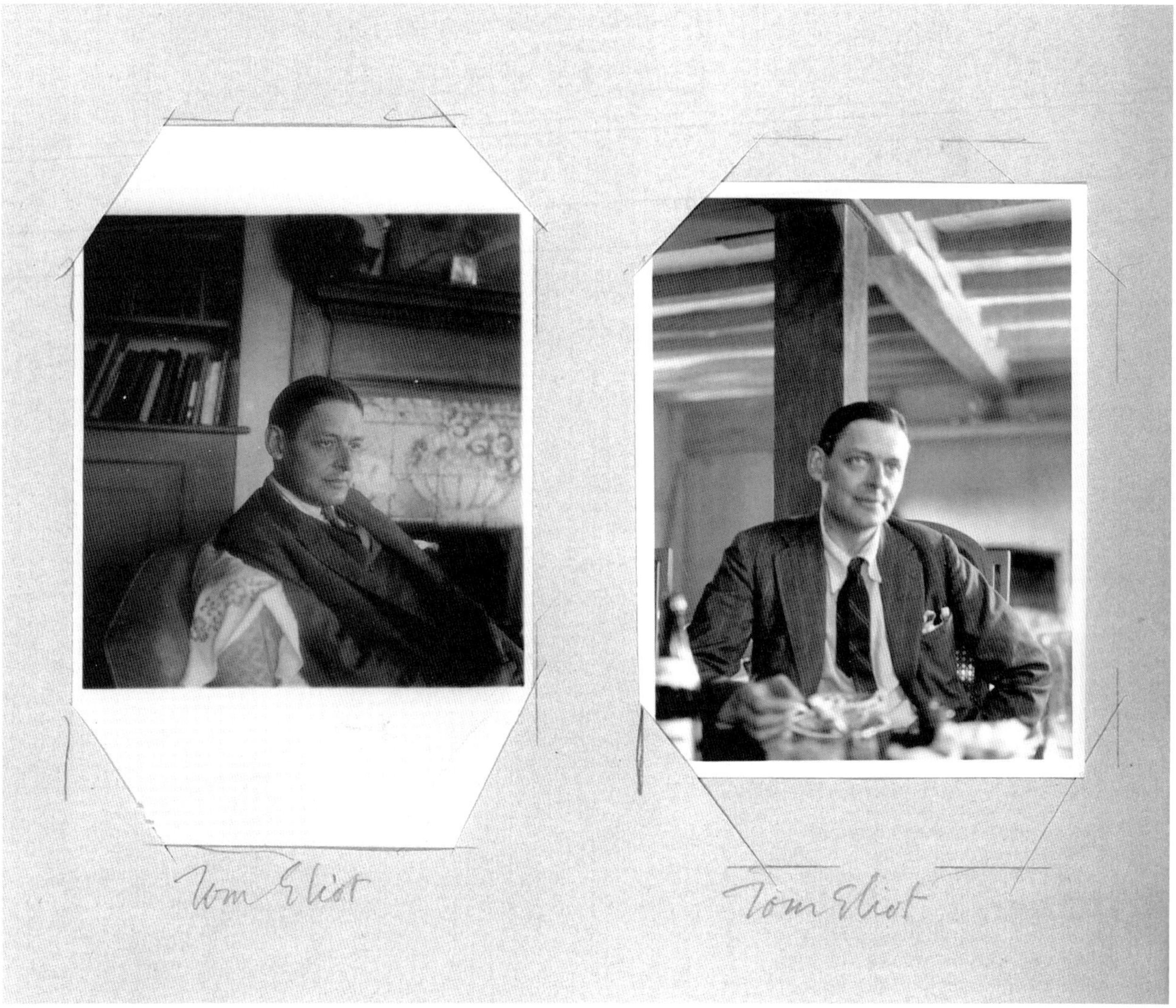

157. T. S. Eliot, September 1933. Monk's House Album 3, p. 68. Reprinted by permission of the Harvard Theatre Collection, the Houghton Library. "A glorified boy scout . . . he is tight & shiny as a wood louse (I am not writing for publication) But there is well water in him, cold & pure. Yes I like talking to Tom" (D, 4:178).

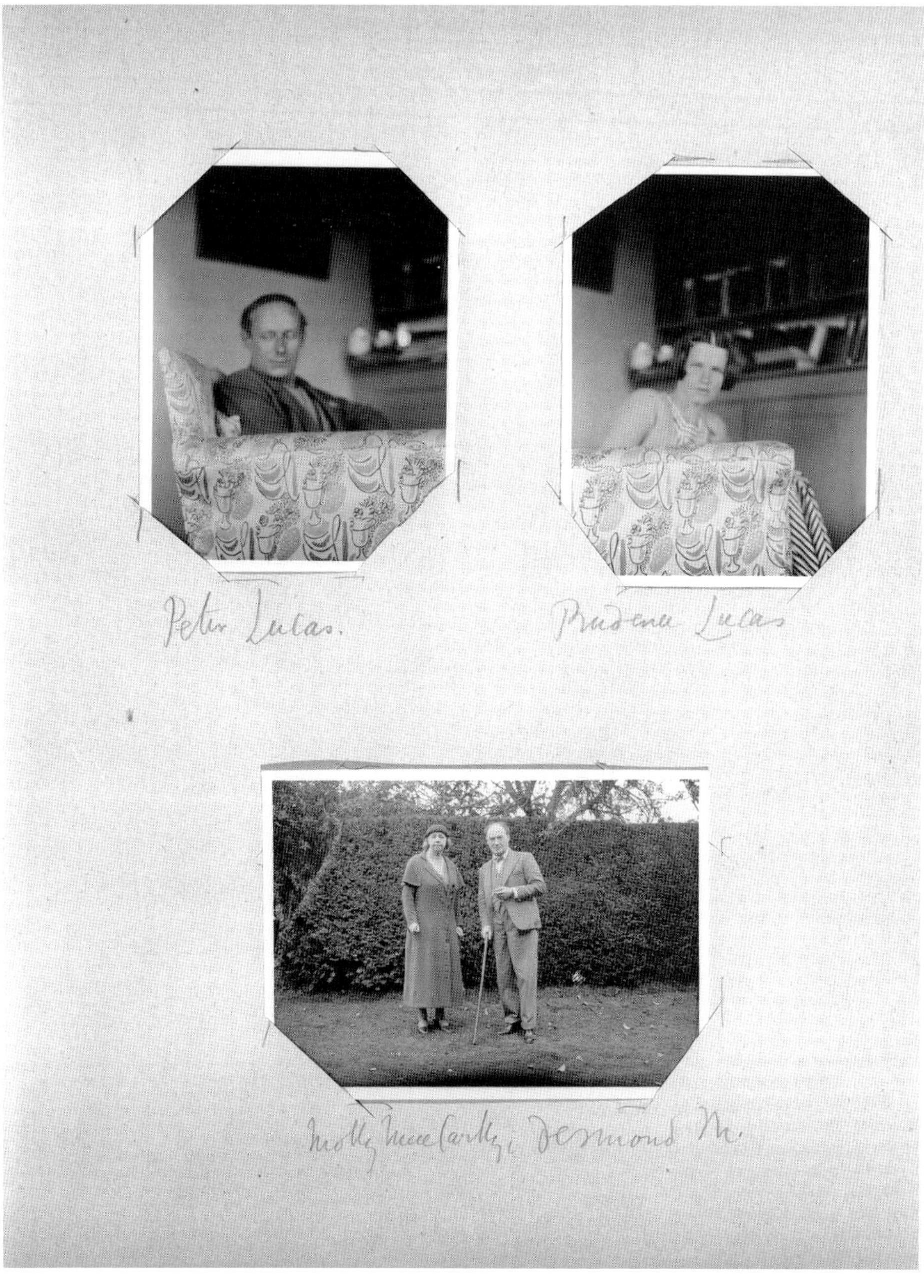

158. Peter and Prudence Lucas, ca. September 1933; Molly and Desmond MacCarthy. Monk's House Album 3, p. 38. Reprinted by permission of the Harvard Theatre Collection, the Houghton Library. "Peter & Prudence . . . she is one of the direct shorthaired terrier kind, breaking, unexpectedly, into loud barks. Why Peter, the fastidious, should commit himself for life to her" (*D*, 4:180).

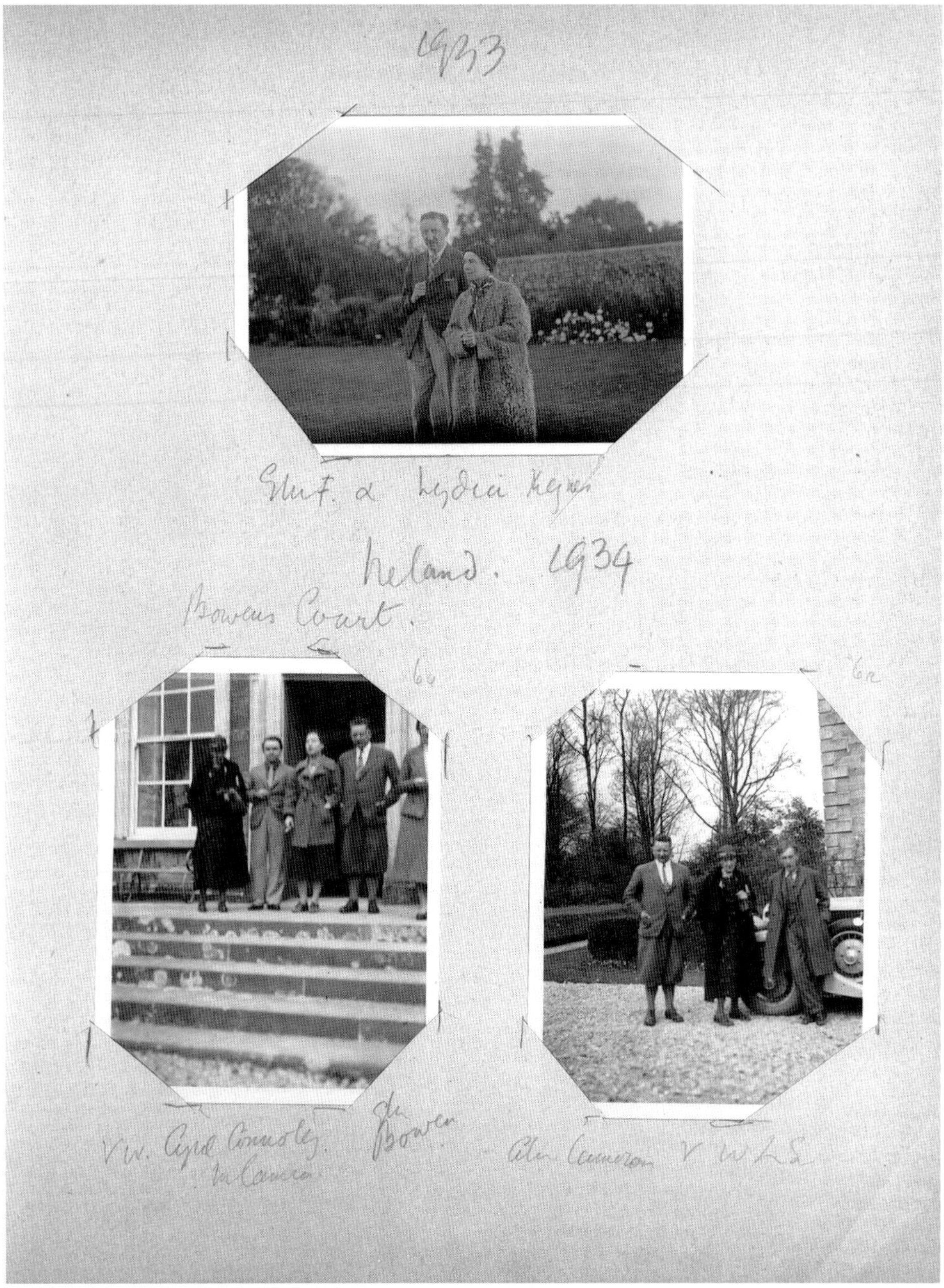

159. E. M. Forster and Lydia Keynes, 1933. Leonard and Virginia Woolf, Cyril and Jean Connolly, Alan Cameron, and Elizabeth Bowen. Bowen's Court, Ireland, 1934. Monk's House Album 3, p. 40. Reprinted by permission of the Harvard Theatre Collection, the Houghton Library. "We spent one night, unfortunately with baboon Conolly [*sic*] & his gollywog slug wife Jean . . . everywhere desolation & pretention cracked grand pianos . . . & yet with character & charm" (*D*, 4:210).

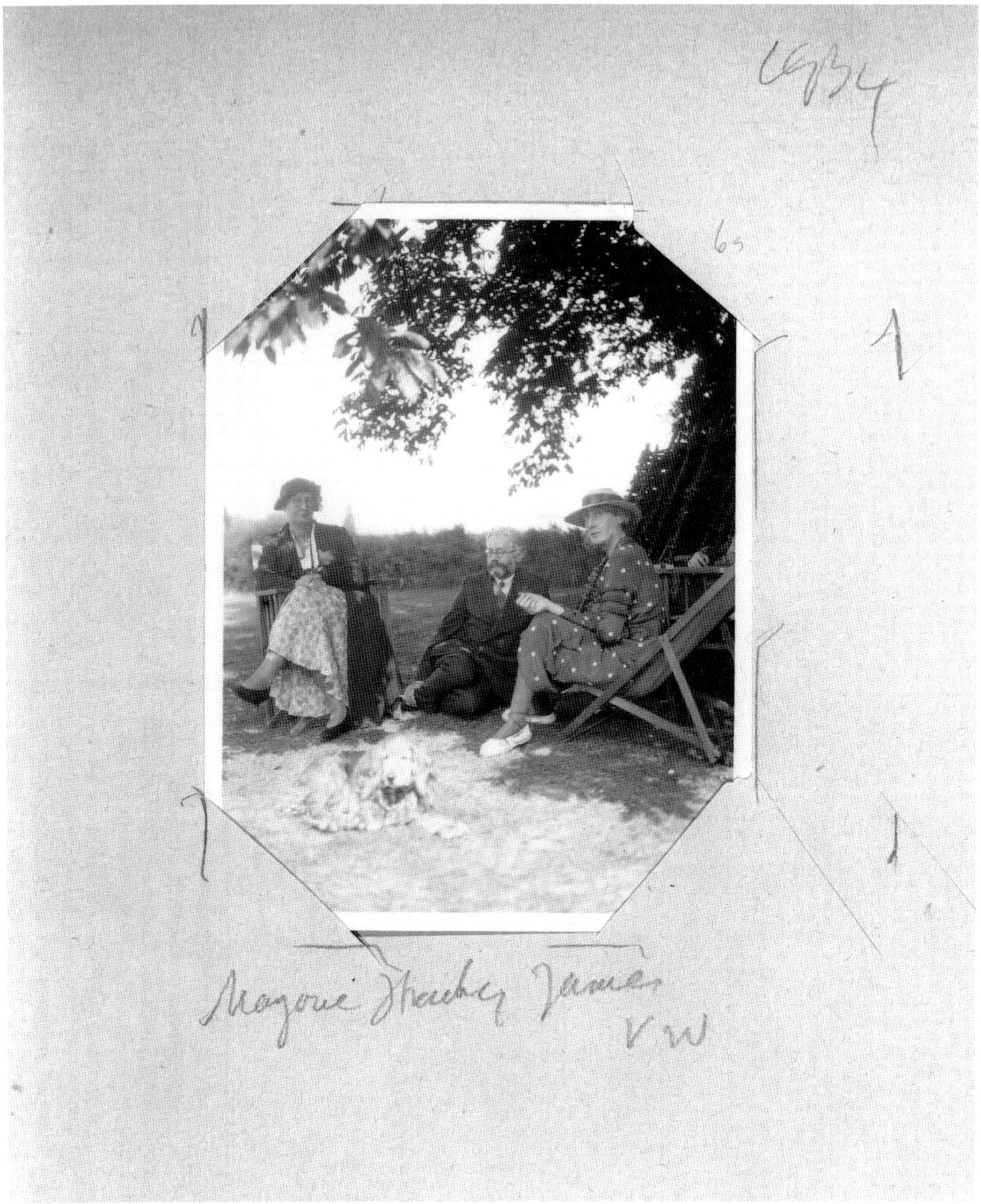

160. Marjorie and James Strachey, Virginia Woolf. June 10, 1934.
Monk's House Album 3, p. 42. Reprinted by permission of the Harvard Theatre Collection, the Houghton Library. The Stracheys lunched before Glyndebourne, which opened in that year.

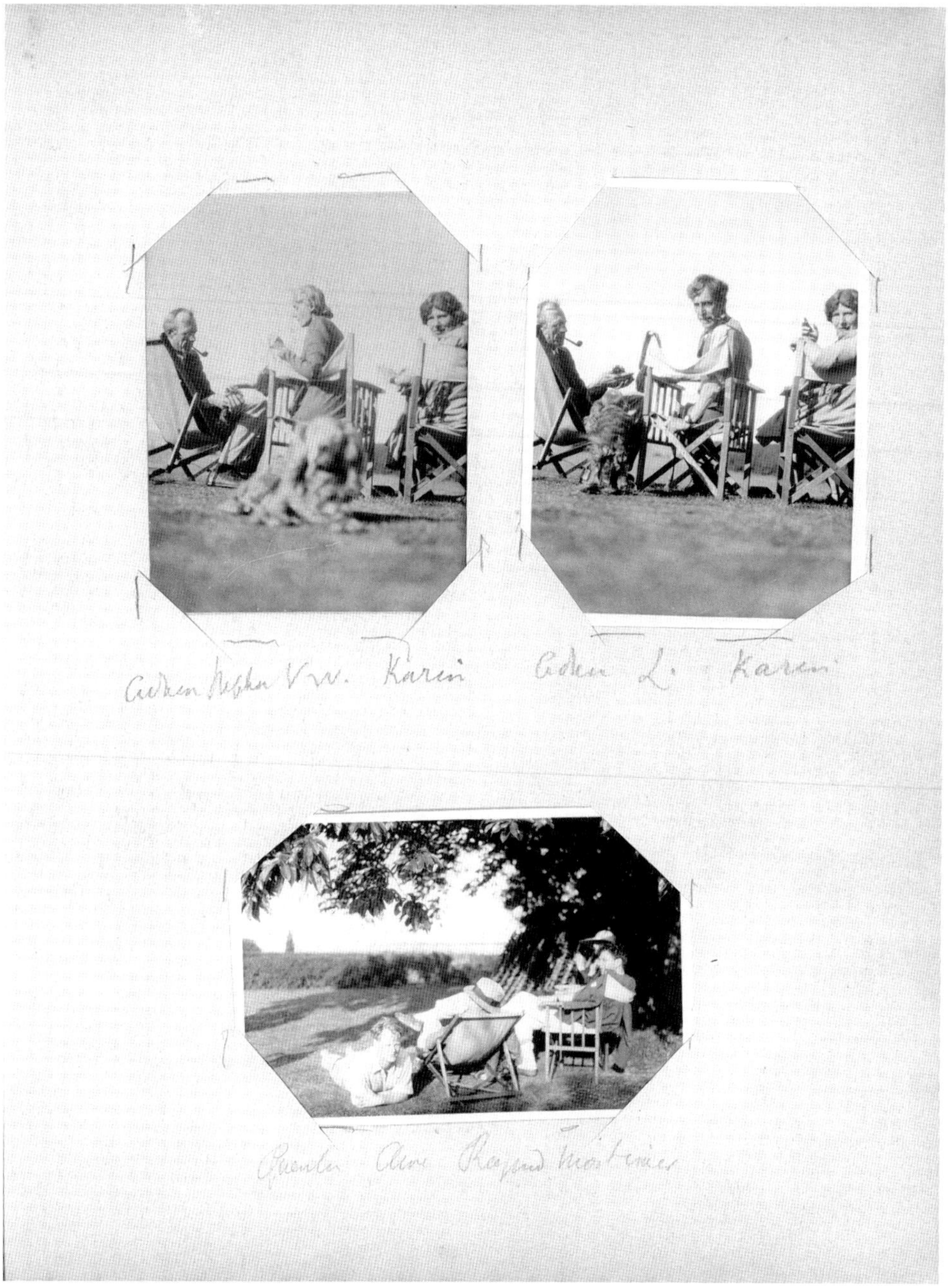

161. Virginia and Leonard Woolf, Adrian and Karin Stephen, Quentin and Clive Bell, Raymond Mortimer, Virginia Woolf, ca. August 1934. Monk's House Album 3, p. 44. Reprinted by permission of the Harvard Theatre Collection, the Houghton Library. "Yesterday just as we had done tea, Adrian's gaunt form appeared; Karin's touseled shape, grown very thick & large . . . Clive & Julian [it was Quentin] & so on to tea today" (*D*, 4:234–235).

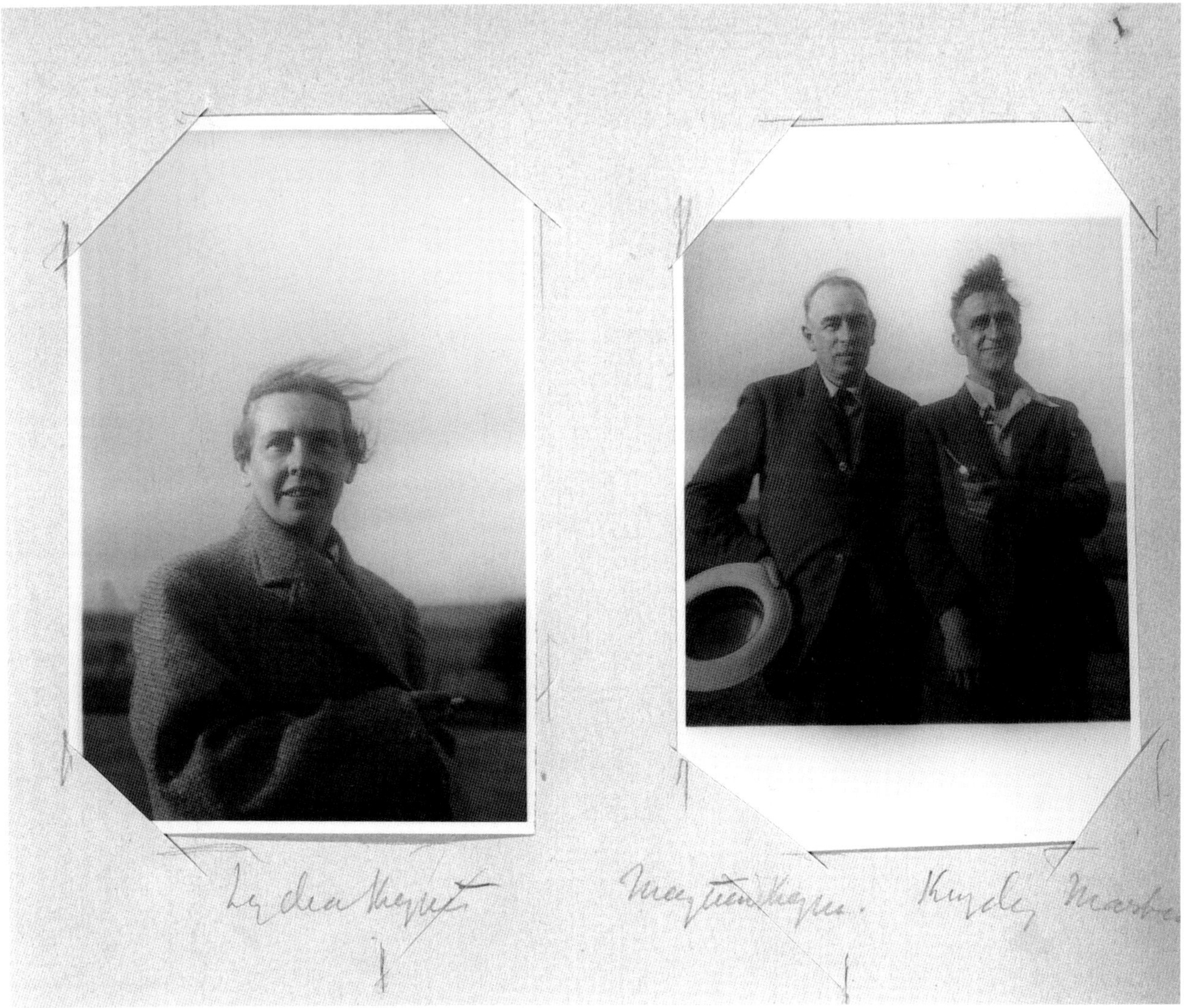

162. Lydia and Maynard Keynes, Kingsley Martin (editor of the *New Statesman*). September 1934. Monk's House Album 3, p. 54. Reprinted by permission of the Harvard Theatre Collection, the Houghton Library. "True, he's [Kingsley Martin] not quite in his right mind; but how tiring . . . with no ear or eye; no reflective faculty" (*D*, 4:305).

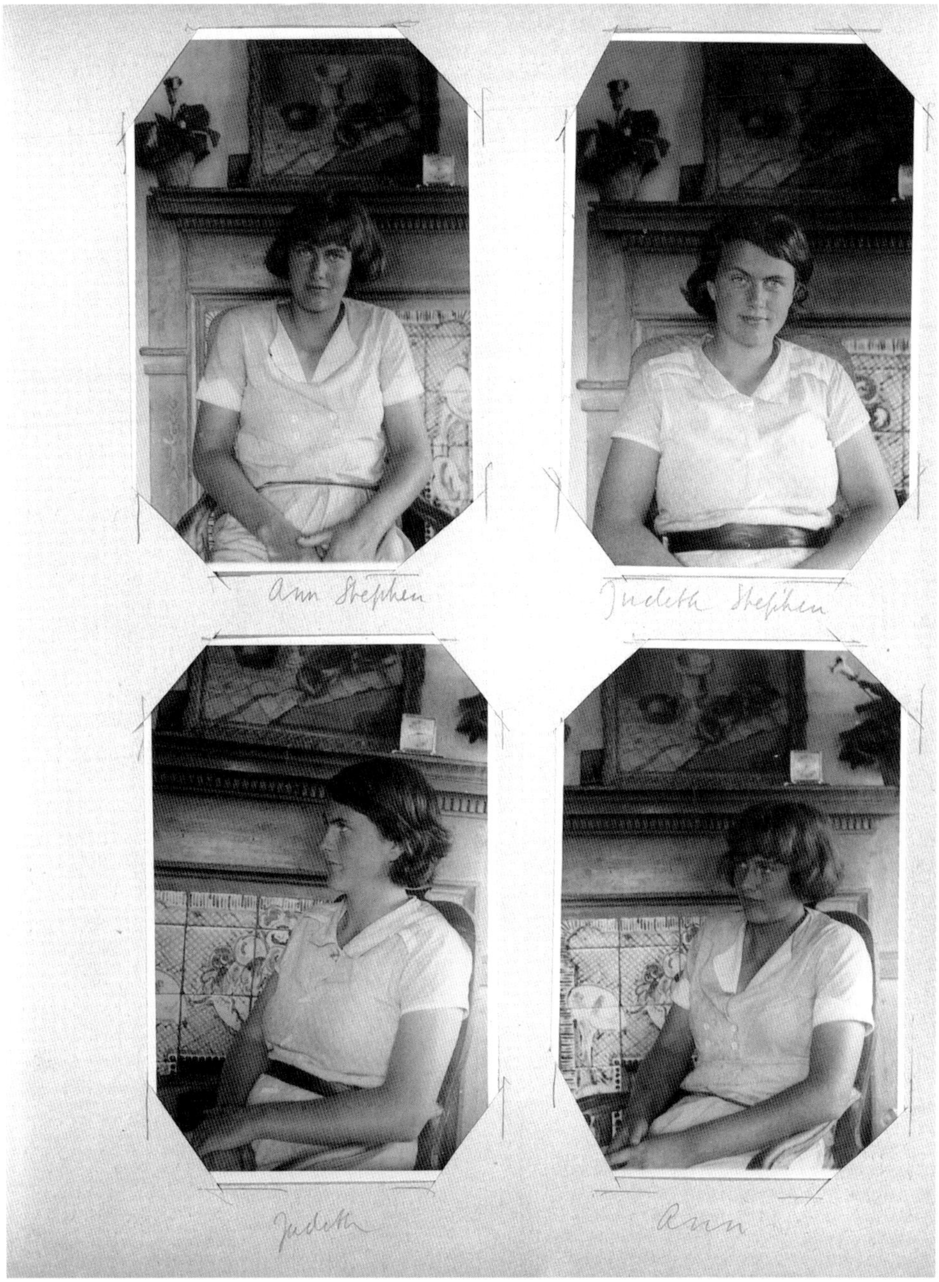

163. Ann and Judith Stephen, September 1934. Monk's House Album 3, p. 55. Reprinted by permission of the Harvard Theatre Collection, the Houghton Library. "A. & J. came . . . great brown naked legged colts . . . they dont wipe their mouths & eat so much" (*D*, 4:243–244).

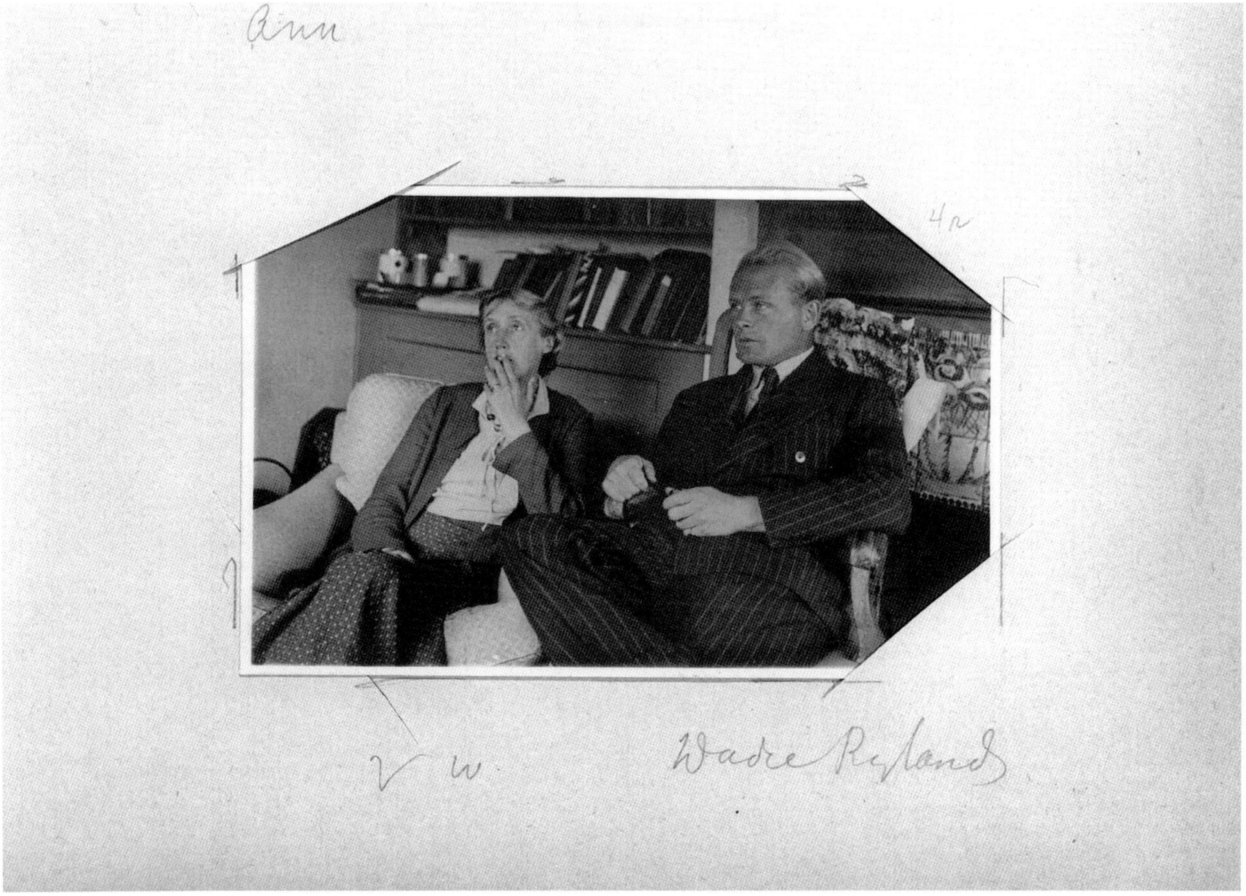

164. Virginia Woolf and George "Dadie" Rylands, September 1934. Monk's House Album 3, p. 56.
Reprinted by permission of the Harvard Theatre Collection, the Houghton Library.
"Dear old Dadie very charming & affectionate . . . he was donnish, serious, very measured; believes in education; in measuring the mind" (*D,* 4:244).

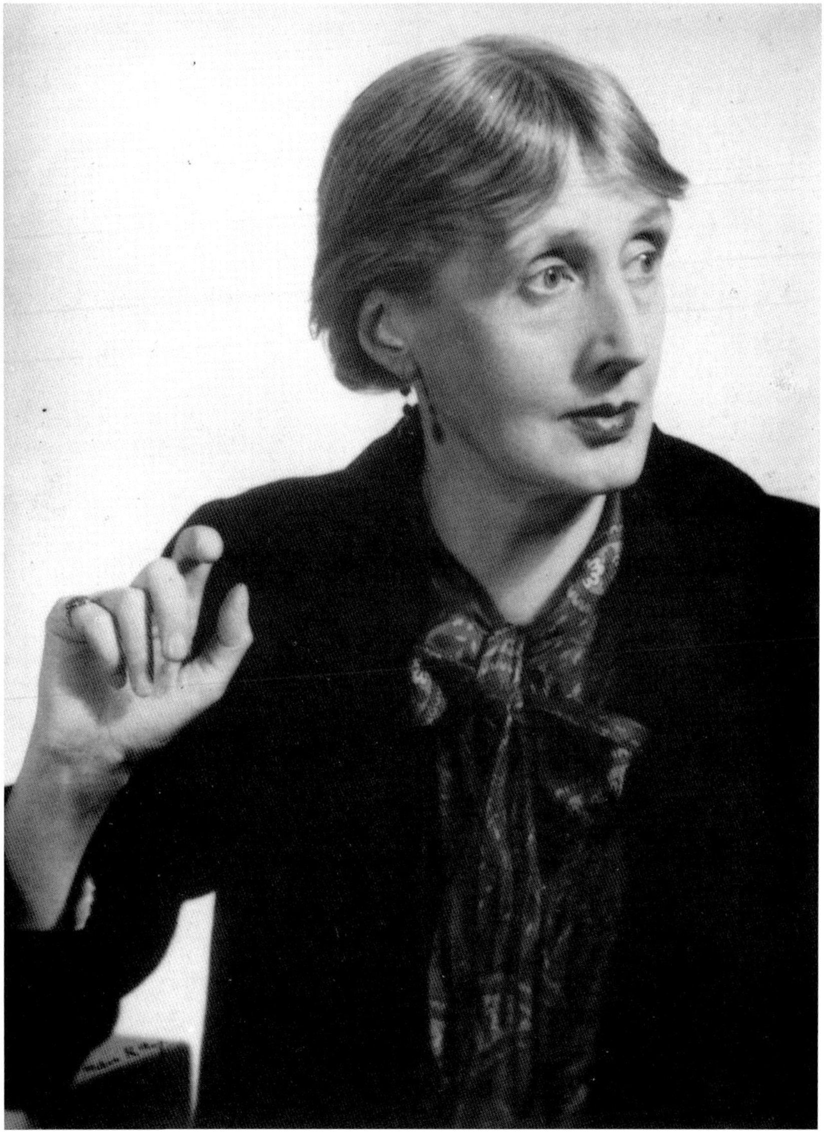

165. Virginia Woolf. Photographer: Man Ray. November 27, 1934, in Curtis Moffat's studio? (the photographer and friend of Man Ray; Man Ray had no London studio). Box 2, folder 3. Reprinted by permission of the Harvard Theatre Collection, the Houghton Library. "Virginia Woolf, whose ascetic face was framed in a severe arrangement of her hair —I had to put some lipstick on her mouth, to which she objected at first, but I explained that it was for technical reasons and would not show in the picture. When she left, she forgot to remove the rouge" (Man Ray, 189).

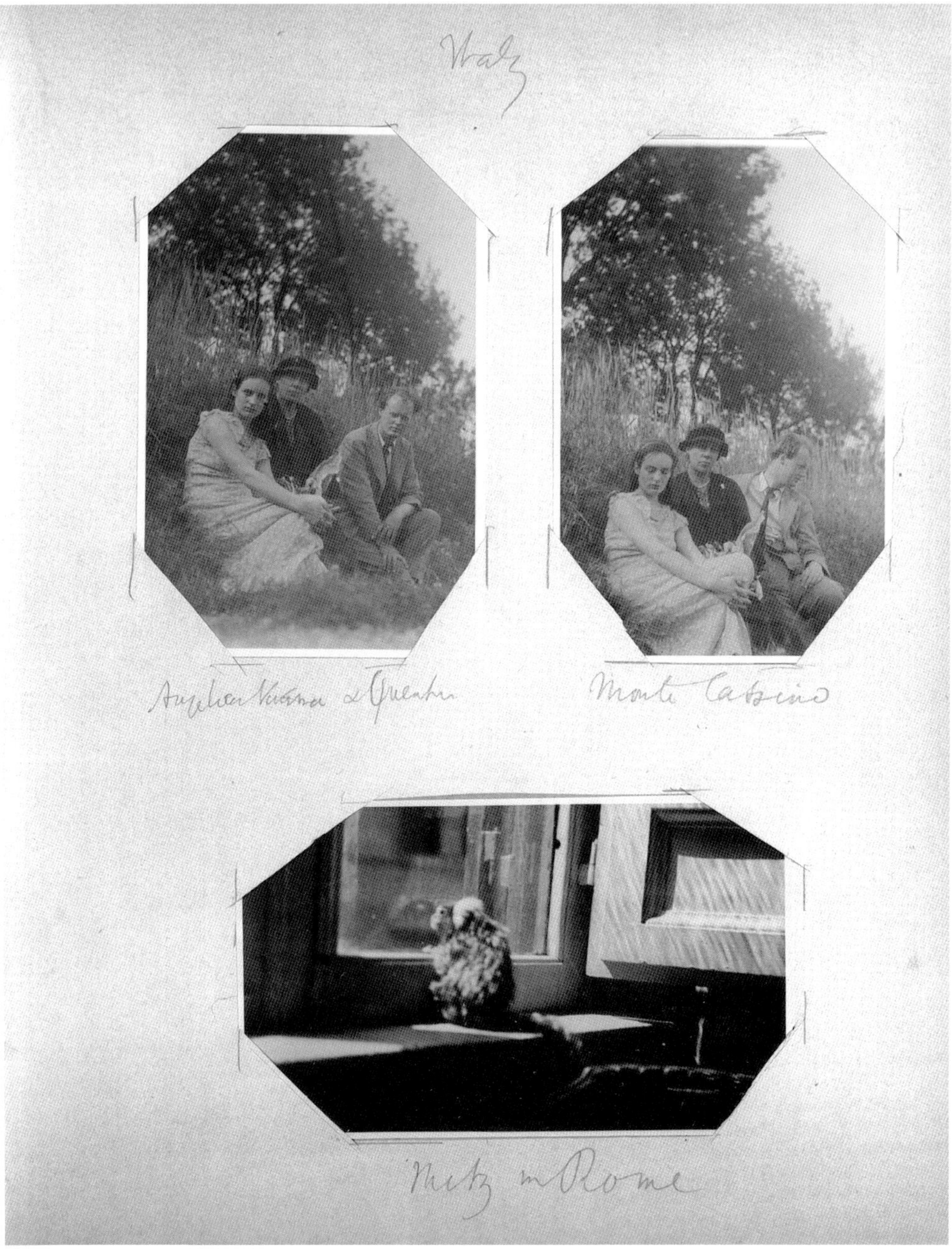

166. Angelica, Vanessa, and Quentin Bell, Italy. Mitzy the marmoset, Rome. May 1935. Monk's House Album 3, p. 60. Reprinted by permission of the Harvard Theatre Collection, the Houghton Library. "I am going to float off the drive home from Cassenlino [Cassino] this evening . . . for the sunset was pouring gold all over us" (*D*, 4:312).

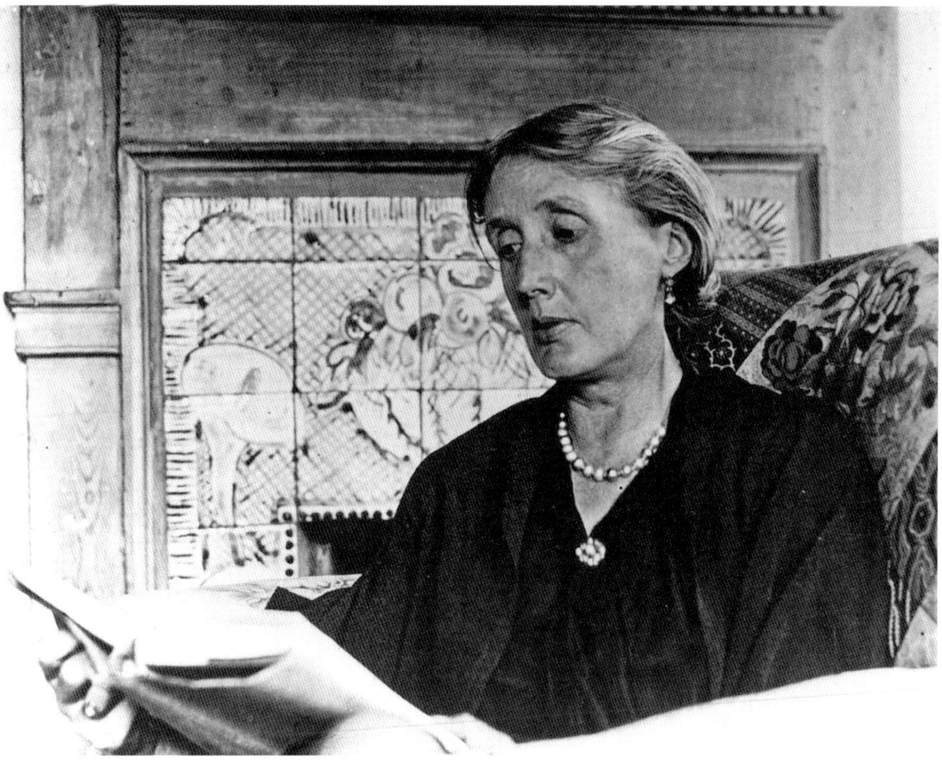

167. (ABOVE) Virginia Woolf, Monk's House, ca. 1933–1935. Box 4, folder 4-1. Reprinted by permission of the Harvard Theatre Collection, the Houghton Library. Tiles were installed September 1, 1931. "Isnt it odd how much more one sees in a photograph than in real life?" (*L*, 5: 455).

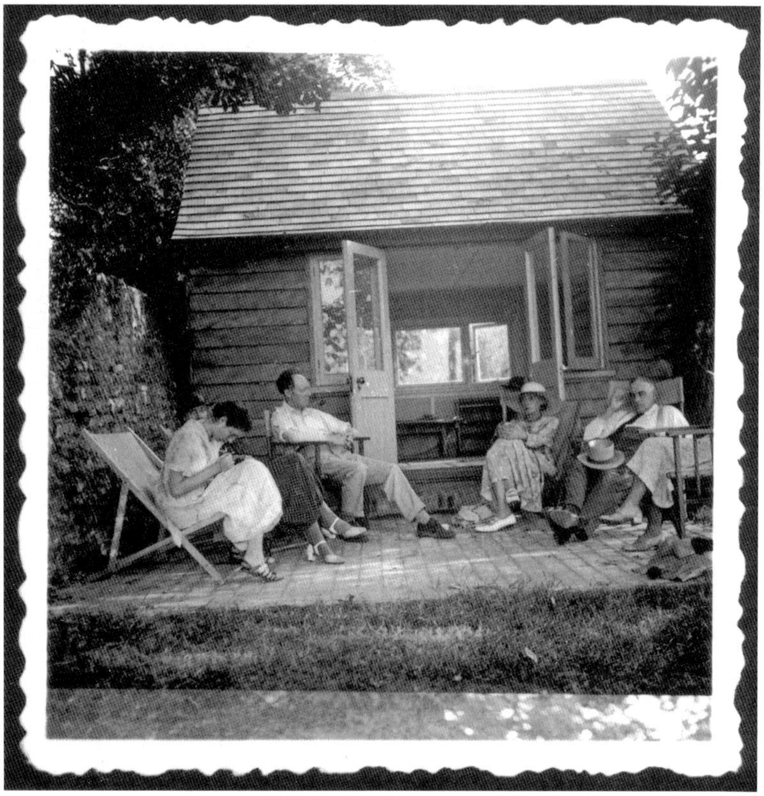

168. (RIGHT) Angelica and Clive Bell, Virginia Woolf, and Maynard Keynes. Monk's House, August 6, 1935. Box 2, unmarked folder. Reprinted by permission of the Harvard Theatre Collection, the Houghton Library. "Since coming here I have poured out tea for 15 self-invited guests . . . it is roasting hot here, and incredibly beautiful" (*L*, 5: 423–424).

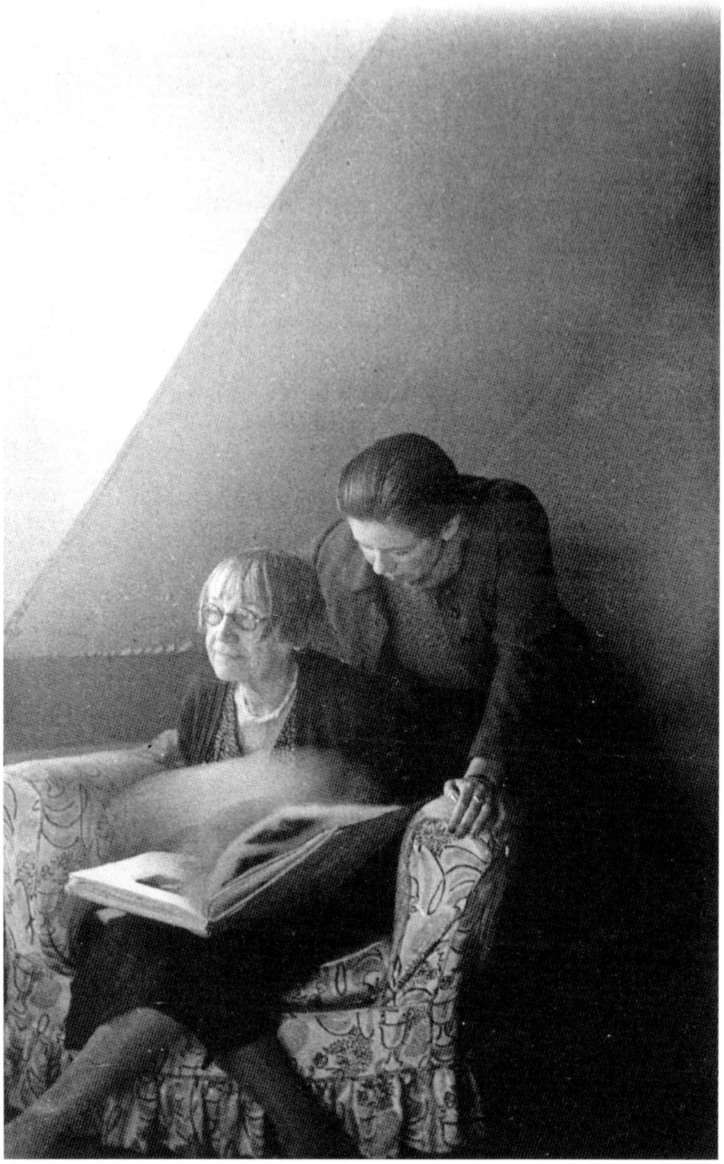

169. Dorothy and Jane Bussy, ca. 1936–1938. Monk's House Album 5, p. 46.
Reprinted by permission of the Harvard Theatre Collection, the Houghton Library. "My dear Dorothy, is there any chance that you could give us a night here before you go—the tea was so transient . . . it would be a delight to both of us to see you again" (*L*, 6:71).

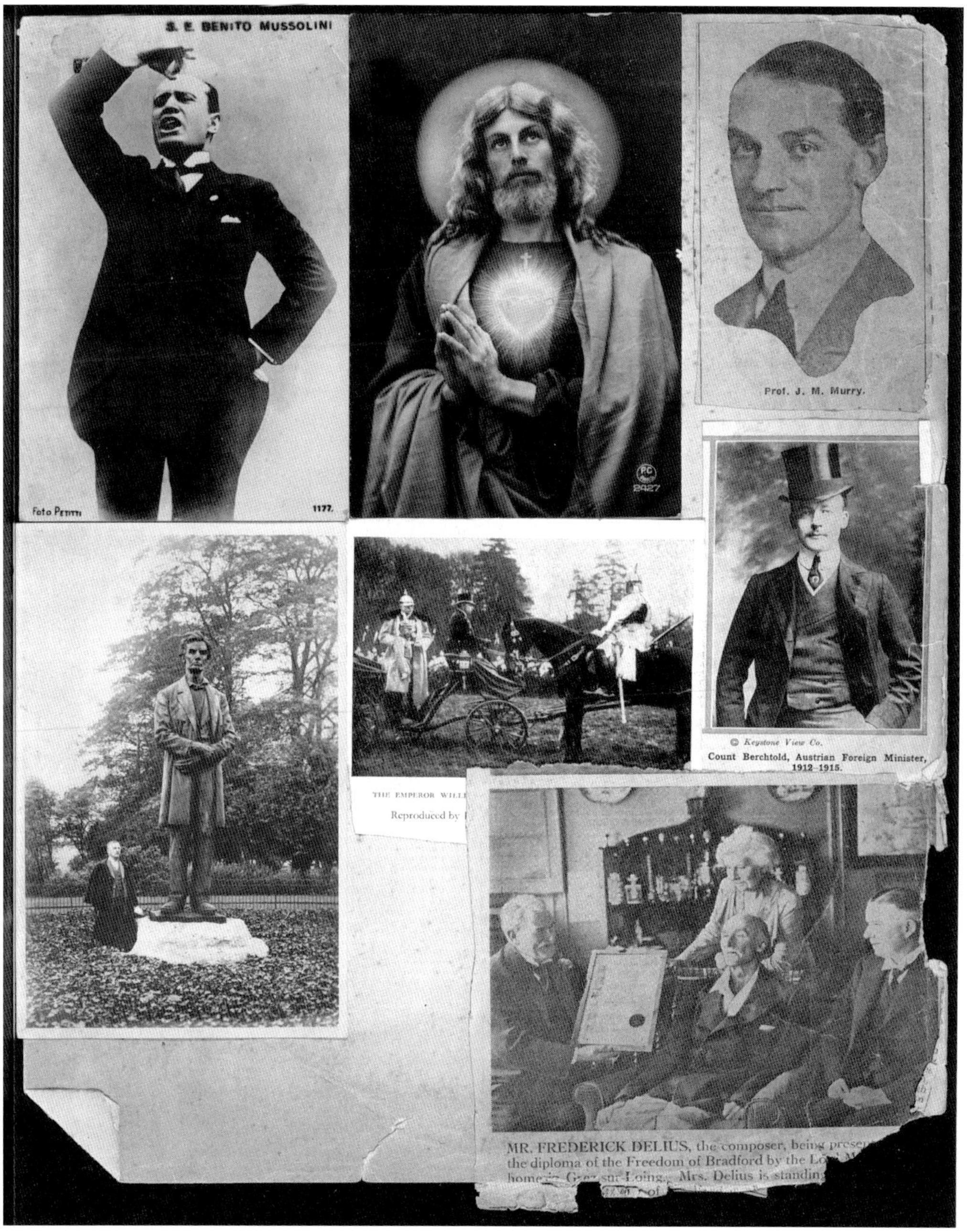

170. Scrap page with cuttings: Mussolini, Christ, Prof. J. M. Murry, Abraham Lincoln, Emperor Wilhelm, Count Berchtold, Frederick Delius. No date. White folder. Reprinted by permission of the Harvard Theatre Collection, the Houghton Library. A photographic preparation for *Three Guineas* resembling its working title, "Men Are Like That"? This was also a phrase of Stella Duckworth's. "Your world, then, the world of professional, of public life, seen from this angle undoubtedly looks queer" (*RO/TG*, 133).

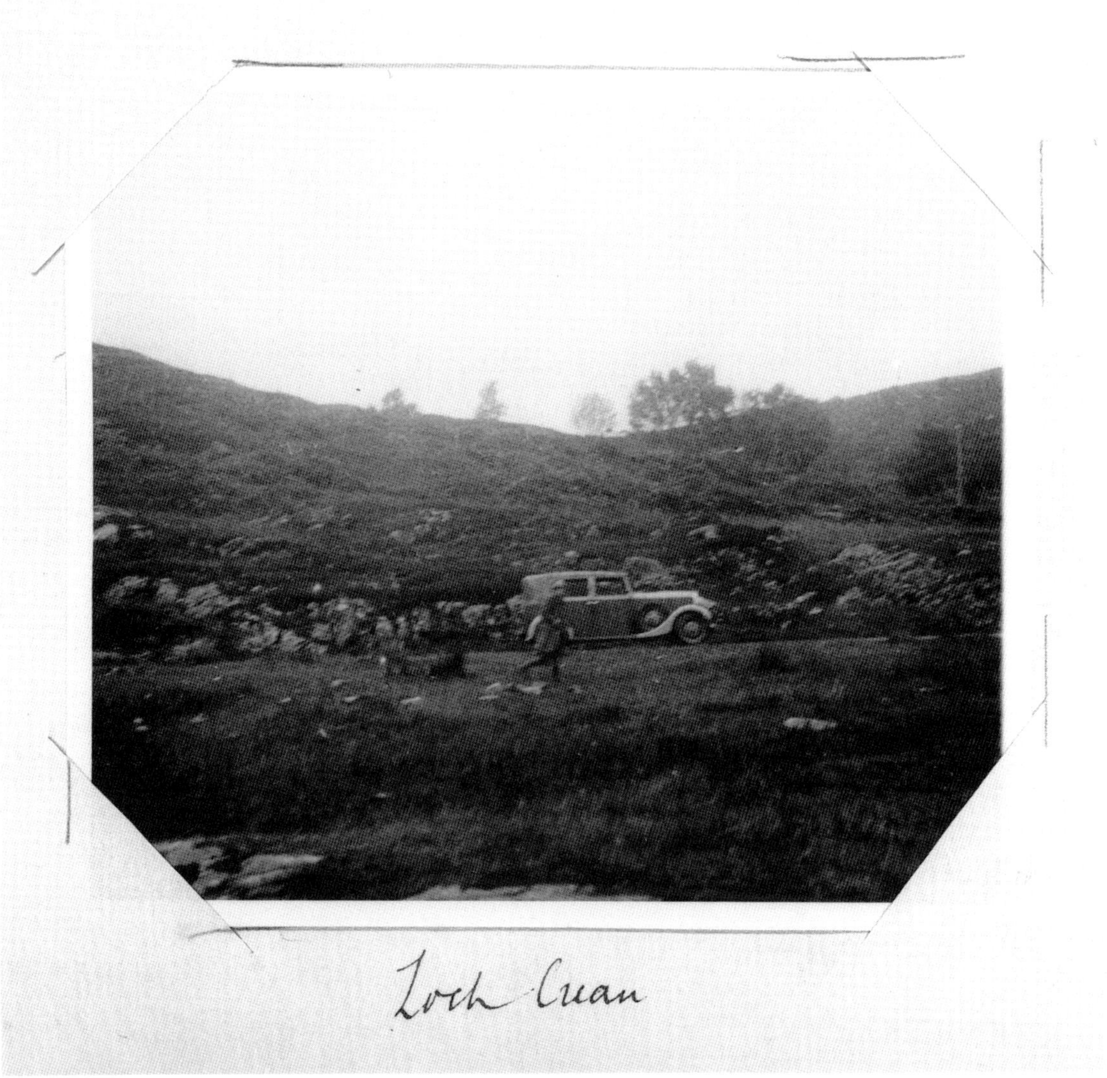

171. Virginia Woolf, Scotland, June 1938. Monk's House Album 5, p. 68. Reprinted by permission of the Harvard Theatre Collection, the Houghton Library. "We had a terrific drive yesterday in one of the worst known gales, over the wildest passes. Trees were hurtling; rivers simply cataractuous, but very beautiful . . . our petrol gave out" (L, 6:249).

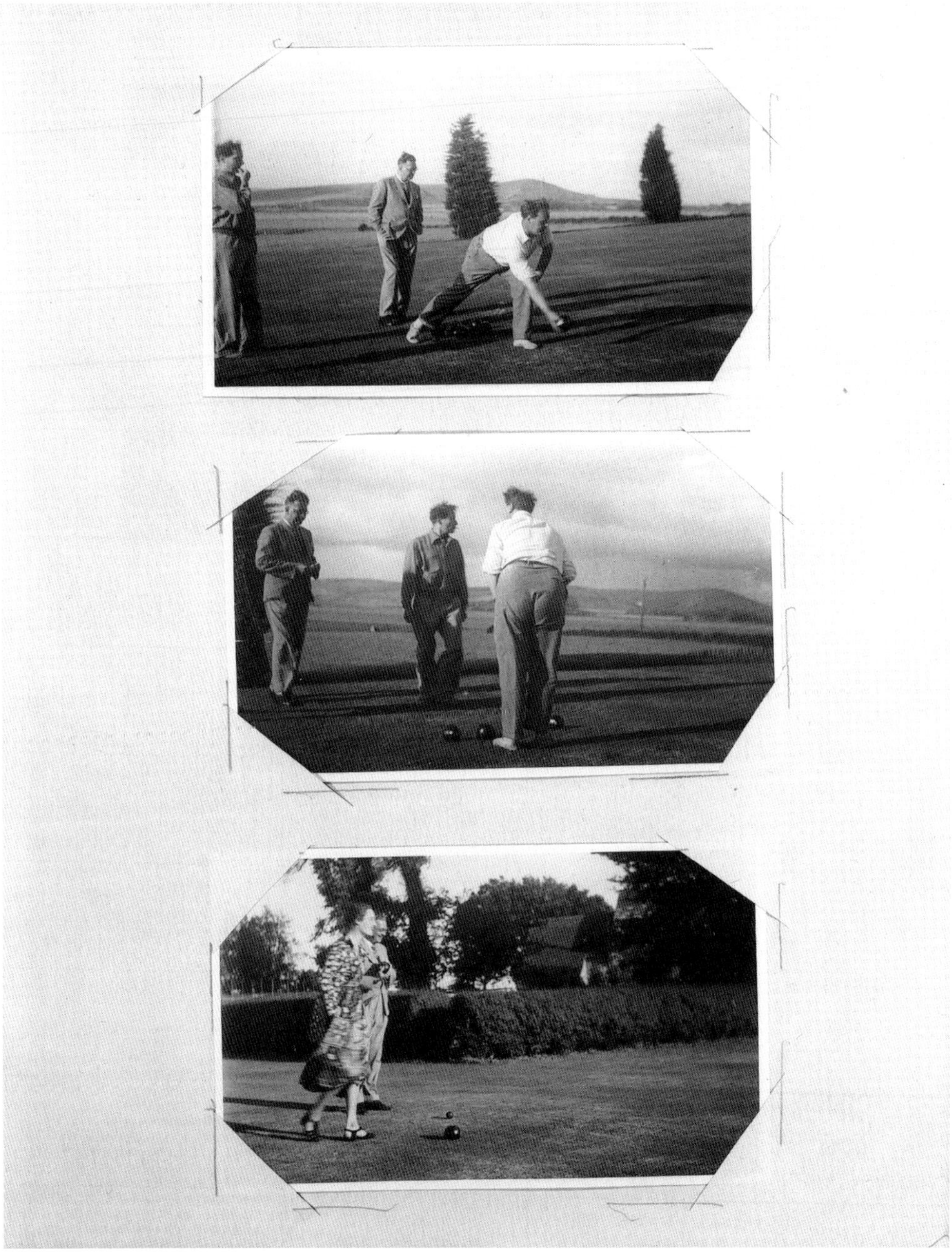

172. Duncan Grant, William Plomer, and Quentin Bell, ca. August 1938. Angelica Bell. Monk's House Album 5, p. 72. Reprinted by permission of the Harvard Theatre Collection, the Houghton Library. "All Charleston & William Plomer yesterday: a lovely thin blue day. Bowls" (*D*, 5:163).

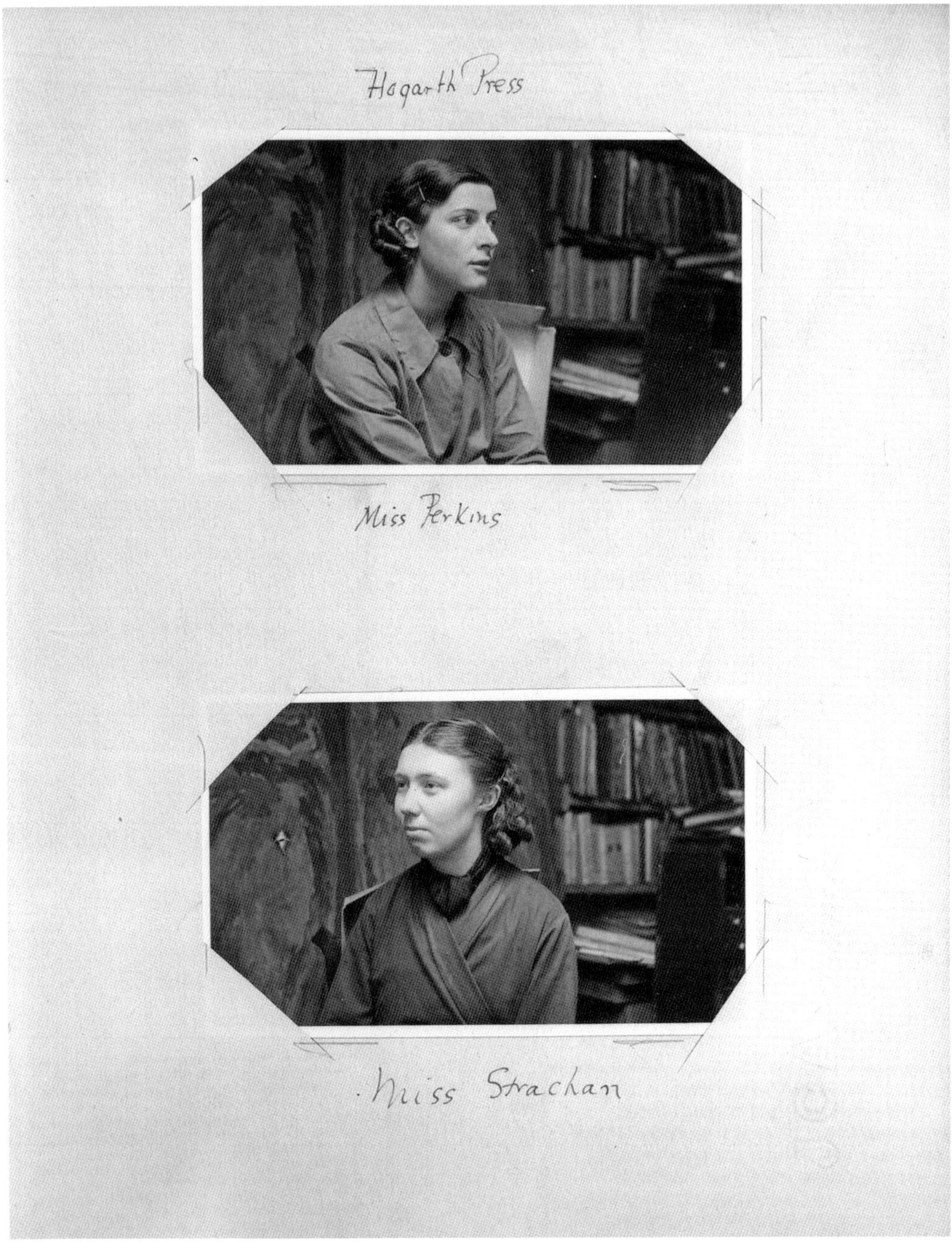

173. Miss Perkins; Miss Strachan. Hogarth Press, ca. 1938. Monk's House Album 5, p. 52. Reprinted by permission of the Harvard Theatre Collection, the Houghton Library. "Everyone was certain it was war . . . found that L. had arranged that the Press was to go on; but the clerks to go away into the country if they liked . . . the clerks wanted to go on, as they had no place in the country; and of course no money. . . . Miss Perkins preferred to sit in the stock room, which she had partly prepared with mattresses" (*L*, 6:276).

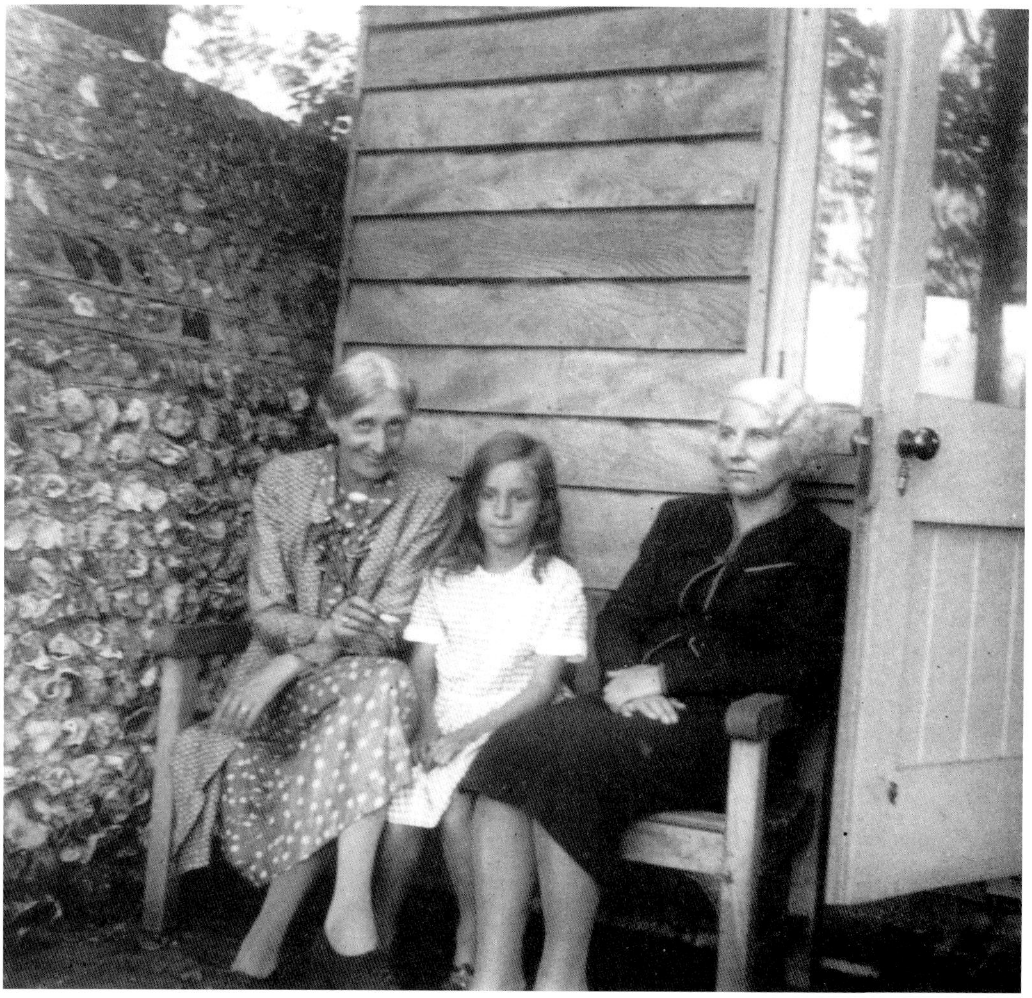

174. Virginia Woolf, Noel and Virginia Richards, ca. 1938. Monk's House Album 5, p. 79. Reprinted by permission of the Harvard Theatre Collection, the Houghton Library. "We've had innumerable visitors . . . Noel very solid badgerly and dependable: my goddaughter [Virginia] a nice little elf" (*L*, 6:274).

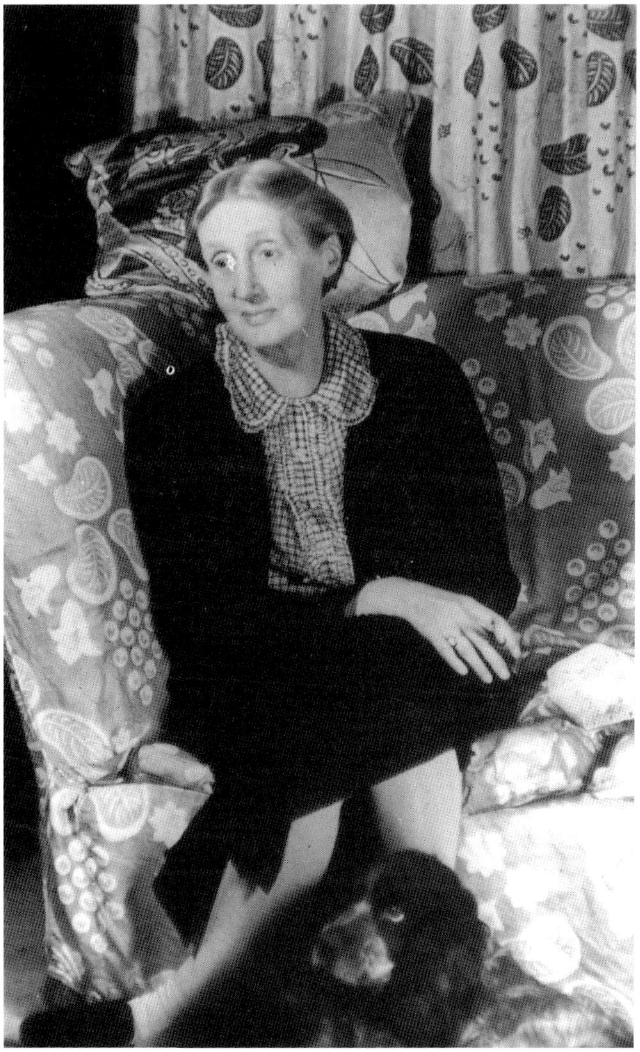

175. Virginia Woolf, 52 Tavistock Square, June 1939. Photographer: Gisèle Freund. Box 2, folder 1. Reprinted by permission of the Harvard Theatre Collection, the Houghton Library. "Ocampo bringing Giselle [*sic*] Freund & all her apparatus . . . oh curse this petty vulgar photography-advertising stunt . . . so my afternoon is gone in the way to me most detestable" (*D*, 5:220).

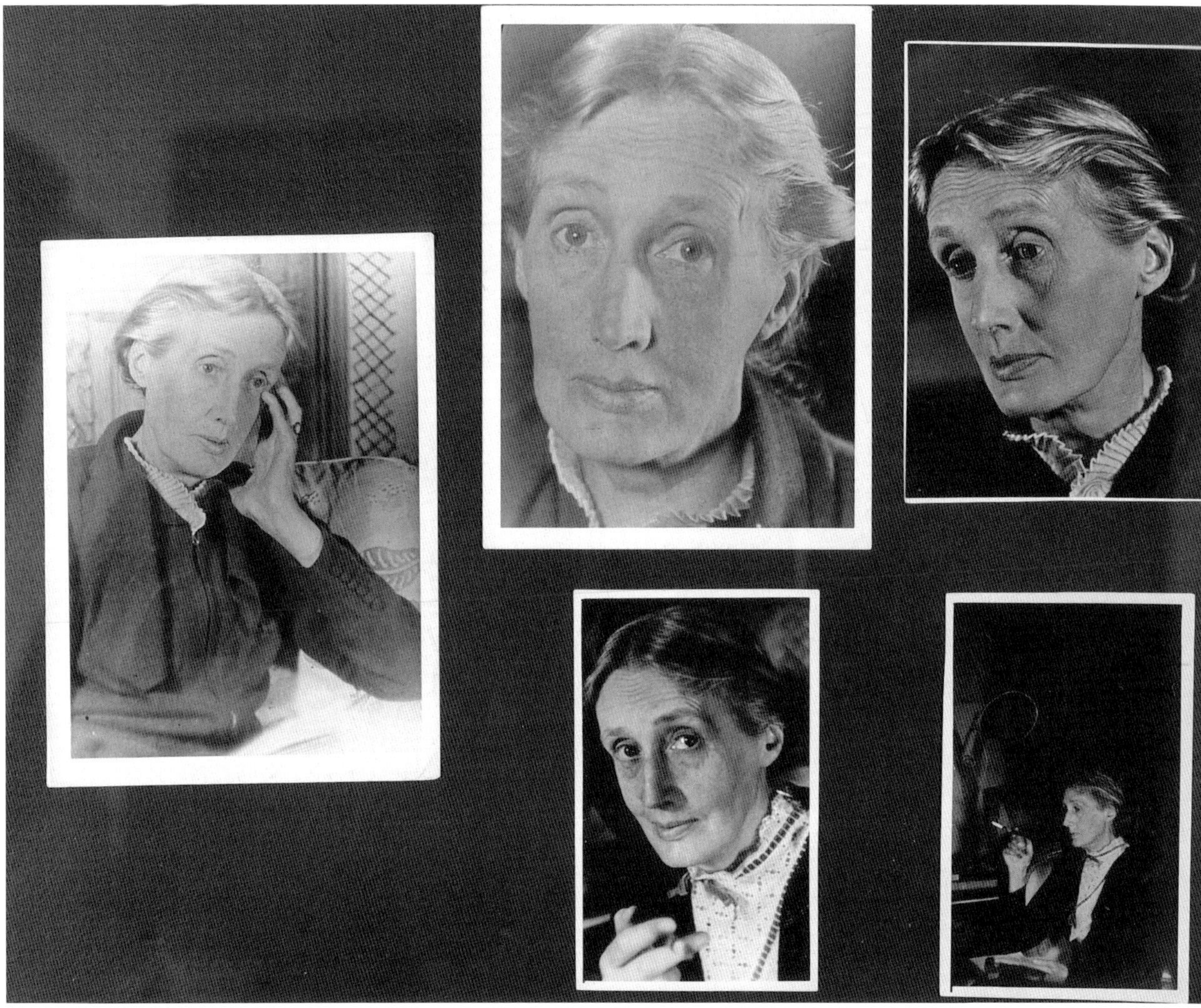

176. Virginia Woolf, 52 Tavistock Square, June 1939. A composite of loose photographs. Photographer: Gisèle Freund. Reprinted by permission of the Harvard Theatre Collection, the Houghton Library. "I loathe being hoisted about on top of a stick for any one to stare at" (*L*, 6:351).

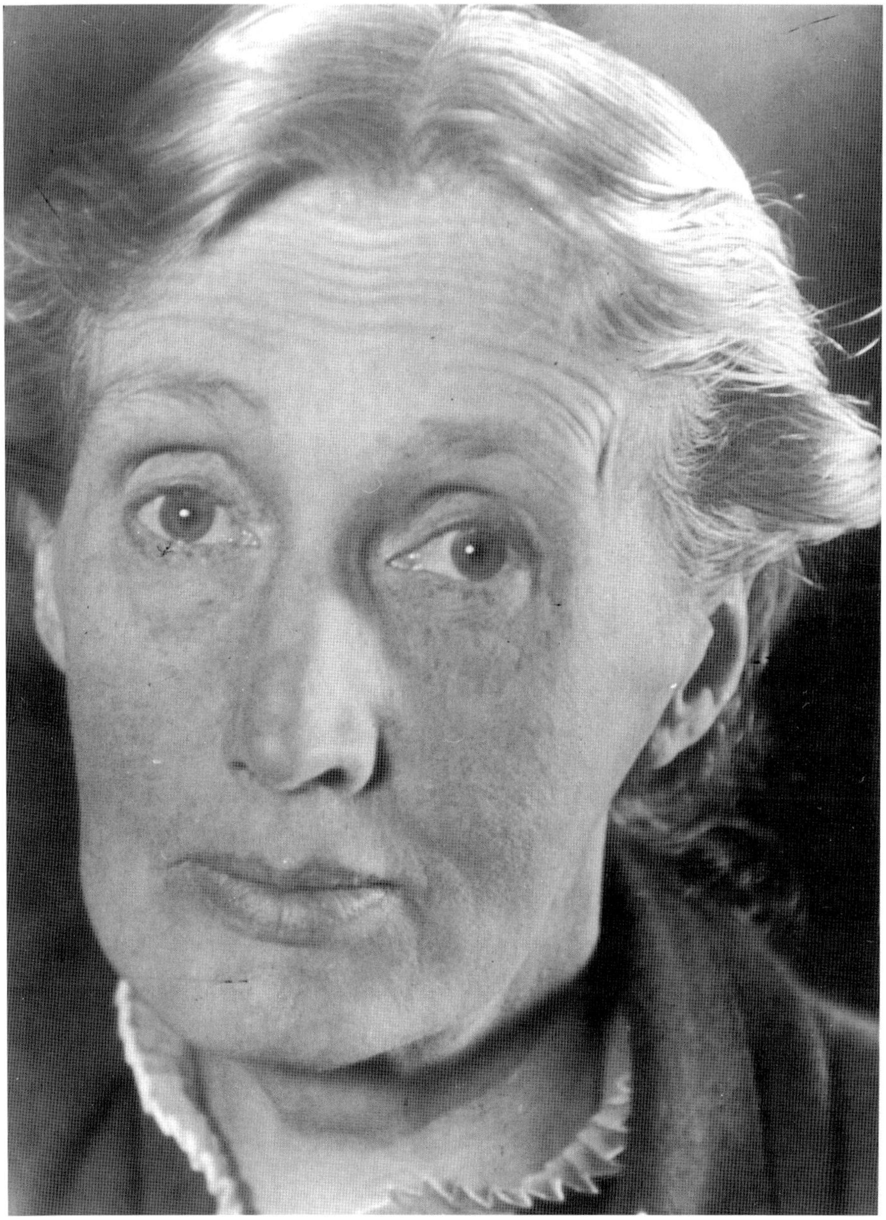

177. Virginia Woolf, 52 Tavistock Square, June 1939. Photographer: Gisèle Freund. Box 2, folder 3. Reprinted by permission of the Harvard Theatre Collection, the Houghton Library. "That devil woman Giselle [*sic*] Freund calmly tells me she's showing those d---d photographs" (*L*, 6:351).

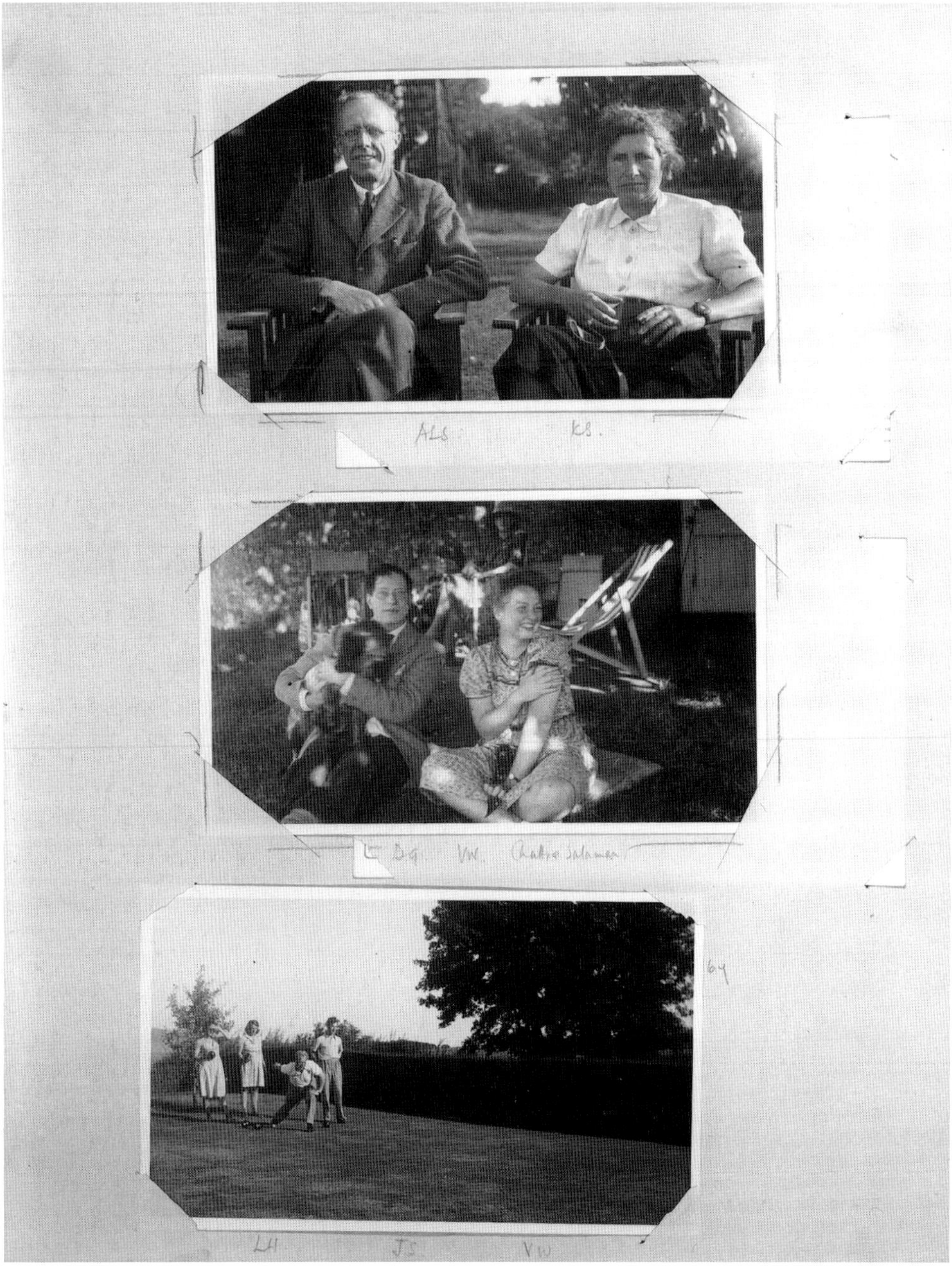

178. Adrian and Karin Stephen; Duncan Grant, Virginia Woolf, and Chattie Salamon; Ann Stephen, Chattie Salamon, Leslie Humphrey, and Quentin Bell, ca. 1939–1940. Monk's House Album 4, p. 31. Reprinted by permission of the Harvard Theatre Collection, the Houghton Library. "As for gossip, we've seen a good many refugees of sorts. . . . Duncan for ever hitching up his trousers which are of blue corduroy and for ever coming down" (*L*, 6:368).

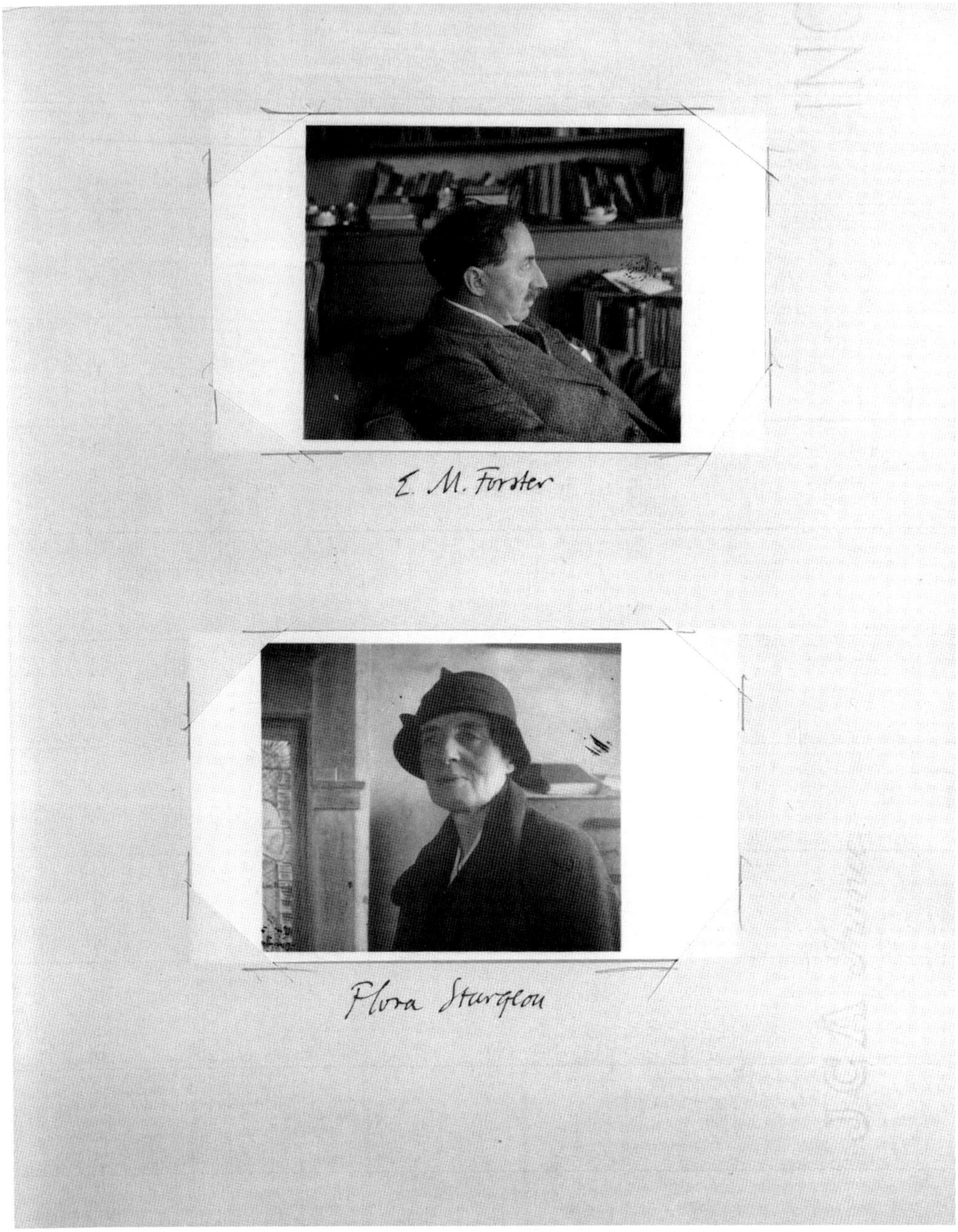

179. E. M. Forster; Flora Sturgeon (Leonard's sister). January 1940.
Monk's House Album 4, p. 23. Reprinted by permission of the Harvard Theatre Collection, the Houghton Library. "Sussex has been sociable . . . then Flora; then Morgan; then London, from which we came back this afternoon to frozen pipes" (D, 5:257).

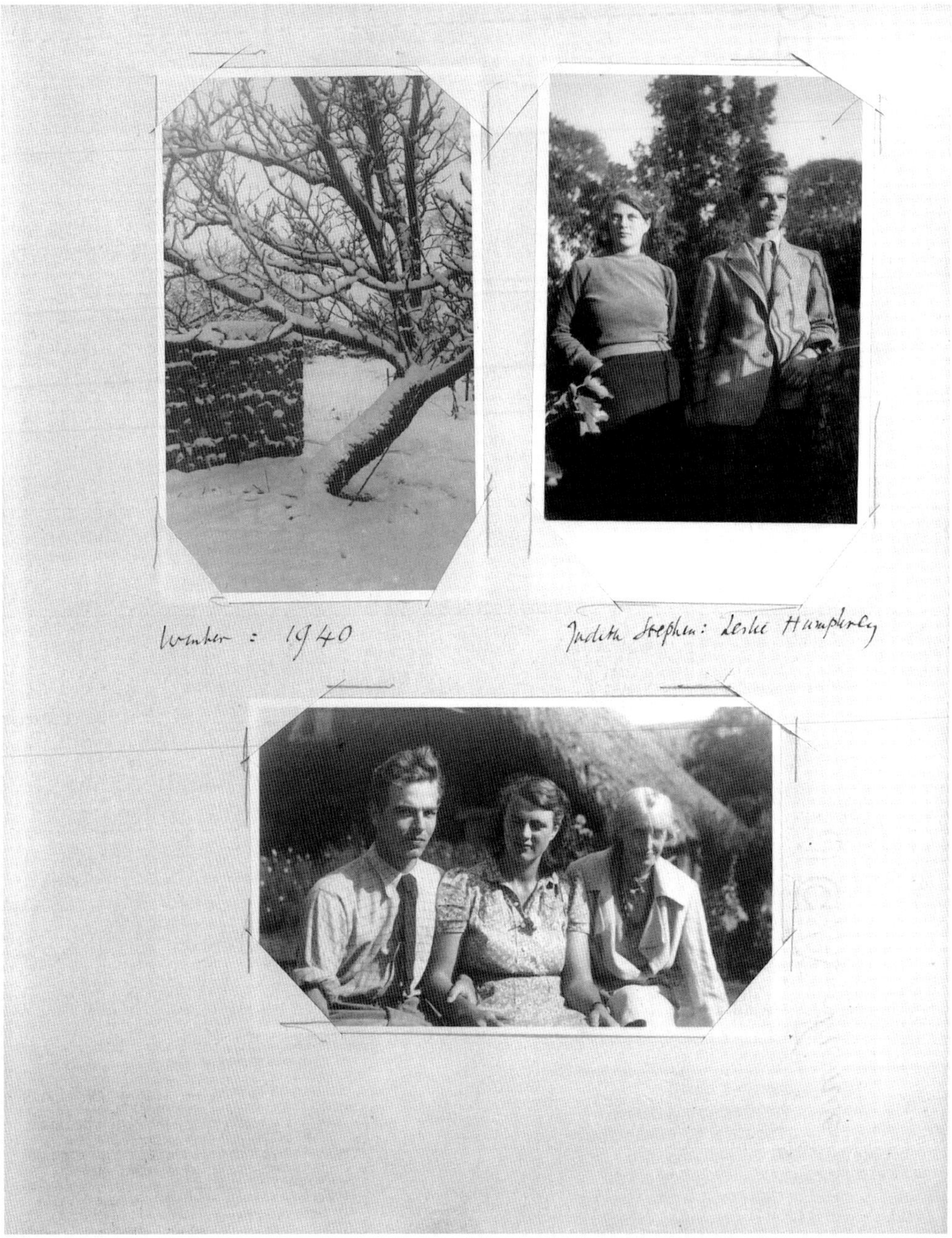

180. Judith Stephen, Leslie Humphrey, and Virginia Woolf. August 1940. Monk's House Album 4, p. 20. Reprinted by permission of the Harvard Theatre Collection, the Houghton Library. "We went out on the terrace, began playing. A large two decker plane . . . Leslie saw the German black cross . . . saw 2 planes very high. They made for us. We started to shelter in the Lodge. But they wheeled & Leslie saw the English sign . . . it wd have been a peaceful matter of fact death to be popped off on the terrace playing bowls" (*D*, 5:313).

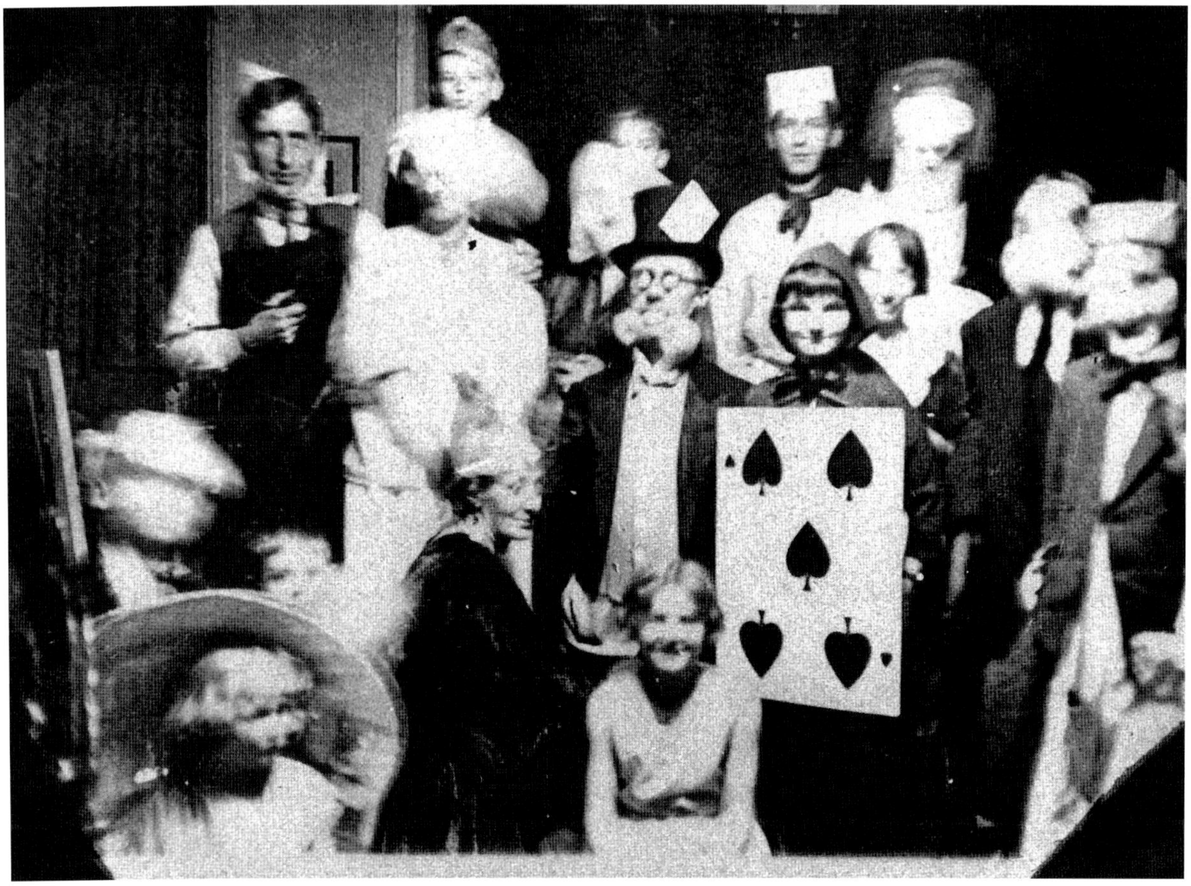

181. Leonard and Virginia Woolf, Adrian Stephen, Julian Bell, Raymond Mortimer, Angelica Bell, Jack Hutchinson, Vanessa Bell, and others, 8 Fitzroy Street, January 1930. Alice in Wonderland party for Angelica's birthday. Bell Album 5, p. 24 A15. Copyright Tate, London, 2004. My dress "a pair of hare's paws (you remember the March Hare) . . . Roger [as the White Knight] had taken the place by storm . . . he was a masterpiece, having called out all the resource and ingenuity of Woolworths stores. Candles, mousetraps, tweezers . . . Leonard, wearing a green baize apron and a pair of chisels as the Carpenter came in conflict with the police on behalf of a drunken prostitute . . . 'why dont you go for the men who began it? My name's Woolf, and I can take my oath the woman's not to blame. She called them bugger; but they called her whore'—and so on—holding his apron" (L, 4:128–129).

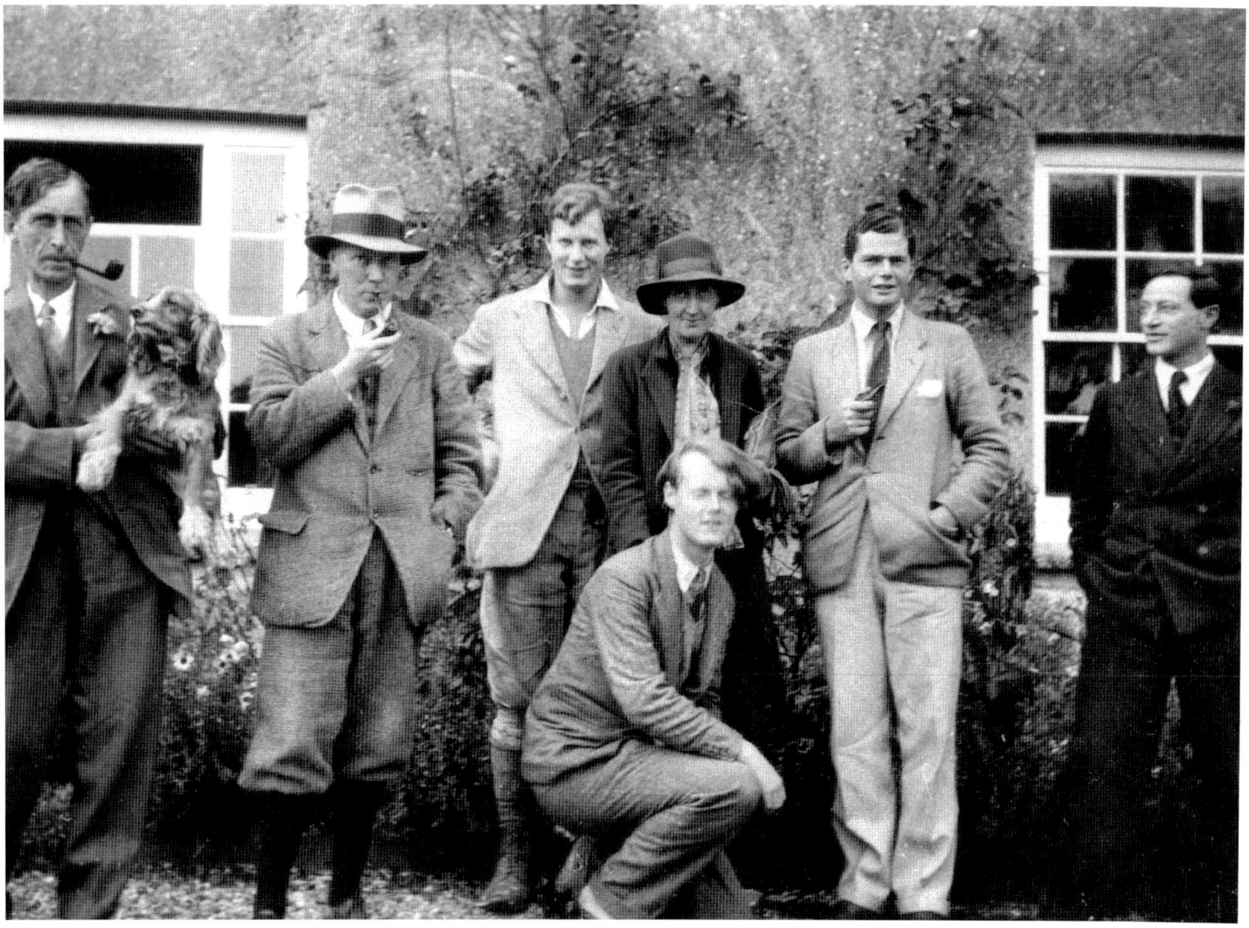

182. Leonard Woolf, Clive and Julian Bell, Virginia Woolf, Auberon Duckworth (son of George), Duncan Grant, and Quentin Bell (in front), 1930. Charleston Bell Album 5, p. 38 AI19. Copyright Tate, London, 2004. "On Wednesday, you'll be amused to hear, Nessa is giving a luncheon party to Sir George Duckworth and his son. He says he is about to die" (*L*, 4:220).

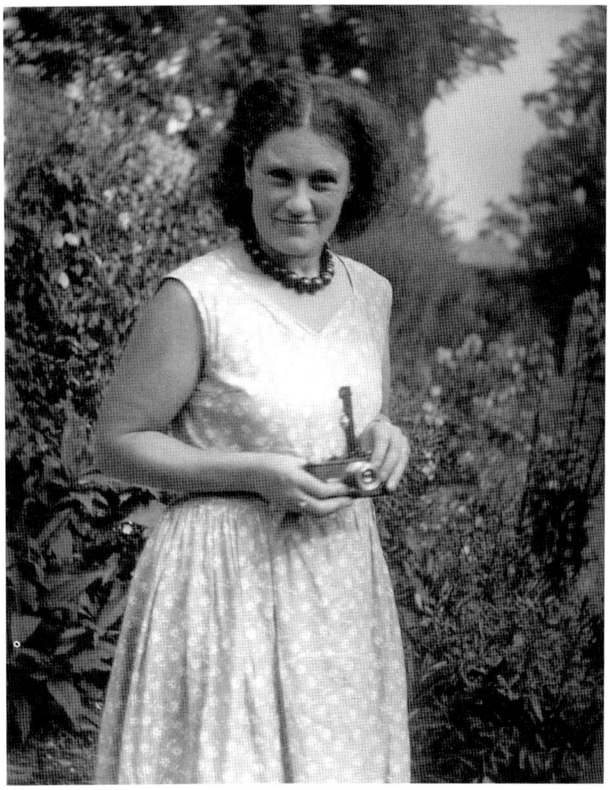

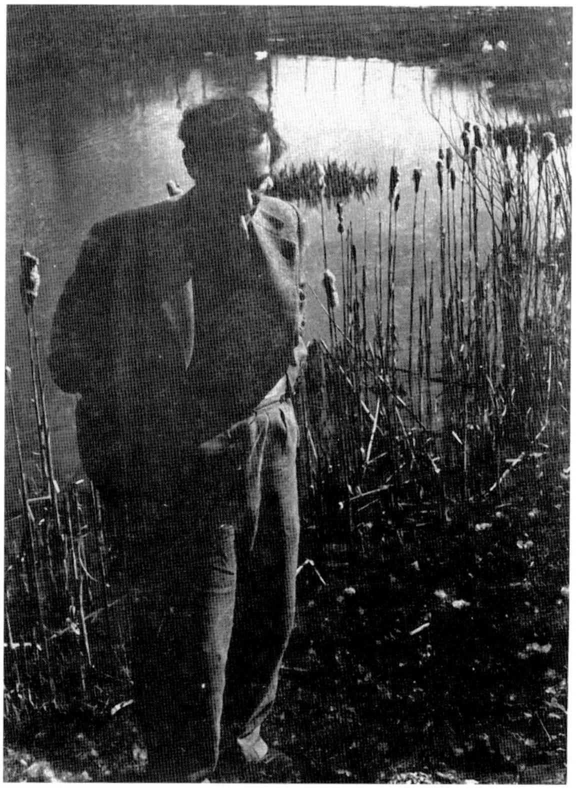

183. (LEFT) Lettice Ramsey, ca. 1932. Charleston Bell Album 7, p. 16 L8. Copyright Tate, London, 2004. "With Julian & Lettice Ramsay [*sic*] last night—why not simply become fluid in their lives, if my own is dim?" (*D*, 4:135).

184. (RIGHT) Duncan Grant, Charleston, ca. 1933–1935. AC17. Copyright Tate, London, 2004. "Q [Quentin] has grand projects for a stream, to meander through the orchard, making one or two large pools, by the side of which Duncan will grow water plants" (VB/L, 423).

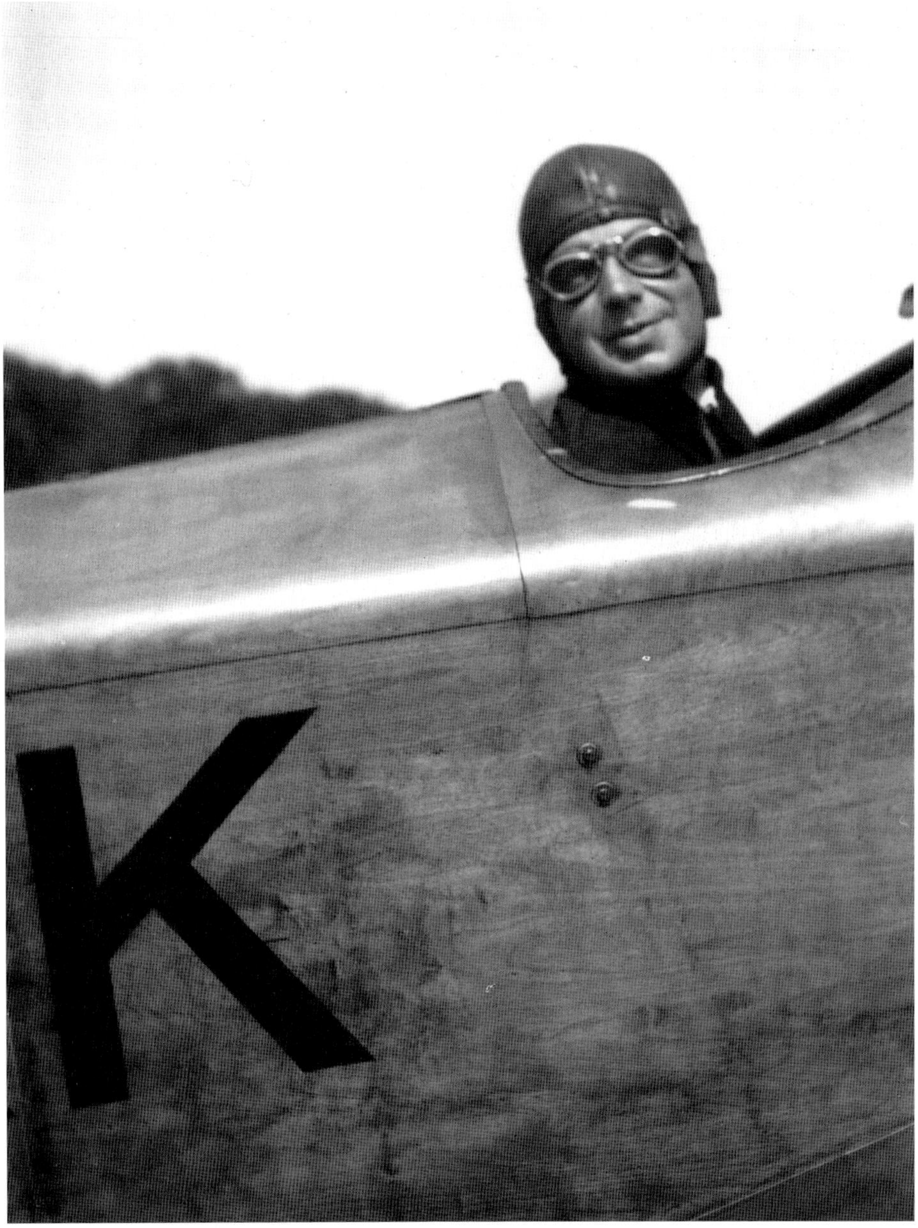

185. David "Bunny" Garnett, Moth aeroplane, Charleston, 1933.
Bell Album 7, p. 27. Copyright Tate, London, 2004. Amy Johnson's solo flight in a Gypsy Moth, England to Australia, was May 5, 1930, taking nineteen days. "[Bunny] talks like a heavy wardrobe . . . How-do-you-start-an-aeroplane?" (*D*, 4:246).

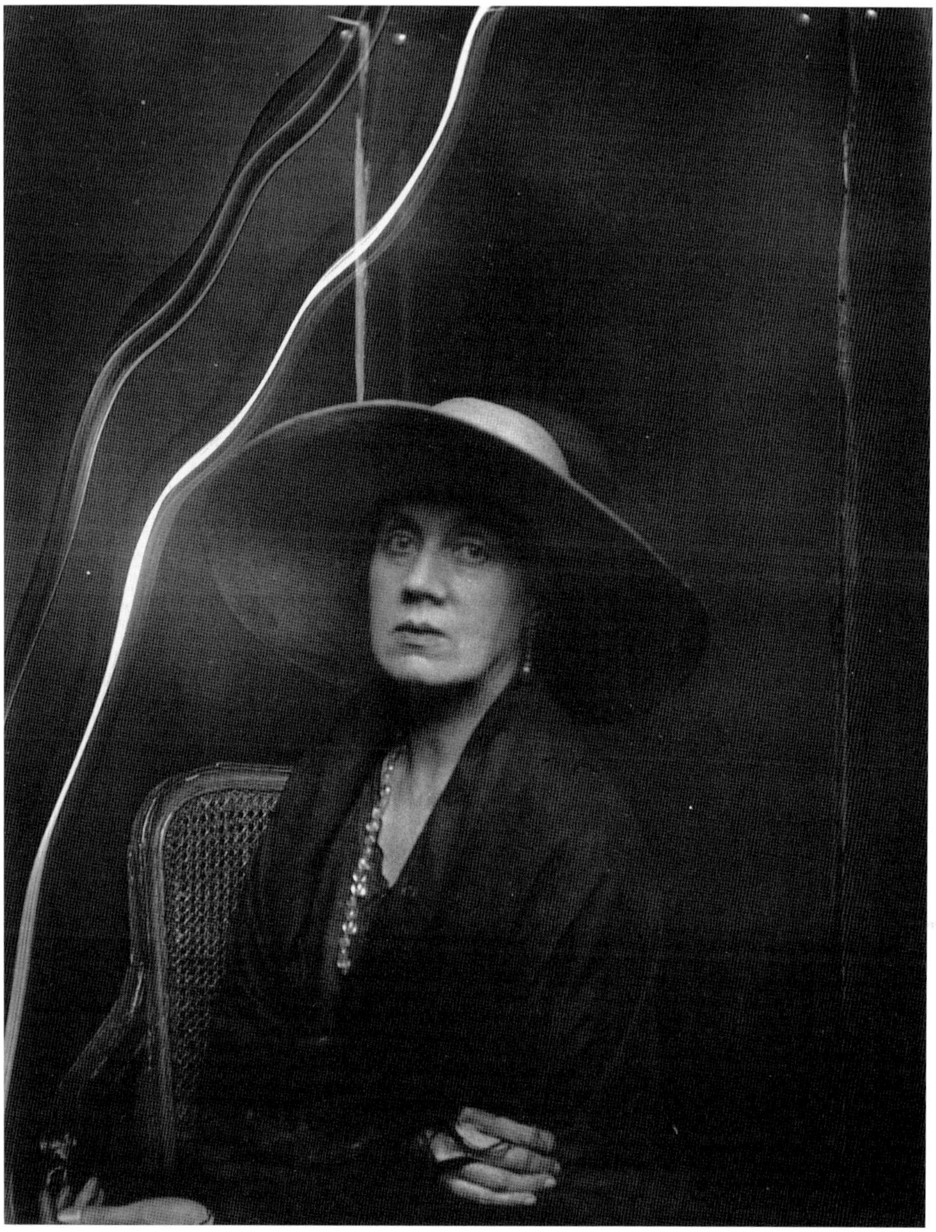

186. Vanessa Bell, 8 Fitzroy Street, 1934. Q50. Copyright Tate, London, 2004
In 1934? Vanessa, saddened by the death of Roger Fry. "A photograph is the best token there is of her [Vanessa] appearance . . . you see the soft, dreamy and almost melancholy expression of the eyes" (R, 28).

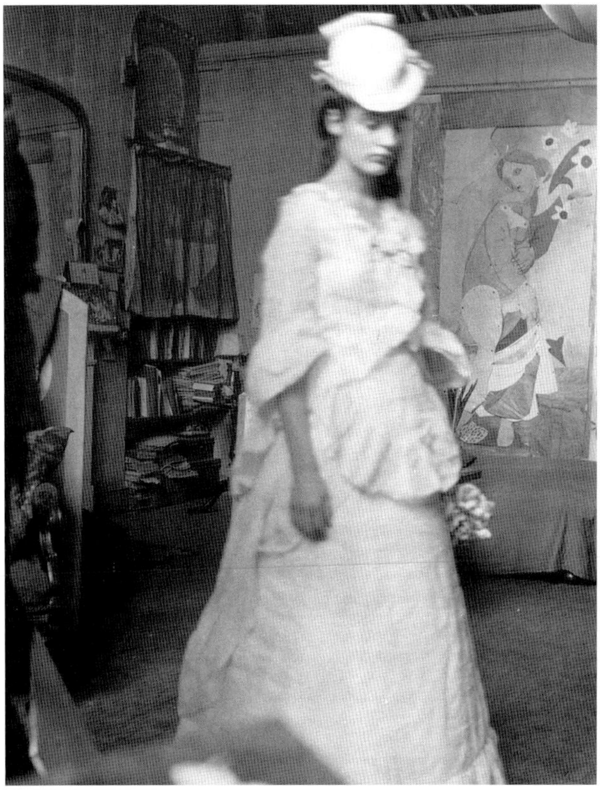

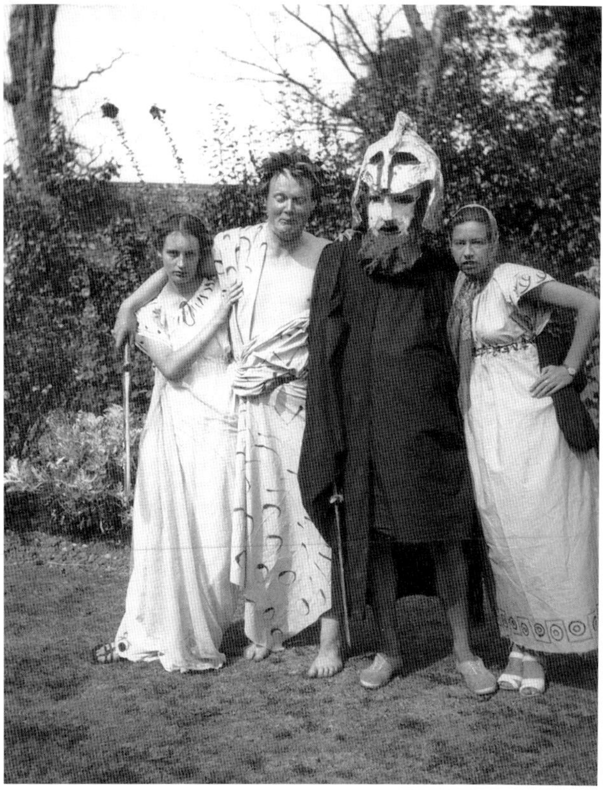

187. (LEFT) Angelica Bell as Ellen Terry, 8 Fitzroy Street, January 18, 1935. Bell Album 7, p. 36 AA38. Copyright Tate, London, 2004. The rear painting is an early version of Duncan Grant's *Design for the Queen Mary* (1936; oil on board). "The play came off last night . . . Angelica ravishing of course, but of course too grown up for my taste" (*D*, 4:274).

188. (RIGHT) Angelica and Julian Bell, Duncan Grant, Jane Bussy. Charleston, 1935. Bell Album 8, p. 14 D2. Copyright Tate, London, 2004. "What an uncomfortable relation, Aunt & nephew. And how nice he [Julian] is, & how obtuse" (*D*, 4:281).

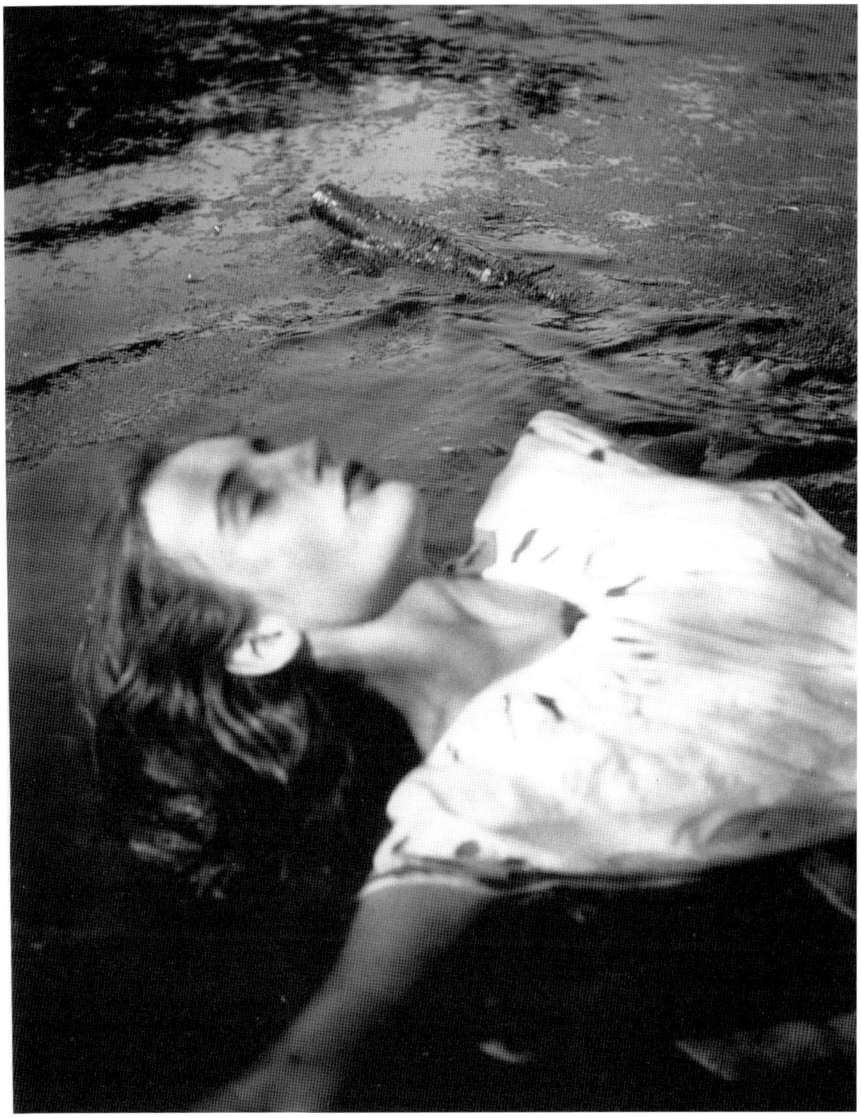

189. Angelica Bell as Ophelia, Charleston, ca. 1935. Bell Album 8, p. 16 AA37. Copyright Tate, London, 2004. In Woolf's *Freshwater,* staged 1935, Angelica played Ellen Terry, who is also presumed drowned.

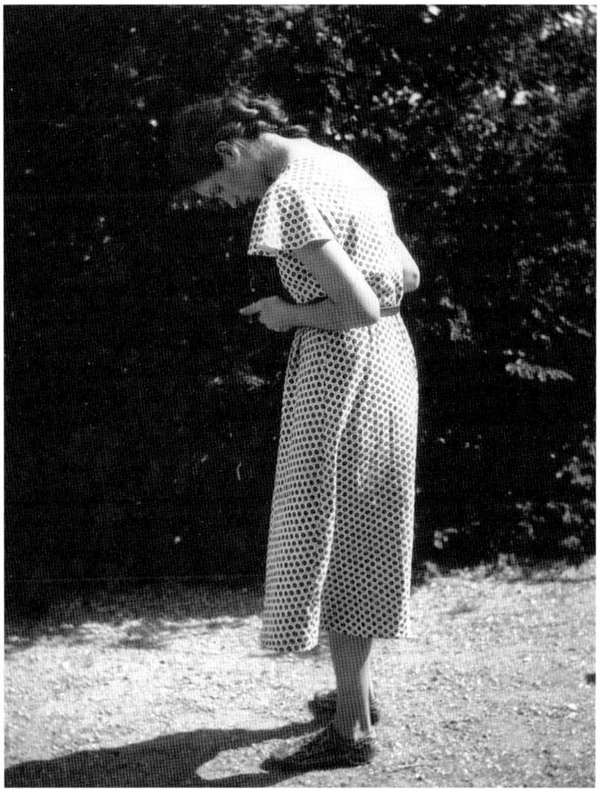 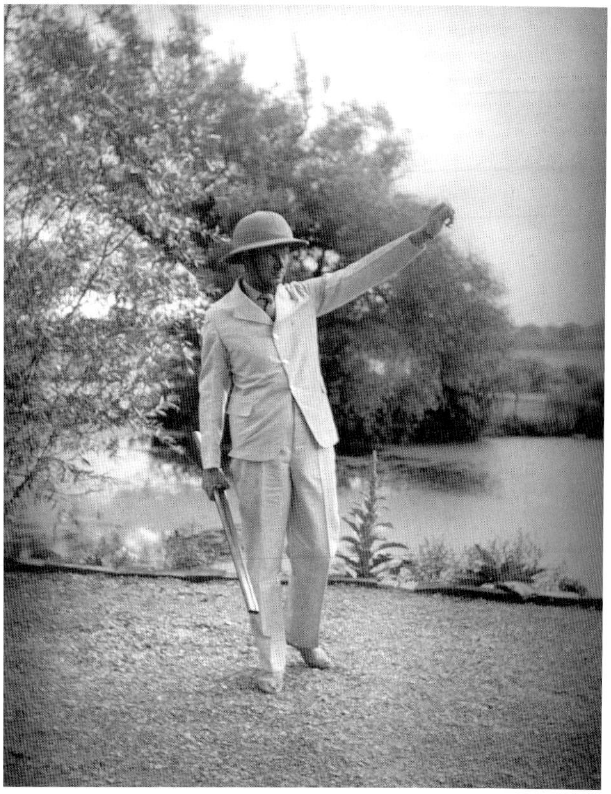

190. (LEFT) Angelica Bell, Charleston, 1935. Bell Album 8, p. 10 D30. Copyright Tate, London, 2004.

191. (RIGHT) Julian Bell, Charleston, 1935. Bell Album 8, p. 15 D14. Copyright Tate, London, 2004. "To dine at Charleston. Julian a little depressed . . . we think of going to China, at any rate think so, to mitigate the parting [of Julian to the National University of Wuhan]" (*D*, 4:335–336).

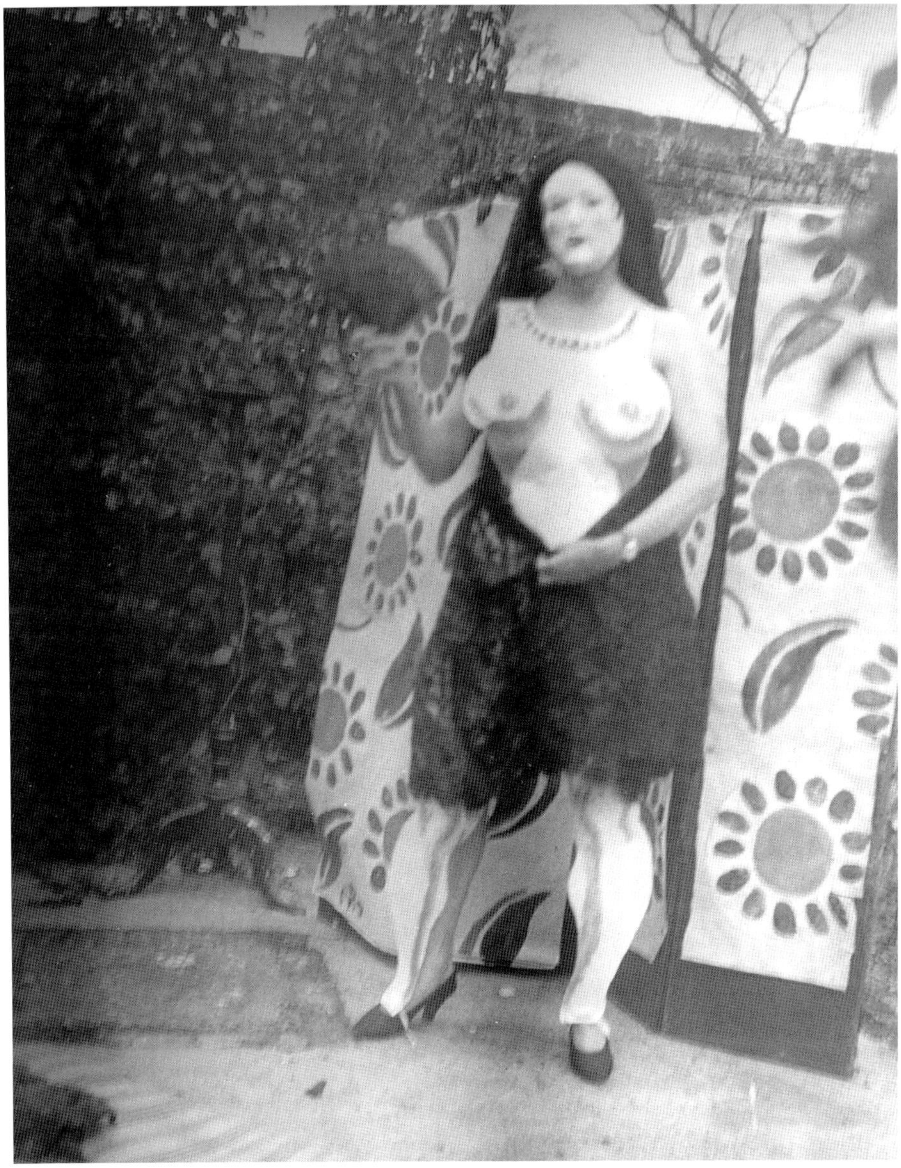

192. Duncan Grant as a Spanish dancer, Charleston, 1936.AA43. Copyright Tate, London, 2004. "Congratulations to all the actors last night. We thought it the most brilliant of all the performances" (*L*, 6:69).

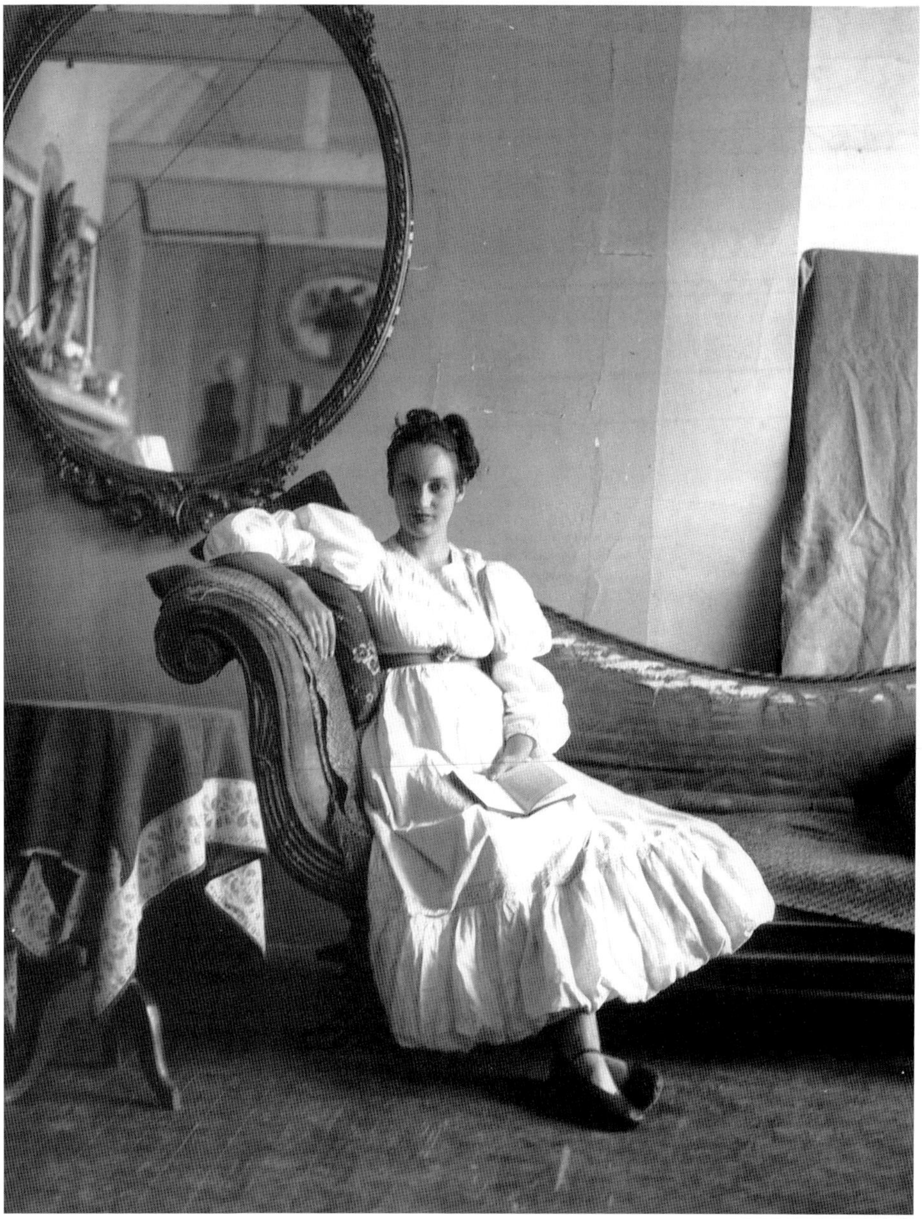

193. Angelica Bell, 1937. Bell Album 9, p. 3 A50. Copyright Tate, London, 2004. "I don't think I can paint portraits at present. It needs a special kind of effort which I don't think I'm capable of [following Julian's death, July 1937]. Sketching Angelica is different" (VB/L, 441).

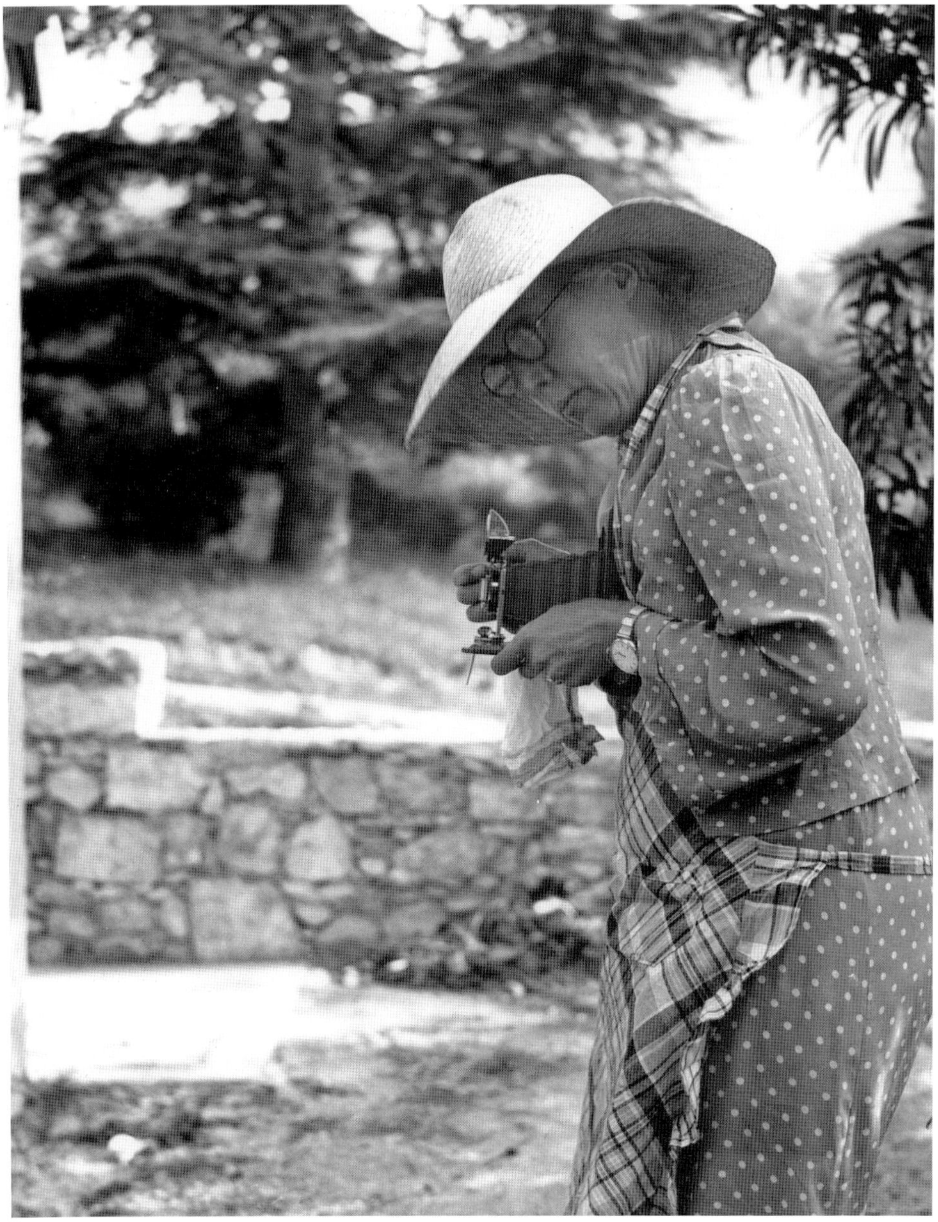

194. Vanessa Bell, Cassis, 1938. Bell Album 9, p. 8 Q32.
Copyright Tate, London, 2004.

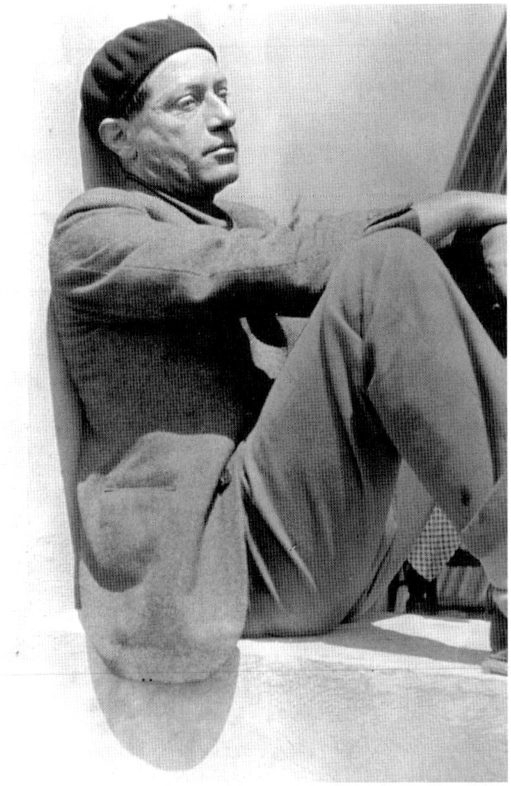

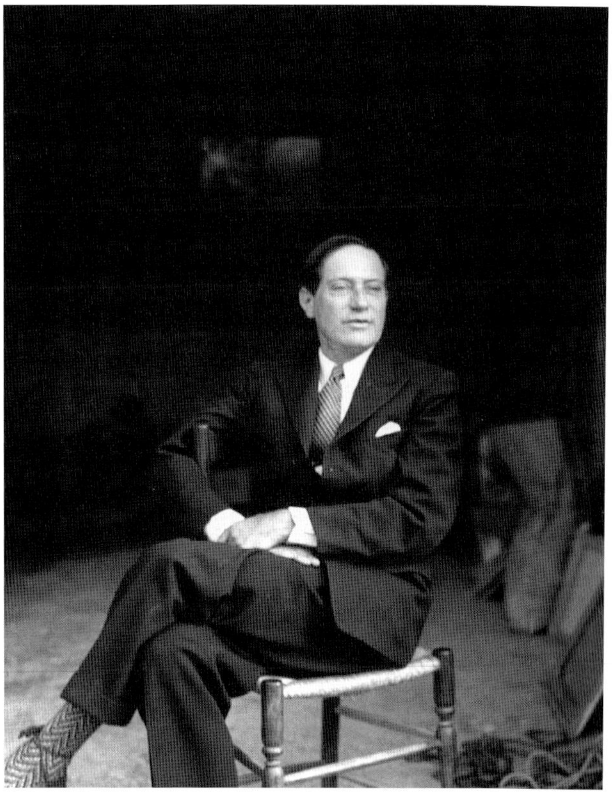

195. Duncan Grant, La Bergère, Cassis, 1938. AA27. Copyright Tate, London, 2004. "We have lunch on the terrace and one could sit in the sun all day. This is almost the most beautiful moment too, with the vines now turning crimson" (VB/L, 449).

196. Duncan Grant, Cassis, 1938. G5. Copyright Tate, London, 2004. "A letter from Duncan. Complete bliss at Cassis" (*D*, 5:186).

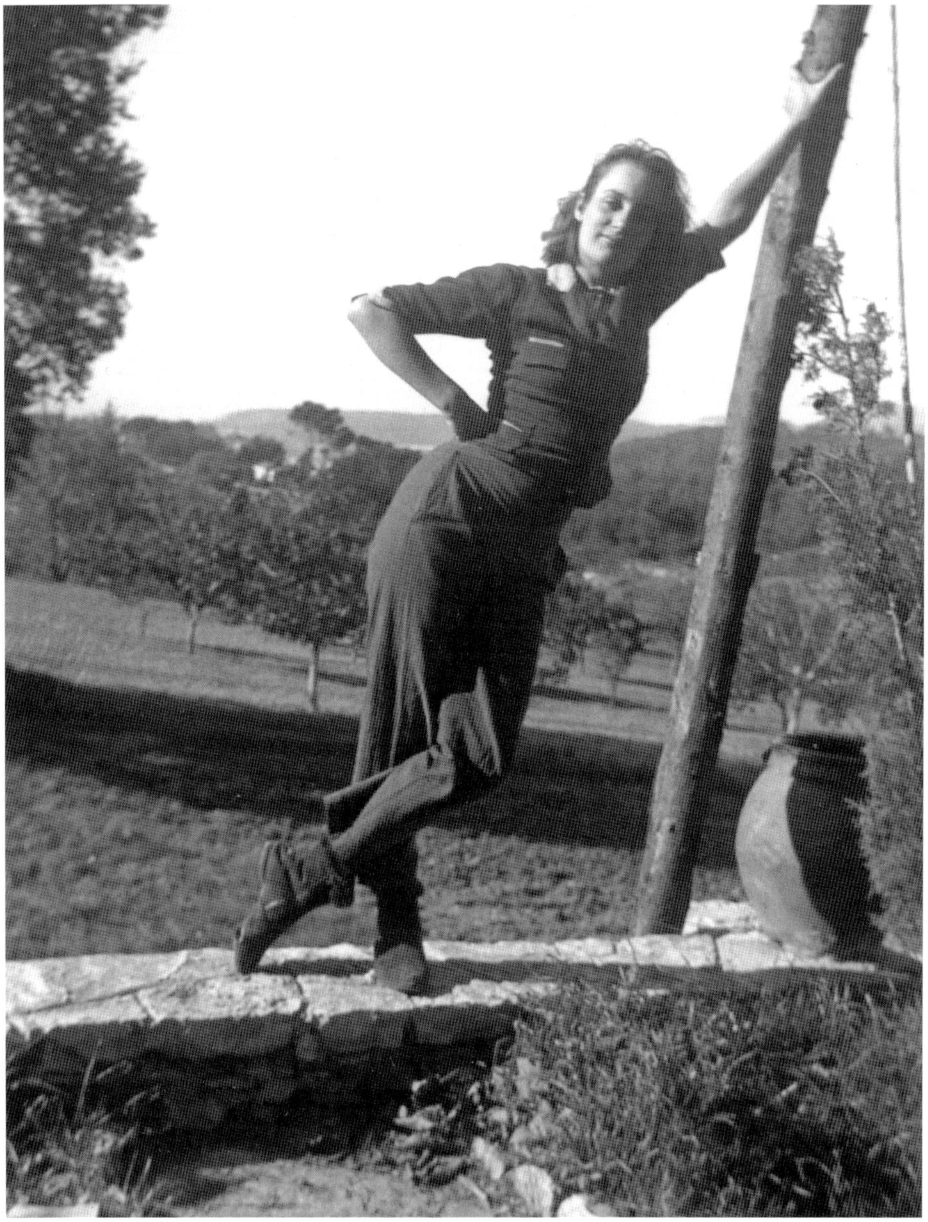

197. Angelica Bell, Cassis, ca. 1938. K29. Copyright Tate, London, 2004.
"You [Duncan] and she [Angelica] and Quentin make life possible, give me such intense happiness constantly" (VB/L, 448).

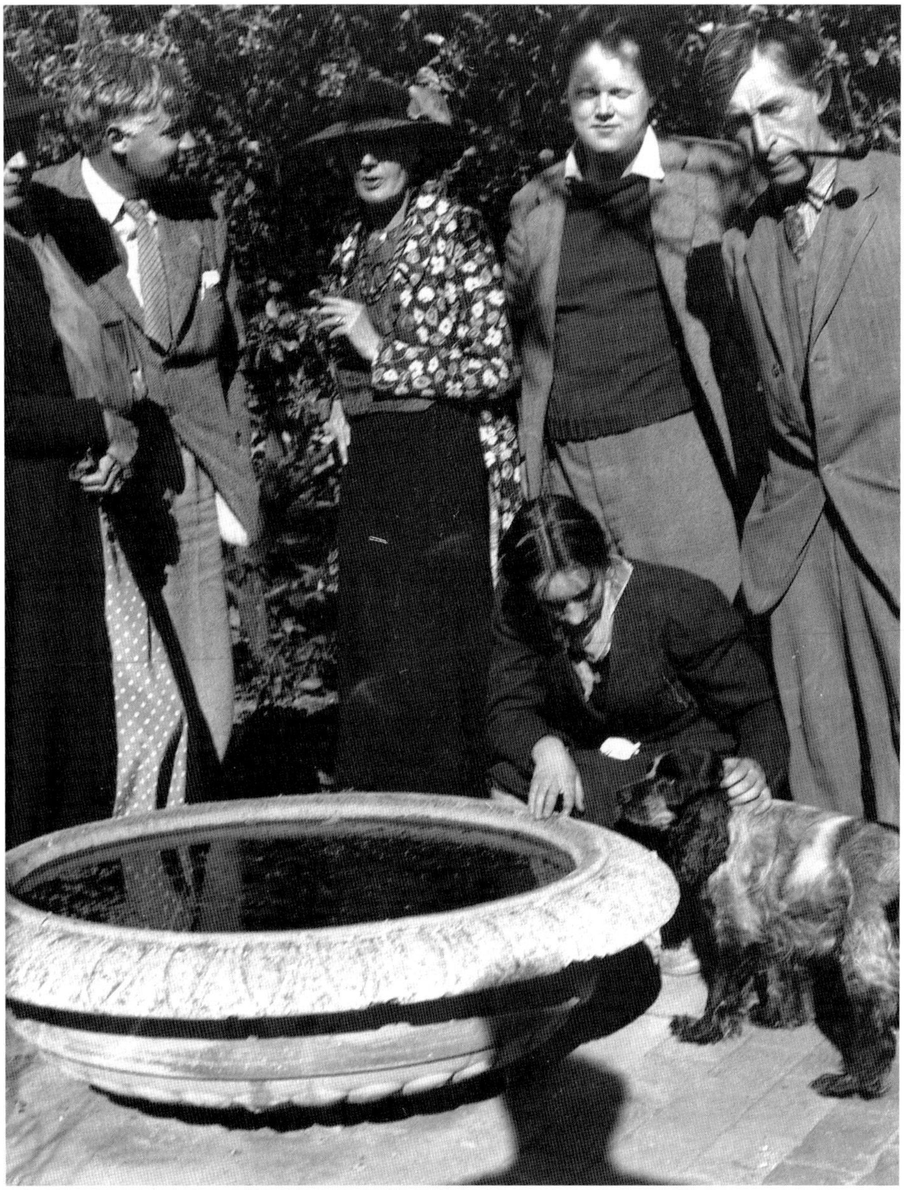

198. Vanessa Bell, David Garnett, Virginia Woolf, Quentin Bell, Leonard Woolf, and Angelica Bell with Sally. Monk's House, 1940. Q38. Copyright Tate, London, 2004. "Angelica there: I diagnose strain; a little defiance, restlessness. And feel in Q. [Quentin] something heavy, mature, depressed" (*D*, 5:307).

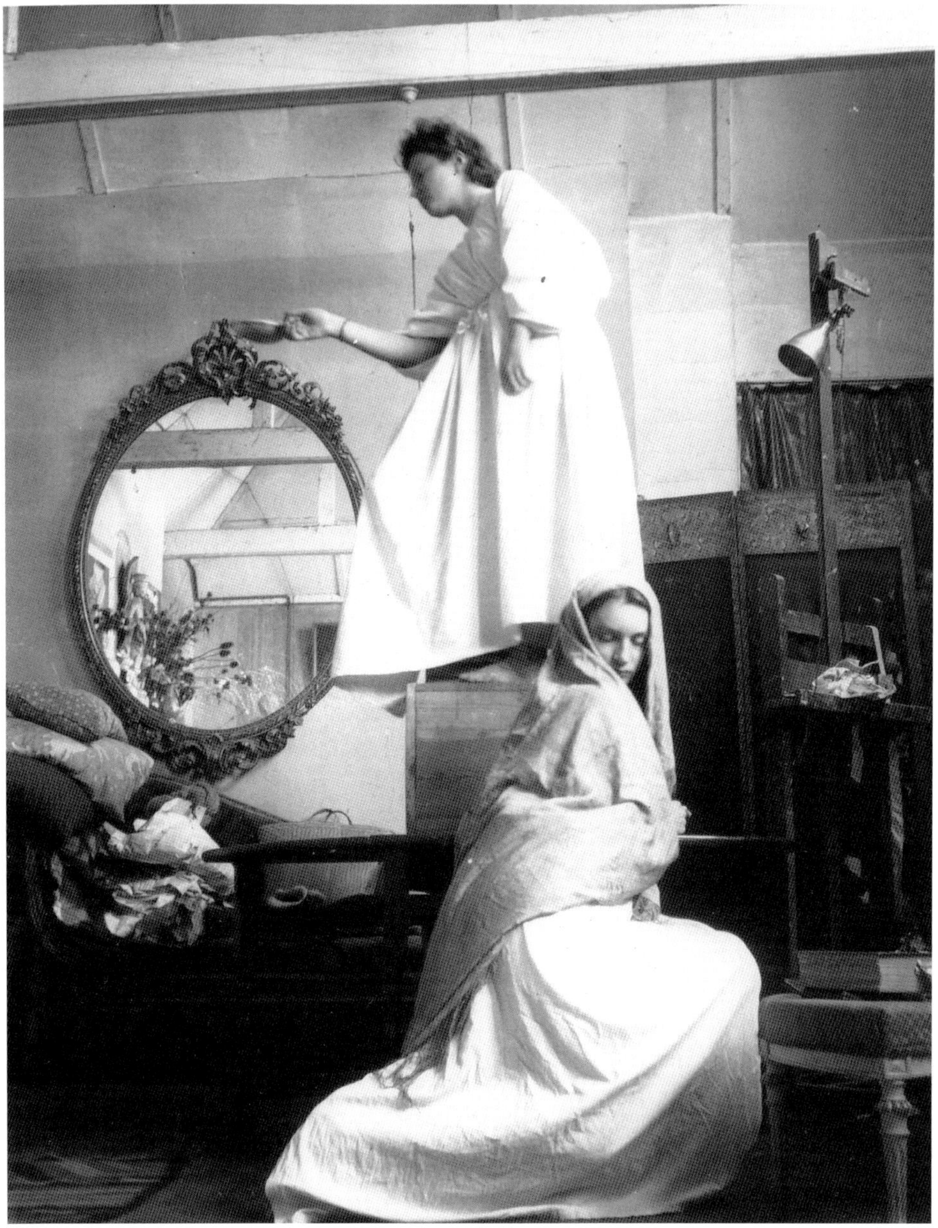

199. Chattie Salamon and Angelica Bell, 1941. S42. Copyright Tate, London, 2004. Posing for *The Wise and Foolish Virgins* by Quentin Bell for Saint Michael and All Angels murals. "We accept every suggestion and read our Bibles diligently . . . Q. [Quentin] of course doesn't get very much time—he's planning the Wise and Foolish Virgins climbing an immense staircase seen from below" (VB/L, 472).

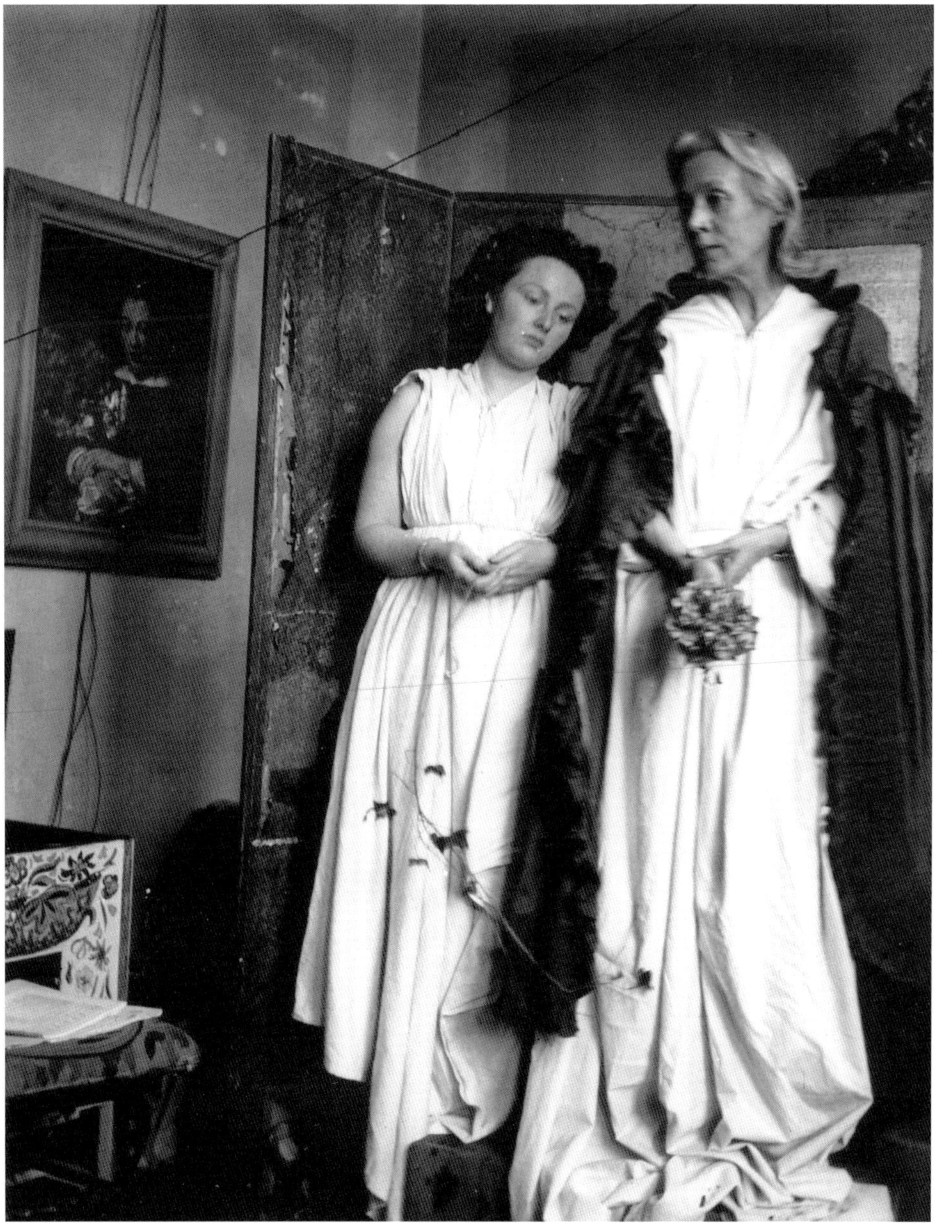

200. Chattie Salamon and Vanessa Bell, 1941. Bell Album 9, p. 27 Q30.
Copyright Tate, London, 2004. Posing for Saint Michael and All Angels murals.

PART THREE

Catalogue of the Monk's House Albums

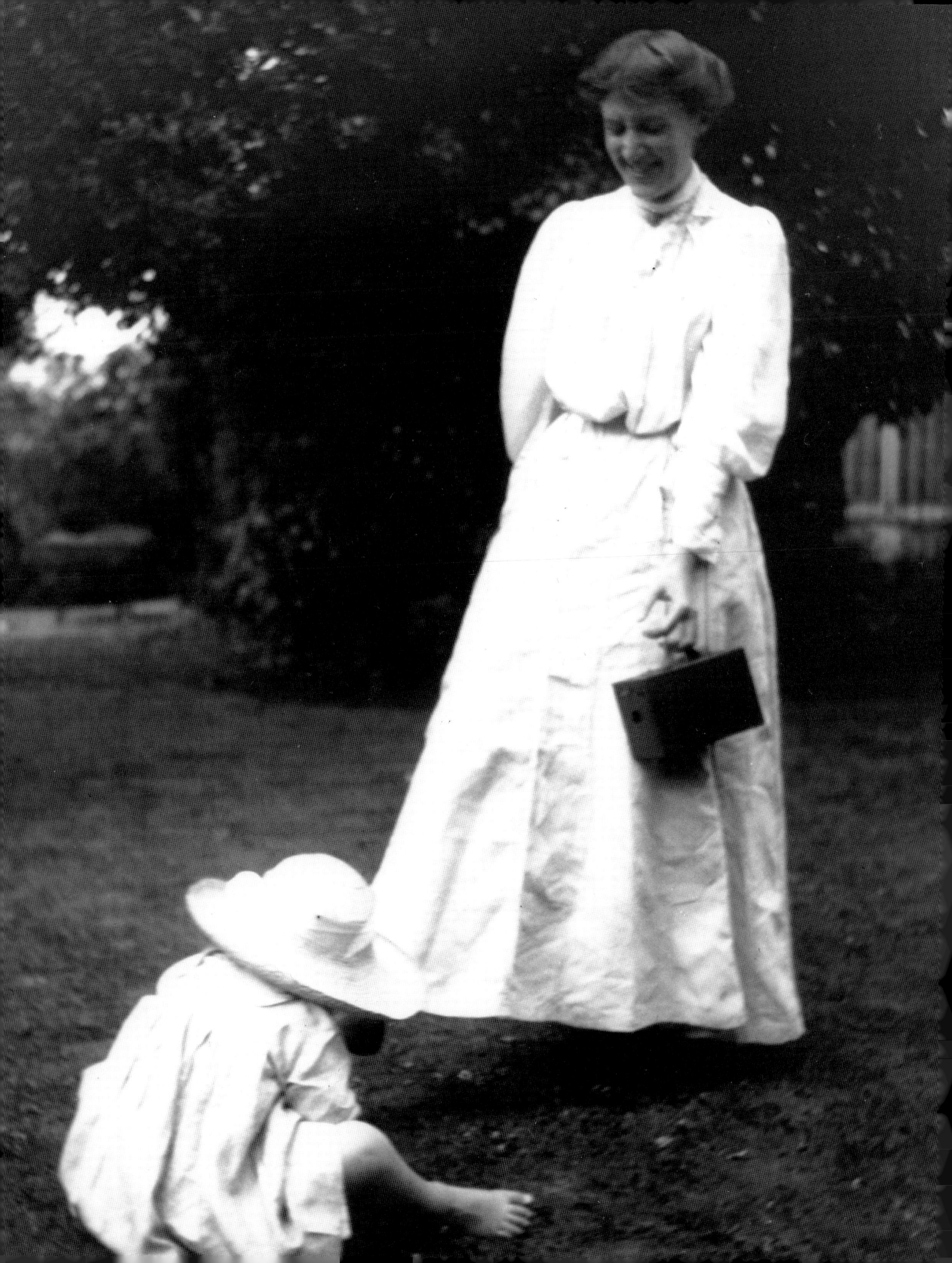

The Monk's House Albums: The Woolfs' Domestic Photographs

FIGURE 73 Julian Bell with Virginia Stephen (with Frena camera), Blean, 1910. Copyright Tate, London 2004.

THE HARVARD THEATRE COLLECTION, Houghton Library, Harvard University, houses the Frederick R. Koch Collection of seven albums (Monk's House Album 1, or MH-1, through MH-7) as well as four boxes (two of which contain two of the albums) of loose photographs. Other photographs are in an additional brown envelope, a large white folder, and envelopes of negatives (of nitrate stock and currently not printable at Harvard). As Elizabeth P. Richardson records in *A Bloomsbury Iconography*, these were sold at Sotheby's on December 15, 1982, lot 277.

The photographs in the albums are not arranged chronologically. Many of the loose photographs may have once appeared in the albums but were removed to serve as illustrations, particularly for Leonard Woolf's publications and the "authorized" *A Marriage of True Minds* by George Spater and Ian Parsons (the husband of Trekkie Parsons, Leonard's later companion). For example, eighteen of my illustrations taken from the loose photographs appear also in *A Marriage of True Minds*. Bet Inglis (formerly of Sussex Library), in an illuminating discussion following my Annual Virginia Woolf Birthday Lecture in 2002, describes partially reassembling the albums after photographs were returned following the Woolf and the Spater and Parsons publications.

Given that a majority of Leonard Woolf's and Spater and Parson's illustrations are now among the loose photographs rather than in the albums suggests that the remaining album contents and their layout are possibly largely as they were before the deaths of Virginia and Leonard. Certainly the lack of chronology is deliberate, as is evident from the occasional dates in the Woolfs' handwritten captions. In addition, because Leonard only very briefly continued mounting photographs after Virginia's death in 1941 (Monk's House Album 4), it seems likely that album construction was more often the work of Virginia. Because, as Richardson suggests, "few pages or mounted photographs are given specific dates," the listings that follow include caption dates and other information written in the albums. Where this information is not in place, I have noted "unidentified" or "unknown" for the figures and omitted dates. The dates in my own captions to each photograph included in this text draw partially on the albums, on my research of the Woolf oeuvre, on other texts both primary and secondary, and on research in other archives, including the Berg Collection and the St. Ives Archive. Many of the photographs are not listed in Richardson, and some listed photographs have inaccurate information.

In the albums the Woolfs refer to themselves as LW and VW, and to Vanessa, Julian, Quentin, and Angelica Bell as VB, JB, QB, and AVB. Occasionally full first names are given. Virginia and Leonard shared the taking of photographs as well as the annotations.

The layout below simulates that in the albums: each album page has several photographs, often arranged in duplicates. The spaces between each photograph's data simulate the album spaces, as does the above/below positioning of data. Dates, places, people, and photographers are those listed in the albums in the main, but I add additional information where appropriate.

Monk's House Album 1 (MH-1)

The covers of Monk's House Album 1 are of thick cardboard (11 × 14½ inches) tied together with string. It is not a commercial photograph album—the mounting slots for the photographs are cut by hand. The cover has a childlike inscription:

PHO-
TO-
GRAPHS.

PAGE 1. Cartes-de-visite (2½ × 4 inches; photographer: Les Brothers).

Fawcett	L.S.	C. B. Clarke
Ferrers	Gildart	King

PAGE 2. Cartes-de-visite (2½ × 4 inches).

Chalker	Talbot	Rolph
Schweitzer	Anderegg	Macgregor

PAGE 3. Cartes-de-visite (2½ × 4 inches).

Gardner	Longman	Lumley Smith
Short	Mellor	Guy Dolfi

PAGE 4. Cartes-de-visite (2½ × 4 inches).

Hardy	Ware	Gunson	
Campbell	Kelly	Davidson	

PAGE 5. Cartes-de-visite (2½ × 4 inches).

C. B. Clarke	Mathews
Moore	Unidentified (but with George Washington stamp on reverse, Washington St., Boston)
Anderegg	Bertlin

PAGE 6. Cartes-de-visite (2½ × 4 inches).

Besant	Gibbs		
Bennen	Morgan	A. O. Hughes	Macdonald of Cambridge (in running clothes)

PAGE 7. Cartes-de-visite (2½ × 4 inches).

W. Holmes 1866	Mckett		Fitzroy
Brown (Fawcett Society)		Paley	Brown

PAGE 8. Cartes-de-visite (2½ × 4 inches; photographer: Lock and Whitfield).

Sir J. F. Stephen	Lady Stephen	Old Lady Stephen
C. E. Stephen	Mrs. R. Gurney	Fan (dog)

PAGE 9. Cartes-de-visite (2½ × 4 inches; photographer: Hawkins).

Mrs. Dicey	Dr. Jackson	Mrs. Bailey
Herbert Fisher (as child)	Jo Fisher	Arthur Fisher

PAGE 10. Cartes-de-visite (2½ × 4 inches).

Millicent Vaughan (as child)	Millicent Vaughan	George Duckworth (missing)
Julia with George (as baby)	Val Prinsep	Unidentified

PAGE 11. Cartes-de-visite (2½ × 4 inches).

Unidentified	Macnamaras (as children)	Unidentified
Henry Mackimera aged 5 years	Unidentified (girl with doll)	

PAGE 12. Cartes-de-visite (2½ × 4 inches; photographer: W. Mudford, Tiverton).

Unidentified	Unidentified	Cousin Mid
Janet Symonds	F. Fraser	Willie Duckworth

PAGE 13. Cartes-de-visite (2½ × 4 inches).

Unidentified (man and woman)

Castle entrance (small manor house) | Madame Lind Goldschmidt (Jenny Lind)

Unidentified | Capt. Annenstedt

PAGE 14. Professional photographs (4 × 5 inches; photographer: Lock and Whitfield, and van de Weyde).
VB (as child) J.T.S. (Thoby Stephen)

PAGE 15. Professional photographs.
Mrs. Francis Unidentified Fitzgerald
Unidentified Russell Gurney

PAGE 16. Cartes-de-visite.
Mrs. Jackson Madame Hallé
Unidentified woman Arthur Prinsep Sir J. Clark

PAGE 17. Professional photographs.
Unidentified (four children in fancy dress)
Martineau Herbert and Billy Ritchie

PAGE 18. Blank; missing a large photo of J.P.S (Julia Prinsep Stephen, presumably).

PAGE 19. Large sketch (possibly over an original photo, 10½ × 4½ inches; unidentified figure) with the initials W.S.

PAGE 20. Photographs of Adrian and Vanessa playing cricket and Annie Macnamara with two children.

PAGE 21. Both photographs are 6 × 4¼ inches.
S.D. (Stella Duckworth) Violet Dickinson

PAGE 22. A missing photograph (initials A.T.S.) and two professional photographs of Julian Bell as a baby (date and photographer not identified).

PAGE 23.
Madge Vaughan and children (mounted on card and therefore treasured)
Fred Maitland VW and LW (missing)

PAGE 24. Professional photographs.
Augusta and Will Vaughan Renshaw Mrs. Fawcett
Unidentified CB Clarke's cat Wolstoneholme

PAGE 25. Five missing photographs.

PAGE 26. Holiday photographs.
Unidentified (people sitting on rocks in Sweden) Houses and sea
LW and friends on a boat, *Najaden* (2¼ × 3⅛ inches) LW, BL, and Mrs. Ross against a fence (4½ × 2¾ inches)

PAGE 26. Four missing photographs.

PAGE 27. Leonard's Ceylon photographs.
Empire Day in Kandy Library at Kandy (missing) Bungalows in Kandy

PAGE 28.
Winter scene sketch (unidentified) LW with three friends (unidentified) and a dog in Ceylon
A river scene

PAGE 29. Three photographs of Ceylon (4½ × 3⅝ inches).
Crowd scene Ceylonese male (unidentified) Official parade

PAGE 30. Two photographs of Ceylon.
LW and dogs White soldiers lowering the Union Jack

PAGE 31. Two photographs of Ceylon (3 × 4 inches).
LW and friends (unidentified) with guns, holding elephant feet and tusks.

PAGE 32. Photographs of Ceylon.
LW and Bella (Woolf)
Two photographs of Leonard One photograph of the lowering of the flag
(from a different viewpoint to above—a crowd scene)

PAGE 33. Three photographs of Ceylon.
LW (on horseback) A roof scene in Kandy
Pearl fishing

PAGE 34. Five photographs of Ceylon (all missing).
Kandy Boat scene House with pool Two unidentified

PAGE 35. Five photographs of Ceylon (four missing).
Suez Canal Kandy
Boat scene Two photographs of Baron Blixen with Leonard Woolf

PAGE 36. Five photographs of Ceylon (all missing).
Pearl Banks Other spaces unidentified

PAGE 37. Four photographs of Ceylon (two missing).
Kmama Tank (twice) Tangaka Unidentified space

PAGE 38. Five photographs of Ceylon (three missing).

LW (on horseback with dog)

Baron Blixen

Two unidentified spaces

Flora Woolf as a young girl

PAGE 39. Four photographs of Ceylon.

Daughters of Kandyan chiefs

Baron Blixen after hunting

Two scenes of Ceylon

PAGE 40. Five photographs of Ceylon.

LW in Ceylon (with two dogs; on reverse in Virginia's hand, "the author in Jaffna")

Four photographs of golf players

PAGE 41. Five photographs of Ceylon (four missing).

LW (on horseback)

Four unidentified spaces

PAGE 42. Five photographs of Ceylon (one missing from unidentified space); the remaining four are of Leonard with dogs and horse (3¼ × 4 inches).

PAGE 43. Four photographs (two missing).

Soldiers at front (unidentified)

Two little girls (unidentified)

PAGE 44. One missing photograph and one family photograph (unidentified).

PAGE 45. Five photographs of JB and QB naked, presumably taken by Vanessa Bell, ca. 1913 (sizes 4 × 3 inches and 4⅛ × 3⅛ inches).

PAGE 46. Three photographs of JB and QB (one missing) and one photograph of QB, JB, and VB (3⅛ × 4 inches; date and photographer unidentified).

PAGE 47. Four photographs of JB and QB (one a duplicate of fig. 28 in Humm, *Modernist Women*).

PAGE 48. One photograph of Madge Vaughan (no date and taken at the Cameron studio).

PAGE 49. One photograph of Janet Case in mortarboard and gown (mounted on card and paper; original photograph 2¼ × 3⅜ inches).

PAGE 50. Stella Duckworth in profile (studio portrait; 7 × 9½ inches; taken in Rome).

PAGE 51. Five Victorian photographs.

Lady Stephen and C. E. Stephen | Laura as a baby with Leslie Stephen | House (unidentified castellated)
Man in army uniform (unidentified) | Woman (unidentified)

PAGE 52. Victorian photographs (Hill and Saunders are photographers of the three children).

Thackeray | Mrs. Freshfield | Three children (unidentified)
Montage of four photographs of an unidentified woman

PAGE 53. Professional photograph of Will Vaughan (date and photographer unidentified; mounted on paper and card).

PAGE 54. Small river scene (unidentified).

PAGE 55. Three photographs missing.

PAGE 56. Three photographs missing.

PAGE 57. Two photographs missing.

One photograph of a group of children near the sea (unidentified)

PAGE 58.

H. M. Stephen (Victorian photo) | George Herbert Duckworth on horseback | L.T.S. (Leslie Stephen)
Ceylon House

PAGE 59. A group portrait for the Zanzibar Hoax, March 2 MDCCCCV [1905] (photographer: W. Wright, 83 Bishopsgate).

PAGE 60. Three photographs of Leslie Stephen, one with Virginia.

PAGE 61. Four professional photographs of Thoby Stephen (4 × 6 inches; photographer: G. Beresford).

PAGE 62.

"Lake Hunt" (unidentified group of men) | C. E. Stephen seated by window

PAGE 63. Repetition of two of the photographs of Thoby (p. 61) and one of the photographs of Leslie Stephen (p. 60), and one photograph of Leslie with an unidentified male.

PAGE 64. Blank.

PAGE 65. July 1914.

Asheham House in winter

LW with G. E. Moore (missing)

Shot and Max dogs at window

Desmond MacCarthy (missing)

PAGE 66. Photographs are 3 × 4 inches with white margins.

D. MacCarthy (missing) Lily and Anny in garden (two photographs) G. E. Moore and LW in garden

PAGE 67.

G. E. Moore in garden (missing)

LW with G. E. Moore in garden

LW and Adrian in garden (two photographs; one missing)

PAGE 68.

VB on terrace (date and photographer unknown)

Gertrude Minnheimer
(date and photographer unknown)

VB and Duncan Grant with flowers on the terrace at Asheham
(copy of photo on p. 39, *Vanessa Bell's Family Album*)

LW and VW with Roger Fry 1912

PAGE 69. 1912.

LW, VB, and VW VW and Ka Cox 1912

Adrian wearing a bowler, outside at Fitzroy Square 1910

PAGE 70.

J. P. Stephen (missing)

PAGE 71. Professional photograph (date and photographer unknown).

Beatrice Thynne

PAGES 72 to 77 are blank.

Monk's House Album 2 (MH-2)

Monk's House Album 2 is a bound black album with brown paper leaves (10½ × 13½ inches).

PAGE 1.

LW and Noel Olivier

VW holding folio size paper sitting on a chair

LW in deck chair with dog

CB with Mary H (Hutchinson)

PAGE 2. James Strachey and Desmond MacCarthy, and a photograph of two unidentified males.

PAGE 3.
LW and three others (unidentified) LW and J.B.S. with unidentified figure
Pippa (Strachey) holding a copy of O'Henry's *Heart of the West*
Group of three (one Adrian, two unidentified) playing cards

PAGE 4. The two Sanger photographs are 3¼ × 4 inches.
Marjorie Strachey with Sanger (Charles) Sanger
Mrs. Woolf and Bella with two unidentified males
Leonard with unidentified woman

PAGE 5.
Annie and Lily (two photographs) Mrs. Woolf and Bella outside a door VW sitting in a chair

PAGE 6.
VW Cornwall 1916 (two photographs)
Margaret Llewelyn Davies (MLLD) and Lilian Harris Cornwall, 1916 MLLD in doorway

PAGE 7.
MLLD Cornwall 1916 LW and VB at Charleston 1916 (missing)
LW at Zennor with MLLD

PAGE 8.
VB and QB in doorway Roger Fry and VB, Charleston with dog
Annie with dog D. MacCarthy in deckchair

PAGE 9. Four missing photographs of VB, QB, and JB.

PAGE 10.
D. MacCarthy (as p. 8, from a different angle) Annie with dog (as p. 8, from a different angle)
Unidentified woman with child

PAGE 11.
Unidentified child with two servants VB and QB (missing)
Saxon (Sydney-Turner) on snowy moor (3 × 4 inches)

PAGE 12. Studio portrait of unidentified child.

PAGE 13.

E. M. Forster
Judith Bagenal
SST (as p. 11)
Mrs. Woolf (1¾ × 2¼ inches)

PAGE 14.

LW among trees
L (unidentified male, arm in bandage) and Lucas at Charleston
Charleston AVB, JB and QB with VB
L. Strachey and Alix (3 × 4 inches)

PAGE 15.

Lytton (Strachey)
VB and AVB

PAGE 16.

TSE (Eliot) and VW outside at Monk's House with ladder
The same walking to camera
VB and AVB, and Lytton and Alix (repeat of photographs on pp. 14, 15)

PAGE 17.

Photograph (unidentified). The reverse side reads: "you didn't know what a fine house I had, did you? RHL 11. 05. 09"
Photograph of Bagenal with two children; on reverse: "With love to you and Leonard from Barbara Xmas 1921" (mounted on card)

PAGE 18.

Rodmell 1922
LW (with unidentified male) in car with dog

PAGE 19.

Servants under tree
Noel Olivier playing with a string of beads, (3 × 4 inches, with white margins)

PAGE 20. Five photographs.

Lytton Strachey
Alix outside a window
Mary Hutchinson and CB
LW and VB with flowers
Group photograph of four servants; only "Grace" captioned

PAGE 22.

Lytton
E. M. Forster and TSE (with picture)

PAGE 23.

Charleston
Lytton in chair
AVB, QB, and JB, and unidentified boy
Asheham, one male and two females (unidentified)
VB, CB, and Duncan (Grant)

PAGE 24.

CB, VW, and VB

EMF (Forster) and LW

PAGES 25 to 38 blank.

Monk's House Album 3 (MH-3)

Monk's House Album 3 is bound in patterned paper with ties. The inner pages are white and measure 9½ × 12½ inches.

PAGE 1. The photograph, a large portrait of Julia Stephen (6 × 7½ inches), was taken at the same sitting as one in the Mia Album that Julia Margaret Cameron gave to her sister Maria (Mia). Graham Ovenden dates this photo ca. 1863–65 and, because of the signature, rather doubtfully attributes it to the photographer O. J. Rejlander (Ovenden, plate 113).

PAGE 2. Photograph of Leslie and Julia Stephen seated in the St. Ives library with Virginia in background. It was taken by Vanessa and dated 1892 (2¾ × 2⅞ inches, and mounted on a 6 × 4 inch buff-colored card).

PAGE 3. August 1931.

LW and VW in chair (same pose, one photo each)

LW outside at Monk's House (two photos, one with him smoking a pipe and the other in a chair)

PAGE 4.

LW in a doorway

LW in an interior chair

PAGE 5.

Shelley House Lerici (4¾ × 6¾ inches)

PAGE 6.

Lerici Singer 1933 (4¾ × 6¾ inches; but the Woolfs traveled to Italy in the new Lanchester)

PAGE 7. Two group photographs, with different poses in each, of VB, CB, AVB, Roger, VW, DG, and RM (Raymond Mortimer) (4 × 3 inches).

PAGE 8.

LW and VW (two photos, with each posing in front of the same flowers)

RM reading in a chair

LW and dog near garden urn

PAGE 9.

Sibyl Colefax (two photographs; 3 × 4 inches)

Lydia Keynes, taken for the BBC; the reverse side reads:

January 4th 1938 *Tilton Firle, Sussex*

Dear Leonard

I was so glad to hear from Virginia that the temperature went down and that you have a Jewish-german doctor. I am sure that he will find something in your kidney: in the meanwhile diet is important no frying pan, grill and boil your food. I look when you and Maynard are feeling well. The photo was taken by the B.B.C.

Affectionately Lydia *All possible good wishes to you and Virginia for 1938.*

Roger Fry in chair

PAGE 10.

Four photographs of dog on chair

Three versions of a group photograph

PAGE 11.

LW and Mrs. Woolf and two others (unidentified)

VW and Mrs. Woolf (VW in same pose as LW)

QB, JB, and VW at Charleston

Duncan, QB, VW, CB, Mary H.

PAGE 12. Four photographs of Ethel Smyth, from different viewpoints, 1931.

PAGE 13. Four photographs of J. M. Keynes and Lydia Keynes, with differing glances, 1931.

PAGE 14.

AVB (*Orlando* photographs)

Maynard and Lydia (missing)

Hugh Walpole and friend (unknown) Manenty Park

PAGE 15.

John Lehmann and VW, Monk's House pond

Photograph repeated with LW instead of VW

JL and LW (another angle)

John Lehmann

PAGE 16.

VW (in chair)

John Lehmann and VW

Quentin Bell

Julian Bell

PAGE 17.

JB (on bench)

VW (missing)

H. Lintott

LW (missing)

PAGE 18. All photographs measure 3 × 4 inches.

VW on chair with books

LW (same chair/books)

VW outside

LW (repeated image)

PAGE 19. Postcard from the Acropolis.

LW, VW, Roger Fry and Margery Fry, May 1932

PAGE 20. Greece, 1932.

Roger Fry reading on a donkey

Margery Fry reading on a bench

VW and Roger Fry

Roger (missing)

PAGE 21.

Margery emerging from a doorway

Aegina group (unidentified) waiting for a boat

Aegina

Photographs of a lion statue

PAGE 22. Three views of the Acropolis and a duplicate of the previous photograph of a lion statue.

PAGE 23. Two views of the Acropolis.

PAGE 24.

Acropolis

Olive field

A Greek theater (two photographs)

PAGE 25. Four long-distance views of Sparta and Corinth.

PAGE 26. Three photographs of Greek buildings and churches.

PAGE 27. Four views of Greece.

PAGE 28. Three views of Greek exteriors.

PAGE 29. 1932.

Alice Ritchie in chair

TSE & VE (Vivienne Eliot) & VW in garden

Angus Davidson in chair

PAGE 30.

Alice Ritchie (same chair, different angle)

Tom Eliot & Vivienne Eliot and dog

Charles Siepmann (in chair)

PAGE 31. Three photographs in the same chair (3 × 4 inches).

William Plomer   Vita Nicolson   Charles Siepmann

PAGE 32.

William Plomer   Vita with dog

PAGE 33. Italy, 1933: three views in long shot, two of boats.

PAGE 34. Four photographs of Vita with VW on the grass bank at Monk's House.

PAGE 35.

T. S. Eliot, Mary, and St. John Hutchinson   T. S. Eliot (indoors)

T. S. Eliot (in garden)

PAGE 36. Four photographs taken of figures in the same chair, at the same angle.

Rosamond Philipps   Wogan Philipps

Eve Younger   Angelica Bell

PAGE 37.

Wogan Philipps (looking left)   Rosamond Philipps (looking right, same chair)

Ethel Smyth (looking down)

PAGE 38. Peter and Prudence Lucas are in similar poses, in the same chair.

Peter Lucas   Prudence Lucas

Molly MacCarthy and Desmond

PAGE 39.

Maynard Keynes and E. M. Forster   Lydia Keynes   Roger Fry

Elizabeth Read   JB   Molly MacCarthy   Desmond MacCarthy

PAGE 40. Most photographs now are 3 × 4 inches, suggesting the use of the Zeiss camera predominately.

E. M. Forster and Lydia Keynes

Ireland 1934, Bowen's Court: VW, Cyril Connolly, E. Bowen, A. Cameron, J. Connolly

A. Cameron, VW, and LW

PAGE 41. 1934.

Killarney (long-distance view)

PAGE 42. 1934.

Marjorie Strachey, James Strachey, and VW (in garden with dog)   Killarney (long-distance view)

PAGE 43.

Angelica, Julian, and Lettice Ramsey (two similar photographs)

PAGE 44. LW and VW photographed individually in the same chair, same positions.

Adrian, VW, Karin, and dog — Adrian, LW, Karin, and dog

QB, Clive, Raymond (Mortimer), VW

PAGE 45.

Angelica and Susan Henderson (two similar photographs)

QB, Clive, Raymond, and VW (duplicate of the photograph on p. 44)

PAGE 46.

Garsington cat

Lytton, VW, and "Yeats" (actually "Goldie" Dickinson)

Leslie Hartley, David Cecil, VW, and P.G. (photograph missing; I cannot determine who P.G. might have been)

PAGE 47. Near Nauplia, 1932 (view; 4¼ × 6¼ inches).

PAGE 48. Two similar photographs of Stella Benson and VW, 1932,

LW (missing) — LW (with two dogs in front of garden urn)

PAGE 49. Prints are of differing sizes—2⅛ × 2⅛ inches and 5⅛ × 3¼ inches—which suggests a use of two Kodaks.

Fish in pond — Lyn Irvine

VW and Ethel — William Plomer (smiling, leaning against garden statue) — W. Robson

PAGE 50.

Pinka (dog) — Mitzy (marmoset) — Lyn Irvine

PAGE 51. The Plomer and Irvine photographs are similar.

Mitzy (missing) — William Plomer (standing with book)

Lyn Irvine reading a book — View from Monk's House of the Downs

PAGE 52. The first three photographs are all 2⅛ × 2⅛ inches; the fourth one is reproduced on a 2⅛ × 2⅛ inch postcard. They were all, therefore, taken with a Kodak.

Harold Woolf — George Rylands

Judith and Ann Stephen (beside a statue) — Monk's House pond

PAGE 53.

W. Robson — Ann and Judith (similar to p. 52)

Dog swimming (two photographs) — Karin, Judith, and Ann (missing)

PAGE 54.

Lydia Keynes (3¼ × 5 inches, on postcard) | Maynard and Kingsley Martin

PAGE 55. Four photographs of Ann and Judith Stephen (3¼ × 5 inches); the sitters are in duplicate positions/chairs.

PAGE 56.

Ann (similar to p. 55) | VW and "Dadie" Rylands

PAGE 57. Lady Strachey (6⅓ × 8⅓ inches).

PAGE 58. Two views of Holland, 1935 (street scene and canal on postcard; 5¼ × 3¼ inches).

PAGE 59.

Germany, the Rhine (view) | Italy, bridge at Verona (view)

PAGE 60. Italy (all prints are 3¼ × 4 inches).

AVB, Vanessa, and Quentin (similar prints) at Monte Cassino

Mitzy in Rome

PAGE 61. Four photographs that duplicate the chair and positioning (5¼ × 3¼ inches).

Mrs. Brian Easdale | Joan Easdale

PAGE 62.

Monk's House (trees in snow) | Man (unidentified)

Mitzy (with hat)

PAGE 63.

LW with dog | Lydia Keynes

AVB, VB, CB, VW, Maynard, Lydia (outside VW's workroom)

PAGE 64.

AVB, VB, CB (against external wall)

PAGE 65.

Stephen Tennant and W. Robson (missing) | Sally

PAGE 66.

Marie Woolf, Pippin (by pond/statue) | Sally

Mitzy | Eve (Younger)

PAGE 67.

Pippin Woolf — Marie and Pippin — Marie (duplicating Pippin's positioning)

PAGE 68. Tom Eliot (two duplicates of earlier prints).

Monk's House Album 4 (MH-4)

Monk's House Album 4, marked 1939, is bound in cardboard with red, art deco paper covers and has white leaves. The various sizes of prints indicate use of at least two Kodaks and a Zeiss. Leonard continued the album after Virginia's death, but both photographs and layout from this date are less artistic.

PAGE 1. Roger Fry (9½ × 12½ inches; photographer: Lenare).

PAGE 2. Clipping from the *News Chronicle*, May 5, 1938, of Lady Baldwin addressing wives and mothers about the formation of babies' welfare clubs (presumably the clipping was kept for *Three Guineas*).

PAGE 3.

Lytton, VW, and Goldie Dickinson (at Ottoline Morrell's, 1923; 4 × 6½)
Marjorie and Lytton playing chess (the reverse reads 1931)

PAGE 4.

Lytton at 10 Gower Street (4 × 6½ inches; presumably by Ottoline Morrell)
Carrington, R. Partridge, Lytton, Ham Spray, 1930

PAGE 5. Photographs are 3 × 2 inches, except for the first, which is 3 × 5¼ inches

Ham Spray, Lytton (close-up in chair) — Lytton (looking from window)
Lytton, Carrington, and Ralph Partridge — Lytton (from different window)

PAGE 6. The second two photographs are 5 × 3 inch postcards, presumably developed by Kodak.

Sally — Five trees in snow — Digging a grave in winter

PAGE 7.

Monk's House door in snow — Three landscape views — Monk's House in snow

PAGE 8. Monk's House in winter (two snow scenes).

PAGE 9. Brittany, six views: there are no people; three are of a castle from different angles; the others are water, a beach scene, and a harbor.

PAGE 10. Brittany, six views: no people, harbor scenes, Douarnenez, Carnac stones, moated castle.

PAGE 11. Brittany, six views: three of a castle, two of beaches, no people

PAGE 12. Brittany, six views: no people, two of Carnac and Les Rochers, two of trees.

PAGE 13. Brittany, four views: church, townscape, two of a market.

PAGE 14. Loose photographs by Gisèle Freund, July 1939.
VW smoking — LW and VW (Tavistock Square; on reverse, 12 Rue Lalande, Paris XIV).

PAGE 15. JB (a professional print mounted on an 8 × 6 inch card; photographer: Lettice Ramsey?).

PAGE 16. QB (a professional print mounted on an 8 × 6 inch card; photographer: Lettice Ramsey?).

PAGE 17. Seven bowling scenes, 1939 (2⅛ × 2⅛ inches).
VW and Angus Davidson (missing) — Stephen Spender (twice, one missing)
Stephen Spender, Duncan, AVB, M. Longman
AVB, M. Longman — AVB, Duncan, Longman — AVB
N. Nicholls

PAGE 18.
Sophie Farrell 1890 — LW (missing) — Snow scene

PAGE 19. Winter, 1940. Three landscapes from Monk's House (postcard prints; 5 × 3 inches).

PAGE 20. Postcard prints (5 × 3 inches).
Winter 1940 view — Judith Stephen, Leslie Humphrey — L. Humphrey, Judith, and VW

PAGE 21. The first three photographs are 2¼ × 2¼ inches; the last is 3 × 5 inches on postcard.
1940 snow scene — Judith Stephen, Leslie Humphrey — Judith (alone)
E. M. Forster

PAGE 22. The photographs are 3 × 5 inches and printed on postcards.
Molly Sturgeon (same chair, position as Forster, p. 21) — Winter 1940 pond frozen
Monk's House

PAGE 23. Forster and Sturgeon are seated in similar positions (3 × 5 inches).
E. M. Forster — Flora Sturgeon

PAGE 24. The photographs are on 3 × 5 inch postcards.

Desmond MacCarthy and George Moore (garden with statue) — Pond at Monk's House

PAGE 25.

Monk's House in snow — Miss Griffiths — Elizabeth Bowen (missing)

PAGE 26.

Adrian and Karin 1940 — Bowling scene (three women and man unidentified) — Judith Stephen bowling

PAGE 27. Close-up of Judith Stephen bowling.

PAGE 28.

Scenic view — Cat

PAGE 29.

Adrian, Karin — E. Bowen (missing) — Group bowling scene (unidentified)

PAGE 30. Three scenic views of Downs.

PAGE 31.

Adrian, Karin (similar to p. 29) — Duncan Grant, VW, Chattie Salaman

Judith Stephen, Leslie Humphrey, and VW bowling

PAGE 32. Two cat photographs.

PAGE 33.

Nick Bagenal (3 × 3 inches) — 1946 two people (unknown) with beehive (2¼ × 2¼ inches)

Scenic view — Cat and dog on lawn

PAGE 34.

1947 woman (unidentified) with cat and dog — Sappho (two prints)

1946 woman (unidentified) in conservatory — Woman (unknown) and cat

PAGE 35. These are 3 × 5 inch postcards.

Sappho 1947 — Sappho and Pluto 1947 — Phillip and Babs 1947

PAGE 36. Two prints of cacti.

PAGE 37.

Woman (unidentified) against doorway — Three swimmers

PAGES 38 to 102 blank.

Inserted loose are the following: "A Sixteenth Century Prayer for a Blessing on the Garden" and two loose pages (pp. 68–69) from *Sussex Life*, May 1965: "Leonard Woolf at Home" by Tom Sobey, "at a time when LW Clerk of Rodmell Parish Council."

Monk's House Album 5 (MH-5)

Monk's House Album 5 is cardboard covered with green mottled paper with a French watermark. JCA France. Its size is 9¼ × 12¼ inches.

LOOSE PHOTOGRAPHS: three of Leonard; George Duckworth and VW (about fifteen years old); Sally on a camp chair; a photograph inscribed "with love from Marie, Alan and Simon"; William Plomer at Monk's House with statue; and a press photograph of Monk's House (6 × 6 inches, undated).

PAGE 1. Leslie Stephen (3½ × 5½ inches; art photo by Fleet Street Photographers).

PAGE 2. Same photograph as that on page 1, mounted as oval.

PAGE 3. St. Ives, August 1892 (both photographs are 2¾ × 3¾ inches).

Stella, Vanessa, Virginia, Thoby, Leslie, Julia, Lily and Dick Norton, Adrian, Gratwick | Shag (dog)

PAGE 4. August 1892.

George Duckworth, Stella, Jack Hills (missing)

Vanessa with Lisa Stillman at cooking range (2¾ × 3¾ inches)

PAGE 5. August 1892.

Jack Hills, Stella Duckworth (missing)

Virginia, Hilary and Gladys Holman Hunt, Adrian, Vanessa, George Duckworth (missing)

PAGE 6. St. Ives, 1892.

L. Stephen, Lady Albutt, Vanessa, Virginia, Gerald, Sir C. Albutt, Adrian, Julia

Two garden scenes (2¾ × 3¾ inches)

PAGE 7. August/September 1892, Talland House.

Charles Booth | J. A. Symonds (Julia Stephen in rear)

PAGE 8.

A. Ll. Davies

Sophie Farrell (shelling peas)

Paddy gardener

Ellen Eldridge

PAGE 9. Bayreuth.

Adeline Fisher, Stella, George, Stephen Massingberd, Mildred and Margaret Massingberd

PAGE 10. 1892.

Photograph similar to the group photograph, p. 6

Amy Norris seamstress (2¾ × 3¾ inches)

PAGE 11. St. Ives, 1892.

Virginia, Vanessa, Walter Headlam, Jack Hills (missing)

Woman (under tree, unidentified)

Woman in chair (unidentified)

PAGE 12.

Dick Norton

Virginia and Vanessa (missing)

Woman (in hammock, unknown)

PAGE 13. St. Ives, 1892.

Paddy gardener

Amy seamstress

Delivery boy with Ellen Eldridge (two prints)

PAGE 14. Photographs are identified as taken by Gerald Duckworth.

Postman

Sandray signalman with wife

Pascoe boatman

Mr. John Roach fisherman

PAGE 15. Cornwall, 1936.

Son of Lyn Newman (on reverse: "this is Edward. I did enjoy seeing you both again")

Ka Arnold Forster (missing)

PAGE 16.

Cobb

Lyme Regis

Coverack

PAGE 17.

Ka A. Forster (writing at desk)

Coverack

Sea view

PAGE 18.

Scenic view

Dosmary Pool

Sally Graves and Richard Chilver (in front of VW's workroom)

PAGE 19. Three photographs of R. Braithwaite and Margaret.

PAGE 20.

Flowers indoors — Quentin, Angus Davidson (in garden with statue)

Sally Graves and Richard Chilver (sequential shot to that on p. 18)

PAGE 21. Quentin.

PAGE 22.

Hugh Walpole with dog — Sissinghurst (missing)

PAGE 23. Sissinghurst, with Nigel, Vita, Benedict Nicolson, and VW. Postmarked Argyll House, on postcard to LW, dated August 14, 1936, posted in Paddington W2, with a red one-penny stamp: "Yes in September I hope" (illegible signature; Argyll House belonged to Sibyl Colefax).

PAGE 24. Two photographs of hops garden.

PAGE 25. Albi, 1937 (6 × 4¼ inches; looks a professional postcard).

PAGE 26. France, 1937; four scenic views (LW among trees, landscape, Rocamadour).

PAGE 27. Four views: Nohant, G. Sand's house, Albi.

PAGE 28. Four views: Dordogne, Cahors.

PAGE 29. Four views: Albi, Loches, Dordogne.

PAGE 30. Three views of Najac.

PAGE 31. Four views: Souillac market, Nohant.

PAGE 32. Four views: Chartes, Albi, Valençay.

PAGE 33.

Garden, Monk's House — Yvonne Joseph, AVB (playing bowls)

Yvonne, Joseph, VW (missing) — C. Mauron, AVB, H. Anrep (bowling scene)

PAGE 34. Bowling scenes.

E. Playfair, H. Anrep — AVB, Yvonne Joseph

PAGE 35. Two photographs of Charles Mauron and AVB (bowling scenes).

PAGE 36. Three views of Rodmell (sheep, farm buildings, Downs).

PAGE 37. Three views of Rodmell (village, church, farm).

PAGE 38. Three views: bridge, Downs.

PAGE 39. View of Downs.

PAGE 40. Two views: cows, Downs.

PAGE 41.
Sissinghurst (professional postcard) | View of sheep

PAGE 42.
Sally (on chair) | Eddie Playfair (in garden with statue)
Sally (among trees)

PAGE 43.
Louie | Eddie Playfair (as on p. 42) | The two elm trees

PAGE 44.
Sally (on sofa) | Statue | LW, Judith Stephen, and dog

PAGE 45.
Sally (on chair) | LW with dog on chair | T. S. Eliot (indoors)

PAGE 46.
Dorothy and Janie Bussy | Judith Stephen
AVB and QB (bowling scene)

PAGE 47.
Dorothy and Janie Bussy (repeat of p. 46, from different angle)

PAGE 48.
AVB, QB, and Portia Holman (bowling scene) | T. S. Eliot (missing)

PAGE 49. William Plomer (in garden with statue).

PAGE 50. John Cornford.

PAGE 51. 1938.

John Lehmann (missing) | Garden scene | Mitzy

PAGE 52. Hogarth Press.

Miss Perkins | Miss Strachan

PAGE 53.

Miss Woodward | Orchard, Monk's House

PAGE 54.

Mud House (home of Ray and Oliver Strachey, Friday's Hill, Haslemere)

Ray Strachey | Marjorie Strachey (among trees)

PAGE 55.

Marjorie, Oliver, Ray | Garden tree

PAGE 56.

Mitzy | Sally with Mitzy

PAGE 57.

Orchard | Miss Hepworth (surrounded by Hogarth books)

Two garden scenes

PAGE 58.

Orchard | Long shot of Monk's House

PAGE 59.

Fence | Pamela Diamond and Roger (mother and baby, three photographs, 1¼ × 1¼ inches)

Ray Strachey

PAGE 60. 1938.

Scotland and Skye | Thorney | Peterborough | Croyland Abbey

PAGE 61.

Croyland Abbey | The Roman Wall, Housesteads

PAGE 62.

Chollerford Bridge | Two views of Roman Wall

PAGE 63.

Roman Wall, Housesteads | Ben Nevis | Flodigarry | Skye

PAGE 64.

Vallum, Thirwall Castle | Flodigarry | Skye

PAGE 65.

Dunvegan | Loch Cluanie

PAGE 66. Two scenic views of Skye.

PAGE 67. Two scenic views of Skye .

PAGE 68. Two views of a Scottish loch (one with VW in front of car).

PAGE 69. Two views of a Scottish loch.

PAGE 70. 1925.

QB and JB | JB and AVB

PAGE 71.

JB | Sally at Charleston with QB | JB at Charleston with QB (dated on reverse 1935, by VW)

QB and AVB (also dated 1935 by VW)

PAGE 72. Bowling scenes: Duncan, William Plomer, and QB.

PAGE 73. Bowling scenes: AVB, Duncan, and QB.

PAGE 74. Bowling scenes: Duncan, AVB, QB, and William Plomer.

PAGE 75. Bowling scenes: Duncan and AVB.

PAGE 76.

Ann (Davies, in chair before mantelpiece) | Richard (Davies, in chair before books)

PAGE 77.

Richard, Ann Davies | Sally joins for second photograph

PAGE 78.

John Lehmann in garden | Ann L. Davies indoors

PAGE 79.
Barbara Bagenal VW, Noel, and Virginia Richards

PAGE 80.
VW, Noel, and Virginia Richards (repeat of p. 79) Richard L. Davies

PAGE 81.
Richard and Ann L. Davies

PAGE 82. Christmas, 1938.
Sally Monk's House (in snow, two exteriors)

PAGE 83. View of trees in snow (as on p. 82).

PAGE 84. Monk's House exterior in snow.

PAGES 85 to 89 blank

Loose Photographs

The location of the photographs in boxes and folders is given as it was in 2004.

BROWN ENVELOPE

The brown envelope contains a photograph of VW (marked "rough proof please return"; 5¾ × 4 inches); Trieste postcard from LW and VW, "the Woolfs have missed the Fry's greatly. V is being taught chess"; Stephen children playing cricket at St. Ives; portrait by H. H. Cameron, 70 Mortimer St., marked "S to S 1893" (6½ × 4 inches), of Stella; photograph of Lytton mounted on card (5½ × 4 inches); and Vita Sackville-West, the Lenare portrait, with the Lenare "signature" (recumbent lion).

WHITE FOLDER

The white folder contains a pastel of Leslie Stephen made during his final illness (no date, artist unknown; Wm. Rothenstein's drawing was 1903); dog sketches (dates, artist unknown); scrapbook arrangement of newspaper photographs of Benito Mussolini, Christ with exposed heart, Prof. J. M. Murray, Abraham Lincoln, Emperor William II, Count Berchtold, Austrian Foreign Minister Bismarck on his eightieth birthday, and Frederick Delius being presented with the Diploma of the Freedom of Bradford (these presumably were part of the research for *Three Guineas*); tennis party; page "from a sketch book dated 1890," by Sir Wm. Rothenstein of Julia Stephen; a sketch of Julia Stephen on an H. H. H. Cameron photograph, 1893 (sketch by Lisa Stillman?); print of painting of Vita Sackville-West, stamped on reverse "Paul Liab. Fine Art Photographer. Thistle Grove Basingstoke"; print of tennis party (unknown); photograph of LW with Malcolm Muggeridge, at Monk's House with his dog in the conservatory; press photograph of LW at Sussex University for an honorary doctorate; LW with camera (possibly a Rolliflex); LW on arrival in Ceylon 1960.

ENVELOPES OF NEGATIVES IN THE KOCH COLLECTION

All the negatives are on nitrate film and unreproducible at Harvard. The negative envelopes list the location of the photograph in the main (for example, box 4, folder 2, and so on). They include VW on sofa; G. E. Moore and LW; LW, marked "pictures of Ceylon 1904–1911"; VW, box 3, folder 1; VW, box 4, folder 1 of 2 ; VW, box 4, folder 1-4; VW, Cornwall 1916, MH-2; VW, box 4, folder 4-2—VB's painting; Marie Woolf, box 4, loose; VW and LW, Ireland, Bowen Court, box 4, loose; VW with Vita, box 4, loose; Monk's House exterior, box 4, folder 4-2; Jacques Raverat, box 4, folder A; VW and Lytton, box 3, folder 2; VW, JB, and Lydia, box 3, folder 2; LW with dog, box 3, folder 2; VW with Noel and Virginia Richards, MH-5; scenes from Monk's House; LW in Cornwall, 1916, MH-2; Molly Sturgeon, MH-4; Monk's House, winter 1940, MH-4; VW and LW, July 1939, MH-4; Angelica, Vanessa, and Quentin in Italy, MH-3; VW, QB, and JB, MH-3; Julia, Leslie Stephen, and Virginia, 1892, MH-3; T. S. Eliot, Vivienne Eliot, and VW, MH-3; Clive Bell, Mary Hutchinson; Vanessa, Clive, and Duncan, MH-2; VW with Ka Cox, 1912, MH-1; Asheham House, 1914, MH-1; Laura with Leslie Stephen, MH-1; Stella Duckworth, MH-1; Man Ray photograph of VW; Virginia and Vanessa playing cricket at St. Ives; LW, VW, and Roger Fry, MH-1; VW with group (unknown); VW smoking on bench; VW and Vita with two dogs.

BOX 1

Box 1 contains a small album, MH-6, with ring binder, green, 11½ × 9 inches, with brown cardboard leaves. It contains some loose photographs: one with handwriting on reverse, "Mrs. Loxo Bradley of Loxo Manor wife of Samuel Glazebrook" (9 × 5½ inches). Another photograph is a studio portrait, undated, of Empress Eugenie. The album photographs are largely cartes-de-visite, and the names given here are as listed in the album, one photograph per person (unless otherwise indicated).

PAGE 1. Victorian portraits of a woman (unidentified) with pug dog and a man and woman (unidentified).

PAGE 2.

Gambetta	Thiers	Grevy
MacMahon		Prince Gostichdkoff, St. Petersburg

PAGE 3.

Mr. R. Davies	Dr. Jowett	Mr. Gaskell (photographers: Elliott and Fry, Baker Street)

PAGE 4.

Sarah Bernhardt   Ellen Terry as Ophelia   Mrs. Langtry
Elizabeth Barrett Browning   The Late George Eliot   Mrs. Gaskell

PAGE 5.

Hubert Parry   Dr. Michael Costa   Professor Beeley
The Late Mlle Tietjens

PAGE 6.

Lady Carlisle   Lady Mary Murray   Princess Royal
Edmund Gurney

PAGE 7.

Pere Hyacinthe   Baboo Keshab   Chindu Sen
Cardinal Newman   His Holiness Pius IX   Leo 13th (pope)

PAGE 8.

Westcott, L.L. Davies, Scott   F. D. Maurice
Cardinal Newman   Bishop Lightfoot   Cardinal Manning

PAGE 9.

Basse (priest)   Patriarch of Greece   Cardinal Wiseman
Dean Stanley

PAGE 10.

Gladstone   John Arthur Roebuck   Huxley
Professor Owen   Faraday   Louis Napleon

PAGE 11.

Male (unknown)   Charlotte Yonge   Mrs. Gaskell

PAGE 12.

Renan   Victor Emmanuel   Bismarck

PAGE 13.

Robert Browning   Tennyson   Tom Hughes   Goldwin Smith

PAGE 14.

Mrs. Crompton   Ethel Sargant   Mrs. Garrett Anderson

PAGE 15.

Lincoln (two photographs) General Lee Jefferson Davis Grant
Lloyd Jameson

PAGE 16.

Lincoln Emerson Chase

PAGE 17.

W. E. Gladstone Herbert Gladstone Marquis of Hartington
Lord Salisbury John Bright Disraeli

PAGE 18.

Lord Palmerston Earl Granvelle Earl Russell
Earl of Beaconsfield Earl Carnarvon John Bright

PAGE 19.

Moltke Todleben Lord Napier
Garibaldi Cavour Crown Prince of Germany

PAGE 20.

Mazzini Gambetta
Garibaldi (two cards, on one of which he is writing to Gladstone)

PAGE 21.

Mrs. Gladstone, W. E. Gladstone, Herbert Gladstone Lord Selborne
Lord Lingen Alexander the Second

PAGE 22.

General Garfield (twentieth U.S. president)

PAGE 23. Unknown male.

PAGE 24.

Gladstone Duke of Argyll Rt. Hon. Stafford Northcote
R. A. Cross Rt. Hon. W. E. Forster MP W. H. Smith Esq. MP

PAGE 25.

Charles Dilke Parnell Marquis of Hartington
Sir Henry James Mandella Cobden

PAGE 26.

Male (unidentified) Anton Rubinstein

Madame Norma-Neruda (violin player) Joachim

PAGE 27.

Stanley (African explorer) J. A. Froude Longfellow

Carlyle Kingsley James Martineau

PAGE 28.

Group (unidentified; on reverse, "with love to Margaret Llewelyn Davies 1892, Arthur Weston Photographer")

J. S. Mill

PAGE 29.

Darwin Marchison Herbert Spencer Prof. Malden

K. Bunsen Roscoe Tyndall

PAGE 30.

Mandella Charles Buxton George Washington

Arnold Toynbee

PAGE 31.

John Dillon Mr. Justice Grove Mrs. Langtry

PAGE 32.

Lady Mary Murray Lady Carlisle Princess of Wales

Mrs. Crompton

PAGE 33.

LW's father Henry Crompton (two prints) Mr. Justice Crompton

PAGE 34. F. J. Furnivall, February 6, 1901.

PAGE 35. Arnold Toynbee.

BOX 2

The following descriptions of people, places, and possible dates are my own. I record any information inscribed on the reverse side of a photograph.

FOLDER 1. LW and Vita with dogs, Monk's House; print by Gisèle Freund taken at the Tavistock Square 1939 sitting, stamped on rear "Gisèle Freund 12 Rue Lalande, Paris XIV" (4¾ × 2½ inches); VW with dog, Monk's House; VW on sofa with dog at feet (3 × 5 inches).

UNMARKED FOLDER. Two prints, one of Angelica, Vanessa, Clive, VW, and Maynard Keynes outside VW's workroom, and another without Vanessa; one is a postcard (1¼ × 1¼ inches).

FOLDER 3. Two prints by Gisèle Freund, sitting as above; two Man Ray prints, 1934, sitting; a Lenare print of VW.

FOLDER 4. VB and VW playing cricket at St. Ives; two prints of VW with John Lehmann at Monk's House.

FOLDER 5. Empty.

FOLDER 6. Negative of photograph of T. S. Eliot wearing a cape.

FOLDER 7. All photographs probably taken at Monk's House ca. 1933–1935. VW against urn; VW against bookcases; VW in chair, upper room; VW with James and Alix Strachey; LW in front of flowers in garden; Vita with LW and dogs; VW in chair in front of mantelpiece; LW against urn with dog; VW with dog on leash in garden.

YELLOW FOLDER. T. S. Eliot at Monk's House.

FOLDER 9. T. S. Eliot at Monk's House (2⅛ × 2⅛ inches); VW on chair, Monk's House; Virginia, Vanessa, Thoby, and Adrian with bike, St. Ives; Gerald and George Duckworth, Virginia, Thoby, Vanessa, Adrian, Julia, and Leslie Stephen.

FOLDER MARKED "L. Woolf—photographs of Ceylon." Photographs taken by Leonard when in Ceylon; they include fishing boats, views of Colombo, and postcards of Ceylon.

FOLDER MARKED "L. Woolf Monk's House and garden." Print by Marcel Kemp, Broadwick St., of Monk's House interior; exterior of house on postcard; two views from the street; Sappho, 1950, long shot with view of trees, flowers; trees, with date on reverse side, 1936; a March 1968 color enlargement of a garden statue.

FOLDER OF L. Woolf pictures of Ceylon, 1904–1911. Negative of a group photograph; picture postcard to LW at Clifford's Inn from Ceylon; photograph of the Suez Canal.

FOLDER OF L. Woolf pictures, marked "People, Monk's post war and animals." Negative of LW in garden with animals; CB and VW in chairs; photograph marked on reverse, "pleasures of old people Ian T. R. Cochrane and their children"; several photographs of animals; Asheham House, 1914, marked as such; Tavistock Square; one photograph marked "Philip Cecil Marie and children" on reverse; 1963 photograph of Synge and family; Mitzy in Rome; duplicate of group outside VW's workroom (VW, VB, CB, Maynard Keynes, William Plomer); Victorian photograph of children (unknown).

BOX 3

FOLDER 1. LW at Monk's House; duplicate of VW in tartan skirt, and of Lytton and VW at Garsington; VW and Vita; VW, upper room Monk's House.

FOLDER 2. VW, VB, Janet Case, at Firle Park, 1911; VW, Julian Bell, and Lydia pulling a rope; duplicate of Lytton and VW, Garsington; one marked "LW with Mitz and animals" on reverse.

FOLDER 2, BOX 3-3. Professional photograph of VW in furs and one for Hogarth Press; LW, VB, QB, and family, Judith and family, 1942; LW in garden reading; three Ceylon photographs; photograph of Sydney Woolf inscribed "to my darling Leonard on the 9th anniversary of his birthday from his loving father Sydney"; LW in garden by pond; slide of LW's statue by Tomlin; print by Gisèle Freund from the Tavistock Square sitting, stamped on reverse, "Foto Gisèle Freund Tres Sargentos 436 Buenos-Aires."

FOLDER marked "From V. Woolf, L. Woolf." VW *Vogue* photographs. VW in front of bookcase, Monk's House; a horizontal album, MH-7 (14¾ × 10 inches), with three photographs of Elia, Gertrude between Lysekil and Fishbrackil, Sweden, July 28, 1911; the remaining thirty pages of the album are blank.

BOX 4

ENVELOPE OF negatives on nitrate stock and unreproducible at Harvard. These photographs appear to have been taken at Monk's House unless otherwise indicated. T. S. Eliot; two of VW with Stella Benson; LW at Asheham; LW in front of books; Adrian and Karin Stephen; Lydia in garden; Roger Fry in Greece, 1932; JB, close up and farther away; Maynard Keynes, interior; two of William Plomer; Louie Mayor in kitchen; LW in chair; VW with Noel and Virginia Richards; group (unknown); two of Sibyl Colefax; VW in front of trees; VW in front of bookcase; VW with Sally in garden; Ethel Smyth, four poses; two of LW's family on bench, with LW and VW substituting for each other; Ka Arnold Forster; VW, James, and Alix Strachey; two of John Lehmann; VW, T. S. Eliot and Vivienne; VW reading, interior; VW, LW in Ireland; Adrian and Karin in garden; Eddie Playfair in garden; John Lehmann; Barbara Bagenal in chair; Vita and VW; VW and Roger Fry, Greece, 1932; Elizabeth Bowen at Monk's House; VW, JB, QB; QB in deckchair; E. M. Forster, Fry, Lydia and Maynard Keynes; two of Lydia, interior; two of Vita in garden; Fry in chair; T. S. Eliot in shorts in garden; several Plomer negatives; Roger Mortimer in profile, interior; VW, long shot, exterior, with dog; T. S. Eliot and Vivienne; the elm trees; VW, CB, exterior; LW with dog and pipe, exterior; F. Lucas, interior; Angelica; Vita with dog, interior; VW, Cyril and Jean Connolly, A. Cameron, Mrs. Cameron, Elizabeth Bowen, at

Bowen's Court, Ireland; Nicolsons at Sissinghurst with VW, in doorway; N. Bagenal, upper room; VB, CB, Angelica in garden; four of R. Lehmann; M. Keynes and Kingsley Martin (used by LW in *Downhill*, p. 177); T. S. Eliot and M. Hutchinson, exterior.

FOLDER 1 of 2. Duplicate photograph of VW in chair; print by Gisèle Freund, Tavistock Square sitting; three of Thoby; two Victorian photographs of two males with dogs (unknown), taken at Stearns Studio, Cambridge; Duncan Grant and Maynard Keynes by VB; VW, Fritham 1900, reading Hakluyt; Bella Woolf; St. Ives group photograph ca. 1889 of Virginia, Stella, Gerald and George Duckworth, Adrian, Mr. Wolstoneholme, dog (before Shag, who came in 1892), and Arthur Hart, taken by Wm. Trevorrow; VW, Firle Park, 1911; VW with Stella Benson; Victorian photograph of two women (unknown) from the London Photographic Co., Regent Street; VB in front of mirror.

FOLDER A. Photographs all taken in Monk's House unless specified. Jacques Raverat, French professional photograph; two of LW with dog; two of Stephen and Natasha Spender; Lydia and Duncan; William Plomer; Victorian photograph of servant (unknown); Vita Sackville-West on donkey in Persia; VW in Brunswick Square; Roger Fry in chair, QB in deckchair; Lytton Strachey, Lords Wood, 1917, card marked "with kind regards Moore"; VW and LW, July 23, 1912, engagement photograph; rough print of a page from the Stella Duckworth album, Berg Collection, New York; Vanessa, Virginia, Thoby, and Adrian, St. Ives ca. 1892; Stella Duckworth studio portrait, Rome.

FOLDER 2 OF 2. Two studio portraits of VB taken by Lettice Ramsey; photo of VB taken by B. Bagenal; VW from rear, exterior; professional photograph marked on reverse, "children of Samuel Glazebrook, Maud Glazebrook, mother of Peggy Hanty and Ann Bradley Glazebrook."

WHITE FOLDER (4-1). Photographs of VW with book; Vita and VW; LW and VW, July 23, 1912; VW, exterior of Monk's House; Charleston group in Scottish chair; Vita with dog in chair; T. S. Eliot and Vivienne; Ethel Smyth.

FOLDER. Postcard of Rodmell; photographs of Mitz; Tavistock Square exterior.

FOLDER. Print (by A. C. Cooper of New Bond Street) of VB's painting of VW.

FOLDER (UNMARKED). LW at Monk's House 1966; VW at Garsington 1923.

FOLDER LW autobiography, Vol. 2. Some color slides, large professional photograph of Leonard's honorary doctorate at Sussex University.

FOLDER Trekkie Parsons. Late photographs for Leonard's autobiographies; and Victorian photograph of Madge Vaughan, "with love from this family Xmas 1900."

FOLDER. A few late photographs of Leonard: with Malcolm Muggeridge, with Nehru; two by Gisèle Freund, dated 1966, of LW in his library and of VW's workroom, Monk's House; Victorian male (unknown) astride a chair, print marked "Chamonix."

The Vanessa Bell Photo Albums: A Note

The Hyman Kreitman Research Centre, Archive and Special Collections, at the Tate houses Vanessa Bell's photo albums. Because these are catalogued, with a personal name index, and are easily accessible to researchers, I do not duplicate that catalogue here. There are some inaccuracies and omissions in the catalogue, and my captions correct these where appropriate. In addition, Richardson does not list all the Bell photographs that are in the Tate archive. I have included some of these photographs in *Snapshots* and given full annotations. Not all the archive photographs, including some reproduced here, are in the albums.

In my captions to the reproduced photographs, I include album and page numbers as well as the Tate archive details to assist scholars researching the albums.

Abbreviations

The following abbreviations are used in this volume to cite works by Virginia Woolf, Leonard Woolf, and Vanessa Bell. Works by other authors are cited by the author's last name and, if needed for clarity, a shortened title. Full bibliographic information for all titles can be found in the bibliography.

WORKS BY VIRGINIA WOOLF

AS "Am I a Snob?" In *Moments of Being*, ed. J. Schulkind.

D, 2 *The Diary of Virginia Woolf, 1920–24*. Vol. 2. Ed. A. O. Bell.

D, 3 *The Diary of Virginia Woolf, 1925–30*. Vol. 3. Ed. A. O. Bell.

D, 4 *The Diary of Virginia Woolf, 1931–35*. Vol. 4. Ed. A. O. Bell and A. McNeillie.

D, 5 *The Diary of Virginia Woolf, 1936–41*. Vol. 5. Ed. A. O. Bell and A. McNeillie.

EJ *A Passionate Apprentice: The Early Journals, 1897–1909*. Ed. Mitchell A. Leaska.

F *Freshwater a Comedy*. Ed. L. P. Ruotolo.

IL "Introductory Letter." In *Life as We Have Known It by Co-operative Working Women*, ed. M. L. Davies.

L, 1 *The Letters of Virginia Woolf, 1888–1912*. Vol. 1. Ed. N. Nicolson and J. Trautmann.

L, 2 *The Letters of Virginia Woolf, 1912–22*. Vol. 2. Ed. N. Nicolson and J. Trautmann.

L, 3 *A Change of Perspective: Collected Letters, 1923–28*. Vol. 3. Ed. N. Nicolson and J. Trautmann Banks.

L, 4 *A Reflection of the Other Person: Collected Letters, 1929–31*. Vol. 4. Ed. N. Nicolson and J. Trautmann Banks.

L, 5 *The Sickle Side of the Moon: Collected Letters, 1932–35*. Vol. 5. Ed. N. Nicolson and J. Trautmann Banks.

L, 6 *Leave the Letters Till We're Dead: The Letters of Virginia Woolf, 1936–41*. Vol. 6. Ed. N. Nicolson and J. Trautmann Banks.

OB "Old Bloomsbury." In *Moments of Being*, ed. J. Schulkind.

R "Reminiscences." In *Moments of Being*, ed. J. Schulkind.

RO/TG *"A Room of One's Own" and "Three Guineas."* Ed. M. Barrett.

SK "A Sketch of the Past." In *Moments of Being*, ed. J. Schulkind.

WS *Walter Sickert: A Conversation*

WORKS BY LEONARD WOOLF

BA *Beginning Again*

LW/D Diaries and related notebooks of the Leonard Woolf Archive

S *Sowing*

WORKS BY VANESSA BELL

VB/L *Selected Letters of Vanessa Bell*. Ed. R. Marler.

Bibliography

Adorno, Theodor. *Aesthetic Theory*. Trans. C. Lenheued. London: Routledge and Kegan Paul, 1984.

Aleksiuk, Natasha. "A Thousand Angles: Photographic Irony in the Work of Julia Margaret Cameron and Virginia Woolf." *Mosaic* 33, 2 (2000): 125–142.

Anderson, Benedict. *Imagined Communities: Reflections on the Origins and Spread of Nationalism*. London: Verso, 1983.

Anderson, Carol M., and Elaine S. Malloy. "Family Photographs: In Treatment and Training." *Family Process* 15 (1976): 258–267.

Ardis, Ann. *Modernism and Cultural Conflict, 1880–1922*. Cambridge: Cambridge University Press, 2002.

Ardis, Ann, and Leslie W. Lewis, eds. *Women's Experience of Modernity, 1875–1945*. Baltimore: Johns Hopkins University Press, 2003.

Armstrong, Carol. "Cupid's Pencil of Light: Julia Margaret Cameron and the Maternalization of Photography." *October* 76 (1996): 115–141.

Baer, Ulrich. *Spectral Evidence: The Photography of Trauma*. Cambridge, MA: MIT Press, 2002.

Barkway, Stephen. "'What Tiara Did You Wear?': Lady Aberconway and Mrs. Woolf." *Virginia Woolf Bulletin* 15 (January 2004): 4–21.

Barthes, Roland. *Camera Lucida*. Trans. R. Howard. New York: Hill and Wang, 1981.

Bell, Quentin, and Angelica Garnett. *Vanessa Bell's Family Album*. London: Jill Norman and Hobhouse Ltd., 1981.

Bell, Vanessa. Photo Albums, 1896–1939. Tate Archive, London.

——. *Selected Letters of Vanessa Bell*. Ed. R. Marler. London: Bloomsbury, 1993.

Benjamin, Walter. *Charles Baudelaire*. Trans. H. Zohn. London: Verso, 1983.

——. "A Short History of Photography." *Screen* 13, 1 (Spring 1972): 5–27.

Berger, John, and Jean Mohr. *Another Way of Telling*. New York: Vintage Press, 1995.

Blomfield, R. *Modernismus*. London: Macmillan, 1934.

Bourdieu, Pierre. *Photography: A Middle-Brow Art*. Cambridge: Polity, 1990.

Branson, Noreen, and Margot Heinemann. *Britain in the Nineteen Thirties*. London: Panther, 1973.

Cameron, Julia Margaret. *Annals of My Glass House*. Seattle: University of Washington Press, 1996.

Campany, David. "Almost the Same Thing: Some Thoughts on the Collector-Photographer." In *Cruel and Tender: The Real in Twentieth-Century Photography*, ed. E. Dexter and T. Weski, 33–35. London: Tate Publishing, 2003.

Caughie, Pamela. Introduction to *Virginia Woolf in the Age of Mechanical Reproduction*, ed. P. L. Caughie, xix–xxxvi. New York: Garland Press, 2002.

Caws, Mary Ann, and Sarah Wright Bird. *Bloomsbury and France: Art and Friends*. Oxford: Oxford University Press, 2000.

Clifford, James. "On Collecting Art and Culture." In *Out There: Marginalisation and Contemporary Cultures*, ed. R. Ferguson, M. Gever, T. T. Minha-ha, and C. West, 141–169. Cambridge, MA: MIT Press, 1990.

Coe, Brian, and Paul Gates. *The Snapshot Photograph*. London: Ash and Grant, 1977.

Coward-Williams, Garry. "AP's Great Triumvirate." *Amateur Photographer* 30(October 2004): 39–43.

Cuddy-Keane, Melba. *Virginia Woolf, the Intellectual, and the Public Sphere*. Cambridge: Cambridge University Press, 2003.

Curtis, Vanessa. *Stella and Virginia, an Unfinished Sisterhood*. London: Cecil Woolf, 2001.

DeSalvo, Louise. *Virginia Woolf: The Impact of Childhood Sexual Abuse on Her Life and Work*. Boston: Beacon Press, 1989.

Dexter, Emma. "Photography Itself." In *Cruel and Tender*, ed. E. Dexter and T. Weski. London: Tate Publishing, 2003.

Dickinson, Violet. Album. Berg Collection, New York Public Library, n.d.

Doane, Mary Ann. "The Close-up: Scale and Detail in the Cinema." *Differences* 14, 3 (2003): 89–111.

——. *The Emergence of Cinematic Time: Modernity, Contingency, the Archive*. Cambridge, MA: Harvard University Press, 2002.

Dow Adams, Timothy. *Light Writing and Life Writing: Photography in Autobiography*. Chapel Hill: University of North Carolina Press, 2000.

Edwards, Derek, and David Middleton. "Conversational Remembering and Family Relationships: How Children Learn to Remember." *Journal of Social and Personal Relationships* 5 (1988): 3–25.

Eisinger, Joel. *Trace and Transformation: American Criticism of Photography in the Modernist Period*. Albuquerque: University of New Mexico Press, 1995.

Ford, Colin. *Julia Margaret Cameron: Nineteenth-Century Photographer of Genius*. London: National Portrait Gallery, 2003.

Foucault, Michel. "Of Other Spaces." *Diacritics* 16 (1986): 22–27.

Frawley, Maria. "Modernism and Maternity: Alice Meynell and the Politics of Motherhood." In *Unmanning Modernism*, ed. J. Harrison and S. Peterson. Knoxville: University of Tennessee Press, 1997.

Freud, Sigmund. *New Introductory Lectures on Psycho-Analysis and Other Works*, vol. 22 of *The Standard Edition of the Complete Psychological Works of Freud*. Trans. J. Strachey with A. Freud. London: Hogarth Press, 1960.

Garnett, David. *The Flowers of the Forest*. London: Chatto and Windus, 1955.

Gernsheim, Helmut. *The History of Photography: From the Camera Obscura to the Beginning of the Modern Era*. London: Thames and Hudson, 1969.

Gillespie, Diane Filby. *The Sisters' Arts: The Writing and Painting of Virginia Woolf and Vanessa Bell*. Syracuse, NY: Syracuse University Press, 1988.

Gillespie, Diane F., and Elizabeth Steele, eds. *Julia Duckworth Stephen: Stories for Children, Essays for Adults*. Syracuse, NY: Syracuse University Press, 1987.

Grant, Duncan. "Virginia Stephen." In *Virginia Woolf: Interviews and Recollections*, ed. J. H. Stape, 135–139. Iowa City: University of Iowa Press, 1995.

——. "Virginia Woolf and the Beginnings of Bloomsbury." In *The Bloomsbury Group: A Collection of Memoirs and Commentary*, ed. S. P. Rosenbaum, 97–101. Toronto: University of Toronto Press, 1995.

Green, André. *On Private Madness*. Madison, WI: International Universities Press, 1993.

"Guide to Library Special Collections." *Woolf Studies Annual* 9 (2004): 243–258.

Hamilton, Violet. "Catalogue Text." In *Annals of My Glass House*, by J. M. Cameron, 17–59. Seattle: University of Washington Press, 1996.

Harrison, Barbara. "Photographic Vision and Narrative Inquiry." In *Considering Counter-Narratives: Narrating, Resisting, Making Sense*, ed. M. Bamberg and M. Andrews. Amsterdam: John Benjamins, 2004.

Harrison, Elizabeth Jane, and Shirley Peterson, eds. *Unmanning Modernism: Gendered Re-readings*. Knoxville: University of Tennessee Press, 1997.

Harvey, Benjamin. "Charles and John, or, On Letting Go and Holding On." *Virginia Woolf Bulletin* 17 (September 2004): 17–26.

Heilbrun, Carolyn, ed. *Lady Ottoline's Album: Snapshots and Portraits of Her Famous Contemporaries (and of Herself), Photographed for the Most Part by Lady Ottoline Morrell*. New York: Knopf, 1976.

Hiller, Susan. *The Myth of Primitivism*. London: Routledge, 1991.

Hirsch, Marianne. *Family Frames: Photography, Narrative, and Postmemory*. Cambridge, MA: Harvard University Press, 1997.

Hogben, Carol. "Design Introduction." In *The Thirties*, ed. J. Hawkins and M. Hollis, 63–78. London: Arts Council of Great Britain, 1979.

Hoving, Kirsten A. "'Flashing Thro' the Gloom': Julia Margaret Cameron's 'Eccentricity.'" *History of Photography* 27, 1 (Spring 2003): 45–59.

Howard, Jeremy. *Whisper of the Muse: The World of Julia Margaret Cameron*. London: Colnaghi, 1990.

Humm, Maggie. *Modernist Women and Visual Cultures: Virginia Woolf, Vanessa Bell, Photography, and Cinema*. Edinburgh: Edinburgh University Press, 2002.

Huyssen, Andreas. "High/Low in an Expanded Field." *Modernism/Modernity* 9, 3 (2002): 363–374.

Jencks, Charles. *Heteropolis: Los Angeles: The Riots and the Strange Beauty of Hetero-Architecture*. New York: John Wiley and Son, 1993.

Kurzweil, Edith, and William Phillips, eds. *Literature and Psychoanalysis*. New York: Columbia University Press, 1983.

Langford, Martha. *Suspended Conversations: The Afterlife of Memory in Photographic Albums*. Montreal: McGill-Queen's University Press, 2001.

Laurence, Patricia. "Walking on a Willow Pattern Plate: Julian Bell and Ling Shuhua." Paper delivered at Back to Bloomsbury: Fourteenth Annual International Conference on Virginia Woolf, London, June 2004.

Leaska, Mitchell. *Granite and Rainbow: The Hidden Life of Virginia Woolf*. London: Picador, 1998.

Lee, Hermione. *Virginia Woolf*. London: Chatto and Windus, 1996.

Lemagny, Jean-Claud, and André Rouille, eds. *A History of Photography: Social and Cultural Perspectives*. Trans. J. Lloyd. Cambridge: Cambridge University Press, 1987.

Lothrop, E. S. *A Century of Cameras*. Dobbs Ferry, NY: Morgan and Morgan, 1982.

Lury, Celia. *Prosthetic Culture: Photography, Memory, and Identity*. London: Routledge, 1998.

Maltby, Richard. "'Baby Face' or How Joe Breen Made Barbara Stanwyck Atone for Causing the Wall Street Crash." *Screen* 27, 2 (1986): 22–45.

Man Ray. *Self Portrait*. London: Andre Deutsch, 1963.

McKeown, Jim and Joan McKeown. *The Collector's Guide to Kodak Cameras*. Grantsburg, WI: Centennial Photo Service, 1981.

Mendes, Val. "Carpets and Furnishing Textiles." In *The Thirties*, ed. J. Hawkins and M. Hollis, 87–92. London: Arts Council of Great Britain, 1979.

Meynell, Alice. *Essays*. London: Burns, Oates, and Waterbourne, 1930.

Milgram, Stanley. "The Image-Freezing Machine." *Psychology Today*, January 1977, 50–54.

Mitchell, William J. *The Reconfigured Eye: Visual Truth in the Post-Photographic Era*. Cambridge, MA: MIT Press, 1994.

Mortimer, Frances J. "The Year's Work." In *Photograms of the Year 1937*, ed. F. J. Mortimer, 3–5. London: Iliffe and Sons Ltd., 1937.

Nicolson, Nigel. "The Most Remarkable Human Being." In *Virginia Woolf: Interviews and Recollections*, ed. J. H. Stape, 73–78. Iowa City: University of Iowa, 1995.

Nochlin, Linda. "Why Have There Been No Great Women Artists?" In *Art and Sexual Politics*, ed. E. Baker and T. Hess. London: Collier Macmillan, 1973.

North, Michael. *Reading 1922: A Return to the Scene of the Modern*. New York: Oxford University Press, 1995.

Orvell, Miles. *American Photography*. Oxford: Oxford University Press, 2003.

Orwell, George. *Nineteen Eighty-four*. Harmondsworth, UK: Penguin, 1976.

Ovenden, Graham, ed. *A Victorian Album: Julia Margaret Cameron and Her Circle*. With an introduction by Lord D. Cecil. London: Secker and Warburg, 1975.

Parr, Martin, and Gerry Badger. *The Photobook: A History*. Vol. 1. London: Phaidon Press, 2004.

Reed, Christopher. *Bloomsbury Rooms: Modernism, Subculture, and Domesticity*. New Haven: Yale University Press, 2004.

Reid, Panthea. *Art and Affection: A Life of Virginia Woolf*. Oxford: Oxford University Press, 1996.

Richardson, Elizabeth P. *A Bloomsbury Iconography*. Winchester, UK: St. Paul's Bibliographies, 1989.

Rosenblum, Naomi. *A History of Women Photographers*. New York: Abbeville Press, 2000.

Ross, Cathy. *Twenties London: A City in the Jazz Age*. London: Phillip Wilson, 2003.

Rowbotham, Sheila. *A Century of Women*. Harmondsworth, UK: Penguin, 1997.

———. *Hidden from History*. London: Pluto Press, 1973.

Russell, Dora. *The Tamarisk Tree: My Quest for Liberty and Love*. London: Elek/Pemberton, 1975.

Said, Edward. *Freud and the Non-European*. London: Verso, 2003.

Schaffer, Talia. "Posing Orlando." *Genders* 19 (1994): 26–63.

Serrès, Michel, with Bruno Latour. *Conversations on Science, Culture, and Time*. Trans. Roxanne Lapidus. Ann Arbor: University of Michigan Press, 1995.

Shinkle, Eugenie. "Boredom, Repetition, Inertia: Contemporary Photography and the Aesthetic of the Banal." *Mosaic* 37, 4 (December 2004): 165–184.

Shone, Richard. *The Art of Bloomsbury: Roger Fry, Vanessa Bell, and Duncan Grant*. London: Tate Gallery, 1999.

———. *Bloomsbury Portraits: Vanessa Bell, Duncan Grant, and Their Circle*. London: Phaidon, 1993.

———. "Pictures at Charleston." In *Cézanne in the Hedge and Other Memories of Charleston and Bloomsbury*, ed. H. Lee. London: Collinson Brown, 1992.

Silver, Brenda. *Virginia Woolf Icon*. Chicago: University of Chicago Press, 1999.

Soja, Edward W. *Third Space*. Oxford: Blackwell, 1996.

Sontag, Susan. *On Photography*. New York: Anchor Books, 1989.

———. *Regarding the Pain of Others*. Harmondsworth, UK: Penguin, 2003.

Spalding, Frances. *Duncan Grant*. London: Chatto and Windus, 1997.

———. *Vanessa Bell*. London: Macmillan, 1983.

Spater, George, and Ian Parsons. *A Marriage of True Minds: An Intimate Portrait of Leonard and Virginia Woolf*. New York: Harcourt Brace Jovanovich, 1977.

Spence, Jo. *Putting Myself in the Picture*. London: Camden Press, 1987.

Spence, Jo, and Pat Holland, eds. *Family Snaps: The Meanings of Domestic Photographs*. London: Virago, 1991.

Stephen, Adrian. *The "Dreadnought" Hoax*. London: Hogarth Press, 1936.

Stephen, Leslie. *Sir Leslie Stephen's Mausoleum Book*. Ed. A. Bell. Oxford: Clarendon Press, 1977.

Stephen, Mrs. Leslie. *Notes from Sick Rooms*. Orono, ME: Puckerbrush Press, 1980.

Stephenson, Andrew. "'Strategies of Situation': British Modernism and the Slump, c. 1929–1934." *Oxford Art Journal* 14, 2 (1991): 30–51.

The Studio. Vol. 103 (January–June 1932): 63–64.

Sturken, Marita. *Tangled Memories*. Berkeley: University of California Press, 1997.

Tagg, John. *The Burden of Representation: Essays on Photographies and Histories*. London: Macmillan, 1988.

Tickner, Lisa. "Mediating Generation: The Mother–Daughter Plot." *Art History* 25, 1 (February 2002): 23–46.

———. *Modern Life and Modern Subjects: British Art in the Early Twentieth Century*. New Haven: Yale University Press, 2000.

Turnbaugh, Douglas Blair. *Duncan Grant and the Bloomsbury Group*. Secaucus, NJ: Lyle Stuart Inc., 1987.

———. *Private: The Erotic Art of Duncan Grant, 1885–1978*. London: Gay Men's Press, 1989.

Vaughan, Janet. "Cousin Virginia." In *Virginia Woolf: Interviews and Recollections*, ed. J. H. Stape, 9–11. Basingstoke, UK: Macmillan, 1995.

Warner, Marina. "Parlour Made." In *Creative Camera: Thirty Years of Writing*, ed. D. Brittain, 220–225. Manchester: Manchester University Press, 1999.

Watney, Simon. *The Art of Duncan Grant*. London: John Murray, 1999.

Williams, Val. *The Other Observers. Women Photographers in Britain, 1900 to the Present*. London: Virago, 1994.

Wolff, Janet. *AngloModern: Painting and Modernity in Britain and the United States*. Ithaca, NY: Cornell University Press, 2003.

Woodall, Joanne, ed. *Portraiture: Facing the Subject*. Manchester: Manchester University Press, 1997.

Woolf, Leonard. *Beginning Again*. London: Hogarth Press, 1965.

——. Diaries and Related Notebooks, 1922–1969. Leonard Woolf Archive, University of Sussex, Brighton.

——. *Downhill All the Way*. London: Hogarth Press, 1967.

——. *Sowing*. London: Hogarth Press, 1961.

Woolf, Virginia. "Am I a Snob?" In *Moments of Being*, ed. J. Schulkind, 182–198. London: Chatto and Windus, 1976.

——. *A Change of Perspective: Collected Letters, 1923–28*. Vol. 3. Ed. N. Nicolson and J. Trautmann Banks. London: Hogarth Press, 1977.

——. *Contemporary Writers*. New York: Harcourt Brace Jovanovich, 1965.

——. *The Diary of Virginia Woolf, 1920–24*. Vol. 2. Ed. A. O. Bell. London: Hogarth Press, 1978.

——. *The Diary of Virginia Woolf, 1925–30*. Vol. 3. Ed. A. O. Bell. London: Hogarth Press, 1980.

——. *The Diary of Virginia Woolf, 1931–35*. Vol. 4. Ed. A. Olivier Bell and A. McNeillie. London: Hogarth Press, 1982.

——. *The Diary of Virginia Woolf, 1936–41*. Vol. 5. Ed. A. Olivier Bell and A. McNeillie. London: Hogarth Press, 1984.

——. *Freshwater: A Comedy*. Ed. L. P. Ruotolo. New York: Harcourt Brace Jovanovich, 1976.

——. "Introductory Letter." In *Life as We Have Known It by Co-operative Working Women*, ed. M. L. Davies, xvii–xxxxi. London: Virago, 1977.

——. *Leave the Letters Till We're Dead: The Letters of Virginia Woolf, 1936–41*. Vol. 6. Ed. N. Nicolson and J. Trautmann Banks. London: Hogarth Press, 1980.

——. *The Letters of Virginia Woolf, 1888–1912*. Vol. 1. Ed. N. Nicolson and J. Trautmann. New York: Harcourt Brace Jovanovich, 1975.

——. *The Letters of Virginia Woolf, 1912–22*. Vol. 2. Ed. N. Nicolson and J. Trautmann. New York: Harcourt Brace Jovanovich, 1976.

——. "Old Bloomsbury." In *Moments of Being*, ed. J. Schulkind, 159–179. London: Chatto and Windus, 1976.

——. *A Passionate Apprentice: The Early Journals, 1897–1909*. Ed. Mitchell A. Leaska. San Diego: Harcourt Brace Jovanovich, 1990.

——. *A Reflection of the Other Person: Collected Letters, 1929–31*. Vol. 4. Ed. N. Nicolson and J. Trautmann Banks. London: Hogarth Press, 1978.

——. "Reminiscences." In *Moments of Being*, ed. J. Schulkind, 28–59. London: Chatto and Windus, 1976.

——. *"A Room of One's Own" and "Three Guineas."* Ed. M. Barrett. Harmondsworth, UK: Penguin, 1993.

——. *The Sickle Side of the Moon: Collected Letters, 1932–35*. Vol. 5. Ed. N. Nicolson and J. Trautmann Banks. London: Hogarth Press, 1979.

——. "A Sketch of the Past." In *Moments of Being*, ed. J. Schulkind, 64–137. London: Chatto and Windus, 1976.

——. *To the Lighthouse*. 1927. Harmondsworth, UK: Penguin, 1964.

——. *Walter Sickert: A Conversation*. London: Hogarth Press, 1934.

Zwerdling, Alex. "Mastering the Memoir: Woolf and the Family Legacy." *Modernism/Modernity* 10, 1 (2003): 165–188.

ABOUT THE AUTHOR

MAGGIE HUMM is a Professor of Cultural Studies at the University of East London. Her books include *Border Traffic, The Dictionary of Feminist Theory* (the first edition of which was named "outstanding academic book of 1990" by *Choice*), the best-selling *Modern Feminisms, Feminism and Film*, and the recent *Modernist Women and Visual Cultures: Virginia Woolf, Vanessa Bell, Photography, and Cinema* (Edinburgh University Press, 2002; Rutgers University Press, 2003).

Humm was an editor of the *Routledge Encyclopaedia of Women* and has been a Distinguished Visiting Scholar and Professor at many universities, including the University of Massachusetts, San Diego State University, Stanford University, Rutgers University, Queen's University of Belfast, and the University of Karachi.

Humm gave the Annual Virginia Woolf Birthday Lecture in 2002 and has given keynote and plenary papers in Brazil, Bulgaria, Egypt, Israel, Italy, Portugal, Slovenia, Spain, the United States, and elsewhere.

A NOTE ON THE TYPE

This book was set in Deepdene, a typeface designed in 1927 by the esteemed American type designer Frederick Goudy. Named for Goudy's modest estate in Marlboro, New York, and originally intended for use in his personal Village Letter Foundery, Deepdene was adapted the following year by Lanston Monotype for machine casting. The digital version used here utilizes OpenType technology, and was released by the newly reorganized Lanston Type Company in 2005.

Designed and composed by Kevin Hanek

Printed in Canada by Friesens